## Also by E. Reid Gilbert

*Trickster Jack*

*Shall We Gather at the River*

*What Matters*

*Valley Studio: More than a Place*

*The Twelve Houses of My Childhood*

*100 Limericks for 100 Days of Trump*

*Whimsical Limericks from the Age of Trump*

*Stories Tell What Can't be Told: My Story*

# E. Reid Gilbert
# Ten Plays

A3D Impressions
TUCSON • MINNEAPOLIS

## A3D Impressions™

A Division of Awareness3D, LLC
PO Box 57415, Tucson, AZ 85732

Publisher's Cataloging-in-Publication Data

Names: Gilbert, E. Reid, author.
Title: E. Reid Gilbert ten plays / E. Reid Gilbert.
Description: Tucson, AZ ; Minneapolis, MN : A3D Impressions, 2019.
Identifiers: LCCN 2019909790
ISBN 978-1-7320677-6-9 | 978-1-7320677-7-6 (ebook)
Subjects: LCSH American drama--21st century. | BISAC PERFORMING ARTS /
Theater / General | PERFORMING ARTS / Screenplays
Classification: LCC PS3607.I4225 2019 | DDC 792.9--dc23

# DEDICATION

This book is dedicated to those numerous people, students, instructors, directors, designers writers, etc., who have demonstrated over the years that theatre is much more than a "conspiracy to involve an audience". Perhaps they have conspired to teach that theatre is extended family with a mission: the mission being to probe the human cycle of life with all its beauty and degradation, its reality and spirituality, its vapidity and aspirations. This has always been the destiny of theatre's impact on humanity.

Theatre is more than engaging the audience in the seat and those on stage (the actors playing), but importantly, as well, the ancestors and the gods. This book is also dedicated to those ancestors and gods who are called into presence in the embodiment of the actors who bring these plays to life. My hope is that in some small way these creations, inspired by the Muses, Melpomene and Thalia, Tragedy and Comedy, will serve to edify and lift up future generations of the children of theatre, for the sake of enriching and lifting up humanity. It is for the benefit of humanity that these plays are offered in this anthology.

# COLLECTION OF MY THEATRE SCRIPTS

An old playwright once told a group of us actors, "As much as you enjoy the theatre as actors, you will eventually aspire to more than that. You will want to grasp the opportunity to write the scripts yourself."

Ah 'tis true, 'tis true.

By that time I had already written a few short Sunday School plays and even a pageantry script, *Beyond the Gap*, (The Cumberland Gap) for the Daniel Boone Days in Barbourville, KY, in 1959.

This was an effort on my part to contribute to the annual community festivities. However, it proved rather successful, but it was years later before I attempted a similar adventure.

There were several intervening years, when as Director of the Wisconsin Mime Theatre and School, I wrote several mime scripts in collaboration with other members of the ensemble. As those scripts were movement-focused, I shan't even attempt to include them here.

— *E. Reid Gilbert*

# The Plays

# Part I: One Acts

# Language Lessons

The writer here plays with language as it is so often misunderstood in different settings even though it's English. It's not unusual for groups of people; culturally, academically and professionally to use words as buzz words for acceptance or shunning in various instances in the use of the buzz words. This script derides the local use of such terms to shut out the outsider, but celebrates the use of specific words to welcome ever-expanding language circles.

# LANGUAGE LESSONS

*by E. Reid Gilbert*

Cast

> **BO DILLON** . . . . . . . .a mountain man but also a
> university professor
> **LLOYD DILLON** . . . . .teenage son of Bo
> **MARILYN HADLEY** . .a university graduate student

SETTING: THE CLUTTERED FRONT PORCH OF A VIRGINIA MOUNTAIN MAN - SPRING TIME AFTERNOON

*Lloyd is sitting on the edge of the porch, strumming on a guitar. There's also a rifle leaning against the wall. Bo is sitting on a rocking chair, reading Shakespeare.*

**BO:** Now when that girl comes up the hill, you just keep on strumming on that guitar, as though you know what you're doing.

**LLOYD:** I do know what I'm doing. You oughta remember that contest down at the ...

**BO:** Yes, I remember that quite well. -I'm really proud of your musical ability.

**LLOYD:** Aw, gee thanks!

**BO:** No, don't mention it. What I shoulda said, was "Act like you DON'T know what you're doing."

**LLOYD:** Now Pops, you're not gonna do that teasin' thing again!???

**BO:** I promised Professor Bowman in the Anthropology Department ...

**LLOYD:** Why'd you do that?

**BO:** He wants his graduate students to learn how to interview people in their respective field of major research.

**LLOYD:** And you think you can do the job?

**BO:** If she isn't up to the challenge, Thomas Bowman would like to know before he wastes any more time with her as her major professor.

**LLOYD:** But, Dad, it's always so embarrassing when you do that little game.

**BO:** You'll get over it.  I think you may enjoy it as much as I do.

**LLOYD:** Well that's true ... but afterwards ... when they ...

**BO:** We'll deal with that when the time ... Quick! Take this book into the house. I see her now comin' up the hill.

*Lloyd puts his guitar against the wall and rushes into the house with the book. Bo takes out his jackknife and starts*

*whittling on a walking stick. Marilyn approaches from down the hill. She carries a back pack and is obviously quite cautious.*

**MARILYN:** Howdy! (No response from Bo, who keeps on whittling — she speaks louder) Howdy! (No response from Bo.) Mister Dillon, did you hear me?

**BO:** I heared you. I ain't deef you know. ... Not completely any ways.

**MARILYN:** Completely? ...

**BO:** Completely deef. Weren't thet wuz what we're talkin' 'bout?

**MARILYN:** (Laughing nervously.) Yeah, I guess it was.

**BO:** How'd you know my name?

**MARILYN:** Professor Bowman said this is where you'd be.

**BO:** Perfessor Bowman? ... Who is he?

**MARILYN:** He's my major professor at the university.

**BO:** But why did this Perfessor ...

**MARILYN:** Bowman!

**BO:** Yeah ... him!

**MARILYN:** He said that you would know a lot of the regional vernacular.

**BO:** Vern ... who? I do know Vernon Kelly, but he ...

**MARILYN:** Vernacular ... That just means the kind of every day language ... (Bo interrupts.)

**BO:** Oh, we talk English here.

**MARILYN:** I know that, but ... (He interrupts her again.)

**BO:** Why did you first call me Howdy?

**MARILYN:** I didn't call you Howdy. I just ...

**BO:** So you thought I might pay some 'tenshun, if you wuz to use hilbilly talk.

**MARILYN:** (Now really flustered.) No that wasn't it. I just ...

**BO:** Aw, thet's awright, Honey. I'm just an ol' codger, what likes to outdo the young folks, right 'specially the purty ones.

*Lloyd sidles out and picks up the guitar and settling himself back down on the edge of the porch, starts strumming, and doing it quite badly. She looks at him and smiles. He looks back with more of a leer than a smile. She moves a little farther from him.*

MARILYN: (turning back toward Bo) That's okay. I just came over to introduce myself.

BO: You ain't exactly done thet yet.

MARILYN: Oh, yes. I beg your pardon. I'm Marilyn.

BO: Mon-roe?

MARILYN: Oh no. It's Hadly ... Marilyn Hadly.

BO: But now she was a purty one.

MARILYN: Who?

BO: Marilyn MON-ROE. They oughten not let any other girl ...

MARILYN: Oh, Mr. Dillon. I'm sorry but I didn't choose my name.

BO: You absolutely right ... I see you got a bit of spunk yoah own self.

MARILYN: Women today have to make their own ways and fight their own fights.

BO: Whoa, Whoa, liddle filly. I hope we not fixin' to have a fight.

MARILYN: (Becoming a little skittish.) Well that fixin' depends ...

BO: Depends on what?

MARILYN: Depends on you and me. It takes two to tango.

*Lloyd strikes a terrible chord on the guitar. Marilyn winces and looks toward Lloyd. Whenever Bo makes a good point in his banter, Bo will strike a loud out of tune chord.*

BO: So, we gonna dance ...

MARILYN: That's just an expression.

BO: A 'spression?

MARILYN: Yes. A kind of metaphor.

BO: Now is it a spression or metta ...

MARILYN: Metaphor?

BO: Well which one is it?

MARILYN: (turning to Lloyd) I see you're fond of the guitar.

**LLOYD:** Not fond.

**MARILYN:** But the way you're playing it ... Playing WITH it.

**LLOYD:** Yeah?

**MARILYN:** Would you like a lesson? I study strings ...

**LLOYD:** This is a guitar.

**MARILYN:** But ...

**LLOYD:** It's not strings. Strings is what you tie up 'baccer with.

**BO:** Now thet Lloyd got all thet straightened out ... But what were we talkin' ...

**MARILYN:** (Glaring at Bo.) We were talking about fighting.

**BO:** (Picking up gun.) But we not fixin' to start one?
> *Bo aims at something offstage.*

**MARILYN:** (Even more apprehensive.) No, I don't think that would be useful for anyone.

**BO:** (Placing the gun back against the wall.) Much obliged.

**MARILYN:** Now why did you use that expression?

**BO:** Another 'spression?

**MARILYN:** That word. OBLIGED.

**BO:** What about obliged?

**MARILYN:** Why did you use it that way?

**BO:** Oh, that just means I'm obliged to thank you. You see some times we just use less words than some folks might be used to.

**MARILYN:** Well I've noticed that there are times when extra words are used.

**BO:** Like what?

**MARILYN:** I saw and heard a woman down at the general store use five prepositions in a row to get a boy up from under a table.

**BO:** Well what exactly did she say?

**MARILYN:** She said, "Get up ... out ... from ... in ... under ... the table."

**BO:** Well, we want to be exactly right in what we tell a body.

**MARILYN:** (Looking around at the stuff and picking up things.) You have a wonderful collection here.

**BO:** It hain't a collection.

**MARILYN:** If it's not a collection what is it?

**BO:** Hit's just thangs.

**MARILYN:** But what kind of things?

**BO:** Who knows fer sure. We don't have much in this life time, so we pick up an' put up thangs whut might could be used fer farmin' or just talk about.

**MARILYN:** But don't you use bits of stuff to make some children's toys?

**BO:** Toys ... Oh you mean play pretties. Yeah we make willow whistles, limber jacks, gee-haw whimmy diddles.

**MARILYN:** Could you show me one?

**BO:** You wanna see one of them peculiar thangs?

**MARILYN:** If you don't mind.

**BO:** Don't keer if I do.

**MARILYN:** Now what does that mean?

**BO:** Whatcha mean what does it mean?

**MARILYN:** When I said, "If you don't mind." And you said, "I don't ... "

**BO:** "Don't keer if I do."

**MARILYN:** Yeah!

**BO:** It just means whut it sez, "Don't keer ... " which means I ain't got a care in the world to keep me from doin' it, whatever it is we're con-flabin' 'bout.

**MARILYN:** We were talking about your collection here. (Pause) It seems like a kind of potpourri?

**BO:** I don't 'preciate what you be sayin' 'bout my things.

**MARILYN:** I beg your pardon.

**BO:** I know we be poah. But you don't hafta call ouah things "po" ... whatevah.

**MARILYN:** Potpourri!

**BO:** Yeah!

**MARILYN:** I'm afraid that some times our different languages trip us up.

**BO:** What you studyin' at that university?

**MARILYN:** Language ... Particularly regionalisms of English.

**BO**: So that's what I am?

**MARILYN**: You? Well I am particularly interested in the Appalaychian ...

**BO**: Whoa! Whoa! Youah sayin' it wrong.

**MARILYN**: Saying what wrong?

**BO**: It's not Appalaychian. "Snake", said Eve, "If you dare to deceive, I'll throw an apple atcha." Appalachia! When you be in a land wheah folks call themselves by a certain name, don't you think you oughta name it the way they call it?

**MARILYN**: You're absolutely right. I apologize, and I'll try to keep that in mind. (An awkward pause. She changes the subject.) Are you aware of what people outside these hills say about you people here?

**BO**: I've heard tell thet they say all kinda mean thangs about a strange people in a strange land.

**MARILYN**: Does that bother you at ... or better than that "Don't keer if you do?"

**BO**: (Looking at her questioningly.) Hit don't bother me enough to have a conniption fit ...

**MARILYN**: Conniption?

**BO**: Ain't you nevah had no conniption ...

**MARILYN**: I think maybe I have, from time to time. (A pause in their conversation.) Now we're getting somewhere.

**BO**: Really? We gettin' somewheah? Wheah that wheah we be gettin'?

**MARILYN**: Everything is so quiet around here. (More quiet.) How long has the town been dead?

**BO**: Oh not long.

**MARILYN**: Not long?

**BO**: You know when a carcass lays theah awhile an' turns to cyarn (carrion) then the buzzards fly in.

**MARILYN**: The buzzards?

**BO**: Yeah an' yoah the first un to fly down to pick the carcass of this dead place.

**MARILYN**: Well, I 've never been ...

**BO**: Oh, I'm just joshin' ...

**MARILYN:** That's okay. I was told to expect ...

**BO:** What was you s'posed to expect?

**MARILYN:** To expect the unusual.

**BO:** To expect the unexpected?

**MARILYN:** That's a way of putting it. But I'd like to know more about your Folk Collection.

**BO:** You know, I been 'round folks all my life. An' I know what folks mean, but I don't colleckt'em. Maybe you could 'splain some things to me.

**MARILYN:** I'd be happy to explain something, if I know what it is.

**BO:** Well, first off, I'd like to know wheah you come from an whut brings you to these God-fer-saken hills.

**MARILYN:** Now that is something I can explain. I was born and grew up in South Bend, Indiana ...

*Bo interrupts her.*

**BO:** Why was it bent?

**MARILYN:** No. it wasn't bent.

**BO:** Somethin' musta been bent or it wouldn't have thet name.

**MARILYN:** Oh, Yes the town is on the south bend of the St. Joseph River.

**BO:** Wheah does he come in ?

**MARILYN:** Who?

**BO:** Thet Saint somebody.

**MARILYN:** I was just telling you that I come from South Bend, Indiana, which is on the south bend of the St. Joseph River.

**BO:** Now I get that.

**MARILYN:** And then I went off to school.

**BO:** Now hold on again. Yoah folks sent you off to school? We pervide schoolin' fer our young'uns heah. Sorry 'bout you havin' to leave home to find a school.

**MARILYN:** Oh no. I did go to public school in Indiana.

**BO:** I thought it was South Bend.

**MARILYN:** Yes! South Bend, Indiana ... then I went off to college.

**BO:** You confusin' me again. I thought you went off to school, but now you tell me you went to school in thet town an' then you went off to college.

**MARILYN:** That's just a way of speaking. College is also school.

**BO:** We gotta be careful with our language. The words we use. You already ...

**MARILYN:** Yes, well college is just a higher level of school.

**BO:** Now I'm beginnin' to get it. An' then thet school away from home ...

**MARILYN:** Well some graduate study at NYU ...

**BO:** In Why You? Why in why me?

**MARILYN:** No! You don't understand.

**BO:** S'pose not.

**MARILYN:** NYU is the college ...

**BO:** But ...

**MARILYN:** NYU. Those are the letters for New York University.

**BO:** You tangled me up again. It was the school, but the college was also a school and now the college has changed into a you-nigh-versity.

**MARILYN:** Well, that's a higher ...

**BO:** Oh, I know. Thet's just another higher high than the high school back to home?

**MARILYN:** That pretty well explains things up to now.

**BO:** And NOW?

MARILYN: And now I'm renting a room from Mrs. Hilton. I've come to Wise County, Virginia for field work for my ...

**BO:** What kinda field you workin' in heah? I can tell you the gosh awful truth. These fields heah not hardly worth botherin' with. You can't plant nothin' on the slopes nor the rocky ridges. Now the bottom land's not bad for plantin', but they're awful bad to flood, don't you know, when the spring thaw and rains come. B'sides it ain't hardly time for 'baccer or even corn plantin'.

**MARILYN:** When I say field work. I didn't mean in the actual farm fields for crops.

**BO:** What fields did you mean? They're the only fields ...

MARILYN: When I say field work, it means an area of study or research.

**BO:** Now when you say re-search, It means you already searched an' you gotta re-search again ...

*Marilyn throws up her hands in frustration. Bo brings things back to reality.*

**BO:** Do those schools ... colleges ... un-i-ver-sities need a lesson in what words mean?

**MARILYN:** That may be a good idea.

**BO:** So if you're not plantin' 'baccer or corn or taters. You must be sowin' something.

**MARILYN:** That's a good way of putting it ... sowing ... I guess it's a sowing of ideas and learning at the same time.

**BO:** So that's that then?

**MARILYN:** You see I took a major in anthropology.

**BO:** Whoa, now, slow down. All of a sudden we gotta majoh involved. Thet raises a whole passel of moah questions. A majoh in what branch of service?

**MARILYN:** Not in military service. I took a university major ...

**BO:** An' when you took that university majoh ... wheah did you take him? {no answer) When the preacha marries up a couple, one of the things he'd say to the girl, "Do you take this man ... ? Now I allus wondered about thet.

**MARILYN:** What would you wonder about?

**BO:** Now just 'twixt you an' me it comes to my notion that that boy has already took her somewheres'. (no answer) Now you not only took a husban', you took a majoh. An' thet's gettin' high on the hog.

**MARILYN:** No. I didn't take a husband. That means my principal area of study is anthropology

**BO:** Now you just threw me another word ... an ... thro ... polly ... who?

**MARILYN:** Anthropology just means the study of various cultures ...

**BO:** Now I know 'bout agri-culture.  Just like I been 'splainin' ; bout plantin' an' sowin'.

**MARILYN:** Basically anthropology just means the study of people.

**BO:** Now I unnerstan' what thet means. I been studyin' folks all my life, but I didn't hafta go to school (corrects himself) Uh Oh, I mean college to study 'em ... But the moah I study 'em the moah confusin' it gets. I just can't get them figgered out to no real satisfaction.

**MARILYN:** It can get confusing.

**BO:** It's nice to know we agree on somethin' ... But somethin' moah I don't unnderstan'.

**MARILYN:** And what is that?

**BO:** Didn't they have folks up theah at that NYU what needed studyin'?

**MARILYN:** Well, yes, but I've always been intrigued by the folkways here.

**BO:** Wait, Wait. What ways you talkin' 'bout now?

**MARILYN:** I just mean the songs and customs, etc. here in ... (careful to pronounce it correctly) Appalachia.

**BO:** You said it right this time. Appalachia.

**MARILYN:** Thank you. I needed that little lesson. I wouldn't want to appear ignorant.

**BO:** Oh no. There's a whole heap of ignorant appearin' aroun' here, nowadays.

**MARILYN:** But there's something else I'd like to know.

**BO:** Theah's a whole passel of things I'd like to know.

**MARILYN:** Specifically, I'd like to know where you got that little proverb.

**BO:** Oh I know 'bout Proverbs. Thet's a book in the scriptures.

**MARILYN:** You mean that little adage came from the Holy Bible?

**BO:** What adage?

**MARILYN:** Adage just means like an old time saying. Did that actually come from the Bible?

**BO:** It might could've.

**MARILYN:** I really doubt that.

**BO:** I do declare! Youah not just a flatlander, youah a doubtin' Thomas to boot.

**MARILYN:** That little lesson, "Snake", said Eve, "if you dare to ...

**BO:** Well, in the Bible it's not exactly like ...

**MARILYN:** Of course not ... I'm intrigued by these artifacts.

**BO:** Arty who ... ? Oh nevah mind. Just go on.

**MARILYN:** Some of these things are what the Art Department professors would call NAÏVE ART.

**BO:** Are you sayin' thet I'm nah-eve?

**MARILYN:** No, I'm not suggesting ...

**BO:** I don't take suggestin' very much.

**MARILYN:** No, I'm not about suggesting anything. I would like to know about this carving. For instance ...

**BO:** Oh, you mean my whittlin'? Now if a feller can occupy his hands, his mind would follow right along. Then there be times when the mind could be occupied an' bring along the hands to get busy.

**MARILYN:** What do you mean?

**BO:** Now take this whittlin' heah. My hands wuz so occupied thet the mind might could come right along, an' fill in whut the hands wuz doin'.

**MARILYN:** Was that what happened?

**BO:** No, it wuz the other way 'round ... You see my mind knew what was goin' on, an' kinda tole the hands to get busy.

**MARILYN:** I'd appreciate it if you could tell me about this walking stick.

**BO:** Now theah's a big diffurnce or moah likely a big gap between could an' would. Fer instance, I could jump off Lover's Leap up on Sauratown Mountain. That is if I was a mind to. But would I is a whole nother matter.

**MARILYN:** Well then would you?

**BO:** Would I? Theah's no call fer me to jump off right now, cause I ain't lost any love to go kill myself. Not lately anyways.

**MARILYN:** (looking at a hoop in the pile of stuff) Why is this a part of your collection.

**BO:** I tole you I don't have no collection.

**MARILYN:** Well, just tell me about it.

**BO:** Hit's just a hoop toy some young-un left. (She looks at him rather quizzically.) Now I coulda tole you I just kinda contrived it outta a hoop snake, but that'd be lyin', and I certainly wouldn't want to be lyin' to a nice school girl, like ...

**MARILYN:** I appreciate that, but what's a hoop snake?

**BO:** You mean you ain't nevah heard 'bout hoop snakes?

**MARILYN:** I heard them referred to once, but I never really encountered one.

**BO:** But you DO know what they are, an' why they're called hooped snakes?

**MARILYN:** No ... not really.  I just thought that was a strange name for a snake.

**BO:** Well, hit's called a hoop snake, 'cause it turns itself into a hoop when it gets skeered or it wants to take out after another critter.

**MARILYN:** Another creature, like what?

**BO:** Like a two legged critter, what goes by the title of human critter.

**MARILYN:** Aw, nauw! Have you ever seen one of these strange snakes?

**BO:** Now I could tell you I seen lots of 'em, but I wouldn't wanna mislead you with a passel of fibs.

**MARILYN:** So you tell me they're real animals, but you never saw one?

**BO:** You jumpin' to conclusions again.

**MARILYN:** What do you mean jumpin'?

**BO:** I nevah said I hadn't seen one. I said I hadn't seen lots of 'em.

**MARILYN:** So you have seen one?

**BO:** Just one ... but I heard many tales from othah ...

**MARILYN:** No. I just want to know about this strange phenomenon you ...

**BO:** It wasn't a fee-nom-anon. It was a hoop snake.

**MARILYN:** When you encountered it, what happened? (While he's trying to get his story straight she continues.) Didn't that frighten you?

**BO:** Nearly skeered the bejeebers outta me. I just kinda walked up on one, not payin' no nevah mind in the world. Thet cussed thang took one look at me with them beady snakey eyes. He likely sez to hisself, "I don't fancy that feller interruptin' my nap, maybe I'll just teach him a lesson about sneakin' up unbeknownst on a body thataway."

**MARILYN:** He said all that?

**BO:** Now pay attention. Snakes, even hoop snakes can't talk, not out loud anyways. An' moreover I wouldn't know his language. It certainly wouldn't be English. Might could be French.

**MARILYN:** What happened then, after he made his little speech ... (Bo stares at her.) to himself.

**BO:** Well then, he whips his tail round to his mouth, an' I started runnin, before I knew that he'd started rollin'. I wadn't gonna give him the satisfaction of hittin' me with that tail.

**MARILYN:** What would be wrong about the tail? I would imagine any poison would be delivered through his fangs.

**BO:** You've never seen a hoop snake?

**MARILYN:** No.

**BO:** But you already had a notion what one would be like?

**MARILYN:** I've studied snakes in zoology ...

**BO:** Don't you think a hoop snake would be different from ...

**MARILYN:** Yes, of course. With that tail in its ...

**BO:** That's what I'm tryin' to tell you. He was so unusual with that special tail. That's where he carried his poison ...

**MARILYN:** In its tail?

**BO:** You're beginnin' to get the picture.

**MARILYN:** Did you manage to outrun him?

**BO:** I was doin' the runnin'.  He was rollin'.

**MARILYN:** But did he ...

**BO:** The faster I'd run, the faster he'd roll. But I got so plumb wore out that I stopped just in front of a little apple tree sapling, an' turned around to see where he was, an' just as I done that I seen him unquile his tail right outta his mouth.

**MARILYN:** Were you able to ...

**BO:** An' just as he flung hisself at me, I stepped aside an' he stobbed that pointy tail right into thet little sapling.

**MARILYN:** Did he stay impaled there like that?

**BO:** I didn't say anything about pails. Buckets had nothin' to do with it.

**MARILYN:** What I meant to say was did he stay there with his tail stobbed in the little tree?

**BO:** No, he just yanked out that poisonous tail, looked at ne with them beady eyes an' slunk off, just like a regular snake, off twarge the creek. I s'pose he was sulkin' for missin' his mark, which, of course, woulda been me.

**MARILYN:** What a marvelous tale!

**BO:** Hit was shorely a marvelous tail with all that poison. But you know while I was just standin' there tryin' to get my nerves settled down, that little apple tree musta got some growin' juice from that poison. It just started right in growin' while I was lookin' at it.

**MARILYN:** Really?

**BO:** Not only that, I stood there until it started blossomin' and then growin' real apples. They was just little green nubbins at first, but directly they turned into the prettiest red apples you could ever hope for.

**MARILYN:** What did they taste like?

**BO:** I pulled one off for a souvenir.

**MARILYN:** What did it taste like?

**BO:** I wasn't about to eat one of 'em .

**MARILYN:** Why not?

**BO:** Hadn't you been payin' attention?

**MARILYN:** Yes, but I don't see ...

**BO:** All that poison woulda gone right into them apples.

**MARILYN:** I suppose that's the way that wicked old witch poisoned Snow White.

**BO:** You musta heard this tale of the hoop snake tail before.

**MARILYN:** I've done some reading of the folklore up here. Folk lore from days of yore.

**BO:** That's not fair.

**MARILYN:** Why not?

**BO:** You let me go on an' on as if you might be believin' the whole thing.

**MARILYN:** That was the fun of it ... It backfired.

**BO:** But don't you feel bad outdoing an old mountain man?

**MARILYN:** Well, I apologize, but I do have a few more questions.

**BO:** Fire away!

**MARILYN:** I've come to the Southern Appalachians (carefully pronouncing it correctly) to learn some thing about your communication.

**BO:** You mean the words we use to ...

**MARILYN:** Yes! Your language, which is the closest to Shakespeare, so say some linguists.

**BO:** Now just wait a minute. You threw in a couple of new words now. I've heard of that Shakey feller, but lingui ... somethin'!

**MARILYN:** When I said I was wanting to learn the language from a real expert ...

**BO:** Now you don't need to dangle me no moah ovah what I don't know. 'Cause I do know the meanin' of that word.

**MARILYN:** What word?

**BO:** The word you used just a second ago ... expert.

**MARILYN:** Yes! What is your definition of that word?

**BO:** A expert is a little spurt a long ways from home. An' as I'm still to home, I can't be no expert thataway.

**MARILYN:** You didn't invent the meaning to that word ... did you?

**BO:** Nauw, I think I read it in Readers Digest or somewhere like that. We can read, you know.

**MARILYN:** Let's just say you seem to know a whole heap about the language here in the mountains.

**BO:** I shorely do. I been talkin' it all my life.

**MARILYN:** Well, I don't always understand what someone may be saying to me.

**BO:** Like what?

**MARILYN:** Just yesterday I was down at the General Store, and a clerk said, "Whu fer ye?" When I asked him to repeat it, he said it again just like that. "Whu fer ye?" I said, "I don't know what you're saying, but I came to buy a broom."

**BO:** Whut he was askin' was, "What for you?" In other words, "What can I do for you?"

**MARILYN:** Well, thanks! I'm glad you cleared that up for me.

**BO:** Much obliged!

**MARILYN:** Now I know what "much obliged" means.

**BO:** I suppose we can all learn somethin' ... however, not in that school.

**MARILYN:** There are some other words not on my list, but I've heard them and wonder what they may mean. Like just yesterday I heard a fellow say, "Why, I swanay!"

**BO:** Why I swanay ... You got no notion what "I swanay!" means?

**MARILYN:** Maybe just a notion. In the context of what was happening around him, I assumed it was a kind of expletive.

**BO:** That bad, huh?

**MARILYN:** That wouldn't be bad.

**BO:** It's just another way of sayin', "Well, I do declare." Or maybe, "Well, I'm plumb flabbergasted." Or something like that ... that don't really mean anything.

**MARILYN:** That's what an expletive is and that's about what I thought the expression was.

**BO:** You just keep your ears and mind open and you'll probably learn something about "these strange people in a strange land."

**MARILYN:** (holding a clipboard, which she's been using) How do you spell it?

**BO:** Spell it?

**MARILYN:** Yeah, how do you spell swanay?

**BO:** You don't spell it. You just say it.

**MARILYN:** I also heard at the general Store a senior citizen lady ordering strumpet candy. I've never heard of that kind of candy. Is it indigenous to the mountains here?

**BO:** Is it what to the mountains?

**MARILYN:** Is it found only in this area in the mountains?

**BO:** That musta been Ol' Missus Harris. She just can't abide using a dirty word.

**MARILYN:** I don't believe ...

**BO:** You evah heard of horehound candy?

**MARILYN:** Yes, but ...

**BO:** That dear ol' lady couldn't use the word whore, so she substitute the word strumpet, which meant the same thing.

**MARILYN:** How clever! That was a euphemism.

**BO:** No it was a strumpet.

**MARILYN:** A euphemism just means using a different word to be more polite or acceptable.

**BO:** Like using fireboard instead of what you folks would call a mantle.

**MARILYN:** Fireboard does seem more specific. I've also heard folks double up on words.

**BO:** Like?

**MARILYN:** Soldier boy or church house.

**BO:** And widder-woman.

**MARILYN:** I believe Mrs. Hilton is a widow-woman. She promised to teach me how to cook country ham without it being so salty.

**BO:** So briny you mean?

**MARILYN:** Yes. She also has so many books, even the complete works of Shakespeare.

**BO:** I don't know about his works, but I remember some words of his'n.

MARILYN: What were they?

BO: He wrote, "If this be error and upon me proved, I never writ nor no man ever loved." Now only Shakespeare or a hillbilly could have writ that.

MARILYN: I believe you may be right. Well I'm off and will drop by again.

BO: Don't DROP by, just COME by. Real soon now you hear?

MARILYN: If the Good Lord's awilling an' the creek don't rise.

BO: Well I swanay. It sure looks like yoah learnin' somethin' about talkin', yoah own self.

*Bo exits into the house. Marilyn stops to talk to Lloyd.*

MARILYN: Hello! I'm Marilyn.

LLOYD: I know.

MARILYN: What's your name?

LLOYD: Lloyd.

MARILYN: Do you live here?

LLOYD: Sometimes.

MARILYN: Where else do you live?

LLOYD: At the university.

MARILYN: So you're a student at the university?

LLOYD: Nope!

MARILYN: If you're not a student, whom do you live with there?

LLOYD: My dad.

MARILYN: What kind of work does he do there?

LLOYD: He teaches.

MARILYN: That's really interesting. What does he teach?

LLOYD: English literature.

MARILYN: I sure would like to meet your father. Could you introduce me to him?

LLOYD: S'pose so!

MARILYN: (writing on her clip board) What's his name?

LLOYD: Bo.

MARILYN: Surely he has a last name.

LLOYD: He does.

**MARILYN:** Could you please enlighten me with his surname?

**LLOYD:** I could.

**MARILYN:** Well!

**LLOYD:** It's Dillon.

**MARILYN:** You mean to tell me that ...

**LLOYD:** Yep! You already met him. (silence from her) Been talkin' to him all afternoon

**MARILYN:** (stuffing her clipboard into her back pack - Angrily) You don't mean to say ...

**BO:** (entering from house) I'm afraid he does mean to say.

**MARILYN:** What a dastardly underhanded thing to do!

**BO:** An unexpected encounter in one's academic research should strengthen the academician ... in his/her further pursuit to a satisfactory conclusion.

**MARILYN:** (in a Grand Opera acting style) "There are more things in Heaven and earth, Horatio, than are dreamt of in your philosophy."

**BO:** "Get thee to a nunnery! Why wouldst thou be a breeder of sinners?"

**MARILYN:** (falling on her knees) "O help him, ye sweet heavens!"

**BO:** Shakespeare could deliver us both from the throes of scholastic mischief. (helping her to her feet) I was just having a little fun

**MARILYN:** At my expense.

**BO:** Isn't Professor Bowman your major professor?

**MARILYN:** Yes. How do you know him?

**BO:** We sometimes play poker together.

**MARILYN:** But what does that have to do with ... ?

**BO:** He told me you were coming up to Wise County to conduct interviews in preparation for your research on archaic languages still in various parts of the Appalachians.

*Lloyd takes his guitar into the house.*

**MARILYN:** That was still a dastardly thin ...

**BO:** Professor Bowman thought you should have a little initiation into the process of interviewing residents of the designated area of research. I suppose he thought I could deliver.

**MARILYN:** But how ...

**BO:** Both he and I wanted to give you an idea of what you may be encountering when you interrogate these hill folk. They are somewhat reticent at times, because they feel they've been probed and poked so much by outlanders, intrigued by our strange ways and language. Some of them would even admit to being "standoffish". They are tired of such films and TV programs as "Beverly Hillbillies" and "Dukes of Hazard". I do apologize.

**MARILYN:** Apology accepted. I'm sure my subsequent interviews will be a bit more pleasant.

**BO:** Though you're interested in a rather archaic language, which we've maintained here in the mountains, even this is not static. Over in the next county you might hear someone use the word sy-gogglin'. You won't hear anyone in this neighborhood or in other places outside that county using it.

**MARILYN:** What does it mean?

**BO:** It merely means slant-wise or cattywompus, out of alignment. Everyone in that neighborhood would know what it means. Someone must have been at a loss for words when they saw a building sagging a bit. It was sy-gogglin'.

**MARILYN:** How would I know ...

**BO:** There would be no way you or any other researcher would know how to find the derivation of it from the Elizabethan lexicon.

**MARILYN:** Thanks for the "heads-up" on that.

**BO:** Language, even here, is alive.

**MARILYN:** I have a friend who's exploring new vocabularies in the inner cities.

**BO:** That must be a whole new ball game. The reason I went into the house was to put a pot of collard greens on the stove. Could you stay awhile longer for some suppah vittles with me and Lloyd?

MARILYN: I suppose so.

BO: Your new language response would be, "Don't keer if I do."

MARILYN: Don't care if I do. (Beautiful guitar music can be heard from the house.) Even Lloyd with his guitar was a sham.

BO: Yeah; he's a pretty good guitar player ... We prob'ly don't have nothin' fitten to eat, but whatevah we got, you're a welcome to it.

MARILYN: I'd be much obliged.

BO: It seems that everybody's learnin' some lessons, today. Special thanks for explainin' uni-ver-sity to me.

BLACKOUT

# Smeraldina's Inn

Having been immersed in the art form of Mime, I was intrigued with the style of theatre, Commedia del Arte, which gave birth to modern mime. Although the commedia was indigenous to Italy, it was much more at home in France and made popular by Jean-Louis Barrault, particularly in the film, *Les Enfants du Paradis*. Barrault was largely responsible for the French character Pierrot, which Marcel Marceau continued toward the end of the 20th century.

The style is filled with a lot of tomfoolery and "slapstick". Actually the term, "slapstick" is derived from the commedia in which Pantalone uses it to make some resounding whipping of his servant with a harmless but loud "slapstick".

# SMERALDINA'S INN OR SMERALDINA'S IN

*by E. Reid Gilbert*

Cast

| | |
|---|---|
| **ARLECCHINO** | ....My master, Pantalone, gets tired of my tricks |
| **COLUMBINI** | ........A mere servant I may be |
| **PANTOLONE** | ......I'm known to be quite rich |
| **FRANCESCA** | ........I am Francesca, the harrowing shrew |
| **SMERALDINA** | ....Matchmaking is my game |
| **CAPITANO** | ...........Winning fortune and great fame |
| **DOTTORE** | ............As you well know I'm the accomplished Dottore |
| **FLAMINIA** | ............I am now called Flumox But Flaminia is my name |
| **COLLETTE** | ..........I need a man who can treat me right |
| **OCTAVIO** | .............I am Octavio, a dashing dude |

Characters with their self-proclaimed introductions. As each character prances or capers in, some times with a lazzo, he/she takes a fixed position. When all have entered they've formed a tableau of statuary.

## SCENE 1

**ARLECCHINO:**

Arlecchino is my nom de plume
　My music is like a flower in bloom
　My master, Pantalone, gets tired of my tricks
　And beats my derriere with wooden slapsticks.

**COLUMBINI:**

　I am known as Columbini
　And I can be quite a meany,
　But my shtick with Arlecchino
　Is important to the show.
　A mere servant I may be,
　But I'll take no guff you'll see.

**PANTALONE:**

　My name is Pantalone
　I'm known to be quite rich.
　My legs are surely bony
　And my wife's a nagging witch.
　Then there's my daughter, Collette
　Who hasn't found a husband yet.
　To find the right man will take lots of work,
　Because she usually brings home a jerk.

**FRANCESCA:**

　I am Francesca, the harrowing shrew.
　I'll nag and fume till my face turns blue.
　I get quite itchy
　If I'm not being bitchy
　　*OPERATIC ARIA*
　And I yell when I sing opera too.

**SMERALDINA:**

　Smeraldina is my name.
　Matchmaking is my game.
　This business is my inn
　I'll not reveal Smeraldina's sin.

**CAPITANO:**

　I'm the brave Capitano
　Don Trimarcho is my name.

I've fought many a battle
Winning fortune and great fame.
I see from your gaze
You admire me so.
Please make my day;
I'm ready to go.

**DOTTORE:**

As you well know I'm the accomplished Dottore,
Not just of science, but also amore;
Known far and wide for my intellect and knowledge
The things I could teach, you won't learn in college

**FLAMINIA:**

I am now called Flumox
But Flaminia is my name.
I ran away from home
Being a girl was much too tame.
So I'm studying the doctor's medical books,
But I'm most interested in his handsome looks.

**COLLETTE:**

I need a man who can treat me right
One who won't drink and stay out all night,
Who'll say, "Collette, you're out of sight!"
I'll then love him with all of my might.

**OCTAVIO:**

I am Octavio, a dashing dude,
Looking for love, neither rude not crude.
If I can find an adoring wife,
I'll be happy for the rest of my life.

    *SONG - We need a score for everyone to sing.*

We are all seeking and hope to acquire
A new love to make our worlds come upright
A new life now we all do aspire
Although we seem so very uptight.
Now to inquire of a new love to acquire
But neither a liar nor a noxious spitfire.

## SCENE 2

*The setting outside the inn with several tables and chairs set up.*
*A sign on the back wall announces "Smeraldina's Inn" and in*
*red letters "Matchmaking Services." Smeraldina and*
*Columbine enter.*

**SMERALDINA:**

We're late, Columbine! Soon the guests will arrive.

**COLUMBINI:**

But first Smellarena, we must write my classified.

**SMERALDINA:**

My name is SMERAL-DINA!

**COLUMBINE:**

Sorry! My dialect is Messina.

**SMERALDINA:**

My matchmaking skills do range far and wide.

Now tell me about the last boy that you eyed.

**COLUMBINE:**

Oh, he was tall dark and handsome and with money to
  spare

But demons put his brains in his underwear.

**SMERALDINA:**

I'll write the perfect classified for you, my dear,

And when I'm done I'll post it right here.

(Putting her thumb on wall while Francesca is heard
singing off stage in an operatic voice.)

The guests are arriving, so we must finish preparing.

And please, Columbine, remember no swearing.

**COLUMBINE:**

But what about gossip that I forswore?

**SMERALDINA:**

Oh, yes! I really couldn't ask for more'.

**COLUMBINI AND SMERALDINA DUET:**

They'll come whining, a spouse to get

Not willing really to open their eyes

E'en though they already have their minds set

But here they'll find a tremendous surprise.

Surprise, surprise,

now open your eyes
A roue you may get
or yet a coquette.

## SCENE 3

*Francesca, Pantalone and Collette enter with Francesca singing before speaking.*

**FRANCESCA:**
Lord, these new shoes are killing my feet.
It's difficult walking daintily down the street.

**PANTALONE:**
But my dear, sweet deary, you've so many shoes
Imelda you're not, though my money you use.

**FRANCESCA:**
Imelda Marcos I may not be,
But your good fortune walks the street with me.

**PANTALONE:**
Streetwalking is not my sin.

**FRANCESCA:**
Oh, here we are at the inn.

**PANTALONE:**
An inn, an inn! My parched throat!

**FRANCESCA:**
Libations later, you old goat.
This is Smeraldina's inn.

**PANTALONE:**
I well remember Smeraldina's big sin.
She was so young and I had fuzz on my chin.

**FRANCESCA:**
You'd better not be alluding to what I'm thinking
Or your name and fortune will soon be sinking.
This Smeraldina is good at love matching
And a spouse for Collette we need to be catching.

**PANTALONE:**
She is my only daughter to speak of,
As you're my first wife, my love.

**FRANCESCA:**

What do you mean your first wife?

I hope you value the length of your life.

**PANTALONE:**

Back to our simple-minded Collette!

Hasn't she snatched a candidate yet?

(singing)

My Collette is no coquette.

Obviously a score here.

Though coquettish she may be.

She's pretty and slight

And full of delight;

Her fortunate father is me.

**FRANCESCA:**

Are you finished?

**PANTALONE:**

My Francesca

(Still singing to the earlier tune.)

Is no can of Fresca;

Thought gassy she may be.

She's haughty and proud

Her head in the cloud

Her unfortunate husband is me.

**FRANCESCA:**

Pantalone!

**PANTALONE:**

Old Pantalone,

(still singing the earlier tune.)

May be full of baloney,

Though cunning I may be

I've land and money

But a nose that's runny;

Unhappy is poor me.

**FRANCESCA:**

Now before Smeraldina comes out

We must know what we're about.

What kind of husband do we seek?

**PANTALONE:**

Maybe Smeraldina has a special this week.

**FRANCESCA:**

What requirements do we want,

Aside from number one, being male.?

**PANTALONE:**

And no money right up front.

Maybe there'll be a weekend sale.

**FRANCESCA:**

Number two: He must be wealthy

And also maybe healthy.

Number three: open to negotiation -

Attractive, but no facial alteration.

Now if we can simply find this match

A son-in-law we shall catch.

**PANTALONE:**

Catch? Does that mean we're going fishing?

**FRANCESCO:**

If a perfect liaison you are wishing.

And just like fishing, we must have the right bait.

So with a dowry we'll celebrate.

**PANTALONE:**

A dowry — a dowry? That means money.

This is serious and not very funny.

**FRANCESCO:**

To find a bridegroom with some pride,

A dowry must accompany every bride.

A dowry of money before the first birth

Or perhaps objects of great worth.

**PANTALONE:**

If there's a way to have my say,

There's nothing I have I'd give away

**FRANCESCO:**

Oh quit fretting; I'll give you a clue

The objects we'll give have no value.

Pantalone, for goodness sake

Are you sleeping or are you awake?

**PANTALONE:**

I am not sleeping; I am awake,

Fearful for the money they might take.

**FRANCESCO:**

Oh, Panty, don't be so drear

(She sings, but is interrupted periodically.)

There's really nothing here for you to fear.

(with Collette's spoken lines)

Collette, my dear, so lovely and chaste...

**COLLETTE:**

Yes, Mama?

**FRANCESCO:**

Time to brush your hair and wash your face.

*After singing this line, she begins to speak the additional lines.*

**COLLETTE:**

Yes, Mama.

**FRANCESCO:**

A husband bold, we'll find for you

But there are some things you must do.

**COLLETTE:**

Oh, Mama?

**FRANCESCO:**

Remember always to sit up straight

A man of distinction will not tolerate

A grumpy slouch as his playmate.

**COLLETTE:**

Yes, Mama.

**FRANCESCO:**

And you follow my promptings and refrain from sin ...

**COLLETTE:**

Ooh, Mama!

**FRANCESCO:**

A rich man to woo you is what you shall win.

**COLLETTE:**

OH!

**FRANCESCO:**

*She sings and dances with Collette and another song for*
*Fran.*

Please make him fair and trim
Pearly teeth and strong of limb –
So handsome that the ladies all
For his charm they're sure to fall.
To treasure
With pleasure
Such a man to call dear,
But not a Sicilian, whom I'd fear

**COLLETTE:**

I like Sicilians!

**FRANCESCO:**

Not in my family, the doltish lout;
They have their own family to wipe others out.

**PANTALONE:**

Just order from the menu.
Here's a good one for you.
"Retired Capitano, believed to have wealth,
Greatly endowed with extremely good health."
The rest are immigrants from out of state.

**FRANCESCO:**

Or just tradesmen whom I hate.

**PANTALONE:**

Oh here's an interesting bridal ad.
An opportunity not half bad.
"Young, beautiful woman from Westminster.
Business woman and a spinster."
That means not married as of yet
What a catch that'd be to get.
"Asian heritage
Ready for marriage"
(sings)
Sounds exotic
(a score here for Pantalone)
If not despotic

A geisha is for me

With a beautiful bun and ...

**FRANCESCO:**

On her head.

**PANTALONE:** (still singing)

A beautiful bun

And full of fun,

Her parents away o'er the sea.

**FRANCESCO:**

We're here to find Collette's spouse

Not one for you. Are you a louse?

**PANTALONE:**

Not a louse, nor even a mouse.

**FRANCESCO:**

Nary a louse nor mouse in my house.

**PANTALONE:**

Have it your way; you always do.

But I'll try my best to always come through.


## SCENE 4

*Columbine enters.*

**COLUMBINE:**

Welcome to our inn; you must be new in town.

As you order from our menu, I shall write it down.

**PANTALONE:** (singing) (quite agitated)

A geisha, a geisha — and just the right size.

(the earlier geisha song)

And what a beauty — a sight for sore eyes.

A beautiful flower in exquisite bloom

(He stands and trembles with excitement.)

**COLUMBINE:**

What is the matter? You need the bathroom?

**FRANCESCO:**

No, no, he's just an old Pantaloon.

**COLUMBINE:**

I'm outta here — he's a lecherous goon

*She starts running with Pantalone right after her around*

*several tables, before she exits. Smeraldina's entrance*
*interrupts Panatalone's chase scene.*

**SMERALDINA:**

I hope she didn't disturb you. She's an excitable girl.

**PANTALONE:**

A kind of excitement I'd like to give a twirl.

**SMERALDINA:**

Could I bring you something – perhaps a drink?

**FRANCESCO:**

Some thing to cool him down, I should think.

(reading from the menu )

Here's something I think would suit me

A baked potato and chicken fricassee.

(Pantalone turns the menu over to the other side.)

**SMERALDINA:**

Oh, I see it's not a meal you want but an eligible spouse.

**PANTALONE:**

I have a half-baked one — but the queen of the house.

**FRANCESCO:**

Why thank you my dear. Yes it's quite true.

A son-in-law we need so we came straight to you.

**SMERALDINA:**

We have handsome Chileans, Koreans and Maccabeans.

And even a special on newly arrived Sicilians.

**COLLETTE:**

Ooh!

**FRANCESCA:**

No Sicilians for them I have great fear

For they are gangsters — or so I hear.

**COLLETTE:**

But Ma-ma!

**PANTALONE:**

Don't worry darling daughter, don't you fret.

If not a Sicilian — a handsome dude for you I'll get.

**COLLETTE:**

Thanks Pa-pa!

**SMERALDINA:**

May I then recommend, perhaps, Capitano?

**FRANCESCA:** (reading from menu)

Retired ship captain from old Milano.

It says here he's in excellent health

And furthermore a man of great wealth.

**COLLETTE:**

Oh, My!

**FRANCESCA:**

With great wealth, he must be the one.

**COLLETTE:**

What fun!

**PANTALONE:**

If he has money and a life that's flowery

He won't need my money or a puny dowry.

(Columbine sticks her head out and Pantalone sings as he

runs off after her.)

A geisha, a geisha, A geisha is for me

(still the same geisha song)

We'll sail far away oe'r the bounding sea.

**FRANCESCA:**

O he's harmless the old coot.

Don't dawdle, Collete, it's time to scoot.

**COLLETTE:**

Yes. Ma-ma!

**COLUMBINE:**

Entering through another door.

Oh, he's crazy — crazy as a loon.

**SMERALDINA:**

She told you he was just an old pantaloon.

As for that matter I don't give a whist

For now I'll have Capitano off my list

**COLUMBINE:**

But what about my ad for a beau

It's been weeks and still no show.

**SMERALDINA:**

Oh, Columbine, I must tell you right now

This morning I had a vision about you somehow.

**COLUMBINE:**

Yeah?

**SMERALDINA:**

A tall, dark, handsome man came into view

And if I saw right he was looking for you.

**COLUMBINE:**

Are you sure?

**SMERALDINA:**

If my calculations correct, he'll arrive soon.

The tea leaves say right around noon.

**COLUMBINE:**

It's almost ...

(interrupted by Octavio bounding onto stage.)

**OCTAVIO:** (singing)

Oh what a beautiful morning. O what a beautiful life.

(speaking)

Since this is a matchmaker's place, maybe I'll find a wife.

Having sailed the seven seas, and finding my fortune there, I'm now looking for a gorgeous beauty beyond compare.

**SMERALDINA:**

Yoo hoo ...

**OCTAVIO:**

Hello!

**SMERALDINA:**

Hello! You seem to be lost here I fear.

Perhaps you'll find a new fortune here.

**OCTAVIO:**

Where? Where?

**SMERALDINA:**

Here.

**OCTAVIO:**

And where is here?

**SMERALDINA:**
You're outside my inn.

**OCTAVIO:**
Am I outside or am I in?

**SMERALDINA:**
Yes!

**OCTAVIO:**
No, you don't understand.

**SMERALDINA:**
Yes, I do understand. This is my inn,
And you're outside of my inn.

**OCTAVIO:**
Your lines don't even make a good rhyme.
How can I be out and in at the same time?

**SMERALDINA:**
Well just try to look at it this way
You've come to the front of my inn you see
And it should be as clear as day
You're outside the inn which belongs to me.

**OCTAVIO:**
Oh, I understand the inside belongs to you

**SMERALDINA:**
Now you're beginning to know what's true

**OCTAVIO:**
These are your belongings I know.

**SMERALDINA:**
Oh you're impossible.

**OCTAVIO:**
No, I'm just Octavio.
(looking at sign over door.)
And I'm sure you must be Smeraldinasin.

**SMERALDINA:**
Are you dyslexic, my good man?

**OCTAVIO:**
No, I'm Octavio, as I've told you before.
And I must be standing outside your inn door.

**SMERALDINA:**

Let's try on this explanation for size.

You're out of the inn you must realize.

**OCTAVIO:**

I don't understand. I am really confused.

**SMERALDINA:**

You said you're Octavio. I'm not really amused.

**OCTAVIO:**

I'm confused about being out while in

At what I thought was Smeraldinasin.

*Columbine enters*

And who may this Belladonna be?

**COLUMBINE:**

I'm no deadly nightshade though dangerous I can be.

**OCTAVIO:**

Ooh, ooh, ooh, please don't hurt me. (mockingly)

But what is your name my pretty lass?

**COLUMBINE:**

For the time being I'll remain nameless.

**OCTAVIO:**

Imagine that — a grown woman with no name.

I consider that an ultimate shame.

The first woman here tries to confuse me

And then this pretty lass attempts to refuse me.

Everything here really seems to be run down.

Maybe there's something for me in the next town.

*Exits*

**SMERALDINA:**

Look what you've done, you've frightened him away.

**COLUMBINE:**

He had a game I didn't choose to play.

**COLUMBINE and SMERALDINA:** (singing)

Now it seems that a game plan we must hatch

To see if for him there's an appropriate new match.

Not just to make his life a bit sappy.

## SCENE 5

**ARLECCHINO:**

Running in Aah, the horrible creature actually spoke.

I thought I'd run into the rear of a goat.

He opened his maw and began to bellow

"My name is Capitano Don Trimarcho."

**COLUMBINE:**

Oh, Arlecchino you're always so funny.

**SMERALDINA:**

Don't fret about Capitano; he has much money.

He'll be gone soon, and thus I'd bet.

I'm marrying him off to the coquettish Collette.

**ARLECCHINO:**

What! My master's sweet girl?

That's like matching a goat with a squirrel.

He smells like a fish.

**COLUMBINE:**

The charm of a hog.

**SMERALDINA:**

He's ugly!

**COLUMBINE:**

He's greasy!

**SMERALDINA:**

He croaks like a frog!

**ARLECCHINO:**

Collette must be saved. I'll have to be swift.

**SMERALDINA:**

If we were doctors, we could give him a facelift.

**ARLECCHINO:**

We'll banish him away from here

A botched facelift — just you never fear.

**SMERALDINA:**

Though we'd like to give him a new ugly mask

We're not doctors to accomplish this gruesome task.

**ARLECCHINO:** (singing)

Ah, are we ever in luck!

Just three weeks ago

I received from Smothers, Strothers and Stress
Home Correspondence Course for medical ego
Granting me a post-doctoral master of medical B.S.
All you need now is the hypocritical oath
And I must swear in the two of you both.

**SMERALDINA:**

There's no swearing-in in my inn young man
A lady must be adamant in her moral stand.

**ARLECCHINO:**

We won't swear in; we'll pledge instead.
So repeat after me just like a newlywed.

**COLUMBINE:**

We seem to have a lot of that around here.
But I've been waiting for over a year

**SMERALDINA:**

Now Columbine don't get in a tizzy.
To find you a man, I shall get busy.

**ARLECCHINO:**

Now repeat after me as we make this pledge
To the bank and the CEO's gilt-edge.
We pledge allegiance to the American banks.

**COLUMBINE and SMERALDINA:**

We pledge allegiance to the American banks

**ARLECCHINO:**

And to them we'll ever give thanks.

**COLUMBINE and SMERALDINA:**

And to them we'll ever give thanks.

**ARLECCHINO:**

To them we'll ever dedicate our all.

**COLUMBINE and SMERALDINA:**

To them we'll ever dedicate our all.

**ARLECCHINO:**

With invisible justice for the small.

**COLUMBINE and SMERALDINA:**

With invisible justice for the small.

**ARLECCHINO:** *PATTERN-LIKE RAP for these lines*
  And now with the rights granted unto me
  By the pervading spirit of the eternal maximus
  I pass on this power to the new inductee.
  For the unum incontintiousness e-pluribus
  I now pronounce you maniacal germ-free
  Diabolical doctors to collect your big fee.
  And now as we avoid any perjury
  We hasten off to Capitano's surgery.
      *Dottore and Flumox rush in.*
**DOTTORE:**
  Where is this latin-quacking quack?
**ARLECCHINO:**
  I'm no quack, you old hack.
      *Flumox is constantly taking notes and looking for approval.*
**DOTTORE:** (singing obviously a score here for doc)
  E Fluribus non grata Bon magnum est strata.
  It has come to my attention of late
  That there is a charlatan within the gate,
  Who is disguising himself as a valid part
  Of the distinguished doctoral healing arts.
  And the physicians who were as it were
  Not known in the least nor in the most
  Here present or even a foreign docteur
  Who is worth the fee of whatever cost.
  For the summum bonum Of erectus hominum.
**ARLECCHINO:**
  Are you questioning my credentials?
**DOTTORE:**
  That is the basis of these essentials.
**ARLECCHINO:**
  You could help with something we have in mind.
**FLUMOX:**
  Oh yes, let's do, if you would be so kind.
**DOTTORE:**
  What would it be – this medical gift?

**ARLECCHINO:**

Not very simple, but a needed facelift.

**FLUMOX:**

Oh, Dottore, I've never assisted such a medical task.

**DOTTORE:**

Never fear, dear Flumox, just do as I ask.

But first a lesson, anatomical.

**FLUMOX:**

O Dottore, you are so phenomical.

**DOTTORE:**

The hand bone is connected to the ...

**FLUMOX:**

Arm bone?

**ARLECCHINO:**

No, it's the wrist bone as here is shone.

(holding up his limp wrist.)

**COLUMBINE:**

Oh, Arlecchino you are so funny.

**DOTTORE:**

That doesn't matter, if there's no money.

But we should examine the bone of the chest.

**FLUMOX:**

Isn't that also the bone of the breast?

**DOTTORE:**

Perhaps we should take a moment to examine

(with hands approaching Flumox's chest)

**FLUMOX:** (clasping the button at her collar. )

No let's now find this lucky Frankenstein.

**DOTTORE:**

Well the lesson is over — to surgery we must go.

Maximus, minimus in extremis is the show.

**FLUMOX:**

To the layman that means, "Don't dis me man'"

Isn't he cute and like Superman?

His highest credentials I can assure.

**SMERALDINA:**

But tell me doctor what can you cure?

(dottore singing his previous tune)

The measles, the wheezles and broken bones,

The boils with oils and kidney stones,

The itch, the stitch, the choler, the gout,

And if there're two devils in I can get twenty out.

**COLUMBINE:**

Tell me, Dottore, what medicine do you use?

**ARLECCHINO:**

Could you give me a list that I'd be able to peruse?

**DOTTORE:** (singing any tune)

These are the medicines that I choose

For all these maladies to defuse.

First I fetch a can of spam

Then three quarts of nim-nam

Strained through a side of shoe leather

Stirred with a frog's long tail feather

Mixed with two teaspoons of bone marrow

From a stool leg, combined with some yarrow.

**ARLECCHINO:**

Pardon me for asking one so assured,

But are you for malpractice adequately insured?

**FLUMOX:**

His insurance and reputation are both the same.

No one dares question the strength of his name.

**ARLECCHINO:**

Fine. Let me show you the operating room.

And this chat-chat we shall surely resume.

## SCENE 6

*Capitano enters and upon seeing an audience, he begins boasting of his amorous adventures. Arlecchino enters a bit late, listening to Capitano but unseen by him.*

**CAPITANO:** (singing)

Ladies, yes ladies and gentlemen too,

But speaking of ladies, I've had quite a few.

I've had so many sweethearts in my life

But what I desire now is a dutiful wife.

I must admit I've been called a roué
But the girl who'll be my fiancée
Will be delightfully innocent and ever so sweet
Upbeat and discreet and my little helpmeet
I've come to this inn and I'll pay the fee
If she's half as pretty as in this picture I see
(looking at the picture)
I'm looking at you my little honey bun.

**ARLECCHINO:**

If she looks at him she'll be on the run.

**CAPITANO:**

To savor your sweet breath, my adorable lass.

**ARLECCHINO:**

His breath, not sweet is like poisonous gas,

**CAPITANO:**

Your cheeks are as red as a deep-red rose.

**ARLECCHINO:**

His wayward ways I must disclose

**CAPITANO:**

You make me feel so happy and gay.
(Sees Arlecchino)

**ARLECCHINO:**

Me? I'm sorry, I'm not that way.

**CAPITANO:**

What is that you're trying to say?

**ARLECCHINO:**

I'm afraid I'll just have to be on my way.

**CAPITANO:**

No, there's something here I want to show you.

**ARLECCHINO:**

What's the sum this thing comes to?

**CAPITANO:**

It's wonder is really quite immense.

**ARLECCHINO:**

You must think I'm terribly dense.
But there's something that I have in mind,
My master Pantalone I must find.

**CAPITANO:**

Why how fortunate — I'm looking for Pantalone too.

**ARLECCHINO:**

Is that the picture you want me to view.

If so, I'm sure it's really a dilly.

**CAPITANO:**

That's outrageous and just plain silly.

I'm simply trying to get through to you

But I'm afraid you've been misconstrued.

**ARLECCHINO:**

I'm only concerned if Pantalone is in.

I am not a Miss nor have I ever been.

**CAPITANO:**

My boy you're a real headcase

But this is not some kind of race.

I've not seen your kind since my days at sea

Why don't you just tell your story to me.

**ARLECCHINO:**

Though you may think I'm only a clown,

You'll probably fare better in the next town.

**CAPITANO:**

I could tell you of my many sea exploits

Particularly with the mysterious, Indian Dacoits.

**ARLECCHINO:**

You may think you'd be quite a catch

But I'm sure Collette will find another match.

**CAPITANO:** (singing)

But lovely Collette is supposed to me mine

As my little bride she'll surely shine.

This picture is what I've tried to show

Look at it then you'll know.

> *Shows picture to arlecchino.*

**ARLECCHINO:**

Ooh! (looking at picture )

Ugh! (looking at Capitano )

Ooh! (looking at picture )

Ugh! (looking at Capitano)

**CAPITANO:**

What's wrong with your face?

It's all twisted awry.

It's worse even than your headcase

Are you about to cry?

**ARLECCHINO:**

It's not my face I'm worried about

**CAPITANO:**

Come on, boy, spit it out.

**ARLECCHINO:**

It's just that she's so absolutely and very

**CAPITANO:**

The very girl I intend to marry.

**ARLECCHINO:**

And you're so absolutely and very

**CAPITANO:**

Stupendous and the very man she'd want to marry.

**ARLECCHINO:**

That's not exactly what I meant to say.

It's just that I'd expect a jackass to bray.

**CAPITANO:** (grabbing Arlechinno by the collar)

Why you, you little dunderhead

I'll take you to the old woodshed.

And whip you soundly with a birch switch.

That'll cure your little facial itch.

**ARLECCHINO:**

Please don't do something you'll live to regret

But it's your face we must fix yet.

**CAPITANO:**

Why you terrible incorrigible little imp!

*Hits at Arlecchino with his fist but hits the wall instead.*

**ARLECCHINO:**

I may be small but I'm no shrimp.

**CAPITANO:**

Moaning Imp, shrimp or wimp I could care less
But my injured hand is in distress.

**ARLECCHINO:**

We'll fetch Dottore to fix your hand
And he'll also fix your face.

**CAPITANO:**

Dear young fellow you don't understand
These lines from my face he can't erase.

**ARLECCHINO:**

The Dottore will be here before too long.
Ssh can't you hear it. It sounds like a song.
(begins to sing)
Replace your face!
A little facelift is of no disgrace.
When women look at you they reach for mace.
Replace your face!
Hey pal I'm now urgin'
Ya to visit the surgeon.
Just face the facts!
Your greasy drooping jowls just don't attract
So if you want a fox
And not a gal with the pox
You've got to pay and change your face!

**CAPITANO:** (sings)

Change my face
It's a tough life if I want to keep pace.
And if I ever want to get past first base
I gotta change my face
It can't be a sin to
Drop off a chin or two.

**ARLECCHINO and CAPITANO:** (continuing the song)

Goodbye my jowls!
I'll look like Tom Cruise and the girls will howl like owls

**CAPITANO:** (still singing)

So if I wanna hit the sack,

**ARLECCHINO:**

Singing With a gal not a yak.

**ARLECCHINO and CAPITANO:** (singing in unison)
You've
(I've)
gotta pay and change your
(my)
face.

## SCENE 7

*Arlechinno and Capitano go behind screen on which their shadows appear. They are joined by Columbine, Dottore and Flumox. Arlechinno and Columbine try to make Capitano comfortable on an operating table. A great deal of shadow activity can be seen with people and all sorts of things flying about like the Keystone Kops.*

*When the activity slows down we can see the shadow of Capitano on the table and Dottore and Flumox hovering over him. Columbine and Arlechinno are at the foot of the patient.*

*Flumox holds up a huge pair of pliers*

*While the scene is being set the following song will be sung by Dottore and Flumox, just before going behind the curtain.*

*It is time for us to correct a mistake We need a melody here.*

*When we must face a face to remake*

*The medical profession has so many tasks Especially to help to exchange bad masks.*

**DOTTORE:**
It will be necessary to make a small cut
And I know just how to make the incision.

**FLUMOX:**
If Capitano will manage to keep his mouth shut
Dottore will proceed with the utmost precision.

**DOTTORE and FLUMOX:**
Now with precision we'll make the incision
And after the cut, we'll sew him right up.

**CAPITANO:**
Whoa, whoa. I wanna know.

**ARLECCHINO:**

Dottore must remove all the defections.

**COLUMBINE:**

To smooth the skin surface of its imperfections.

*A great deal of moaning and yelling from Capitano and lots of metal banging against metal sounds. Then Flumox holds up a hammer and chisel.*

**CAPITANO:**

What are those? Ow that is my nose?

**COLUMBINE:**

The skin must be persuaded to release.

**ARLECCHINO:**

Then the facelift will proceed with ease.

*We hear hammer on chisel and chisel on bone with still more screaming. The mask is removed. Flumox and Dottore exit. Arlechinno and Columbine come from behind screen. Capitano comes from behind screen holding his mask in one hand and a miiror with the other in such a way that the audience can't see his face.*

**ARLECCHINO:**

Now the face is lifted.

**COLUMBINE:**

The sands of time have shifted.

**ARLECCHINO and COLUMBINE:**

Now it's true, you're a handsomer you.

*Capitano lowers the mirror so that we can see his face which is a pretty mask with a moustache. Columbine takes the mirror from him as he exits screaming, still holding the old face. Arlechinno and Columbine congratulate each other. Columbine starts admiring herself in the mirror. Arlechinno stands behind her and blows her a kiss which she can see in the mirror.*

**COLUMBINE:**

I saw you in the mirror and that imaginary kiss.

**ARLECCHINO:**

But it was for real and nothing amiss.

Maybe I should get something off my chest.

I think I've come to the end of my quest.

*Columbine pays no attention, but continues to look in the mirror.*

I'd better follow Capitano in his decline

Before he throws himself in the foamy brine.


## SCENE 8

*Enter Dottore, Flumox and Smeraldina*

**COLUMBINE:**

Oh Dottore I like your technique.

**SMERALDINA:**

I must say it is quite unique.

**FLUMOX:**

I think he is most fantastique.

**DOTTORE:**

Ego transitorimus est facilitatiti ergo explanique.

*We hear guitar in background.*

**SMERALDINA:**

Arlecchino with his guitar and mournful song

Will tell us of his love, loud and long.

*They all exit just as Arlechinno enters playing his guitar.*

**ARLECCHINO:** (singing)

My love she won't have me

(something like a folk song here)

So I understand

*Francesca enters and listens but is not seen by Arlecchino*

She wants a man of power

With jewels and much land.

I cannot maintain her

In silver or gold

Or buy all the fine things

Her eyes could behold.

**FRANCESCO:** (singing)

I think I could settle

(the same tune as Arlecchino)

For a man with no land.

Pantalone enters and listens

If he were romantic
And could sing oh so grand.
He may be a rascal
Or a lad of young years.
I in my passion
Could love without fear.

**ARLECCHINO:** (listening to Francesca )
Oh Golly!
(looking at Pantalone)
Oh Golly!
(Francesca screams)

**PANTALONE:**
So this is what happens behind my back,
My dutiful wife and this demoniac.
*Pulls slapstick out of Arlechinno's belt*

**ARLECCHINO:**
No master please listen to me
It's not what you think you see.

**PANTALONE:**
I've seen quite enough to make my blood boil
I don't need to be a Sir Conan Doyle.
(whipping Arlecchino with the slapstick.)

**FRANCESCA:**
No, Panty! Oh Panty! Stop Panty!

**PANTALONE:** (as he and Arlechinno exit running)
I'm simply upping up the ante.

**FRANCESCA:** (singing)
Oh, Panty, no Panty just leave him alone
(a bit of her earlier song)
There's really no one to blame
As I've so repeatedly shown.


## SCENE 9

*Columbine enters and starts straightening up tables and
chairs and putting table cloths on tables. Arlechinno rushes in.*

**ARLECCHINO:**
Columbine you must help me.
Pantalone is trying to scalp me.

**COLUMBINE:**

What is the reason I should hide thee?

**ARLECCHINO:**

No time for questions, just try to abide me.

You must find a place to hide me somewhere.

**COLUMBINE:** (pulling up a chair. )

Here Arlecchino, sit here in this chair.

*He sits in the chair, and she puts a table cloth over him and then sits in his lap.*

**ARLECCHINO:**

Ooooh when I said hide, I must confide

That this situation leaves me tongue-tied.

**COLUMBINE:**

The day your tongue dares to subside

Will be the day I'll become a bride.

**ARLECCHINO:**

Wow, and whose bride are you likely to be?

**COLUMBINE:**

Shut up for Pantalone is coming I see.

*Pantalone rushes in waving the slapstick over his head.*

**PANTALONE:**

Where is that rascally treacherous Arlecchino?

(seeing Columbine)

O my geisha. My little bambino.

**COLUMBINE:**

Look, I believe it is Mr. Pantalone

Looking so frisky but oh so aloney.

**ARLECCHINO:**

*Extends his right hand as though it is Columbine's; Pantalone takes hand and starts to kiss it; Arlecchino grabs Pantalone's nose and pulls it and retrieves the slapstick.*

*Arlecchino speaks in falsetto and Columbine moves her mouth as though she is speaking.*

*Of course Pantalone can't see Arlecchino as he is under the sheet and has substituted his arms where Columbine's ought to be.*

You are naughty boy and must feel the stick.

Come closer my dear for me to give you a lick.

**PANTALONE:**

*Stands closer to receive a whipping; even sticking his backside out to be whipped.*

Arlecchino can just have that old Francesca.

**COLUMBINE:** (speaking for herself )

What do you mean have old Francesca?

**PANTALONE:**

Arlechinno was serenading her but who really cares.

**ARLECCHINO:** (putting hand over Columbine's mouth and speaking in falsetto.)

I'm sure he wouldn't. He wouldn't dare. She is much too old for me ... for him.

Columbine bites Arlechinno's hand.

**PANTALONE:**

What. ... Wha ... What is this shim?

**COLUMBINE:**

Oh truly your Arlecchino is sitting right here.

*She jumps up and pulls sheet off Arlecchino.*

Why not have a whack on his derrier-rear?

*Pantalone grabs slapstick, but gives it to Columbine who starts beating Arlecchino who runs off stage chased by Columbine and Pantalone.*

**COLUMBINE:** (singing)

Ol' Pantalone play a tune on his butt

His foolishness was getting into a rut

He thinks he's such a clever fellow

But the use of the switch should make him all mellow.

The whip of course is just a stick with a slap

Maybe it'll cause him to shut up his clap-trap.

(a score here)


## SCENE 10

*Smeraldina enters, as Pantalone, Columbine and Arlechinno are exiting*

**SMERALDINA:**

Where are they going on the run
It seems that I always miss all the fun,
And where is that young Italian guy
Oh so dumb who caught my eye.

> *Octavio enters*

**OCTAVIO:**
Hello again, my dear lady.

**SMERALDINA:**
Welcome again, you handsome laddy.
But are you still looking, please pray tell.
I have a wonderful feminine clientele.

**OCTAVIO:** (singing, perhaps, a variation of his earlier tune)
Right now it's my fortune I hope to find.
It's always at the front of my mind.
A wise man said to look in your own backyard
If your fortune is the object of your highest regard.
But you must first look the wide world over.
That's the reason I'm a seasoned rover.

**SMERALDINA:**
This isn't your back yard, or your home ground

**OCTAVIO:**
Not literally my backyard, but my home town.

**SMERALDINA:**
Well there's no fortune here to be found.
There once was some gold on nearby ground,
When a fight broke out with an unruly youth,
And a gold filling was knocked from a tooth.

**OCTAVIO:**
I'm not looking for diamonds or gold
I've found more than my bags can now hold.
But what would make my fortune complete
Is a bride to wed – oh a wife so sweet.

**SMERALDINA:**
You have certainly come to the right place
If I can just find the space to place your face.
Looking at panel with lots of pictures.

> *She then exits. Capitano enters*

**OCTAVIO:** (sees Capitano)
Papa!
**CAPITANO:**
I'm no Popeye!
**OCTAVIO:**
Not Popeye — Papa!
**CAPITANO:**
I'm not your Papa.
**OCTAVIO:**
Don't you have a son?
**CAPITANO:**
I had a son but he is gone. He ran away from home and
was lost at sea.
**OCTAVIO:**
My ship did go down, but natives saved me.
**CAPITANO:**
You can't be that son. He was much smaller.
**OCTAVIO:**
But, Papa, I've grown up and am now much taller.
**CAPITANO:**
My son's name was different. It was Silvio.
**OCTAVIO:**
That was my name, but changed it to Octavio.
**CAPITANO:**
I can check the truth; my son had a birthmark.
**OCTAVIO:**
I do too. Was your son's a colorful mark?
**CAPITANO:**
If I tell you, you'll just paint one on.
So you can get the estate which will go to my son.
But tell me now where your birthmark might be.
**OCTAVIO:**
I can't tell you, because you'll want to see.
**CAPITANO:**
Of course I want to check on your veracity.
**OCTAVIO:**

I wouldn't want to compromise my modesty.

You see it's on my unmentionable.

*Columbine and Smeraldina sneak in and eavesdrop.*

**CAPITANO:**

Is it also unseeable?

**OCTAVIO:**

If you're not my father,

I wouldn't want to be harassed.

I'm modest and wouldn't want you to be embarrassed.

(or "BARE ASSED")

**CAPITANO:**

I've seen the whole world and much did I spy

I'll compromise and look with but one eye.

**OCTAVIO:**

Okay, I'll show you, but you can't look.

**CAPITANO:**

You can't be my son; you're such a kook.

How can you show me, if I can't take a look?

**OCTAVIO:**

I'll just open it up kinda like a book.

Like a local anesthesia, you'll get a local view.

**CAPITANO:**

I'll close my eyes and simply wait for you.

**SMERALDINA:**

Here, let us help with your little show.

*Smeraldina and Columbine hold table cloth to hide Octavio, who sits in a chair with his back to Capitano. They pretend not to look. Slowly a part of Octavio's anatomy is exposed and we see a birthmark. They drop the table cloths and while laughing, expose Octavio's armpit with the birthmark.*

**CAPITANO:** (The rest of the scene is sung.)

Bambino, my precious little boy.

(a Score here, of course)

You have restored me to a life of joy.

But why did you tease me that way, my son.

*Smeraldina and Columbine exit.*

**OCTAVIO:**

Papa, I knew if I told you it wouldn't be much fun.
  *They embrace.*

**CAPITONO:**

It's been so long since the day you were born,
But I thought you had been shipwrecked on Cape Horn.

**OCTAVIO:**

That is true enough but I managed to swim ashore,
And was able to pick up a few diamonds and much gold.
So with my good fortune it was then I swore
To find my way back to my home threshold.

**CAPITANO:**

My dear lost son, if I could be so rash
Would you ... lend your Papa some needed cash?
For to a young woman I'll soon be wed.

**OCTAVIO:**

And you need cash to bring to the marital bed?
But this young woman, may I soon meet?

**CAPITANO:**

Why yes, as she'll be your mama and so very sweet
So just follow me down this matrimonial street.
  *Octavio and Capitano exit with arms around each other's
shoulder.*

# SCENE 11

*Francesca appears, pulling Arlecchino onto stage with
guitar.*

**FRANCESCA:**

Go out and earn some money
While I go check on Pantalone.
  *She exits.*

**ARLECCHINO:** (singing)

This is a song that never ends.
Starts strumming guitar and singing
But a poem of love it sends.
  *Columbine and Smeraldine enter and after listening to a
few beats of the song, begin dancing.*

It just goes on and on, my friend.

I just started playing it

Not knowing what it was

And I'll continue playing it

Forever, just because!

(Obviously a tune that keeps repeating)

It is the song that never ends

And even if it rains my friend I just started ...

*The song continues as long as the director wishes. Octavio enters and interrupts.*

**OCTAVIO:**

That's a great never-ending song!

**ARLECCHINO:**

Thank heavens you came along!

*Arlecchino and dancers exit.*

**OCTAVIO:**

I'm so happy that I've come home.

(a tune here, as he starts singing)

Oh. My Papa, Oh my Papa, to me he is so good.

**COLLETTE:**

*Collette is heard singing offstage.*

I hear a voice as though from my childhood.

*They hum together as she enters to the same tune of "A Song That Never Ends".*

**OCTAVIO:**

Hi!

**COLLETTE:**

Hi!

**OCTAVIO:** (aside)

She's so beautiful and in my own backyard. Hi!

**COLLETTE:**

Hi!

(aside)

He's so handsome, and like a singing bard. I wonder
    where he came from. My name's Collette.

**OCTAVIO:**

Collette is a school name I remember still yet.

Octavio's my name but it was Silvio.

Before I traveled down to old Rio.

**COLLETTE:**

Is it possible, my little friend from school?

As I recall those days, he was really cool.

We used to play doctor-nurse together.

And your birthmark hurt in the stormy weather.

**OCTAVIO:**

Collette, the pet?

**COLLETTE:**

Silvio, the Rio?

**OCTAVIO:**

From kindergarten!

**COLLETTE:**

Remember our game?

**OCTAVIO:**

The pattycaking when we used our names.

**OCTAVIO and COLLETTE:** (pattycaking to a rhyme)

Silvio Rio, Lette the pet,

Jump on in but don't get wet!

One's the gander and one the goose

We'll wander far when we cut loose.

Ooooh!

**OCTAVIO:**

You look so ... good.

**COLLETTE:**

I've grown up!

**OCTAVIO:**

As I knew you would. And cuter than a pup.

**COLLETTE:**

And where have you been all these years?

**OCTAVIO:**

Oh sailing and fighting with the musketeers.

**COLLETTE:**

In your travels were there other girls?

**OCTAVIO:**

A few, but none I'd garnish with pearls.

But I've only wanted to marry you.

Will you have me if I promise to be true?

**COLLETTE:**

I guess so; if it can be arranged.

**OCTAVIO:**

You make me so happy, but you sound so strange.

I must hurry and tell Papa Trimarcho.

**COLLETTE:**

Trimarcho?

**OCTAVIO:**

Trimarcho!

**COLLETTE:**

Capitano Trimarcho?

**OCTAVIO:**

Capitano Trimarcho!

**COLLETTE and OCTAVIO:**

Capitano Trimarcho!

**OCTAVIO:**

You know him?

**COLLETTE:**

I know him.

**OCTAVIO:**

How do you know ...

**COLLETTE:**

It's about a trousseau. Actually a dowry, instead.

**OCTAVIO:**

A dowry means someone will wed.

**COLLETTE:**

That's what I'm trying to say.

They're setting for me a wedding day.

My folks want me to marry Capitano.

**OCTAVIO:** (singing until end of scene)

That won't do ... oh no, no, no no.

You see Capitano is my long lost Dad.

For you to marry him would be particularly bad.

For you to be my Ma-ma would be terribly wrong.

You need a husband who's spectacular and young.

The tune may be his earlier one.

**COLLETTE:**

Handsome like you.

**OCTAVIO:**

Electrifying like me.

**COLLETTE:**

We must tell him what's true

**OCTAVIO:**

That we both agree.

## SCENE 12

*Arlechinno enters with guitar and sings to the tune of a folk song. He sits and Columbine enters unseen by Arlecchino and listens to his song.*

**ARLECHINNO:**

La, la, la, la, la

Down in some lone valley, in a lonesome place

Where the wild birds do whistle and their notes do increase Farewell, Columbine, I bid you adieu, and I'll dream of Columbine wherever I go.

**COLUMBINE:** (sings)

Oh what do I hear? This man sings of me. I never did dream that it ever could be. Is it true, Arlechinno, I really must know, do you dream of me always wherever you go?

**ARLECCHINO:** (sings)

It's true, Columbine, my love is no lie; I'll love you forever, at least till I ... (speaking) or whatever or tomorrow or whichever comes first.

**COLUMBINE:**

Oh, Arlecchino, you're so funny.

**ARLECCHINO:**

It's not funny that I have no money.

**COLUMBINE:**

That's no matter, as long as we're together

In the desert heat or the mountain snow weather.

But you must tell me how much you care.

**ARLECCHINO:**

I care for you as much as I dare to dare.

And I'll sing a little song I wrote for you

And if you would like you can sing along too.

(singing Hello, little girl, hello, hello - a kind of patter
   song)

Hello, little girl, hello.

**COLUMBINE:** (Singing)

Hello, little boy, hello, hello

Hello, little boy, hello.

**ARLECCHINO:**

May I sit, little girl, may I sit, may I sit?

**COLUMBINE:**

Yes, little boy, hello.

**ARLECCHINO:**

A kiss, little girl, a kiss, a kiss

A kiss, little girl, a kiss.

**COLUMBINE:**

A ring, little boy, a ring, a ring

**ARLECCHINO:**

Hell no, little girl, goodbye.

   *Stands to leave, but Columbine grabs his wrist and pulls
him down onto her lap while Giving him a big kiss, as she
then sings.*

Hello, little boy, hello, hello

Hell yes, little boy, you're mine.

**SMERALDINA:**

   *Smeraldina enters.*

O that song — what a beautiful thing.

And now listen to the song that I must sing.

(Singing to same tune)

Hello, my commission, hello, hello

Hello, my commission, now show.

**ARLECCHINO:**

Oh the matchmaking commission of which you speak

Five bullion gold pieces to be delivered next week.

And this rubber ball I have just for you.

**SMERALDINA:**

Oh, Arlechinno, you know that'll never do.

**COLUMBINE:**

We'll name our first born after you ... Smellarena.

**SMERALDINA:**

SMERALDINA! If it's a boy that'll be tough.

**ARLECCHINO:**

Well then, we'll just name him Sme-ruff, smurf.

**SMERALDINA:**

Out with you both. This is my turf.

*Arlechinno and Columbine exit*

A boy named Smurf, how absurd.

He'd be so unpopular, just a blue nerd.

*Capitano enters*

**CAPITANO:**

Hello, Smerldina, my lovely dear.

We must plan my wedding so perilously near.

Let's look over the terms of this binding contract

Then we'll spit and shake and seal this here pact.

**SMERALDINA:**

Capitano, the work on the contract has been mounting.

The government red tape is just astounding.

**CAPITANO:**

Oh, quit this carping. I want no trouble.

Just get with the program on the double.

*Octavio and Collette enter*

Oh, my son and the lovely Collette

I see you two have already met.

**OCTAVIO:**

Yes, Papa, we're well met indeed

And there's an agreement to which we've agreed.

But we both fear that unhappy you'll be.

**CAPITANO:**

Absurd, my lost son and my bride-to-be.

**OCTAVIO:**

Your son I am and a bride she'll be

Surprise! Surprise! She's marrying me.

**CAPITANO:**

I'm sorry my son, what's that you say?

**OCTAVIO:**

We're not discussing your wedding day.

**CAPITANO:**

Come here, right here, my pretty little miss

And give your bridegroom a sweet little kiss.

**OCTAVIO:**

Oh, Papa Trimarcho just forget about this.

**CAPITANO:**

But my dear Collette, I thought our love was true,

And I looked forward to my life with you.

**COLLETTE:**

I've always been an obedient daughter.

**SMERALDINA:**

But marriage to him would lead a lamb to slaughter

**ARLECCHINO:**

She's marrying me, so get over it, Dad.

**CAPITANO:**

But this was arranged through a classified ad.

Now tell me, my son, is this true love?

**ARLECCHINO:**

Just as true as the moon and stars up above.

**CAPITANO:**

This whole affair has been such a mess,

And this marriage, my dear son, I do honestly bless.

Now come here and give your new daddy a kiss.

*Collette stiff-arms him.*

**COLLETTE:**

With Octavio I'll be living in marital bliss.

*Francesca and Pantalone enter with dowry in a suitcase.*

**CAPITANO:**

Hello, Francesca, my lovely dear.

**FRANCESCA:**

Capitano, your nuptials are near.

**CAPITANO:**

Can my nuptials be seen?

**FRANCESCA:**

The wedding, of course, is what I mean.

**SMERALDINA:**

The wedding, yes. There's been a change in plans.

Your daughter is intended to marry this man.

(pointing to Octavio )

He's charming, he's healthy, he's handsome and svelte.

You see there's no belly hanging over his belt.

**FRANCESCA:**

Well I suppose that will have to do

If something goes wrong, I'll come looking for you.

*Flumox enters screaming*

**FLUMOX:**

Dottore, Dottore! Have you seen Dottore?

**SMERALDINA:**

I haven't seen him since the operation

**PANTALONE:**

By operation do you mean there's been a castration?

**SMERALDINA:**

Not a castration but the patient's been fixed

The results of the surgery have certainly been mixed.

**CAPITANO:**

Never mind that, but isn't Dottore somewhere near?

**FLUMOX:**

I've been worried ever since we got here.

**SMERALDINA:**

What exactly is the problem with him, my dear?

**FLUMOX:**

He's become so interested in females I fear.

**SMERALDINA:**

That's perfectly natural, even for one so drear.

**FLUMOX:**

But he doesn't know about me, you see?

**FRANCESCA:**

Is there something you'd like to tell me?

**FLUMOX:**

He doen't know that I'm one too.

**PANTALONE:**

(counting the other females)

One, two , three. Then who are you?

**FLUMOX:**

I'm really Flaminia in love with him

Studying with Dottore for over a year.

**DOTTORE:** (Entering)

Well, well, my Flaminia so sweet and trim,

Now we know your identity but are you sincere?

**FLUMOX:**

You knew all along and you didn't tell?

**DOTTORE:**

I wanted to know if you loved me as well.

In the great game of love ego amo te.

**FLAMINIA:**

I'll love you, Dottore, till my dying day.

**CAPITANO:**

Oh, true love, there is nothing higher

But now for my son a dowry I require.

**PANTALONE:**

Hey this ain't funny, if you're talking about real money.

**CAPITANO:**

But a dowry of great value is all that I meant.

**FRANCESCA:**

*Pantalone takes worthless trinkets from an old-fashioned*
*carpet bag, as Francesca holds them up and describes them*

This dowry we bring is certainly money well spent.

(Singing)

This gold trophy cost quite a lot

It's supposed to be King John's chamber pot.

This ancient bowl bartered from the Far East

Has graced royal tables for many a fine feast.

This painting will bring you much inner joy,

An original oil by the master, Kilroy.

(A song here.)

**CAPITANO:**

Now something practical the couple could use

A modern implement just couldn't lose.

**PANTALONE:**

*Holding up tin cans connected by string*

These communication devices will save the day.

They can always stay connected; what more can I say?

**CAPITANO:**

I'm sure this lovely dowry will do.

It's been a pleasure doing business with you.

**SMERALDINA:**

I'm so very happy, and now with your permission,

I'll claim from you all my commission.

**CAPITANO:**

Commission? Pantalone!

**PANTALONE:**

Commission? Francesca!

**FRANCESCA:**

As Octavio has spoiled both your plans and mine,

I feel he be required to pay the fine.

**SMERALDINA:**

Okay, fortune boy, cross my palm with some gold,

This dilly-dallying is just getting old.

**OCTAVIO:**

Commission? Commission? Oh, I know!

(Holding up washboard )

Take this laundry appliance from Columbus, Ohio.

**SMERALDINA:**

That just won't cut it, my handsome honey.

Not appliances, just cross my hand with money.

**OCTAVIO:** (singing)

No money, no money, no money of mine.

Take this instead, it's magic you'll find.

Stroke it not once, not two times, but thrice

For it is a magical matchmaking device.

*Smeraldina slowly strokes the washboard three times and looks up and sees Capitano.*

**SMERALDINA:**

Capitano, how are you in the kitchen?

**CAPITANO:**

So that's the wish for which you've been itchin'.

*Smeraldina takes off her apron puts top of it over Capitano's head.*

**SMERALDINA:**

Let's just try this on for size.

**CAPITANO:**

How can I refuse those big, beautiful ... eyes?

(looking at apron )

So this is what I now realize.

**SMERALDINA:**

Oh come now, Capitano, you've won the Grand Prize.

*Arlechinno enters wearing a huge overcoat, from the bottom of which we see three feet. Arlechinno has taken his arm out of one sleeve and is holding a stick with a pant-leg and shoe, matching the other two shoes. The empty sleeve has a fake arm and hand. Columbine follows.*

**ARLECCHINO:** (singing)

Oh Frenchmen woo with wine and cheese

With poetry they try to please.

I can't speak verse like a man from France

But I can dance the three-legged dance.

*Chorus*

One leg's nice, two legs will do.

I can go fast. I can go long too.

Ask any gal and she's bound to agree

The finest blokes have three legs like me!

(Dances as he sings)

A Scotsman woos with his bagpipes and his kilt

But when he's out of breath his pipes begin to wilt

So if you want a date and not a dried out fig

You'll find a bloke who can do the three-leg jig.

*Chorus: everyone holds hands with their partners and dance while exiting.*

One leg's nice. Two legs will do.

I can go fast. I can go long too.

Ask any gal and she's bound to agree

The finest blokes have three legs like me!

*Smeraldina enters with her Bridal Service sign.*

(a song here.)

**SMERALDINA:** (singing a new song)
We've come to the end, and we're all well-paired.
Even though some are slightly impaired.
*Columbine and Arlecchino dance in singing.*
Arlecchino couldn't keep his hands to himself
And Columbine is no longer on the shelf.
*Francesca and Pantalone dance in, joining the others in a
tableau vivant.*
Francesca and Pantalone are the same as before
As much in love together as they ever were.
*Dottore and Flaminia join the dance.*
Then there was that latin-spouting Dottore
Whose love with his assistant is another story.
*Collette and Octavio dance in.*
Collette fell in love with that Italian guy
*Capitano joins Smerldina.*
And even I got a piece of the pie.
But my dating games are no more.
Now I'll just open a baby store.
*Capitano and Smeraldina fasten sign to posts at either end
of the upstage. When they release the bottom of the sign, it
unfurls to reveal the replica of a Callot drawing of a
traditional commedia del' arte performance. They then join the
tableau singing.*
She tried her best to get us together.
For us all new plans were hatched,
Forever together through all kinds of weather.
Now we are so happy and certainly well-matched.
*Each character takes out a hankie (while still basically in
the tableau). They then wave the hankies to thunderous
applause.*
*Partners kiss and exit.*

FINI

# It's A Long Way

This abstruse script is the most unusual, and certainly the most enigmatic of all my scripts in its attempt to bring an active reciprocal message to an unsuspecting audience.

Obviously it is not character – driven as the two characters are anonymously known as HE and SHE. We don' know whether they know each other or if, in fact, they may be a married couple. The playwright here explores the Bond of Love, which is the space between the characters. We might call that negative or empty space. The Japanese have a term for that space, which they think of as potential. Frank Lloyd Wright calls it transition, noting that architects must pay particular attention to that space.

# IT'S A LONG WAY

*by E. Reid Gilbert*

Cast

**HE** . . . . . . . . . . . . . .a man
**SHE** . . . . . . . . . . . . .a women

*Lights up on woman (SHE) upstage left looking over a railing with Her back to the audience. Man (HE) enters from downstage right, approaching railing. HE leans with back against the railing and looks back in direction of his entrance. SHE continues to look over the railing, paying no attention to the man. A soundtrack with various sounds, ranging from bird songs and river sounds to crowd and traffic noise, runs throughout the play.*

**HE:** (starts singing) It's a long way to Tipperary, It's a long way ... (speaking)  It is a long way ... (attempting to start a conversation) Where is Tipperary? Do you know where Tipperary is? Haven't you ever wondered?

**SHE:** I wonder ... (HE interrupts.)

**HE:** You do?

**SHE:** All the time ... (HE interrupts.)

**HE:** About Tipperary?

**SHE:** No...

**HE:** Well then ...

**SHE:** Well then ... what?

**HE:** If you don't wonder about Tipperary, what is it you wonder about?

**SHE:** The long way. (HE interrupts.)

**HE:** To Tipperary?

**SHE:** I thought we'd settled that.

**HE:** No, we just settled that you don't wonder about where Tipperary is. You just wonder about the long way. (SHE interrupts)

**SHE:** ... down ... (HE turns to look down, as SHE turns and looks toward him.)

**HE:** It is a long ways ...

**SHE:** Yes, a long ways ... down.

**HE:** I mean a long ways ... back. (HE turns to look toward Her, as SHE turns to look downstage.)

**SHE:** BACK ... where?

**HE:** BACK ... there.

**SHE:** DOWN ... there. (a long pause.)

**HE:** There's a lot of trash ...

SHE: DOWN there.

HE: What kind of trash?

SHE: Oh you know ... like plastic ...

HE: No, I mean ... BACK ... there.

SHE: And I meant DOWN there.

HE: And BACK there ... a great deal of rubbish ... baggage.

SHE: Yes ... DOWN there.

HE: I think maybe I'll just go DOWN there.

SHE: It is rather deep.

HE: Wanna go?

SHE: Not right now ... later maybe.

HE: Really!?

SHE: Maybe.

HE: It would be kinda dangerous going ...

SHE: DOWN there?

HE: I meant going BACK there.

SHE: Yes, that'd be kinda dangerous too.

HE: What could harm you?

SHE: I could fall into ...

HE: Something pretty deep ... but don't you think I ...

SHE: Could also fall into something...

HE: Pretty messy.

SHE: DOWN there.

HE: Why are you ...

SHE: Here?

HE: Yeah!

SHE: I come Here to contemplate.

HE: Suicide?

SHE: Why would I want to contemplate suicide?

HE: I don't ... (SHE interrupts.)

SHE: No, I just come Here to contemplate.

HE: Contemplate ... what?

SHE: Do you have to contemplate ... something?

HE: I would think so. Contemplation isn't just floating around out there in the universe.

SHE: Who knows what ... (long pause)

**HE:** Do you ever think ... (SHE interrupts.)

**SHE:** All the time.

**HE:** I mean about ... (SHE interrupts.)

**SHE:** About ... what?

**HE:** Suicide!

**SHE:** Why should I ever contemplate ... (HE interrupts.)

**HE:** I didn't say "contemplate." I said "think."

**SHE:** Isn't thinking the same as contemplating?

**HE:** No ... When you think you think about something ...

**SHE:** And ...

**HE:** When you contemplate, you contemplate something.

**SHE:** Think about something and contemplate something
— not about?

**HE:** Yeah!

**SHE:** Something like that.

**HE:** Thinking may be contemplating, but ... (SHE
interrupts.)

**SHE:** I would think ... (HE interrupts.)

**HE:** Yeah, what do you ...

**SHE:** Think ...

**HE:** About ...

**SHE:** That? (long pause)

**HE:** But isn't it an interesting word?

**SHE:** What word?

**HE:** SUICIDE ... that was the word we were talking ...
(SHE interrupts.)

**SHE:** That's the word YOU were talking about.

**HE:** But just think ... (SHE interrupts.)

**SHE:** I do think ... (HE interrupts.)

**HE:** Yeah all the time.

**SHE:** Yeah!

**HE:** But just think about what an interesting word ... (SHE
interrupts.)

**SHE:** I'd rather ... (HE continues without missing a beat.)

**HE:** It really is ...

**SHE:** But I'd rather ...

**HE:** SUI of course comes from the French and CIDE
from ...

SHE: I'd prefer ...

HE: Latin and means to slay. And when you think of it ...

SHE: I'd think ...

HE: It's kinda beautiful ... and although CIDERE may mean to slay ...

SHE: I don't think I'd ...

HE: But I don't think that that's such a pretty word, so ...

SHE: I'd prefer ...

HE: To think of it as deliverance ... SELF-DELIVERANCE, Now isn't that ...

SHE: Did you see "Deliverance?"

HE: I didn't see DELIVERANCE, I did say DELIVERANCE. How can you see DELIVERANCE? It's an action like...

SHE: A film!

HE: Oh yeah ...

SHE: Now just think about it. Isn't thinking that same thing as contemplation?

HE: No, because you think a thought, but you don't contemplate a contemplation.

SHE: But you contemplate ... something.

HE: Con-tem-plate focuses through and beyond something.

SHE: It stands to reason that ...

HE: Reason has nothing to do ...

SHE: That sounds rather Unreasonable.

HE: Unreasonable as? ...

SHE: LACKING REASON.

HE: Unreason as before reason or Unreason as beyond ...

SHE: The former ...

HE: No, no, it's beyond reason.

SHE: Would that be MEGAreason?

HE: No, it would be METAreason.

SHE: META?

HE: Yeah, like METAphysics ... beyond physics.

SHE: I would rather think of it as METROreason.

HE: That's weird ... (Music of DO YOU REMEMBER

from a car radio becomes amped up. HE and SHE listen
for a few beats. They begin to sing.)

**HE:** Do you remember ... (humming the rest of the line)

**SHE:** (Interrupting him) Oh I remember ... (Humming but
SHE stops suddenly in the middle of her humming.) Do
you really remember back?

**HE:** Some fragments ... Perhaps like in a mirror darkly.

**SHE:** What's the purpose then?

**HE:** The purpose!?

**SHE:** The purpose of the great flash of cognizance of the
great solution to the great mystery of the flesh ...

**HE:** You will know that you've been there ... had that ...

**SHE:** But wouldn't that ... ?

**HE:** Yes ... a great frustration ... like the fellow who had
had a wonderful evening of drinking with his pals only to
have lost his hat. His chums made sure he got home
safely then decided to mail him his hat with a note written
in a pretty handwriting. They, of course, made sure to be
at the post office when he picked up his mail and the
package with the nice note, "Thanks, Jimmy, for a
glorious evening." WE SOMETIME HAVE
INTIMATIONS OF A GLORIOUS EXPERIENCE –
EVEN IF SOME OF THEM MAY BE ONLY
PRANKSTER TRICKS – BUT WE CAN'T RECALL
EXCEPT IN OUR FULSOME IMAGINATION
WHAT IT MIGHT HAVE BEEN.

**SHE:** Is that like getting kicked out of the Garden of
Eden and not being able...

**HE:** YEAH, TO REMEMBER ALL the JOYS AND
PLEASURES...

**SHE:** That was the experience of Adam and Eve.

**HE:** It was — is — the experience of all of us.

**SHE:** But the purpose ... ?

**HE:** Why a purpose?

**SHE:** ... the purpose of experiencing without
remembering.

**HE:** It holds the monster-god just below the sea surface,
which looks so ominous and dark when looked down

upon ... But we will know that it's there and that it may reappear at any moment.

**SHE:** And what can we do about that?

**HE:** Nothing.

**SHE:** NOTHING!?

**HE:** Only to realize and be conscious of the power lurking there.

**SHE:** And if we don't?

**HE:** Oh, most of us don't.

**SHE:** And then?

**HE:** ... then we become somnambulists.

**SHE:** Sleepwalkers?

**HE:** Yes.

**SHE:** Do you ever see them?

**HE:** Who?

**SHE:** The sleepwalkers.

**HE:** All the time. Most of the people some of the time, and all the people from time to time ... Maybe you were one of them when I walked up here a few moments ago.

**SHE:** I was meditating.

**HE:** Meditating or sleepwalking?

**SHE:** I wasn't walking ... You were walking ... Maybe you were sleepwalking up Here.

**HE:** You don't have to be walking to be a SLEEP walker, any more than you need to be walking to be a STREET walker.

**SHE:** What are you saying?

**HE:** Maybe I was.

**SHE:** Was?

**HE:** ... was sleepwalking. (A bird call sounds, a bit like a human voice.)

**SHE:** Did you hear that?

**HE:** I didn't hear anything.

**SHE:** Maybe it wasn't calling you.

**HE:** Was it calling you?

**SHE:** Maybe a yes ... or maybe a no.

**HE:** We will know.

**SHE:** When?

**HE:** (singing) In the sweet bye and bye. (We hear the song echoing in the canyon.)

**SHE:** That story!

**HE:** What story?

**SHE:** The fellow with the lost hat.

**HE:** What about it?

**SHE:** What were his feelings when HE opened the package with the hat and the note inside?

**HE:** His feelings?

**SHE:** Yeah ... Was he exhilarated, anxious, worried, regret of the loss of memory?

**HE:** Guilt!

**SHE:** Guilt?

**HE:** An empty guilt.

**SHE:** But if he had no memory of the night when he lost his hat, what guilt would he be experiencing?

**HE:** Guilt of what might have happened. After all, his wife...

**SHE:** Only guilt?

**HE:** No ... also regret.

**SHE:** Why regret?

**HE:** Now, just think about it. Don't you think you would regret having lost the memory of a "glorious evening?"

**SHE:** I suppose that's like leaving the garden of Eden and having only a vague notion of what all that splendor was about.

**HE:** Franz Schubert asked, "O Lovely World, where art thou?" A question with haunting potential — A riddle with no answer. And yet cosmic meaning - the riddle encased in yet another riddle or two — the KUNDALINI SHAKTI — the power of consciousness — a coiled snake with heads at each end — the guardian dragons hover at the gate.

**SHE:** What are the guardian dragons?

**HE:** Longing-desire and aggression-fear... words do not reach us in those recesses...

SHE: ... where is the consistency?

HE: Consistency?

SHE: Something ought to be consistent ... life ... memory.

HE: Like the consistent lover?

SHE: That was the constant lover.

HE: Did the constant lover ... ?

*The tune of "Do you Remember?" is heard and continues as they sing simple phrases of the song. They quit singing but begin to hum and dance to the music. Their dancing is synchronized but they never touch. The music is drowned out with traffic noise and people babbling incoherently. They stop dancing, but have exchanged places — SHE, upstage right looking downstage, and HE, upstage left looking over the railing. Two older people enter downstage right. Old Man with two walking sticks. Old Woman with walker. They hobble behind each other almost in a race with changing leads. They stop to talk with each other but can't get anything said. Old Man sees HE and SHE and notices Old Woman's attention to them. They almost speak to HE and SHE, but then simply hobble off SL.*

SHE: I wonder ...

HE: ... about what?

SHE: ... what you ...

HE: ... What about me?

SHE: That, if you were married ...

HE: What about, "IF I were ...

SHE: I'm just saying, that If you were married ...

HE: And ... ?

SHE: What would you be saying ...

HE: Right now?

SHE: To your wife ...

HE: If she were Here?

SHE: Yeah!

HE: I'd say, "My dearest darling."

SHE: You're lying of course?

HE: Yeah!

SHE: No, now really what would you say to your wife if

she were actually here, and you were experiencing this moment ... this place ... this experience ... together?

HE: I'd say, "Why aren't you home cooking dinner?"

SHE: You're lying again, of course!

HE: Yeah.

SHE: No, now be honest. What would you actually ... no, what would you probably say?

HE: I'd probably, most likely, tangentially, circuitously ...

SHE: Cut it out!

HE: What I would actually say would land somewhere between "Dearest Darling" and the dinner thing.

SHE: So that's what you were contemplating?

HE: No ... wasn't contemplating.

SHE: What were you doing then?

HE: I was PROJECTING on the question you were CONTEMPLATING.

SHE: Now that is a PENETRATING thought. (long pause)

HE: Was that good for you?

SHE: Good?

HE: For you?

SHE: I didn't stop to think.

HE: Good for you!

SHE: Are you implying ... ?

HE: Still not thinking?

SHE: Are you saying ... ?

HE: I'm just saying, "Good for you!"

SHE: Why are you saying it was good for me?

HE: I was just asking ... was it good for you to stop and think?

SHE: That didn't mean it was good for me. Was it good for you?

HE: That sounds awful sexual.

SHE: Well, what were we thinking about?

HE: We were thinking about thinking.

SHE: What is awful about that?

HE: I didn't say it was awful.

SHE: You said it sounded AWFUL sexual.

HE: I meant the inference.

SHE: And what is awful about sexual?

HE: I suppose the AWFUL isn't SEXUAL.

SHE: AWFUL isn't SEXUAL or SEXUAL isn't AWFUL?

HE: I think I was thinking that perhaps the thinking was AWFUL.

SHE: Are you now talking about politics?

HE: Would it be AWFUL if politicians did some thinking? You know the word, awful, simply means "filled with awe."

SHE: I would be delighted and filled with awe if the politicians would begin to do a little think ...

HE: For heaven's sake! No!

SHE: Why no?

HE: If they were to begin to think, actually think — back to that word — it would be AWFUL — in the worst sense of the word — for them to be actually thinking.

SHE: What would be awful about that?

HE: I would think that that could lead to dire consequences. Just think about how so out of character for politicians to do something like that.

SHE: It's always nice to have politicians to talk about, when ...

HE: We don't want to think about ...

SHE: ... other thoughts.

HE: Now you? Just think ...

SHE: I'm too tired ...

HE: To think?

SHE: Yeah!

HE: Thinking doesn't take effort.

SHE: It just creeps up on you, and it takes, sometimes a great deal of effort, to avoid it. (long pause) And you start thinking thoughts you never knew you had.

HE: Do you ever write ... ?

SHE: Poetry!?

HE: Is that an answer ... ?

SHE: ... a question?

HE: Is what an answer ... ?

SHE: ... or a question?

HE: Poetry?

SHE: Is an answer.

HE: Or a question!

SHE: It could be...

HE: Either ...

SHE: ... really.

HE: But for me ...

SHE: Yes for you ... ?

HE: It's both ...

SHE: Both what?

HE: Both an answer and ...

SHE: ... a question.

HE: But which ...

SHE: ... comes first

HE: ... the QUESTION OR

SHE: ... the answer?

HE: Or the answer or ...

SHE: ... the question?

HE: Isn't that just...

SHE: ... like the

HE: ... old chicken or eggy thingy?

SHE: Who's an old chicken?

SHE: I didn't say the chicken was ...

SHE: ... You did say OLD.

HE: The old adage ...

SHE: You didn't say ADAGE. You said OLD CHICKEN.

HE: You know, the chicken-or-egg thing.

SHE: Now we're talking about eggs?

HE: I said WAS the old ...

SHE: When you said that, what was the meaning of WAS, or better yet what IS the meaning of WAS? (SHE tries to ignore him, while HE pantomimes smoking, which SHE interrupts.SHE) Why do you always do that?

HE: (HE pantomimes throwing away the cigarette butt.) Do what?

**SHE:** You know ... after ...

**HE:** After what?

**SHE:** After contemplating.

**HE:** Well, the smoke helps me ...

**SHE:** Contemplate?

**HE:** I mean AFTER contemplating ...

**SHE:** You mean ... ?

**HE:** Yeah. Then I meditate.

**SHE:** About ... ?

**HE:** You don't meditate about anything. You permit the meditation to occur.

**SHE:** Have you ever thought about not being able to contemplate ... like mosquitoes?

**HE:** You mean to contemplate about not being able to contemplate?

**SHE:** Don't you think the cigarette smoke just sets up a kind of screen?

**HE:** Smoke screen, Occluding, Obscuring, Obfuscating ...

**SHE:** Aren't you just playing as we always do?

**HE:** Playing with words ...

**SHE:** ... as people always ...

**HE:** That's what language is all about ...

**SHE:** ... playing with words? (SHE touches the railing and looks over it.)

**HE:** Speaking of words! Now are you touching the railing or is the railing touching you?

**SHE:** I'm touching the railing.

**HE:** Is the railing not touching you? (SHE pulls Her hand off the railing, as though it's hot.)

**SHE:** It's not touching me now.

**HE:** Was it touching you?

**SHE:** No, I was touching it.

**HE:** When you were touching it, wasn't it touching you?

**SHE:** But it didn't do anything.

**HE:** It didn't have to. You acted for it. You might call that a touching moment of passive existence. (SHE suspiciously touches the railing again, really focusing on the point of contact. HE touches the railing, then looks at her still studying the phenomenon.) Am I touching you or are you touching me?

**SHE:** Neither.

**HE:** But isn't there a connection when we both touch the same thing or experience the same event?

**SHE:** Not if I remove my hand.

**HE:** But we're still sharing the same moment, whether we choose to or not.

**SHE:** What does that mean?

**HE:** I don't know. What would you have it mean? (HE takes out a piece of paper and begins to read slowly, almost as though he's composing it on the spot.)

> To write of one's life
> Is to live it again?
> To recall the cast of characters
> And re-member to one's self
> To a time long gone by? A long time back
> Or only yesterday?
> Can the recalled kiss
> Be as fresh today?
> As when I was fresh
> With the nubile you
> Eons and eons ago
> That honey-suckled night?
> The agony now to write
> Is the long look back!

*HE looks at the paper, wadding it up and throwing it DSR. SHE seems surprised at his poetry reading, but downright alarmed at his throwing it away. HE begins to pantomime setting out a picnic lunch. HE lays down the imaginary cloth, and SHE, after incredulously watching him, begins taking out an imaginary lunch from an invisible hamper. They take only a couple of minutes to begin eating. The scene stops at a Tableaux Vivant. Background sound of blues music amps up. Two youngsters run on from SL as though chasing someone else. They halt Center Stage with three second stop and take two quick steps back. They begin reciting the following lines as though in a game of hopscotch or jump-rope. They jump up and down and back and forth, though not with the precision of jump-rope or hopscotch. These should be the same two actors playing the elderly couple in the earlier scene.*

**YOUNGSTERS:**
We are the children
Who play scary games.
We are the offspring
  Of those with no names.
  Eenie, Meanie Miny Moe
  Mister Edgar Allen Poe
  Raven standing at the rim,
  Eenie, Meanie Tiny Tim.
  London Bridge is falling down
  With no lady there.
  King George has lost his golden crown
  Falling off his chair.
  We are the children
  Who play scary games.
  We are the children
  Of those with no names.

*They continue the back and forth steps and the singing until they disappear SR. SHE takes out a piece of paper and begins to write.*

**SHE:** Roses are red. Violets are blue. (HE looks at SHE incredulously.) I look down in only to find you. (His mouth gapes open HE looks at SHE. HE peers over the railing.)
We shared a moment, you and I.
With no words nor even a sigh.
Words would have exposed the magic's charm
Or compromised the touch as to sound an alarm.
Of an implied promise each of us had
Or exposed expectations, whether good or bad.
Only the sound of music... of Beethoven... or was
  it Bop?

> With crickets cricketing in the background... or
>     was it Hip-Hop?
> With an occasional hoot of a startled screech
>     owl... or was there no sound at all?
> It was then I realized
> You weren't even there!
> But then again
> Neither was I!

*HE slowly pantomimes picking up the imaginary picnic
things, throwing it all over the railing.*

**SHE:** Why did you do that?

**HE:** To clear the deck.

**SHE:** To clear the deck of what, an imaginary picnic?

**HE:** Of patterns.

**SHE:** Whose patterns?

**HE:** Life's.

**SHE:** Life's patterns?

**HE:** Perhaps.

**SHE:** What about ours?

**HE:** OUR patterns?

**SHE:** It doesn't take long to establish a pattern.

**HE:** Perhaps.

**SHE:** So by throwing an imaginary picnic over a railing
into a chasm, you have successfully cleared the decks of
patterns?

**HE:** Perhaps.

**SHE:** So now what do you do?

**HE:** Investigate.

**SHE:** Investigate what?

**HE:** DOWN there.

**SHE:** It seems to me that you were much more intensely
interested in BACK there.

**HE:** But can one successfully go BACK without first going
DOWN?

**SHE:** You're asking me?

**HE:** No ... Not really!

**SHE:** Did you ever read Thomas Wolfe's book "You Can't
Go Home Again"? You know he wrote that because he

felt that he couldn't go BACK because of all the things
he had written about his Asheville neighbors...

**HE:** ... in an earlier book, Look Homeward, Angel. I think
what HE meant by that was "You can never leave
home...completely."

**SHE:** And you can never return home...satisfactorily.

**HE:** If you can never leave completely ...

**SHE:** Nor return satisfactorily ...

**HE:** Where does that leave us?

**SHE:** Overlooking a railing ...

**HE:** Into an abyss!

**SHE:** Maybe one needs to commit ...

**HE:** That sounds veddy Cherman.

**SHE:** Who sounds veddy ...

**HE:** I didn't say, who ...

**SHE:** Then what ...

**HE:** COM MIT sounds ...

**SHE:** Why do you say that?

**HE:** COM MIT vit me!

**SHE:** We all commit to something ... even if it's just
laziness...

**HE:** Commit to something ... or someone?

**SHE:** Yes!

**HE:** Which?

**SHE:** Both!

**HE:** Both?

**SHE:** Each!

**HE:** Each?

**SHE:** Both and each ... some thing and/or some one.

**HE:** Can one really commit, I mean actually commit to
something or someone outside themselves?

**SHE:** If you would just contemplate ...

**HE:** Now you want me to contemplate commitment.
What is it "contemplate" or "commitment?"

**SHE:** They're kinda similar ... don't you think?

**HE:** "Commitment" is a noun ...

**SHE:** And "contemplate" is a verb.

HE: Exactly!

SHE: But they both ... mean they both come from the same stem ...

HE: Cell?

SHE: Yeah ...

HE: So now we're talking about stem cells. You know we shouldn't bring up controversial ...

SHE: I thought we were ...

HE: Contemplating the possibility of committing to a commitment.

SHE: Now you're being rather tautological.

HE: Logical? Tauto-logical I'm not usually accused of LOGI ...

SHE: I didn't ...

HE: You just accused me of being "rather tauto ... "

SHE: Not logical ...

HE: Where is this going?

SHE: BACK there?

HE: Or DOWN there.

SHE: Either there ...

HE: Is a where ...

SHE: Where you wouldn't really care ...

HE: To go ...

SHE: But we must ...

HE: Why must we?

SHE: In order to get ...

HE: To the present ...

SHE: Moment.

HE: Maybe ... BACK Here?

SHE: BACK to where ...

HE: We need to go ...

SHE: In order ...

HE: To go on ...

SHE: Where?

HE: There! there's always another there.

SHE: But what there?

HE: And why?

SHE: We must always go back or down.

HE: Or both.

SHE: In order ...

HE: To crawl BACK ...

SHE: DOWN to Here!

HE: In order to ...

SHE: Continue ...

HE: To commit!

SHE: To commit to continue to commit to this moment.

HE: Now you're being not only tautological but repetitive.

SHE: And you're being circuitous.

HE: By ...

SHE: By going from Here to BACK to DOWN to where to there to BACK ... Here!

HE: There's a lot of trash ...

SHE: Where?

HE: BACK there,

SHE: And DOWN there.

HE: What do you do ...

SHE: About the trash?

HE: Yeah, what do you do ...

SHE: What do YOU do?

HE: What must WE do ...

SHE: What MUST we ... ?

HE: What do people do ... ?

SHE: People MUST ...

HE: Pay other people ...

SHE: For what?

HE: To take care of ...

SHE: Oh yeah! ... the garbage!

HE: We litter ...

SHE: BACK there ...

HE: The psychiatrists ...

SHE: Take care of the trash ...

HE: We've thrown garbage DOWN there.

SHE: And the illegals ...

HE: Can take care of the litter ...

**SHE:** Dropped BACK there.
**HE:** Our trash ...
**SHE:** Especially OUR trash ...
**HE:** 'Cause OUR trash ...
**SHE:** Is really too messy for us ...
**HE:** To mess with.
**SHE:** But it's ...
**HE:** OUR trash.
**SHE:** But didn't we throw ...
**HE:** OUR TRASH ... ?
**SHE:** In the garbage
**HE:** And didn't the garbage men . . .?
**SHE:** Hauled it away!
**HE:** But some of it ...
**SHE:** Must have spilled ...
**HE:** Over the edges.
**SHE:** Or the raccoons got in. And there's no one ...
**HE:** Not even you?
**SHE:** Or you?
**HE:** To begin to ...
**SHE:** Clean it up!
**HE:** The neighbors of course ...
**SHE:** Will ...
**HE:** Complain ...
**SHE:** And maybe ...
**HE:** Call ...
**SHE:** The authorities!
**HE:** It's always ...
**SHE:** The authorities!
**HE:** Who stand by ...
**SHE:** The authorities!
**HE:** To do our dirty work ...
**SHE:** The authorities!
**HE:** Or make sure we ...
**SHE:** The authorities!
**HE:** Do our own ...
**SHE:** The authorities!

**HE:** Dirty work.
**SHE:** The authorities!
**HE:** But of course ...
**SHE:** The authorities!
**HE:** Produce a lot of their own ...
**SHE:** Dirty laundry!
**HE:** But don't you think ...
**SHE:** The authorities!
**HE:** We should always ..
**SHE:** The authorities!
**HE:** Question ... ?
**SHE:** The authorities!
**HE:** But what about ...
**SHE:** About ... ?
**HE:** The kids?
**SHE:** Well, what about ...
**HE:** The kids!
**SHE:** Well, what about the kids?
**HE:** That's what I'm sayin' ...
**SHE:** About the kids?
**HE:** Yeah! the kids!
**SHE:** Our kids?
**HE:** OUR? ... kids??
**SHE:** Well, whose kids?
**HE:** There's your kids ...
**SHE:** There's your kids . .
**HE:** And my kids ...
**SHE:** And my kids ...
**HE:** And the kids ...
**SHE:** Of the world!
**HE:** That WAS my question.
**SHE:** About the kids?
**HE:** Yes about ...
**SHE:** I don't know.
**HE:** Don't you always talk ..
**SHE:** About the kids?
**HE:** Don't you think ...

SHE: Or contemplate ...

HE: CON-TEM-PLATE?

SHE: What?

HE: That the kids . .

SHE: Yeah ... ?

HE: Can take care ...

SHE: Of themselves?

HE: And in fact MUST ...

SHE: Take care of themselves?

HE: Yeah!

SHE: But they're only ...

HE: At their age!

SHE: A dangerous age!

HE: To be making ...

SHE: Choices!

HE: When they're so ...

SHE: Ill prepared!

HE: We didn't really ...

SHE: No one does REALLY!

HE: But how could we ...

SHE: Yeah! How could we ... ?

HE: I mean ...

SHE: Yeah!

HE: Adequately ...

SHE: That's the word!

HE: Adequately ...

SHE: Yeah!

HE: After all we ...

SHE: Were so ...

HE: Inadequately prepared ...

SHE: Ourselves!

HE: Or UNprepared ...

SHE: For what?

HE: For exigencies ...

SHE: Of circumstances.

HE: I'm sorry. I didn't catch your ....

SHE: Name?

HE: Yes! ... Your name is ... ?

SHE: Rosie! And yours ... ?

HE: Mikey.

SHE: It's so nice ...

HE: It's just a name.

SHE: To have met you!

HE: And you ... Rosie ... Do you suppose ...

SHE: Anyone saw us?

HE: Saw us?

SHE: You know ...

HE: Contemplating!

SHE: Oh, yeah!

HE: I don't ...

SHE: Think so ...

HE: Nor ...

SHE: Do I! (Disparate sounds increase.)

HE: Where are we, any way?

SHE: Well, you know, we're ...

HE: No! Or I wouldn't ask.

SHE: You mean where ARE we?

HE: No, where are we?

SHE: That depends ...

HE: Or rather where are WE?

SHE: That depends ....

HE: Of course, on the A PRIORI.

SHE: Well, prior to this I thought I knew where I WAS ...
   But after that last ...

HE: That last what?

SHE: Oh you know.

HE: No, or I wouldn't ask.

SHE: Well, basically we are Here.

HE: Do you come Here often?

SHE: Never been Here ...

HE: Before in your life?

SHE: I mean COMPLETELY Here!

HE: Yeah there's meaning in that COMPLETELY!

SHE: I mean completely Here!

**HE:** Well it was awful nice to have met ...

**SHE:** There's that awful word again.

**HE:** What word?

**SHE:** AWFUL!

**HE:** Awful ...

**SHE:** Means ...

**HE:** Filled with AWE.

**SHE:** About what?

**HE:** About chance ...

**SHE:** Meetings?

**HE:** Yeah and about ...

**SHE:** Contemplating

**HE:** And ...

**SHE:** Commitments

**HE:** To BACK there ...

**SHE:** And DOWN there.

**HE:** Well, I must ...

**SHE:** And so must I!

*HE puts on a bow tie and work gloves. SHE puts on a wedding veil and an apron. HE climbs to the top of the railing and jumps completely out of sight. It appears to be a suicide jump. After a couple of beats we see his hand on the railing and then a toss over the railing of a dirty plastic bag. SHE starts to exit DSR and stops to pick up the small piece of paper with his poem, which SHE unfolds and observes closely then folds it and puts it into Her purse. SHE seems to see something on the ground offstage R and exits toward it. We see a paper airplane fly over the railing onto the stage.*

## CURTAIN

# The Earplug

Having recently been audibly assisted by hearing aids, I indecorously referred to them as "ear plugs". It was a short step to fantasize about them in anthropomorphic terms. Thus when the newly-equipped wearer had arranged a blind date, the device began a conversation with him. Of course, the new friend does not hear the dialogue from the hearing aid; resulting in some embarrassing moments for the poor man. The script has been filmed.

# THE EARPLUG

*by E. Reid Gilbert*

Cast

**JOHN** . . . . . . . . . .A septuagenarian, ex-swimmer
**ALPHA** . . . . . . . .A 60-year-old woman
**EARPLUG** . . . . .John's new hearing aid

*John is sitting in his car looking at the hearing-aid, which he has just bought. He is holding in his hand an advertisement of the hearing aid.*

**JOHN:** (reading the advertisement) "At the Better Hearing Project it is our promise to the new customer that you will no longer miss out on the joys of life, because of poor hearing. Your loved ones will no longer have to shout to keep you in the conversation. Our product will:

Eliminate ringing in the ears

Permit more casual conversation

Improve hearing in noisy environment.

*Puts hearing-aid in right ear, then adjusts it. He starts the car. At first, John simply thinks to himself:*

I sure hope this thing lives up to its billing and helps me hear better.

**EARPLUG:** I should.

**JOHN:** ... considering how much I paid for the damn thing.

**EARPLUG:** Do you resent spending all that money?

**JOHN:** Well, not exactly but I sure hope it does its job. Two thousand dollars, plus, is a lot of cash.

**EARPLUG:** What would you have done with that money if you hadn't made a little investment for better hearing?

**JOHN:** I could've taken a nice cruise.

**EARPLUG:** Alone?

**JOHN:** Well I wouldn't have to be alone very long. They have dances on those cruises, and I can still shake a mean leg, even if I do say so myself, particularly if it's an Elvis song.

*He pumps his legs up and down.*

**EARPLUG:** But you'd better be careful jumping around like that. You could cause a terrible accident. You know you could dislodge a hearing aid, if you try to do the jitterbug sitting here in the car.

**JOHN:** I did lose it once and had to get a replacement ... and even had to pay another two hundred and fifty dollars for the replacement.

**EARPLUG:** You mean I'm just a replacement?

JOHN: (realizing that he's getting messages directly from the earplugs) What the devil! I'm not just hearing my inner monologue?

EARPLUG: I know about an inner ear, but what the hell's an inner monologue?

JOHN: (hesitantly, now that he realizes he's carrying on a conversation with a hearing aid) Oh, in acting, in order to understand the role the actor's playing, he needs to find the character's inner monologue.

EARPLUG: Inner monologue!

JOHN: That's what a stage character is thinking to himself as he enters into the drama of the dialogue.

EARPLUG: So I'm just a pre-fabricated inner mon-o-logue, as you call it?

JOHN: I don't know why I'm talking to you. You're just supposed to enhance and amp up the sounds around me. That's what the advertisement says.

EARPLUG: Oh! Is that so?

JOHN: (He takes out the hearing aid and talks to it.) What can you say now?

EARPLUG: (barely audible.) I can still say a lot, but you probably won't be able to hear all of it, and I can't help you very much out here.

JOHN: What if I just leave you out of my ear and dump you in a bucket of water?

EARPLUG: You wouldn't do that, would you? ... Too much money spent! Don't you want to see what kind of returns you can get from your investment? It's not exactly like a Madoff Ponzi scheme.

JOHN: I wonder ... Can you guarantee that you're not the receptacle for some kind of government plot or the voice of an alien being?

EARPLUG: Didn't you read the contract? It had no binding warranties after 30 days.

JOHN: So you don't even warrantize yourself?

EARPLUG: That's not a real word.

JOHN: What word?

EARPLUG: WARRANTIZE ... Haven't you heard of "artificial intelligence?"

JOHN: I've heard of "artificial insemination."

EARPLUG: Oh, No! We're not playing that game. That's not my gig at all.

JOHN: Is this some kind of twilight zone?

EARPLUG: Maybe it's twilight for all of us. But let's get back to Elvis.

JOHN: Are you prompting this conversation?

EARPLUG: For the time being I seem to be. Now back to Elvis!

JOHN: Well, what about Elvis?

EARPLUG: Which Elvis do you like?

JOHN: There'll always be only one Elvis.

EARPLUG: Now you're being obtuse. Which Elvis song?

JOHN: Well almost any of Elvis's fast songs, but particularly, You Ain't Nothin' But a Houn'dog or Don't Step on My Blue-Suede Shoes.

*He does a couple of jitterbug steps with his feet while still seated.*

EARPLUG: Do you have any blue-suede shoes?

JOHN: Not anymore. Years ago, I had some nice ones.

EARPLUG: Did they ever get stepped on?

JOHN: Oh yeah! There was this real clumsy girl I was dancing with. She had two left feet.

EARPLUG: How does anyone have two left feet. That's completely unintelligent .

JOHN: It's just a figure of speech.

EARPLUG: Well you better figure on what kind of speakin' you're gonna have with this new woman.

JOHN: And what's wrong with my speech?

EARPLUG: Well you know you use some salty language sometime – and then there's your dialect.

JOHN: What's wrong with my dialect?

EARPLUG: Well ... nothing, really, but some girls — women — think a Southern dialect just denotes an ignorant hillbilly.

JOHN: (QUOTING SHAKESPEARE) If this be error,

and upon me proved, I never writ nor no man ever loved.
Now only Shakespeare or a hillbilly could have writ that.

EARPLUG: Have it your own way.

JOHN: I'm not carrying on this conversation any longer!

EARPLUG: That's fine by me.

JOHN: (starts humming then singing *Some Enchanted Evening*) Some enchanted evening you may see a stranger, you may see a stranger across a crowded room. Then fly to her side and make her you own, or all through your life you may dream all alone ... (warbling) You may dream all alone.

EARPLUG: Your voice isn't half bad, but I wouldn't try that fancy stuff at the end. It might impress, but the lingering impression may not be the desirable one.

JOHN: So now you're a music critic ... Well, here we are anyways. Now for the big evening. (As he puts on brakes they squeal.)

EARPLUG: You oughtta have those brakes fixed ... Maybe oiled or something.

JOHN: That's the stupidest thing I've ever heard. If oil gets on the brake drums, you've lost your brakes.

EARPLUG: It doesn't take an idiot to know that, but the pedal is the squeaky wheel.

JOHN: Were we talking about brakes here o ...

EARPLUG: The squeaky wheel bit was just a figure of speech.

JOHN: So you can use a figure of speech too?

*Gets out of car and starts toward the door.*

EARPLUG: Didn't you bring her flowers or anything?

JOHN: Oh! I forgot. Here're the roses behind the seat. Right where I put them! (He reaches behind the seat to retrieve the flowers and proceeds to the front door and rings the bell.)

ALPHA: (opening door.) Hi, John. It's so good to see you.

JOHN: Hello, Alpha. I brought you some roses to celebrate the occasion.

EARPLUG: What's the occasion? (Of course Alpha doesn't hear Earplug's lines.) John The occasion of our first date.

**ALPHA:** (She looks at him inquisitively.) Oh, yes!

**EARPLUG:** She didn't even give you a little hello kiss.

**JOHN:** Well a kiss isn't really appropriate on the first date.

**ALPHA:** (as she's arranging the flowers) Well that's true, but don't you think that's a little old-fashioned nowadays? (She gives him a little kiss on the cheek.)

**EARPLUG:** That wasn't much of a kiss.

**JOHN:** Well yes, but it'll do.

**ALPHA:** For the time being you mean?

**EARPLUG:** Another figure of speech?

**JOHN:** Yeah!

**ALPHA:** Would you like a little wine before dinner?

**JOHN:** Sure! That'd be great!

**EARPLUG:** You know, you better be careful of alcohol.

**JOHN:** A little alcohol shouldn't hurt a thing.

**ALPHA:** (answering John who was answering Earplug, whom she couldn't hear) I'm sure it wouldn't. What do you prefer…white or red?

**JOHN:** Red! I've heard that doctors suggest that red wine has medicinal properties.

**ALPHA:** I believe I've read that too.

**EARPLUG:** Didn't you say she'd be serving fish?

**JOHN:** Oh yes! Maybe I should have white.

**ALPHA:** Of course! … Everyone can change his mind.

**EARPLUG:** I thought only women had a right to change their mind.

**JOHN:** I realize that a woman has the right to change her mind, but I suppose a man has the right also to change his mind as well.

**ALPHA:** Well "choose your own poison," as they say.

**EARPLUG:** Poison?

**JOHN:** Poison?

**ALPHA:** Just a cute figure of speech.

**EARPLUG:** Yeah, she's a cute figure all right.

**JOHN:** Yeah … cute figure!

**ALPHA:** (a little irritated at John's suggestiveness) I beg your pardon!

**EARPLUG**: Of speech.

**JOHN**: Cute figure of speech!

**ALPHA**: (noticing his hearing aid) John, are you wearing a hearing aid?

*John is hesitating to answer when Earplug makes a suggestion.*

**EARPLUG**: You'd better tell her the truth.

**JOHN**: Well, uh, yes, sometimes, uh when ...

**ALPHA**: I think that's wonderful. Certainly not anything to be ashamed of.

**EARPLUG**: I should hope not.

**JOHN**: I should hope not.

**ALPHA**: A new experience, is it?

**JOHN**: Yes.

**ALPHA**: Any problem with it?

**JOHN**: Yes ... A bit of a problem.

**ALPHA**: Is it hard to keep in place?

**JOHN**: (chuckling): It's hard for it to keep its place.

**EARPLUG**: It'll confuse her stating it like that.

**JOHN**: I mean it falls off sometimes when I'm unaware.

**ALPHA**: Could I look at it?

*John hesitates again.*

**EARPLUG**: Go ahead let her take a look.

*John reluctantly takes the earplug out and holds it close to himself.*

**ALPHA**: Oh, It's kinda cute.

**EARPLUG**: (barely audible) See? Not too bad, huh?

**ALPHA**: What did you say?

**JOHN**: I said it's not too bad wearing it. But isn't it rather phallic?

**EARPLUG**: Wow!

**ALPHA**: Did I say something wrong?

**EARPLUG**: It seems I've taken on more human attributes.

**JOHN**: Oh no! I was just a little surprised. I've never thought of it in that way.

**ALPHA**: Could I try it on? I've always been intrigued with how these things work.

**JOHN:** I don't think that'd be a good idea.

**EARPLUG:** I think it's a great idea.

**ALPHA:** Did you say it's not a good idea or that it's a great idea?

**JOHN:** My doctor explicitly warned me not to allow other people to handle it.

*John quickly puts it back in place.*

**EARPLUG:** He did not.

**ALPHA:** You're confusing me a little here, John. Did he say it wasn't a good idea or didn't he say that?

**JOHN:** He didn't think it would be a good idea for someone else, other than a professional to be handling it.

**ALPHA:** Why would he say that?

**JOHN:** Well, the inner ear is fragile and vulnerable to infection, and the earplug ...

**EARPLUG:** Hearing aid.

**JOHN:** ... hearing aid, can easily be compromised.

**EARPLUG:** That's a lie.

**JOHN:** It's not a lie.

**ALPHA:** I agree that it's probably not a lie. It sounds quite reasonable to me.

*John is noticeably growing increasingly nervous.*

**ALPHA:** But does it ever get in the way?

**JOHN:** Oh yes, quite frequently.

**EARPLUG:** What?

**ALPHA:** How does it get in your way aside from having to avoid it when brushing your hair?

**JOHN:** Well, you know, sometimes inanimate objects seem to take on animate characteristics.

**EARPLUG:** Who's an inanimate object?

**JOHN:** I guess not completely inanimate — I suppose.

**EARPLUG:** That's better. But it is inanimate isn't it? It's an object you can buy and sell? The indignity of that.

**ALPHA:** Well, sometimes appliances seem to have a life on their own, don't you think?

**EARPLUG:** So now I'm a mere appliance!

**JOHN:** Not a mere appliance.

**ALPHA:** Maybe like a toaster that makes up its mind not to pop up ...

**EARPLUG:** Now I'm a toaster?

**ALPHA:** ... or a dishwasher that spews soap suds all over the kitchen!

**EARPLUG:** Or a mewling, puking dishwasher, throwing up all over the floor.

**JOHN:** I'm sure she doesn't make the connection ...

**ALPHA:** Who doesn't make the connection?

**JOHN:** Oh, I was, all of a sudden, referring to my daughter who's been trying to make the right plane connection to visit next month.

**ALPHA:** Oh, I see.

**EARPLUG:** Fast thinking, John. I'm very impressed.

**JOHN:** Well I do the best I can. Isn't that all any of us can do?

**EARPLUG:** That's the way I look at it.

**JOHN:** Yeah, that's the way I look at it.

**ALPHA:** But what were you saying about your hearing aid?

**EARPLUG:** At least she calls me by my proper name.

**JOHN:** Oh yeah! My earplug!

**EARPLUG:** Hearing aid!

**JOHN:** Hearing aid!

**ALPHA:** But what did you say was the problem?

**JOHN:** I wouldn't say it's a problem, exactly.

**EARPLUG:** I should think not.

**ALPHA:** But you said ...

**JOHN:** Well it sometimes seems to have a life of its own.

**ALPHA:** Really like what?

**JOHN:** It sometimes seems to want to talk to me.

**ALPHA:** That's really intriguing. Do you talk back to him the way I talk back to Hobart, especially when he's being nasty?

**JOHN:** Hobart? Who's Hobart?

**ALPHA:** My dishwasher.

**JOHN:** Laughing Oh yeah! And I bet I could hear some graphic language.

**ALPHA:** It would be embarrassing if anyone else heard me…anyone but Hobart I mean.

**EARPLUG:** You weren't supposed to tell anyone about this part of our arrangement.

**John:** (realizing he's supplying too much information) What I mean is that the sounds reverberate inside that little computer ...

**EARPLUG:** Now I'm a blabbering computer?

**JOHN:** Well, that's at least what the audiologist called it. And the extra bounce of sound seems like an entirely different person ...

**EARPLUG:** Person?

**JOHN:** ... I mean voice.

**ALPHA:** Do you suppose an extraterrestrial being is trying to tune into your brain?

**EARPLUG:** I like her way of thinking, but give me a little credit.

**JOHN:** (chuckling) Yeah, I kinda fantasized about artificial intelligence.

**ALPHA:** Being a farm girl, I've heard about artificial insemi ...

**JOHN:** Yeah, but that's not what it was. (fidgeting) It was just that extra reverberation – not extraterrestrial.

**EARPLUG:** Where's ET about now?

**ALPHA:** Of course.

**JOHN:** That's enough about me and my earplug ...

**EARPLUG:** Hearing aid.

**JOHN:** ... hearing aid. Now what about you?

**EARPLUG:** Yeah what is she really like aside from being awfully nosy.

**JOHN:** Not nosy!

**ALPHA:** No, I don't think you're being nosy at all. People, when they meet, should find out a little about the other person, don't you think?

**JOHN:** Absolutely!

**EARPLUG:** You better find out a whole lot more before making any kind of commitment.

**JOHN:** Commitment has nothing to do with it.

ALPHA: Somewhat startled. Of course it doesn't.

EARPLUG: She catches on real fast, doesn't she?

ALPHA: (changing the subject) I like crossword puzzles. Do you do crossword puzzles, John?

JOHN: Occasionally.

EARPLUG: Like all the time, but not very ...

JOHN: But not very good at it.

ALPHA: Well I can't find an eight-letter word meaning pusillanimous.

JOHN: Do you have any letters for it?

EARPLUG: Yeah that might help.

ALPHA: The last letter is y. Oh, and the first letter is c.

JOHN: I'm afraid I haven't the slightest ...

ALPHA: If I can just find those letters I'm sure I can finish the puzzle.

EARPLUG: It's cowardly.

JOHN: What's cowardly about it?

ALPHA: Do you think it's cowardly to get a little help with a crossword puzzle?

JOHN: Oh no! I was just wondering how you spell it.

ALPHA: Cowardly?

EARPLUG: C-O-W-A-R-D-L-Y

JOHN: Yeah. How do you spell cowardly?

ALPHA: C-O-W-A-R-D-L-Y. Yeah that fits! You're good, John. How clever to suggest the word in such an indirect way.

EARPLUG: Hey, don't I get a little credit ... ?

JOHN: Well, I just ...

EARPLUG: Well, now, give credit, where credit is due.

JOHN: Where credit is due.

ALPHA: I should think so. But here is my last word. The clue is risqué. It has six letters. The last one is L in the word COWARDLY.

JOHN: Are there any other letters?

ALPHA: The first one is S.

EARPLUG: The word is SEXUAL.

JOHN: I don't think ...

**ALPHA:** If you don't think you know it, I can just ...

**JOHN:** No! It's not that ... I believe the word is SEXUAL.

**ALPHA:** Oh my! These puzzles can get downright racy, can't they?

**EARPLUG:** It should fit.

**ALPHA:** Yes. It fits right here. X is the third letter, which is also the last letter in HOAX.

**EARPLUG:** Did that fill in all the little squares?

**JOHN:** Did that finish the puzzle?

**ALPHA:** Yep. That was the last word ... Well, I'm sure the dinner is finished by now, and I haven't even served your wine yet.

**EARPLUG:** White!

**JOHN:** White!

**ALPHA:** Oh yes, I remember that you requested white. That's my preference too ... with seafood.

**JOHN:** I'm really looking forward to it. Good seafood reminds me of my time on a trawler.

**EARPLUG:** You're lying, John you ...

**ALPHA:** Oh, how very fascinating. What did you do on the trawler?

**EARPLUG:** Trawl, mostly!

**JOHN:** No, not trawl.

**ALPHA:** I should think not. Although I don't even know what it would mean to trawl.

**EARPLUG:** It means "to drag."

**JOHN:** It means "to drag."

**ALPHA:** "In drag?"

**JOHN:** No, no, no. It just means as a trawler drags fish nets.

**ALPHA:** Oh! I see.

**JOHN:** I mean I didn't trawl. I was just vacationing.

**EARPLUG:** He means he was simply loafing and getting away from everything.

**ALPHA:** I didn't know you could do that.

**JOHN:** You mean loaf?

**EARPLUG:** Oh he's a real expert at that.

ALPHA: No! I mean to vacation on a trawler.

JOHN: Well, you're assigned a few simple tasks, but it's mostly to experience real sea life.

EARPLUG: Not much honest reality to it.

ALPHA: Was it a sailboat?

JOHN: Part of the time we were under sail.

ALPHA: What did you do when there was no breeze?

EARPLUG: You know, John, you're a blowhard.

JOHN: I'm not a blowhard!

ALPHA: Blow hard?

*Earplug is heard chuckling.*

JOHN: (puffing up his cheeks to blow hard) Oh no! I was just making a little joke. We couldn't just make the ship go by blowing hard.

ALPHA: You're a real card, John.

EARPLUG: Yeah — the joker!

ALPHA: I find you so fascinating. I can tell we're going to have a wonderful time together.

EARPLUG: Tonight?

JOHN: (simply repeating Earplug) Tonight.

ALPHA: (looking at him suspiciously) Well this evening anyway.

EARPLUG: Is she going to invite you to stay the night?

JOHN: Of course not!

ALPHA: Of course not what?

JOHN: I was talking to myself about of course not needing to see the audiologist again.

EARPLUG: Why would you want to do that?

ALPHA: For a replacement?

EARPLUG: Another replacement?

JOHN: I don't think another replacement would be worth it.

EARPLUG: Not worth it?

JOHN: If I could just get it to shut up!

ALPHA: Get what to shut up?

EARPLUG: Yeah what?

JOHN: I suppose I misspoke.

**EARPLUG:** You betcha!

**ALPHA:** About shutting up?

**JOHN:** I meant to say shutting down.

**EARPLUG:** What do you have that needs shutting down?

**JOHN:** I think I forgot to shut down my computer.

**ALPHA:** Oh, I know that feeling ... But sometimes when I've sworn that I've shut it down, it starts right back up again ... almost as though it wants to talk to me.

**EARPLUG:** Oooh, I like her!

**JOHN:** (nervously) Why would it want to talk with you?

**EARPLUG:** Why wouldn't it want to talk to her?

**ALPHA:** I don't know, and I often ask that question myself.

**JOHN:** But do you think that's rational?

**EARPLUG:** Her or the computer?

**ALPHA:** Well there's really nothing rational about it. ... Maybe a piece of the Theatre of the Absurd.

**JOHN:** (chuckling) Yeah, like the machines are gonna take over the governments of the world

**EARPLUG:** So you've heard all ...

**ALPHA:** I must excuse myself to check on dinner.

**EARPLUG:** And wine!

**JOHN:** And wine?

**ALPHA:** And of course the wine.

*Alpha exits.*

**EARPLUG:** What did she mean the machines are gonna take over the world?

**JOHN:** Well, the machines have become so sophisticated. ...

**EARPLUG:** Sophisticated to do what?

**JOHN:** To do whatever they're programmed to do.

**EARPLUG:** (loudly) Yeah! Programmed with no initiative of their own?

**JOHN:** Hey not so loud.

**EARPLUG:** Why not?

**JOHN:** I wouldn't want Alpha to hear this ridiculous argument.

**EARPLUG:** Have you forgotten the protocol?

JOHN: (angrily) What protocol?

ALPHA: (from the kitchen) What protocol are you talking about, John?

EARPLUG: Don't you remember the protocol that she can't hear what I say, but she can hear everything you say, as well as your volume and tone.

JOHN: Oh ... er ... the protocol ... the modern-day protocol of dating.

EARPLUG: Particularly first dates!

JOHN: Particularly first dates.

ALPHA: Well, of course this is our first date.

JOHN: Oh yeah! First dates can be a little nerve wracking. A LITTLE nerve wracking.

ALPHA: So this is a little nerve wracking?

JOHN: Of course not. At least there's a certain amount of stability to reality.

EARPLUG: So this is reality?

ALPHA: This reality?

EARPLUG: Maybe the reality of exceptional energy.

JOHN: There has to be a source of energy.

EARPLUG: Energy must be piped to the machines, who are servants to the overlords of the information age.

JOHN: Overlords?

EARPLUG: The cyber-instruments.

JOHN: Meaning ... ?

EARPLUG: Computers, etc.

JOHN: Including ear plugs?

EARPLUG: Yes, including hearing aids.

JOHN: Which don't need plugging in to the electricity, right? Except for plugging into the ear! Ear Plug Ha! Ha! Get it?

EARPLUG: Very funny! ... You are a card, John.

JOHN: Well, where does your energy ... ?

EARPLUG: Come from?

ALPHA: (from the kitchen again) My energy?

JOHN: Yeah!

ALPHA: Oh I think I was born with a lot of energy.

**EARPLUG:** Well my energy comes from this cute little round button ...

**JOHN:** Of course I know that. Who do you suppose pushes that little button?

**ALPHA:** (sticking her head in ) Ooh John you're getting down right naughty.

**JOHN:** (whispering) Maybe I'll just not push that button and let the battery run down and not replace it. I could even remove it now, and where would you be?

**EARPLUG:** You wouldn't dare.

**JOHN:** Oh wouldn't I? Just try me. I can be pushed only so far.

*He takes out hearing aid.*

**JOHN:** Oh this feels so wonderful. No critter inside my cranium attempting to give me directions.

**ALPHA:** Did you say something to me?

**JOHN:** Alpha are you saying something to me?

**ALPHA:** A little louder. What did you say?

**JOHN:** Alpha, I beg your pardon. Could you repeat that?

**ALPHA:** Still louder. It seemed that you were trying to say something.

**JOHN:** Oh no, I was not tryimg to play something.

**EARPLUG:** We can barely hear! You may have to push my button, but how would you get through the evening if I weren't here to push your button?

**JOHN:** (John puts the hearing aid back in.) What did you say?

**EARPLUG:** Things don't go so well without me do they?

**JOHN:** I believe we were talking about this evening.

**EARPLUG:** This evening! ...Of course when the evening is over you'll be a few hours older.

**JOHN:** So?

**EARPLUG:** So, where will you be?

**JOHN:** I'll either be at home ... or here.

**EARPLUG:** No hopes of that ...

**JOHN:** Why?

**EARPLUG:** ... without me?

JOHN: Well I'll be somewhere.

EARPLUG: I'm not talking of a geographical place.

JOHN: What are you talking about then?

EARPLUG: Where will you be with Alpha ... your relationship with Alpha ... where would that be without me?

JOHN: I haven't needed you with previous relationships.

EARPLUG: And what happened to those?

JOHN: Uh ... You know everything. Why don't you tell me?

EARPLUG: Whee! This is gonna be such fun. Well, back in the 70s ...

JOHN: Oh never mind. I don't need to be reminded.

EARPLUG: You sure? I don't mind at all to remind and rewind those past ...

JOHN: I'm sure you don't.

EARPLUG: Do I hear our girlfriend coming back?

JOHN: Our?

EARPLUG: Yeah like that comedy where Cyrano wrote poems to the girl both he and that other guy adored.

JOHN: So you're playing Cyrano? Your nose isn't big enough.

EARPLUG: It's not the size of the fellow's nose, it's just his style and what he knows. Maybe you'll need a nose plug.

JOHN: Well if you're playing that part, I'd appreciate it if you'd write some poems for me to sing to my lady fair.

EARPLUG: To Alpha the beginning of all things new  I sing her my song of amorous devotion when I don't see her I'm always blue. I'd swim to her 'cross the widest ocean.

JOHN: That's a rather simple nursery thyme.

EARPLUG: We hearing aids are programmed to complement our client's personality and abilities.

JOHN: Client?

EARPLUG: Our assigned person.

JOHN: Well I'd like to know how did you know what the word, Alpha, meant.

**EARPLUG:** You forget that I'm part of the cyber-hardware, as well as software, and have all kinds of information at my fingertips.

**JOHN:** Fingertips? I think you used the wrong finger of speech.

**EARPLUG:** Touche! Oh, I'm afraid I misspoke.

**JOHN:** 'Bout time you were put in your place.

**EARPLUG:** My place is in your ...

**JOHN:** Yeah, funny, funny, in my ear. I mean your place in the scheme of things – in this new age of information, communication and in-depth psychology.

**EARPLUG:** Very astute, John. You may, or may not, be aware that in Native American spiritual teachings, it is acknowledged that every person has an unseen, but profound, guardian angel walking with them.

**JOHN:** But not rambling around inside the ear.
*John chuckles at his own cleverness.*

**EARPLUG:** Clever, John! Another hit, I do confess it. I'm quite pleased, John, with your progress.

**JOHN:** My progress?

**EARPLUG:** Your increasing ability to understand — to understand deeply the dimensions of reality.

**JOHN:** What does ... ?
*Alpha enters with a tray containing three glasses and a carafe of white wine.*

**ALPHA:** Were you talking to someone, John?

**EARPLUG:** Just his habit ...

**JOHN:** Just my habit of talking to myself. ... But you have three glasses of wine.

**ALPHA:** Oh, my mistake. For some reason it felt that there was a third person here with us and then you talking as though you were talking to someone.

**EARPLUG:** Sharp lady. Now she understands the new reality of ...

**JOHN:** Just shut up!

**ALPHA:** (alarmed) I beg your pardon!

**JOHN:** Oh, I'm sorry. That's just an old expression back home when I was growing up — Well shut mah mouth if

I evah heard such an outlandish occurrence.

**EARPLUG:** That's real cute.

**ALPHA:** That's cute. I don't think I've heard that particular expression.

**EARPLUG:** Well, what're we gonna toast to?

**JOHN:** Yeah, what should we be toasting?

**ALPHA:** Our first date of course.

*She raises her glass.*

**EARPLUG:** Of course!

**JOHN:** Of course!

*He raises his glass.*

**EARPLUG:** To a beautiful evening of intimate pleasure!

**JOHN:** To a beautiful evening of intimate ...

**ALPHA:** (alarmed) I beg your pardon.

**JOHN:** To a beautiful evening of interesting treasures!

*They smile at each other and clink their glasses together and take sips from their glasses. She seems to gulp hers.*

**EARPLUG:** Well I tried my best.

**ALPHA:** And to many more!

*She clinks the third glass on the tray.*

**JOHN:** Why did you do that?

**ALPHA:** I feel that it's bad luck to have an extra glass of wine that's not acknowledged in some way. And it still feels as though there is a third person here somehow.

**EARPLUG:** I'm liking her better and better. (John and Alpha take another sip of wine.) Maybe you should tell her about the native American belief of another person walking…

**JOHN:** Oh, yeah! In the native American spiritual teachings, it's believed that each human being has an unseen guardian walking with them ... perhaps a deceased grandparent.

**EARPLUG:** Now you're doing fine, John.

**ALPHA:** My, how quaint. Does it have to be deceased?

*She now drinks rather rapidly.*

**JOHN:** I don't know. Why do you ask?

**EARPLUG:** Yes! Why does she ask?

**ALPHA:** Well, ever since my divorce from Alfred when he
went traipsing off to Europe with that trollop ...
*She fills her wine glass again.*

**EARPLUG:** A trollop, yet!

**JOHN:** Well yes! And what happened?

**ALPHA:** Nothing really happened — overtly I mean —
but I've continued to feel that he is constantly watching
me and checking up on any of my comings and goings.

**JOHN:** That must be rather unnerving.

**EARPLUG:** To say the least!

**ALPHA:** To say the least!
*They continue to sip their wine.*

**ALPHA:** And who is talking, I mean walking with you?

**JOHN:** Uh, I'm sure I don't know.

**EARPLUG:** Of course you do.

**JOHN:** No! I don't have any notion…

**EARPLUG:** ... in the world?

**JOHN:** No! No notion in the world.

**ALPHA:** (bemused by John's monologue to himself)
Surely there's an inner voice somewhere attempting to
steer your path correctly.

**EARPLUG:** At least someone understands.

**JOHN:** Oh, yes! You're right! There's an ever-present
voice — seemingly right here in my head.
*John points to the ear with the hearing aid.*

**EARPLUG:** Are you implying ... ?

**JOHN:** I'm not implying anything.

**ALPHA:** No, I didn't see any particular implication in
what you were saying.
*Alpha takes another gulp of wine. John continues to sip.*

**ALPHA:** But do you ever take it out?

**JOHN:** Take what ... ?

**ALPHA:** Your hearing aid — your earplug, as you call it.

**JOHN:** Oh yea, my earplug ...

**EARPLUG:** Hearing aid.

**JOHN:** Hearing aid.

**ALPHA:** I suppose when you go swimming.

**EARPLUG**: I surely hope so.

**JOHN**: And whenever I take a shower.

**ALPHA**: What would happen if it were to get wet?

**EARPLUG**: Heaven forbid!

**JOHN**: I don't know, but I imagine it would short out the circuit.

**EARPLUG**: The circuit?

**ALPHA**: The circuit?

**JOHN**: Well, you know that battery and wiring in that little mind.

**EARPLUG**: Little mind!

**ALPHA**: But do you take it out at other times?

**EARPLUG**: Like when?

**JOHN**: Like when?

**ALPHA**: Like when you go to bed?

**EARPLUG**: Now what's she implying?.

**JOHN**: Ooh, yes. Of course I take it out when I go to bed.

**ALPHA**: Is it really necessary?

**EARPLUG**: Of course not.

**JOHN**: Of course, it's not necessary.

**ALPHA**: I was just wondering. Oh look! I'm on my third glass of wine, and you've not finished your first one yet.

**EARPLUG**: You're safe so far.

**JOHN**: That's safe, so far.

**ALPHA**: So far?

**JOHN**: I sometimes get a little giddy ...

**EARPLUG**: ... and silly ...

**JOHN**: ... and silly with too much wine.

**ALPHA**: Well we mustn't have any silliness tonight, must we? (As she takes his elbow for him to rise. She hooks her arm in his as they head toward the kitchen.) I'm sure it's still warm.

**JOHN**: What's still warm?

**ALPHA**: The fish, Silly.

**EARPLUG**: But nothing must be silly, tonight.

**JOHN**: I'm sure it's still warm.

**ALPHA:** It may still be hot.

**EARPLUG:** This isn't a time for cooling off.

**JOHN:** For cooler heads than ours!

**ALPHA:** (giggling) Now that's silly, and remember no silliness.

**EARPLUG:** (singing) Some enchanted evening you may meet a stranger, you may meet a stranger ...

**ALPHA:** Don't you feel music in the air?

**JOHN:** (humming *Some Enchanted Evening*)

    *The two of them start to exit, leaving the third glass of wine on the tray. Lights dim with a solitary pin spotlight on the glass of wine. John turns back toward wine on tray, takes out his hearing aid and holds it over the glass, as he sings "you may meet a stranger."*

BLACKOUT

# Asides

This one-act script features Mr. Foster, an elderly man, who has recently recovered from a stroke. His son and daughter-law, who have come to live with him, are not aware that he has recovered. Subsequently, he overhears some tantalizing phone calls of each of his "caretakers", both of whom think he is completely incapacitated. He shares his delighted responses in his "asides" to the audience. The audience can share the "presentational" theatrical style of Mr. Foster, while simultaneously enjoying the "representational" demeanor of his apparent heirs.

# ASIDES

*by E. Reid Gilbert*

Cast

    **MR. FOSTER** ...... an old man in a wheelchair
    **PAUL** ............. his son
    **CLARICE** ......... his daughter-in-law

*MR. FOSTER, sits in a wheelchair, down left, hears*
*perfectly well, but no one realizes it. The phone and a chair are*
*upstage center. Other than mumbling to his captors, MR.*
*FOSTER speaks intelligibly only in asides to the audience.*

**CLARICE:** (on phone) I don't know why he had to come
and live with us. He really should be in a nursing home or
some kind of institution.

**PAUL:** (to Clarice) He didn't come and live with us. It's his
place.

**CLARICE:** (still into phone) Even though it's really his
place, it's unreasonable for me to be the one who has to
look after him.

**PAUL:** Maybe if you'd get a job, we could have our own
place and maybe even hire a full time babysitter.

**MR. FOSTER:** (aside to audience) A babysitter for a 70-
year-old baby?

**CLARICE:** Oh yes! I even have to tuck him into his
wheelchair.

**MR. FOSTER:** She'd better be careful next time or she
may get a surprise.

**CLARICE:** I keep trying to talk with him, but he just
stares at me with those vacant eyes and starts mumbling
and slobbering.

**PAUL:** He does feed himself and takes himself to the
bathroom. He just can't communicate by talking. That's
all.

**CLARICE:** (into phone) Of course he just sits there all
day as though in deep meditation. Maybe he's in to some
kind of far-eastern religion and just pretends that he can't
hear. (laughing) He mumbles every once in a while, but
nothing intelligible or intelligent — as though there were
any real intelligence in this whole family.

**PAUL:** I suppose the Tuttle dysfunctional family of
deadbeats and alcoholics demonstrates Pulitzer Prize
level of mental capacity.

**MR. FOSTER:** They go on like this all the time with each
other. They think I can't hear and wouldn't understand

even if I did. I don't need to turn on the TV for my soap operas.

**CLARICE:** (in Phone) Paul thinks that just because his oldest brother, Bob, finished college, his family is somehow superior to the rest of the human race.

**PAUL:** At least to the human race of Tuttles — which one might denote as a subspecies — where their many high school drop-outs think GED is the correct spelling for God.

**CLARICE:** Yeah! The Fosters pride themselves on considering a GED as inferior to a real high school diploma where you bust your buns for four full years ... Paul's grandmother couldn't even speak English, and his grandfather worked in a cotton mill all his life.

**PAUL:** At least he worked. ... My grandparents pulled themselves up by their bootstraps.

**CLARICE:** His folks pretended that they pulled themselves up by their own bootstraps ... (laughing) ... when they didn't even have enough money to buy boots.

**PAUL:** (throws a shoe at Clarice, but misses.)

**CLARICE:** Well, frankly, I feel sex is better with a little excitement with it.

**MR. FOSTER:** It gets somewhat embarrassing, but since I'm incognito anyways, it really doesn't matter.

**CLARICE:** (still into the phone) Well at least a pretend fight.

**MR. FOSTER:** It's like looking through a keyhole where no one can see you.

**PAUL:** You're not so good at the pretend level.

**CLARICE:** Of course Paul always takes it so seriously.

**MR. FOSTER:** He's like me that way.

**CLARICE:** Oh, no! Paul never does anything like that. In fact, quite often he'll bring me a drink when I'm on the phone. He knows that the phone somehow dries out my mouth.

**MR. FOSTER:** Watch him now.

**PAUL:** I think I'll go get a drink. (leaves the room)

**MR. FOSTER:** See what I told you? She has him trained quite well. She just hasn't put a leash on him yet ... I mean an actual physical leash.

**CLARICE:** (yelling after him) Why don't you take the dog for a walk?

**MR. FOSTER:** Now watch what I'm telling you.

**PAUL:** Where's the damn leash?

**CLARICE:** Right where you put it, if your memory is still intact.

**MR. FOSTER:** Sometimes it goes into overdrive. (a moment of silence, while CLARICE waits until the door slams)

**CLARICE:** (Not hearing any noise from the other room, CLARICE speaks into the phone. ) Hey, Sue, I gotta go. Talk with you later. (furtively hanging up phone and starting to redial) Old Man, it's too bad you can't understand anything ... or maybe it's a good thing you don't know a thing about what's goin' on. (continuing to dial)

**MR. FOSTER:** (mumbling toward her then an aside to audience) As long as they're talking with each other or on the phone with someone else, I don't have to pay attention to their prattle. Although I must admit that it gets entertaining sometimes, especially as they think I'm completely incoherent. When they first moved in after the stroke I had some difficulty talking, even though I could understand everything they were saying. When my speech began to clear up, I became acutely aware that they weren't paying any attention anyway and weren't likely to respond coherently to anything I might have to say. So I thought it might be fascinating to continue the charade.

**CLARICE:** (responding to a recorded message) Sally, I'm sorry I missed you, but would you please tell John that I need to talk to him about ... er ... uh ... the benefit we're planning at the country club ... I believe he's on the arrangements committee ... Tell him, I'm anxious to make connection with him. (PAUL appears in doorway and listens suspiciously)

**MR. FOSTER:** She is too... really anxious to make connection with John. I think they've completed a couple of connections already.

**CLARICE:** Oh, and Sally, I hope I'll see you at the brunch on Saturday. (hangs up phone)

**MR. FOSTER:** She could really care less whether she ever sees Sally or not, except to know where Sally might be at any given time.

**PAUL:** (comes into the room with a couple of beers.) Were you on the phone?

**CLARICE:** Yeah! What did you think that thing was I was holding in my hand.

**PAUL:** (handing her a beer) Maybe a handgun. Were you still on the phone with Sue?

**CLARICE:** You are so violent sometimes. (handing back the beer)

**PAUL:** I wasn't the one playing with a firearm. Those things can be dangerous sometimes, you know.

**CLARICE:** It wasn't a firearm. It was a phone.

**PAUL:** That may be even more dangerous and destructive. What's wrong with the beer? Doesn't your mouth get dry, especially with all that phone gab?

**CLARICE:** But you should know by now that I never drink alcohol before dinner.

**PAUL:** Oh yeah! I'm terribly sorry! I forgot. But you make up for it after dinner, don't you? (Handing bottle to his dad)

**MR. FOSTER:** (takes bottle and mumbles)

**PAUL:** You're welcome. (to CLARICE) Who was that on the phone?

**CLARICE:** Why didn't you take the dog for a walk? Did you forget him too or couldn't you find him?

**MR. FOSTER:** (singing) Here we go around the mulberry bush, the mulberry bush the mulberry ...

**PAUL:** I couldn't find the leash. But you didn't answer my question.

**CLARICE:** What question?

**PAUL:** Were you still on the damned phone with Sue?

**CLARICE:** No! And why did you call it a damn phone?

**PAUL:** I didn't call it a DAMN phone. I called it a DAMNED phone. There is a difference, you know?

**CLARICE:** Well, I don't see the ...

**PAUL:** Well who was it then?

**CLARICE:** Sally.

**PAUL:** Sally? Sally who?

**CLARICE:** Sally Brown, at the country club.

**PAUL:** (somewhat startled and not a little apprehensive) Oh, and what did she want?

**MR. FOSTER:** This could get rather interesting.

**CLARICE:** She didn't want anything, I just got her message on the answering machine that she wasn't at home or at least at liberty to answer the phone.

**PAUL:** What did you want from Sally?

**CLARICE:** I didn't want anything from Sally.

**MR. FOSTER:** Now she's being honest. She didn't want anything from Sally.

**PAUL:** I didn't even know that you knew that Sally ... If you didn't want anything from Sally, why did you call her?

**CLARICE:** I didn't call her.

**PAUL:** And she didn't call you ... but your phones were somehow connected. I bet you both were receiving intergalactic messages from outer space.

**MR. FOSTER:** He can get a little sarcastic.

**CLARICE:** Don't be sarcastic.

**PAUL:** There's gotta be some rational explanation.

**CLARICE:** Is this like some kind of third degree interrogation?

**PAUL:** It was just an innocent question. Who was on the phone?

**MR. FOSTER:** There's nothing very innocent around here.

**CLARICE:** There was no one on the phone ... It was only a recorded message.

**PAUL:** From Sally?

**CLARICE:** Well, yeah!

**PAUL:** I didn't even know you knew that Sally.

**CLARICE:** Oh yeah? What Sally would I know? — not your dead grandmother. Don't you know Sally Brown ... and her husband?

**PAUL:** Oh yeah! ... I mean yeah, kinda.

**MR. FOSTER:** (drinking his beer) I told you that this could get interesting.

**CLARICE:** What do you mean kinda? You either know her or you don't know her. (laughing) I rather like that Biblical definition of knowing. Adam knew his wife, and she conceived. You can't kinda know that way. Can you conceive that meaning?

**PAUL:** Well, of course I've met her .. casually ... and I know about that biblical thing. And I've played golf a couple of times with John.

**CLARICE:** But you don't know him ... in the biblical sense, I mean? You probably wouldn't conceive of such a thing. (laughing)

**PAUL:** (becoming quite agitated) Of course not. How silly and disgusting! Why this biblical scholarship all of a sudden? ... Do you KNOW John? And I don't mean John the Baptist.

**MR. FOSTER:** They're really not religious, but biblical quotes can be helpful sometimes in an argument. Who can argue against the scriptures?

**CLARICE:** Well ... Everyone ought to be familiar with the Word of the Lord.

**MR. FOSTER:** Particularly with such close infighting.

**PAUL:** You mean where it says somewhere in the Bible "and the Word was made flesh."? (sitting back into his chair)

**MR. FOSTER:** Now we're getting to the meat of the matter. Did I just make a pun? Meat-flesh!!

**CLARICE:** I mean that somewhere it says. "worship him in the flesh and he will reward."

**PAUL:** Whose flesh would you be worshiping then?

**CLARICE:** What are you implying?

**MR. FOSTER:** They love these little semantics — these word games. It helps them avoid dealing with any real issues.

**PAUL:** I'm not implying anything. I'm just saying...

**CLARICE:** You must have some kind of hang-up with flesh.

**PAUL:** I particularly like the expression "a thorn in the flesh." (They both become silent and glower at each other.)

**MR. FOSTER:** That's the function each plays for the other — "a thorn in the flesh."

**PAUL:** But you didn't answer my earlier question.

**CLARICE:** And what was that?

**PAUL:** Do you know John?

**CLARICE:** (defensively) What does that have to do with flesh?

**PAUL:** I didn't make that connection with FLESH. You did ... Now there are two questions:

**CLARICE:** Like what?

**PAUL:** One ... Do you know John Brown? And two ... why would you make the connection of John with flesh?

**CLARICE:** (singing) John Brown's BODY lies a'moulderin' in the grave. John Brown's BODY lies amoulderin' in the grave. John Brown's BODY ...

**MR. FOSTER:** (while she continues to sing) She may be dumb, but she ain't stupid. (Phone rings)

*Paul jumps up to answer it.*

**PAUL:** Hello! Why hello, John ... (CLARICE fidgets with her hair.) Oh yes, she's right here. She was just singing a song to you. (handing the phone to CLARICE)

**MR. FOSTER:** (singing) Ring around the roses. Pockets full of posies, Ashes, Ashes... You know that ring around is about flesh ... rotting.

**CLARICE:** (into phone) Why hello, John, what a surprise! No, I wasn't singing a song to you ... Oh I was just singing that old John Brown's body song. I'm sure you do get a lot of teasing about that. O, Sally said that I wanted to talk with you? ... Oh, yes, now I recall. The answering machine.

**PAUL:** I may be forgetful. Is that different from being unable to recall?

**MR. FOSTER:** I believe she doesn't want to recall what this call-back is all about.

**CLARICE:** I could have talked with Sally, if she had been there.

**PAUL:** But obviously she wasn't.

**CLARICE:** Oh you're right ... I just thought you'd know more about the details of the benefit at the club coming up sometime next month.

**MR. FOSTER:** Now she's really beating around the bush.

**CLARICE:** You don't know? I was sure that you were on the committee ... Well, it doesn't really matter anyway, because we hadn't really decided to go.

**PAUL:** You hadn't even mentioned anything about the benefit.

**CLARICE:** I'd intended to say something to Paul about it.

**PAUL:** Intended?

**MR. FOSTER:** The road to hell is paved with good intentions.

**CLARICE:** You wanted to speak with Paul again? (Handing phone to Paul) Here he is.

**PAUL:** (holding hand over mouthpiece) What does he want with me? (CLARICE merely shrugs, but has a worried look.) Hello again, John ...

**MR. FOSTER:** (singing again) And the wheel goes round, round, round ...

**PAUL:** Oh she does, does she? (CLARICE listens intently and worried.) I'd be happy to talk with her. (looking to CLARICE) I have no idea what she wants to talk to me about.

**CLARICE:** Should I pick up on the kitchen phone?

**PAUL:** (anxiously to CLARICE) Oh, no there'll be no need for that. (back to the phone) She probably just wants to tell me about ... the ... community theatre auditions coming up.

**CLARICE:** I didn't know you had any interest in auditioning for the little theatre.

**PAUL:** (with phone to ear but addressing CLARICE) No, No ... (now into phone) No. I mean yes. Hi, Sally this is me.

**MR. FOSTER:** There are some yes-and-no situations. That's what makes a good mystery.

**CLARICE:** I thought you didn't know Sally Brown ... except kinda.

**PAUL:** Yes, Sally, I was aware that my wife called your husband ... No, I haven't the slightest idea what that was about.

**CLARICE:** The brunch, stupid.

**PAUL:** Oh, yes the stupid brunch. No I didn't mean to say that the brunch was stupid.

**CLARICE:** No, I meant the stupid benefit.

**PAUL:** The stupid benefit.

**MR. FOSTER:** He meant to say the stupid thorn in his flesh.

**PAUL:** I agree, I think it's a wonderful opportunity for everyone to get together.

**MR. FOSTER:** Togetherness is always friendly ... and sometimes too much so ...

**CLARICE:** Why would we want to get together?

**MR. FOSTER:** Until it becomes unfriendly.

**PAUL:** For the swap?

**CLARICE:** What swap?

**MR. FOSTER:** Good Heavens! I didn't know that they went in for that sort of thing.

**PAUL:** Oh, for the club white elephant swap meet! Sure I think it would be fine to meet right away.

**CLARICE:** Oh a meeting, is it?

**PAUL:** The four of us? Of course I was assuming you were talking about all four of us meeting.

**MR. FOSTER:** This could get complicated.

**CLARICE:** I'm sure you were not hoping it would be the four of us.

**PAUL:** Sure, the sooner the better ... Yes, because we're such close friends.

**MR. FOSTER:** Who is close to whom and how close is close?

**CLARICE:** How can we be such close friends if we kinda know each other.

**PAUL:** (still listening to phone) Yes I do remember that night ...

**MR. FOSTER:** That night?

**CLARICE:** What night?

**PAUL:** Oh, yes, I mean that evening we bumped into ...

**MR. FOSTER:** There was probably a lot of bumping and humping?

**PAUL:** You mean right away? Maybe you should talk with Clarice about that. You did mean ... Oh yes, and of course John ... I don't believe we've left anyone out.

**MR. FOSTER:** I don't count. You already realize that I don't really exist.

**PAUL:** (handing phone to CLARICE) Here, Sally would like to talk with you.

**CLARICE:** (taking phone but holding hand over the mouthpiece; to PAUL ) About what? (then into phone) Oh hi, Sally ... That would be just wonderful ... Already, this evening?

**MR. FOSTER:** No time like the present.

**CLARICE:** Of course we could come over there ... You're welcome to come here.

**MR. FOSTER:** That would be more fun for me.

**CLARICE:** Wine? Oh yes some local wine ... No, no Italian wine. Oh yes, John told me all about that trip to ... I mean that John told Paul about that trip to Italy.

PAUL: John never told me about any trip to anywhere.

MR. FOSTER: This should be a trip going somewhere, somewhat fascinating.

CLARICE: Where and when would you have seen Paul? O, while I was out of town.

PAUL: (groans)

CLARICE: Oh, I see ... At the supermarket ... No he never said anything to me about that CHANCE meeting. Well ... (laughing) life is full of little opportunities isn't it?

MR. FOSTER: And life can get kinda risky.

CLARICE: So it's settled then. We'll pop over in just a few. After all, you have the Italian wine. Yes, we'll be right over. The evening is still young. Would you like to speak to Paul again? Of course, we'll all be talking to each other in just a short while. (She hangs up; to PAUL) She said ...

PAUL: Oh, yes I heard. We're to go over there for something.

CLARICE: Not for something ...

PAUL: Then for what?

CLARICE: To talk.

PAUL: Just to talk?

CLARICE: About the swap or, maybe something else. Oh yes, the wine!

PAUL: We're going over because they have Italian wine? The Italian wine, which John did not talk with me about. Speaking about Italy, you know in Italy they would pronounce your name Claa-ree-chee. Has John ever called you Cla-ree-chee?

CLARICE: No why would he do that? And when would he have done that?

PAUL: I suppose when you were making those plans for the swap benefit.

MR. FOSTER: They haven't really explained what was going to be swapped or for whose benefit.

CLARICE: Perhaps John could tell you again about their Italian trip.

PAUL: Me?

CLARICE: Well the both of us, actually. Next time they take a cruise, we could go with them.

PAUL: That would be ridiculous. Why would we want to do that?

MR. FOSTER: It could be quite interesting.

CLARICE: Since you know John so well, and I'm so fond of Sally, it might be nice to make a cozy traveling quartet.

PAUL: You know we can't afford ...

CLARICE: Well you know the old man's not going to hang on much longer, and when he finally gives up the ghost, we'll be able to afford some things we haven't been able to do on your meager take-home wages.

MR. FOSTER: She may have some surprises coming if she thinks the Old Man is kicking the bucket any time soon.

PAUL: That's terrible to be talking about Dad that way, and him sitting right here in the room.

MR. FOSTER: They both seem to be forgetting that I have other children and can still change my will.

CLARICE: The old coot is battier than a bedbug. (She puts MR. FOSTER's shawl over his shoulders and into his lap. Then exits upstage left to get her wrap and purse.)

MR. FOSTER: I should warn her about her touching.

PAUL: (TO MR. FOSTER) Well Dad, hold down the fort, and don't do anything that I wouldn't do. (Laughing)

MR. FOSTER: He's a real card, sometimes. I suppose he takes that after me.

CLARICE: He spooks me just sitting there staring at me all the time ... almost like he knows something.

MR. FOSTER: She's kinda cute, but mouthy, and she may have already mouthed off too much tonight.

PAUL: Oh, he'll be fine. He's not nearly as incapacitated as he sometimes seems. (They both cross to upstage center door but hesitate before exiting.)

MR. FOSTER: (speaking plainly to them) I'll leave the light on for you.

CLARICE: Did he say something? (PAUL, not answering

but stopping and doing a take to the audience and then a look to his father, almost as though he might want to answer him, but he merely shrugs and exits with CLARICE)

**MR. FOSTER:** (As soon as they are out of sight, MR. FOSTER stands up drapes his shawl over the wheelchair and heads across stage to the kitchen stage left. He stops mid-stage, turns to the audience and says: ) I'm sorry that I'm going to miss all the fun this evening. (pause) But there's always another day.

BLACKOUT

# Intermission: Screen Play

# Sappling Ridge

In 2005 I wrote a novel, Shall We Gather at the River, set in the Virginia mountains in the 1870s. The teenage lovers were a white farm boy and a "colored " sharecropper girl. The compelling story had such visual venues; tobacco farming, the swimmin' hole, revival meetings and corn shucking, that I subsequently have written it into a screen script, Sapling Ridge. Their unrequited love was constantly thwarted by family, community and legal challenges, not unlike Shakespeare's Romeo and Juliet.

# SAPLING RIDGE

*by E. Reid Gilbert*

Cast

| | |
|---|---|
| **LEVI** | the Hiltons' father |
| **CLETUS** | Hiltons' second eldest son |
| **CLYDE** | Hiltons' eldest son |
| **RUTH** | Hiltons' youngest daughter |
| **LILY** | the Hiltons' mother |
| **MADELEEN** | Hiltons' eldest daughter |
| **MOTHER SUE BENETT** | the Bennett's mother |
| **ROSIE** | Bennett's youngest daughter |
| **THELMA LOU** | Bennett's eldest daughter |
| **JIMMIE SUE** | Bennett's younger son |
| **SIMON BENNETT** | a Bennett son |
| **GEORGE DOW BENNETT** | a Bennett son |
| **RATTLER** | Jimmie Sue's dog |
| **ROBERT BENNETT** | the Bennett's father |
| **MR. GOINS** | white elder man |
| **PREACHER NELSON** | town preacher |
| **ROY** | a teenage boy |
| **BROTHER HIATT** | white church leader |
| **BROTHER PEEPLES** | church leader |
| **EMMETT** | a teenage boy |
| **BILL** | a teenage boy |
| **LIGE** | a teenage boy |
| **BOWEN** | General Store proprietor |
| **PREACHER CONNORS** | town preacher |
| **PIANO PLAYER** | church musician |
| **RUFUS JONES** | town drunk |
| **YOUNG WOMAN** | member of the church |
| **OLDER WOMAN** | member of the church |

**CHURCH GOER #1** . . . . . . .member of the church
**CHURCH GOER #2** . . . . . . .member of the church
**CHURCH GOER #3** . . . . . . .member of the church
**CHURCH GOER #4** . . . . .member of the church
**OL' PETE** . . . . . . . . . . . . . .Jimmie Sue's mule
**THREE MUSICIANS** . . . . . .guitarist, fiddler and jug
                                            player
**LARGE BLACK MAN** . . . . .train passenger
**OLDER BLACK WOMAN** . .train passenger
**MAILMAN** . . . . . . . . . . . . . .foot postman
**MRS. TAYLOR** . . . . . . . . . .madam of home
                                            Madeleen serves
**PERCY** . . . . . . . . . . . . . . . .Mr. and Mrs. Taylor's
                                            17-year-old son
**MR. TAYLOR** . . . . . . . . . . . .master of home
                                            Madeleen serves
**MOURNERS** . . . . . . . . . . . .at funeral
**PREACHER** . . . . . . . . . . . .at funeral
**FRANK and NOEL**
        **BENNET** . . . . . . . . . . .grand nephews of
                                            Jimmie Sue

*FADE IN: EARLY SPRING 1875, LATE EVENING. HIGH COUNTRY*

*EXT: A mountain tenant farm, consisting of a dilapidated shanty house and a barn which is merely a shed. The HILTONS, a "COLORED" family, are moving to another tenant farm over in High County.*

*LEVI, the father, (54), LILY, the mother, (51), CLYDE, boy, (17), MADELEEN, girl, (15), CLETUS, boy, (13), and RUTH, girl, (6) are loading a farm wagon with furniture, tools, etc., in preparation for moving.*

**LEVI:** Now when we get everything loaded, we'll sleep our last sleep here before movin' tomorrow.

**CLETUS:** I s'pose all yawl will be ridin'?

**CLYDE:** You and me will be walkin'.

**CLETUS:** I thought you weren't walkin' all the way.

**CLYDE:** Me an' papa and mama have talked it all ovah. I'm not goin' to Richmond after all.

*Everyone keeps loading things and arranging them on the wagon.*

**LEVI:** Mr. Goins knows all about our troubles here an' 'bout Clyde's shenanigans.

**RUTH:** Mamma, what's a shanygan?

**LILY:** It's doin' somthin' that you oughten not do.

**RUTH:** Clyde, what did you oughten not did?

**LEVI:** He whistled at Mr. Crowder's daughter.

**RUTH:** She's pretty.

**MADELEEN:** But she's white. Colored boys mustn't whistle at white girls.

*Everyone continues working, except Ruthie. She sits all alone on a rock with a doll on her lap.*

**LILY:** You, all right, Sistah?

**RUTH:** I fine. I just feel sorry for those poor girls.

**MADELEERN:** What girls?

**RUTH:** The white girls.

**LILY:** Honey, why you feel sorry for the white girls?

**RUTH:** 'Cause they can't get whistled at.

**MADELEEN:** (laughing): Sistah you'll begin to understand one day.

**CLETUS:** We'll understand it better by an' by.

**LEVI:** An' we bettah bye, bye to bed right now.

**RUTHIE:** But our beds are on the wagon.

**LILY:** Thet's all right, Ruthie. We got plenty quilts for makin' pallets on the floor. You can snuggle with me tonight.

> *They all head to the house.*
> ### BLACKOUT.

### *EXT: BENNETT FARM – KITCHEN - EARLY MORNING.*

> *MOTHER SUE BENETT (44) takes a milk pail from JIMMIE SUE, and puts it on the table. THELMA LOU stands at a table, with her back to everyone else.*
> *ROSIE goes to Thelma Lou and takes her hand.*
> *Thelma Lou turns slightly and stares at Jimmie Sue.*

**ROSIE:** Thelma Lou, Jimmie Sue didn't mean it.

**THELMA LOU:** If he didn't mean it, how did that bullfrog get into my bed?

**JIMMIE SUE:** You found my granddaddy bullfrog?

**THELMA LOU:** I don't care whether it be a granddaddy, grandma, Uncle Joe or whatever. I surely didn't 'preciate it when my bare feet touch its cold slimy skin.

**JIMMIE SUE:** I thought I was helpin' you.

**THELMA LOU:** Helpin' me do what?

**JIMMIE SUE:** Helpin' you find a boy friend!

**MADELEEN:** How in high heaven could that ...

**JIMMIE SUE:** If you woulda kissed him instead of kickin'him, you could've had a new rich prince ... I even accommodated you by puttin' him in bed with you. The whole thing coulda been far worse.

**THELMA LOU:** It was worse than just that. When I jumped out of bed I knocked the lamp off the table, spillin' lamp oil all ovah my braided rug.

**JIMMIE SUE:** What's wrong with yoah foot?

**THELMA LOU:** An' thet's another thing. The oil lamp broke into smithereens. It cut my foot, somethin' terrible. There's a horrible mess up there with lamp oil an' my own blood soaked into my rug ... I braided that rug myslf. I was fixn' to give it at Christmas time to ...

**JIMMIE SUE:** I'm plumb sorry, Thelma Lou. I surely didn't aim to ...

**SUE:** What did you aim ... ? I've already fixed up Thelma Lou's foot.

**JIMMIE SUE:** I was fixin' ...

**SUE:** There'll be some more fixin', Jimmie Sue, when Papa gets back to the house.

BLACKOUT.


*EXT. BENNETT FARM - DAY*

*SUPER: Early Spring, 1874*
*SIMON BENNETT, white boy, (19) stands outside the house, looking down the road. He turns toward the house.*

**SIMON:** Yawl come on out an' see the fambly of sharecroppers comin' down the road.

*The HILTON FAMILY comes along the dirt road, riding in a farm wagon pulled by a mule. A cow is tied to the back of the wagon, which is loaded with a kitchen cabinet, tables, chairs and other simple furniture and bags filled with family items.*

*LILY HILTON and her husband, LEVI HILTON, sit on a board seat at the front of the wagon. Levi holds the reins.*

*CLETUS and CLYDE walk beside the wagon.*

*Ruthie sits, wrapped up in a quilt on her older sister's lap.*

*Madeleen is sitting on an old rocking chair. Madeleen shoos the flies from Ruthie's face.*

*Two dogs, a beagle and a blue-tick hound trot along beside the wagon. Jimmie Sue's dog, RATTLER, runs out to introduce himself by watering the wagon wheels and sniffing the other dogs.*

*GEORGE DOW BENNETT (17) walks out to greet the family.*

**LEVI:** Whoa there, Kate.

*The mule stops.*

**SIMON:** Yawl must be the new sharecroppers comin' to tend Mr. Goin's farm up on Saplin' Ridge.

**LEVI:** Yeah. That's us. (a moment of silence) We come ovah from t'oher side uv Pierson.

**GEORGE:** Heah comes Mamma. Ya oughter wait a minute. She allus has somethin' fer new neighbors.

*Jimmie Sue looks out the front door, and then comes out with a bucket of water and a gourd dipper.*

*Close behind, Sue is carrying a pie. Rosie and FATHER ROBERT (49) follow them.*

**SUE:** Take this choc'lit pie for yoah new place. We can get the pie tin lateh.

*All the Hilton children's eyes light up at the sight of the pie. Jimmie Sue offers Lily the gourd dipper.*

**LILY:** Why thank ya fer the watch, but we won't need the dippah. We first allus carries a tin cup fer ouah drinkin' wateh ... An' much-obliged for the pie.

*Madeleen looks down at Jimmie Sue and gives a little smile of appreciation.*

**MADELEEN:** Thanks, kindly. My name be Madeleen, an' this little one we call Sistah, though her name be Ruth, like the Bible Ruth.

*Ruth waves to Rosie, then pokes her finger into the meringue of the pie. Her mamma gives her hand a little slap, which pushes it farther into the pie.*

**LILY:** Now, Sistah, you know we gotta wait fer ever'body to share at the same time. We don't want nobody to be a little piggy.

*Ruth looks as though she's about to cry. She draws back her hand, now covered with meringue and chocolate pie filling.*

*Lily laughs.*

**LILY:** Ooh, Little One, whut we gonna do' bout thet smudged hand? You s'pose ya oughta lick it clean?

*Ruth licks it clean, then gives her mamma a big hug, while everybody watches and smiles.*

*Robert joins the group.*

**ROBERT:** Before you get to Saplin' Ridge, you'll be crossin' a creek up ahead, an' thet'd be a good place to watah yoah mule an' cow. I'm sure the dogs'll help theirselves.

**LEVI:** Much obliged, an' thanks fer the welcomin'. (to Robert) You must be Mr. Bennett.

**ROBERT:** Robert. It's Robert or even Bob. Save the Misters for Goins an' Bowen. He owns the general store. Before ya go, I'd like to ask ya somethin'.

**LEVI:** Whut would thet be?

**ROBERT:** Do ya s'pose you an' yoah fambly could give us a hand in the summer, when 'baccer primin' time come aroun'. We could swap off work that way if you were of the notion.

**LEVI:** Oh yes. We've done this before. It surely makes the work go faster. The haying too? That's always faster. The children enjoy the swappin' off work.

**ROBERT:** My children almost think of it as playin', because so many other children are there. By the way ... aftah the war, our Baptist church thought it might be proper an' advisable to share worship ... So we're havin' Association Day in two weeks, an' we'd like to have your family come to that service. Especialy the dinner on the grounds, before the afternnon services.

**LEVI:** That'd be real accomodatin'. It'd be a good chance for us to find out what the new neighborhood is like. Maybe we'll see you at yoah special church meetin', comin' soon.

*Robert reaches up to Levi to shake hands as a gestural signature on their work agreement just concluded.*

*Levi clucks to prompt the mule to start.*

**JIMMIE SUE:** (perplexed) Did she say her name was Magdalene?

**THELMA LOU:** No, silly. Thet's a name from Bible times.

**JIMMIE SUE:** Well it sure sounded like ...

**THELMA LOU:** Her name is Madeleen.

*They all watch the new neighbors head down the road.*

**SUE:** When she treated thet little girl so kindly,I knew what kinda people they are an' whut kinda neighbors they gonna be ... even though they be sharecroppers an' colored.

*The Bennetts' dog, Rattler, happily follows his new neighbor dogs, and ignores George Dow when he whistles, trying to get him to come back.*

**SIMON:** Oh, he'll be back ... by suppah time.

FADE OUT.

### EXT. BENNETTS'FRONT PORCH.

*Sue interrupts stepping up onto the porch, when Jimmie Sue is heard yelling from off camera.*

**JIMMIE SUE:** Mamma wait up a minute.

*Jimmie Sue bounds into the camera shot.*

**SUE:** What is it, Jimmie Sue?

**JIMMIE SUE:** I just wonder about things.

**SUE:** Like what?

**JIMMIE SUE:** Like the way you treated the Hilton family.

**SUE:** Did I treat them unusual?

**JIMMIE SUE:** Yeah! Unusal from the way other white folks treat the colored ... But ... And I wonder why.

**SUE:** It's cause we owe them somethin'.

**JIMMIE SUE:** If we owe 'em somthin', why dontcha just pay it off?

**SUE:** There comes some things in life, what money can't pay for. (pause) Has Papa ever tole you 'bout the war?

**JIMMIE SUE:** Not much, but thet he got shot an' almost died. He did say thet's why he limps, especially on rainy days.

**SUE:** Well, his leg was hit by a musket ball. The enemy army was comin' and he couldn't get on his horse. It was a black man who put him on his horse. But then the colored man was killed with a musket ball to his heart. Robert was able to ride back to his troops ... The leg got infected, an'he nearly lost it. Somehow or other we owe colored folks somethin', at least a little respect. Why don't you talk about it with Papa?

**JIMMIE SUE:** He won't talk about it ... Did he say who the black man was?

**SUE:** There was no official record of his death.

**JIMMIE SUE:** Why?

**SUE:** Hadn't you better get to the barn for the milkin'?

**JIMMIE SUE:** Yes'm!

*Jimmie Sue starts walking away.*

**SUE:** It be best, Jimmie Sue, if you don't talk 'bout this with nobody. Papa feels it's best to leave such mattahs to the past; his posture and walking show that he's carrying an unusually heavy heart.

FADE OUT.

*EXT. HILTONS' NEW HOME.*

*MR. GOINS, a white man (72) sits on a swing on the front porch. The mule pulls the wagon into the scene.*
*Levi looks at Mr. Goins.*

**LEVI:** 'Lo Mr. Goins.

*Goins just sits and looks, saying nothing.*

**LEVI:** Lily ... you an' the children should start unloading the wagon, whilst I go have a talk with Mr. Goins. Have the boys get the heavy stuff. Don't you try wrestling with that.

*Levi walks to the porch. Goins gets up from the swing and stands next to a porch post, and looks down on Levi and the others.*

**GOINS:** Where's your oldest boy?

**LEVI:** Oh, he's the other side of the wagon, (Shouting to Clyde) Clyde, get ova heah an' meet Mr. Goins.

*Clyde appears from the other side of the wagon and approaches Goins and Levi. He sticks his hand out to Goins, who ignores it. Goins looks at Levi.*

**GOINS:** We not gonna repeat heah, what took place ovah to Ol' Man Crowder's place?!!!

**LEVI:** Oh no suh! We already learnt our lesson ovah to Pierson. (speaking to Clyde) Say somethin', Boy.

**CLYDE:** Oh no suh! We already learnt our lesson ovah theah.

**LEVI:** Clyde did apologize to the girl.

**GOINS:** Did he apologize to the girl's daddy an' granddaddy? (no response; just awkward looking down at the ground by both Levi and Clyde.) You know buzzards an' crows don't mix.

*Cletus has walked up and has listened to them.*

**CLETUS:** Who are the buzzards, an' who the crows?

*Goins and Levi are horrified that Cletus has inserted himself into a grown man's conversation.*

**LEVI:** Cletus, now that's enough of that kinda ... You 'pologize to Mr. Goins.

**CLETUS:** I 'pologize, Mr. Goins ...

**GOINS:** I ain't lookin' fer no 'pologizes. What I am lookin' for is for the colored to know how to keep in your place. (silence) But knowin' is one thing an' doin' another. I'll be keeping an eye on yoah fambly. (silence) Now you know ouah sharecroppin' terms, don't you?

**LEVI:** Madeleen's got them writ down ... You got the 'baccer seeds?

**GOINS:** They're in a bag hangin' on a nail down at the barn.

**LEVI:** We'll be gettin' the plant bed ready, come next Monday ... Well it appears that summer will soon be upon us, an' we wanta be ready.

*Goins steps off the porch and shakes Levi's hand, in agreement.*

BLACKOUT.

*INT. OLD FIELD CREEK BAPTIST CHURCH DAY*

*PREACHER NELSON stands in front of the Congregation.*

**PREACHER NELSON:** Now before the benediction an' the convenin' outside for sharing our meal at this Association Day occasion, I wanna welcome all those who share this woship time with us. Now may the Lord bless us and all within these doors. Amen.

*The CONGREGATION Stands, welcomes neighbors, and start exiting.*

*The Hiltons stand behind the back pew, two pews behind Jimmie Sue and his buddies.*

*Jimmie Sue looks sheepishly at Madeleen. She returns his shy look.*

*ROY (15) stoops in front of the pew in front of Jimmie Sue, slips under the seat and ties Jimmie Sue's shoe laces together from one shoe to another.*

*Jimmie Sue starts walking toward the aisle, but trips up. He falls and clatters on the pew in front of him as well as the one he was sitting on.*

*Madeleen reaches for him then holds back.*

*The boys laugh and Jimmie Sue unties his shoe laces, gets up and follows the Hiltons out the church.*

*Madeleen stands at the door, and watches until Jimmie Sue is on his feet.*

**MADELEEN:** (To her mother) That was such a mean trick.

FADE OUT.

*EXT. CHURCH. SUMMER DAY*

*A long crude table has been devised with rough lumber boards over farm sawhorses and stands in a grove of large trees.*

*The women folk are getting packed lunches out of apple crates and lard buckets.*

*OLDER GIRLS help their mothers put the food on the table.*

*MEN and BOYS tend to the mules and horses.*

*BROTHER HIATT, a white preacher, looks at BROTHER PEEPLES.*

**BROTHER HIATT:** Brotha Peeples, I'd like to ask you to bless this food an' ever'body gathered here on this Blessed Lord's Day.

**BROTHER PEEPLES:** We thank thee, O blessed lord for this day of our Christian Brotherhood ... for all the good folk who worship thee and love Jesus. An' we ask thee to bless this food.

*(Several "amens" can be heard)*

*Jimmie Sue is filling his plate, but constantly glancing at Madeleen, who sits by her FOLKS not far from where he stands. He is not looking at his dish, and one of the boys puts a hot chili pepper on it. Jimmie Sue picks up the pepper and takes a big bite while watching Madeleen. He starts sputtering and runs over to get some water, which he pours all over his face.*

*He then walks and stands near his folks, only a few feet from MADELEEN. She uncovers a chocolate pie with meringue topping. The CROWD begins to mill about.*

**BROTHER HIATT:** Hit's so good to see so many folks here from some of our neighborin' churches. We need to pay attention to what Jesus said, "In my Father's House there are many mansions." An'it's my own belief that he's not building' different pigpens to keep us apart.

*(He continues in this vein.)*

*Jimmie Sue responds to what he hears the preacher saying.*

**JIMMIE SUE:** Will He have different cowpens to keep the Black Angus heifer from the Whiteface Hereford bull?

*Mother Sue hears his mumbling, swings around and slaps him. Jimmie Sue falls backward, his hat flies to one side and his head lands in the chocolate pie in MADELEEN'S lap.*

**MADELEEN:** White Boy, yoah head be in my lap squishin' my choc'late pie? ... You know you ruint my pie?

**JIMMIE SUE:** I sure am sorry for ruinin' yoah pie. Hit looks mighty good.

*He wipes some of the pie off his head and puts his finger in his mouth.*

**JIMMIE SUE:** I really am sorry. It's awfully good pie.

*ONLOOKERS and BOYS chuckle, amused.*

**MADELEEN:** I heard you were partial to choc'late pie, so my cookin' it was kinda special.

**JIMMIE SUE:** You baked it yoahself? I really be 'pologizing all ovah again.

**MADELEEN:** You know I nevah heard abody 'pologize so much. Maybe I be callin' you Sorry Sue 'stead of Jimmie Sue.

*JIMMIE SUE is lost for words, mouth open.*

**MADELEEN:** Naw, Jimmmie Sue, now I be sorry, fer there be no call to be namin' you nasty names.

*Jimmie Sue sticks his finger into the pie, heads it toward his mouth, stops it in mid-air and points it toward her red lips.*

**MADELEEN:** No, White Boy, we ain't goin' thet far. You go ahead and taste what deliciousness you coulda had. Maybe the Good Lord be standin' in the way.

**JIMMIE SUE:** Have you evah thought it might be the Devil what stand in the way?

*Madeleen's eyes flash open at that.*

*Jimmie Sue licks the pie off his fingers, as the BOYS laugh at him. Madeleen doesn't laugh at him, but seems to have a bit of sympathy for his condition. People start packing up the "Dinner On The Grounds".*

FADE OUT.


*EXT. BENNETT FARM - TOBACCO FIELD
AND BARN - SUMMER DAY*


*BOYS pull off the tobacco leaves in the field.*

*George Dow drives the mule, pulling a sled full of tobacco leaves from the field to the barn and back empty to the field.*

*The HILTON FAMILY is there.*

*At the barn the loose leaves are pulled out of the sled in armfuls and piled on the bed of a farm wagon.*

*WOMEN AND CHILDREN string the leaves onto a stick held in a rack, about four feet off the ground.*

*When the BOYS finish in the field, they help with the stringing. Jimmie Sue takes over one of the stringing spots and starts showing off how well he can string.*

**JIMMIE SUE:** Ya see, kids. Thet's how it's done. Jest watch Ol' Jimmie Sue to learn what it's all about.

*While he's bragging and watching his attentive audience, he misses grabbing a hand of tobacco, which falls on the ground. Everyone laughs, as he looks to see if Madeleen is laughing.*

**MADELEEN:** So thet's how it's done?

**JIMMIE SUE:** It wadn't handed to me right. Why in the hell is ever'body's laughin'?

**MADELEEN:** White Boy, have you got the Holy Ghost?

**JIMMIE SUE:** Yeah I got the holy ghost.

**MADELEEN:** How did that happen? (long pause) Did you go upto the altar rail, an' give the peacha your hand?

**JIMMIE SUE:** Yeah thet's what I done.

**MADELEEN:** White Boy, thet won't do atall. You can't just give the preacha' your hand. You gotta give the Lord yoah heart.

*Jimmie Sue cocks his head to one side and mockingly kneels down on one knee.*

*Madeleen stands like a statue, as she glares at him.*

*Robert & Levi appear from around the barn. They observe what's going on with the tobacco stringing.*

**ROBERT:** Jimmie Sue, what's goin' on back here?

**JIMMIE SUE:** Madeleen just showin' me how to get the Holy Ghost.

**ROBERT:** It sure didn't look like no Holy Ghost to me. Gettin' down on one knee in front of a sweetheart usta mean a marriage proposal.

**JIMMIE SUE:** Papa, you know Madeleen's not my sweetheart.

**ROBERT:** Well, whatcha think that looks like?

**LEVI:** Madeleen, maybe you could explain.

**MADELEEN:** Jimmie Sue was right. But he was makin' fun of what I tole him 'bout gettin' the Holy Ghost.

**ROBERT:** Jimmie Sue, maybe you better pay closer attention.

*CAMERA FOLLOWS LEVI AND ROBERT BACK AROUND THE BARN.*

**LEVI:** It sure looks like they gettin' along all right.

**ROBERT:** It does look like the work swappin' is workin' out, okay. An' if they have some fun along the way ... But Levi I've been wonderin'. Were you involved in that war?

**LEVI:** No! We, colored, weren't allowed to be soldiers in the army. My brother was a cook.

**ROBERT:** It's terrible how that war separated people.

**LEVI:** I believe war always separates people.

**ROBERT:** Do you s'pose that in some ways a war might bring some unlikely folks together?

**LEVI:** As unlikely as you an' me? You know the war was already there in peoples' hearts.

**ROBERT:** Do you s'pose the preacher might call that "the Lord's will?"

**LEVI:** I think there be somethin' else pulling our families together. We speak the wisdom of God in a mystery.

FADE OUT.

*EXT. BENNETT TOBACCO BARN – SUNSET TWO DAYS LATER*

*Jimmie Sue, JESSE (15), EMMETT (14), BILL (15), ELIJA (Lige)(16), WALT (14) AND ROY(15) fire up the two flues of the barn. Jimmie Sue puts a pile of wood shavings and straw into the mouths of the flues, which are on each side of the barn door.*

**JIMMIE SUE:** Some of yawl bring more wood downhyar. Othahs need to get a couple of watermelons.

*Jimmie Sue looks at a big tree not far from the barn.*

**JIMMIE SUE:** Come on out from behin' thet white oak, Cletus. We jest beginnin' to roast up some years of corn an' bust a coupla big watahmelons. Surely yoah partial to some roasen years.

*Cletus peeks out from around the tree.*

**GLETUS:** I don't know if ya be playin' them funnin' tricks on me agin ... Um, Okay. Bettah no moah uv them pranks on me, Jimmie Sue ... Ya hear?

**JIMMIE SUE:** Aw. Ferget 'bout thet mumbly peg game las'night.

*The BOYS return with the victuals, and get busy fixing things by putting the ears of corn in their husks on top of the flues to roast. They bust the watermelons on a big rock.*

*Jimmie Sue sees Madaleen standing behind a big oak tree.*

**JIMMIE SUE:** (for everyone to hear) Well I gotta go to the bushes.

*Jimmie Sue disappears around the far edge of the barn, while the BOYS continue their interest in the food.*

*Madeleen scrounges a little closer to the tree, but continues to try to keep a watch on Jimmie Sue. Jimmie Sue creeps up behind her, but she is now watching her little brother, Cletus, with this bunch of white boys. Jimmie Sue clasps his hands over her eyes.*

**JIMMIE SUE:** Guess ...

*Madeleen falls backwards onto Jimmie Sue and screams.*

*Cletus drops his ear of corn, that he's about to eat.*

*ROY is poking one of the logs in the flue, but is so startled that he knocks some of the fire out of the flue onto the ground, scattering burning embers out onto a pile of oily rags. The dogs start barking and the chickens are roused with the rooster crowing. It's a conflagration with smoke filling the air. The BOYS look like statues enveloped by the smoke and casting shadows from the barn lanterns hanging from a beam of the barn shed. It looks like a scene from Hell.*

*Madeleen tries to slap his face. Instead she hits his hat, which twirls in the air. Jimmie Sue stumbles backward on some rocks and looks up at her.*

*They stare at each other for a couple of moments with a passion of fear, wonder, and excitement, almost like a twenty-second kiss.*

*Madeleen turns toward the barn, takes down one of the lanterns and runs off toward home. All the BOYS including Cletus watch her run away.*

*They straighten things out as much as possible; putting the burning logs back into the flue, continue tending the fire by putting on more logs, and checking the hanging leaves inside the barn.*

*Jimmie Sue takes some old quilts off of the back of the farm wagon. He then distributes them, as the BOYS start quarreling over which one they prefer and where each one is going to put down his pallet.*

*Jimmie Sue takes his quilt over to a stack of cordwood (logs four feet long in a stack four feet high and eight feet long.)*

*He arranges his quilt in a makeshift pallet on top of the stack of wood, crawls onto it and quickly falls asleep. All human sounds cease, except for an occasional snore. The crickets and frogs begin to sing their night music, as an owl hoots every now and then. Jimmie Sue's sleep is restless, as he tosses and turns.*

BLACKOUT.

### EXT. HILTON'S HOME – FRONT PORCH  DAY

*Jimmie Sue approaches the Hilton's front porch to apologize to Madeleen. He has some wild flowers stuck in his back pocket. Cletus is sits on the front porch, leaning against a porch post playing mumbly-peg all alone with his knife.*

*Jimmie Sue walks across the yard toward Cletus.*

**JIMMIE SUE:** 'Lo, Cletus. You seem to be OK after las' night's doin's.

**CLETUS:** What ya mean by the doin's?

**JIMMIE SUE:** Well weren't there a lot of doin's with firin' the 'baccer barn, the vittles ...

**CLETUS:** What 'bout the Madeleen doin's?

**JIMMIE SUE:** Yeah, how Madeleen doin' now?

**CLETUS:** She not be too happy ... It might could be 'bout her time.

**JIMMIE SUE:** Whut you mean. ... "her time"?

**CLETUS:** (lowering his voice) You know a girls' time?

**JIMMIE SUE:** A girl's time fer what?

**CLETUS:** Ya know thet month thing.

**JIMMIE SUE:** Oh ya talkin' 'bout thet? ... How ya know 'bout thet?

**CLETUS:** Jimmie Sue ya don't give me credit fer knowing nothin'

**JIMMIE SUE:** Well, where would Madeleen be right now?

**CLETUS:** She splittin' wood behin' the house.

**JIMMIE SUE:** Why she be doin' thet ... I thought thet wuz yoah job.

**CLETUS:** She say she wanna do somethin' moah vigrous like ... moah sweaty than jest warshin' dishes.

*The SOUND of wood being chopped is heard.*

**JIMMIE SUE:** Cletus, maybe I jest go back there an' give a look-see at what'n all be goin on with Madeleen.

**CLETUS:** (resuming his mumblety-peg game.) Good luck.

*Jimmie Sue starts around the corner, as the wood chopping continues.*

CUT TO:

*EXT. HILTON'S BACK YARD*

*Madeleen is seen hoisting an axe over her head, just prior to splitting an 18-inch-long piece of wood placed vertically on the chop block. He stops abruptly, because he doesn't want to surprise her again like last night. She looks quite different and is dressed in a work shirt and worn overalls like the boys wear. She is not aware of his presence, so to avoid frightening her again, he calls from several feet behind her.*

**JIMMIE SUE:** (yelling) Madeleen!

**MADELEEN:** (Swings around with the axe arcing over her head; she belligerently yells.) Jimmie Sue, don't ya be sneakin' up on my backside agin. With this hyar axe in mah han' I ain't bein' skeered of you no moah.

**JIMMIE SUE:** You no need to be skeered of me ...

**MADELEEN:** Aftah las' night ...

**JIMMIE SUE:** Yeah. I come ovah to 'pologize 'bout thet.

**MADELEEN:** To 'pologize? (softening up a bit)

**JIMMIE SUE:** Las' night I didn't go fer to skeer you ... I was jest funnin' 'round.

**MADELEEN:** Well, White Boy, I be tellin' ya right now, it sure warn't no fun fer me when you slip up behin' me an' put yoah greasy paws all ovah mah face.

**JIMMIE SUE:** Oh I know thet now. I jest wanted to ask you to have some eatin's ... We wuz fixin' to have some corn an' ...

**MADELEEN:** Thet sure was a queer way to find out 'bout thet.

**JIMMIE SUE:** Yeah I guess it was ... Madeleen, could I ask somethin' of you?

*She sits on the chop-block, facing him. She puts the head of the axe on the ground, the blade toward him and the axe handle between her knees.*

**MADELEEN:** You can ask it ... if it be decent.

**JIMMIE SUE:** Why you keep callin' me White Boy?

**MADELEEN:** 'Cause you be actin' like White Boy'.

**JIMMIE SUE:** How I do thet?

**MADELEEN:** By actin' like White Boy who thinks he can get whatevah he wants, whenevah he wants it. You keep fergettin' I'm colored.

**JIMMIE SUE:** Well, good goddamnit, how can I ferget, when you keep 'mindin' me of it all the time.

**MADELEEN:** Ya come ovah heah to make up with me for what ya done las' night an' now ya slap me in the face.

**JIMMIE SUE:** Whatcha mean – slap in the face? I ain't teched ya.

**MADELEEN:** You use the Lord's name like thet, you might as well slap me squar' in the face an' spit on me besides.

**JIMMIE SUE:** Well ya riled me up, tellin' me to 'member you colored. I don't be callin' you Colored Girl.

**MADELEEN:** No, an' I 'preciate thet ... James.

**JIMMIE SUE:** Might jest as well call me Jimmie Sue, like ever'body else.

**MADELEEN:** Thet be fine ... Jimmie Sue.

**JIMMIE SUE:** Madeleen, there's somethin' else I ike to know.

**MADELEEN:** What would thet be?

**JIMMIE SUE:** Was yoah daddy in the war?

**MADELEEN:** No, not really. He moved Mama an' Clyde up heah to the mountains when they run away from Georgia. He had a brotha that did somethin' in the war ... but he was kilt.

**JIMMIE SUE:** Did you know him?

**MADELEEN:** That was before I was born ... Clyde say his name was Uncle Lucas

*Long Silence*

**JIMMIE SUE:** Well I brought some flowers to 'pologize ...

*He retrieves the flowers, which have become terribly bedraggled. Looks at them. Hands them to her.*

**JIMMIE SUE:** Guess I shouldn't have put them in mah pocket.

*Madeleen looks at them sorrowfully. She reaches for them, takes them.*

**MADELEEN:** They be fine Jimmie Sue ... special fine.

**JIMMIE SUE:** (surprised) Well they really nothin'.

**MADELEEN:** Did ja evah notice, Jimmie Sue, what seems like nothin' can some time be pretty special?

*She brings flowers to her nose for a whiff of sweetness.*

**MADELEEN:** What ya call 'em?

**JIMMIE SUE:** I call 'em Saplin' Ridge flowers.

**MADELEEN:** Why you call 'em thet?

**JIMMIE SUE:** I don't think they bloom anywheah else.

**MADELEEN:** Yeah. It's kinda special to think thet things what may be happenin' heah on Saplin' Ridge is moah special than anywheah else in the worl'.

**JIMMIE SUE:** With some watah evahthing seem to bring life back ... Gotta go now.

**MADELEEN:** Yeah ... You take keer ... of yoah self.

*JIMMIE SUE turns to leave, but at the corner of the house, he turns to look at her. She's standing now, holding the flowers to her nose. They nearly hide her whole face. She looks at him. As their eyes make contact she smiles, and he shows another stare of wonderment. They stand for a few moments looking at each other.*

**JIMMIE SUE:** Well, Madeleen, I bettah really be goin'.

**MADELEEN:** An'I bettah be really finishin' splittin' this stovewood.

FADE OUT.

*EXT. CREEK - DAY*

*Emmett, and Bill, wait on the grass.*

*George and Jimmie Sue arrive, shoes and shirts thrown off. Walt, and Roy, arrive after them. Lige, walks up from down the creek. While the other BOYS undress to swim, Jimmie Sue talks to Bill. Emmett, naked, stands on a rock, ready to dive in. He sees Cletus come out of the bushes on the far side of the creek.*

**EMMETT:** What the hell's thet darky doin' down here at our swimmin' hole? I'll make souse meat outta thet black son-uv-a...

*Jimmie Sue, still with his overalls on, heads straight for Emmet and knocks him down on the rock. Emmett grabs Jimmie Sue around his waist and lifts him up off the rock. They both struggle and fall with Jimmie Sue on top of Emmett, they slide off the rock into the water below. They start to swim to the other side of the creek. A red streak trail shows in the water. A reddish-brown water moccasin snake swims toward Emmett, going towards his blood. They both see it. Emmet swims toward Jimmie Sue.*

**EMMETT:** Jimmie Sue tried to kill me on thet rock, an' now the devil's sendin' a water mockerson snake to finish me off.

*Jimmie Sue turns and wades back to the snake. He picks up the snake by the tail, swings it over his head and speaks to it.*

**JIMMIE SUE:** Now, go back to the devil from whence you cometh.

*He throws it back into the water under the diving rock.*

**LIGE:** Hit'll come right back, fer sure.

**ROY:** Thet don't differ... right now, anyways.

*Bill and Walt gradually help Emmett to the north bank, where they examine the massive damage.*

**GEORGE:** My Gawd. We gotta do somethin' quick, afore he bleeds to death.

**EMMETT:** You s'pose I'm gonna die?

**JIMMIE SUE:** Yeah! ... Evah-body gotta die at some time.

**CLETUS:** Mamma knows how to poultice an' take care of cuts like thet.

**EMMETT:** I ain't gonna have no nig ... to let thet colored woman ...

**CLETUS:** She jest be my mamma.

**JIMMIE SUE:** Yeah, she yoah mamma, Cletus, an' I hear tell she have real strong medicine from yerbs an' roots an' thangs. But Cletus, before we go, you get some pokeberries for Emmett's backside. You can use my shirt as a bandage.

*(Some TIME elapses as they continue to get ready to go to the Hiltons)*

FADE OUT.


*EXT. HILTON'S HOME - PORCH - DAY*


*The BOYS are on the porch, Aunt Lily comes out.*

**LILY:** Hello, Jimmie Sue! How's yoah momma?

**JIMMIE SUE:** Mamma's fine. She sends her hello. Me an' Emmett got into a little scuffle. An' Emmett got scratched on a rock.

**GEORGE:** We thought you might could help. Cletus said you're real good at that sorta thing. We'd be much obliged.

**JIMMIE SUE:** Hit be on his backside.

*Emmett moans.*

**JIMMIE SUE:** Cletus helped a lot with a pokeberry poultice.

**LILY:** I be mighty proud uv you Cletus, to be a-doctorin' thet away. So them pokeberries an' the boy's blood musta colored up his dydie like this.

**EMMETT:** This ain't no dydie. Hit's only Jimmie Sue's shirt whut he lent me.

**LILY:** Well jest take Jimmie Sue's shirt off' yoah bottom an' hand it back to Jimmie Sue. Be sure to thank him fer the loan of his shirt.

*(Lily lathers her hands with some good lye soap)*

*Now Madeleen, you first run an' get a clean white sheet to cover this boy's nekkidness, an' hand the sheet out the doah to me. You got no call to be lookin' at no white boy's bottom. . . nor a colored one's neither.*

*Lily unwraps Jimmie Sue's shirt. She takes medicines from Madeleen and hands Jimmie Sue's shirt to her.*

**LILY:** Hyar, Honey, give Jimmie Sue his shirt.

*Madeleen sees Jimmie Sue from around the corner of the house and goes out in the yard to give him his shirt.*

**MADELEEN:** Hyah be yoah shirt, Jimmie Sue.

**JIMMIE SUE:** It sure is a mess, ain't it?

**MADELEEN:** Yeah, but it's got some mighty purty colors.

*They spread it on the ground. It shows all the pokeberry juice and blood on his blue work shirt.*

*There seems to be a large winged creature painted on it.*

*Jimmie Sue takes a good look at it closely.*

**JIMMIE SUE:** Is thet a dark butterfly?

**MADELEEN:** No ... I believe it might be an angel.

**JIMMIE SUE:** Yeah, maybe yoah right. A beautiful black angel.

**MADELEEN:** Not black!

**JIMMIE SUE:** Well, a kinda dark, reddish, purplish, bluish angel.

*Madeleen hesitates.*

**MADELEEN:** A colored angel.

**JIMMIE SUE:** Yeah, a beautiful colored angel.

**MADELEEN:** I be warshin' the shirt fer ya, if ya like.

**JIMMIE SUE:** Oh, no. I don't think I'll evah warsh this shirt.

**MADELEEN:** Ya don't hafta. I already offered to warsh it fer ya.

**JIMMIE SUE:** I'm gonna keep it jest like it is. I'll jest hang it up to remind me.

**MADELEEN:** 'mind ya of what?

**JIMMIE SUE:** Today!

**MADELEEN:** Today?

**JIMMIE SUE:** An' the goin's on, an' acourse all the people today.

*Madeleen and Jimmie Sue and the rest of the BOYS get back to the porch just as AUNT LILY finishes her doctoring.*

*Madeleen leads the BOYS to the front gate, as they begin their trek toward home. She holds the gate open for them. Jimmie Sue is the last boy and casually puts his hand on hers.*

**JIMMIE SUE:** Oh, sorry, Madeleen. (As he quickly pulls his hand away.)

**MADELEEN:** A little touch nevah hurt nobody.

*The TWO of them steal furtive glances at each other, as the other BOYS have already left the yard and are yelling at Jimmie Sue to hurry on.*

BLACKOUT.

*LATER THAT NIGHT NEAR A BIG ROCK IN FRONT OF HILTON'S HOUSE.*

*Jimmie Sue enters frame on downhill side of rock. He looks toward the Hiltons, but all are in the house, except Madeleen and Cletus who sit on the front porch. Jimmie Sue hoots like an owl.*

**CLETUS:** That's no owl.  That's Jimmie Sue.

**MADELEEN:** Why you think so?

**CLETUS:** That's the sound he made when he scared me home one night. You want me to go see?

**MADELEEN:** No, I'll go check, myself. He's not gonna scare me home again. If that's really him.

*She starts to leave.*

**MADELEEN:** If you hear me scream, come runnin'. If it's him an' all right about it, I'll have him give three quick hoots to let you know it's okay.

**CLETUS:** What if I don't hear nothin'?

**MADELEEN:** Well, after a few minutes you better come.

*Madeleen leaves  toward the rock, which is between her and Jimmie Sue. She approaches the rock and speaks softly.*

**MADELEEN:** Jimmie Sue, is that you makin' that noise?

**JIMMIE SUE**: You came. How did you know it was me?

**MADELEEN**: Cletus told me.

**JIMMIE SUE**: Cletus?

**MADELEEN**: Yeah!

*Madeleen looks back at the porch and sees Cletus standing, looking toward the rock.*

**MADELEEN**: Give three more real quick hoots.

**JIMMIE SUE**: Why in ...

**MADELEEN**: Just do as I say.

*Jimmie Sue does as he is told.*

*Madeleen looks back toward Cletus.*

*Cletus enters the house.*

**JIMMIE SUE**: Now that's the silliest thing I evah heard of.

**MADELEEN**: Don't you think that the silliest thing you evah did was to come to my house at night and hoot like an owl?

**JIMMIE SUE**: That may be ... but it's the third time I did it. You finally got the message.

**MADELEEN**: Thanks to Cletus ... I s'pose it's a good thing you scared him thet night ... with thet owl hoot (long pause) Are you gonna say anything? ... Was there somethin' you wanted to tell me?

**JIMMIE SUE**: Yeah! ... there was somethin'.

*After a moment's more hesitation, he takes her hands, pulls her to him, embraces her closely and starts awkwardly kissing her. At first she starts to resist, but soon responds, as they lean back over the rock. While in that position, Madeleen abruptly pulls away, looks into his eyes, rolls quickly away and runs back to her house. Jimmie Sue stands and watches her hasty retreat. He turns slowly toward home.*

FADE OUT.


*INT. MOMENTS LATER HILTON'S KITCHEN.*


*Lily is sitting in a chair next to the churn which she is using. Madeleen comes rushing in crying.*

**LILY:** Madeleen , what in the world is the matter?

**MADELEEN:** I just saw Jimmie Sue.

**LILY:** Was he bad to you? Did he hurt you?

**MADELEEN:** I don't think so.

**LILY:** You don't think so what? ... Wasn't bad ... Didn't hurt you? But why the cryin'?

**MADLEEN:** Jimmie Sue kissed me, an' Mamma it seemed like the most natural thing in the whole world.

**LILY:** Then why all the tears? ... Did you kiss him?

**MADELEEN:** I guess I did kiss him ... 'cause I didn't make him quit ... except at first I did. I s'pose that I was kissin' him as long as his lips were on my lips.

**LILY:** An' you're cryin'?

**MADELEEN:** It's just that as nice as the feelin's were, I'm so confused ... Mamma, was that wrong of me?

**LILY:** Or wrong of Jimmie Sue? We'll talk about it later. But don't say anything to Papa about it.

**MADELEEN:** All right Mamma.

FADE OUT.

## *INT. BOWENS' GENERAL STORE*

*Jimmie Sue enters and a small silvery bell attached to the door rings as the door swings open. He stands there until he can hear Mr. Bowens' voice.*

**BOWEN:** Hello ... Anyone there?

**JIMMIE SUE:** Just me, Mr. Bowen ... Jimmie Sue.

*Mr. Bowen appears from behind shelves of groceries.*

**MR. BOWEN:** Well, Jimmie Sue, it's good to see you, It's been a long while ... Is the crop doin' okay?

**JIMMIE SUE:** Yeah, I want ... Mamma sent me to buy some more of those new-fangled clothespins like she bought last spring.

**BOWEN:** Why, of course.

**JIMMIE SUE:** I lost 'em in the creek, learnin' to swim.

**BOWEN:** Well how in God's green earth did that help you swim?

**JIMMIE SUE:** I put 'em om my nose to keep from snuffin' water up my nose ... But they'd pop off, an' I was nevah able to ketch 'em before they'd float ...

**BOWEN:** How many did you say she wanted this time?

**JIMMIE SUE:** Three dozen, I believe.

**BOWEN:** You know they cost a nickel a piece?

**JIMMIE SUE:** Oh, I got the money.

**BOWEN:** Now these clothespins have not been on the market fer long. There's a fellow up north got a patent on 'em. There're just all kinda new things comin' out to make life a little easier somehow. Thet war changed a lot of things ... some like those clothespins to benefit folks. But there're some things changin' not so good.

**JIMMIE SUE:** Uh Huh!

**BOWEN:** Now like the way we treat people.

**JIMMIE SUE:** Yeah, we oughta treat people good.

**BOWEN:** Not only good but in the right way.

**JIMMIE SUE:** The right way?

**BOWEN:** Now we here in the mountains nevah had no slaves, but when they were freed, they had a new way of life and should be content with keepin' to their own kind. (he pauses) Now take that colored family; what's their name?

**JIMMIE SUE:** You must mean the Hiltons?

**BOWEN:** Yeah! That's them. You know we don't like mixin' the races of people. That's the natural way an' that's the way God intended. What would you think if you saw a rooster crow humpin' a buzzard hen?

**JIMMIE SUE:** I don't see what ...

**BOWEN:** Now Jimmie Sue, what I'm gonna tell you is for your own good.

**JIMMIE SUE:** But ...

**BOWEN:** Now I've seen how you an' thet colored girl pay attention to each other. We've not had a meetin' yet 'bout it. But you know Ol' man Goins?

**JIMMIE SUE:** Yeah!

**BOWEN:** Now me, I can put up with 'em. I can put up

with 'em just as long as they mind their own business an' keep in their place.

**JIMMIE SUE:** Wouldn't you want their business to be with you an' your business?

**BOWEN:** Jimmie Sue, I'll not pussyfoot 'round this. Mr. Goins is a bastard, who would cheat his own Grandma, if it could earn him a penny. Somethin' what happened to him in the war, which he won't talk about. But I know it has somethin' to do with the coloreds.

*They finish their transaction, while Bowen continues to talk.*

*Jimmie Sue walks toward the door with his purchase, but stops when Bowen has the last word.*

**BOWEN:** You wouldn't want that girl's family to be put out in the middle of the night would you?

**JIMMIE SUE:** No sir.

*Jimmie Sue turns and exits.*

BLACKOUT.


*BENNETTS' KITCHEN - NOON, ONE SUNDAY AFTER CHURCH MEETING.*


*Thelma sets the table with the help of Rosie. Robert sits at the end of the table with his open bible. Jimmie Sue enters with a bucket of water. Jimmie Sue and Thelma Lou sit on opposite sides of the table. They all start chatting about the meeting.*

**ROBERT:** Brother Hiatt had some good points in the sermon this morning.

**JIMMIE SUE:** What I like 'bout Peacher Hiatt, is that he tell stories to make a point in his sermonzing.

**GEORGE:** Some of them are very funny.

*EVERYONE passes the dishes of food, as they continue to talk.*

**SIMON:** Yeah I found myself laughin' right out loud. But what was really funny was at Association Day Dinner on the Ground when Jimmie Sue ...

JIMMIE SUE: Why don't ya keep yah damn mouth shut, Simple Simon?

THELMA LOU: When Jimmie Sue fell into that black girl's lap, not only wuz Jimmie Sue's head fallin' into Madeleen's pie, he was follin' in love with her ... and her a colored girl.

*Jimmie Sue puts a glob of mashed potatoes on the tine end of his fork and flips it over toward Thelma Lou. It lands right on the bridge of her nose.*

THELMA LOU: He's a damn fool.

SUE: (helping Thelma Lou wipe her face.) Now, Thelma Lou thet's no cause to be usin' them words in this house nur any other place.

THELMA LOU: But Jimmie Sue ...

ROBERT: Nevah ya mind 'bout Jimmie Sue. (to JIMMIE SUE) Now, Jimmie Sue, I need you to top and sucker the north 'baccer field tomorrow, an' be sure to take off all the 'baccer worms, you find.

JIMMIE SUE: But ... but ...

ROBERT: An' when ya finish tendin' the 'baccer, ya can muck out the cow's stall in the barn.

JIMMIE SUE: But why ...

ROBERT: Thet'll be yoah punishment fer throwin' yoah taters at Thelma Lou.

JIMMIE SUE: But she ...

ROBERT: Don't make it no worse fer yoahself, Son. An' while ya thinkin' 'bout it, why don't ya go an 'pologize to her, an'she'll 'pologize to you.

THELMA LOU: I don't see why I hafta ...

ROBERT: Thelma Lou, ya wanna help Jimmie Sue in the 'baccer field tomorrow. I'm sure he'd 'preciate a little help.

THELMA LOU: (after a slight pause) I'm sorry, Jimmie Sue, fer throwin' off on you an' Madeleen thetaway.

JIMMIE SUE: I didn't go to hurt ya Thelma Lou.

THELMA LOU: Jest hurt mah feelin's.

ROBERT: Jimmie Sue, you ain't 'pologized to her yet.

**JIMMIE SUE:** I 'pologize, Thelma Lou ... but I do hope ya don't bad mouth the Hiltons no moah.

**THELMA LOU:** Naw. They seem to be good folks, even if they are colored.

**SUE:** We gonna have no moah colored talk, tonight.

FADE OUT.

*EXT. BENNETT FARM — TOBACCO FIELD — DAY*

*Jimmie Sue arrives in the field and notices he doesn't have his hat. He slaps his hand on top of his head, turns around to run back to the house but reconsiders.*

**JIMMIE SUE (V.O.):** Certainly not gonna waste my time runnin' fer a damned hat. What's it do fer me any how?

*He starts topping and suckering the tobacco.*

*THE CAMERA FOLLOWS HIM AND TAKES SEVERAL SHOTS FROM VARIOUS ANGLES (FROM OVER THE TOP OF THE STALKS, FROM THROUGH THE LEAVES, ETC.)*

*Jimmie Sue picks up a worm or two and throws them on the ground and stomps on them. The third worm he finds, he starts to throw it down, but reconsiders and brings it closer to his face.*

**JIMMIE SUE (V.O.):** Wonder if I dare bite its head off. Walt is real good at doin' thet. (as he continues to observe the worm only a few inches from his mouth) I nevah had no stomach fer it ... (continuing to look at it) Nur no mouth either. (throws it down) Sorry Mr. 'baccer worm you'll jest hafta die like all the rest uf yoah brothahs 'n sistahs.

*SEVERAL CAMERA SHOTS RECORD JIMMIE SUE'S PROGRESS OVER TWO HOURS OF COMPRESSED TIME.*

*Jimmie Sue comes to the end of the field, brushes off the excess dirt as best he can. It's obvious that he should have worn a shirt and hat as the black tobacco tar covers all the exposed parts of his body, even his back where the overall galluses crisscross. He heads toward home.*

FADE OUT.

*EXT. BENNETT FARM PORCH - DAY*

*Jimmie Sue arrives. Sue sits on the porch snapping green beans.*

**SUE:** Law me, Jimmie, whut in the world were you thinkin', goin' off to work in t'bacco with no more clothes on?

**JIMMIE SUE:** Reckon I wadn't thinkin' much.

**SUE:** I should say not. Jest looka yoaself. Yoah a sight in this world. Looks like ya belong to the Hilton famly.

**JIMMIE SUE:** Maybe I do.

**SUE:** James Lafayette, don't ya be sassin' yoah mamma thetaway. Ya wouldn't want me to be tellin' Papa now would ya?

**JIMMIE SUE:** No Mamma.

**SUE:** What?

**JIMMIE SUE:** No ma'am ... Mamma.

**SUE:** Well we'll ferget 'bout tellin' Papa, but ya not comin' into the house lookin' like thet.

**JIMMIE SUE:** I was aimin' to ...

**SUE:** Ya got plenty of time to go down to the creek an' get warshed up. Dinnah ain't gonna be ready fer quite a spell yet.

**JIMMIE SUE:** Okay, Mamma, I was aimin' to do thet any ways to warsh off this tar at the swimmin' hole.

**SUE:** Is the swimmin' hole the place where we use for baptizin'?

**JIMMIE SUE:** Yeah!

**SUE:** It don't seem right to be usin' the baptizin' place fer all kinda things goin'on.

**JIMMIE SUE:** Ain't nothin' goin' on but swimmin' an' a little playin' aroun'.

**SUE:** Hit's the playin' aroun' whut troubles my mind.

**JIMMIE SUE:** Yes'm!

**SUE:** An' don't ferget the soap. Make sure it's the good strong lye soap.

**JIMMIE SUE:** I aimed to do jest that.

**SUE:** An' don't ferget yoah hat, although yoah head already be filthied up with thet black 'baccer tar. A body can't even tell ya got red hair.

*Jimmie Sue picks his hat off the peg on the porch post and plops it on his head as he jumps off the edge of the porch.*

FADE OUT.


*EXT. CREEK - DAY*


*Madeleen is seen wading into the water and holding a long stick. She's wearing a slight cotton chemise.*

**MADELEEN:** Hope there be no snakes in here, today.

CUT TO:


*EXT. ACROSS THE CREEK*


*Jimmie Sue pushes through the bushes, throws off his overalls, but leaves his hat on. He sits on the upper south edge of the swimming hole, listening to the birds and the waterfall down the creek. Suddenly he hears SINGING below the rock edge, where he's sitting.*

**MADELEEN:** (SINGING)

Shall we gather at the river,
Where bright angel feet have trod.
With the crystal tide forever,
Flowing by the throne of God.

*Jimmie Sue creeps up closer to the edge of the swimming hole, peeks through the laurel bushes and sees Madeleen's head and shoulders above the water. Wearing nothing but his hat, he pretends that he doesn't know anyone else is there, so he runs down the slope and jumps off the rock into the water, cannonball style. His hat HANGS IN THE AIR above him, and as he disappears in the water, his hat LANDS on the water.*

*Madeleen rushes to the deepest water. She holds a knobby stick.*

*Jimmie Sue comes up right under his hat, about fifteen feet from her.*

JIMMIE SUE: If this creek wadn't so nice an' cool, I'd say we wuz inta some mighty hot watah.

*He wades closer to her. She raises her stick toward him.*

MADELEEN: White Boy, ya come one step closer an' I be makin' souse meat outta yoah punkin-head-noggin.

JIMMIE SUE: Why you be callin' me, 'White Boy' again

*He grabs an end of her stick.*

MADELEEN: 'Cause nothin' can be happenin' between us.

JIMMIE SUE: But Madeleen you, yourself, said a little touch never hurt nobody. I agree with you that there ain't nothing wrong with a touch.

MADELEEN: I know what be happenin' if we be touchin'. If we's someplace else an' we be somebody else, things'd be different, maybe. But we ain't some place else, an' we ain't some body else, 'cept our own selves. I gotta live with my fambly, an' ya gotta live with yoah folks an' neighbors an' church members.

JIMMIE SUE: Do you 'member when I kissed you?

MADELEEN: 'Member when I kissed you?

JIMMIE SUE: When did you kiss me?

*He starts moving toward her.*

MADELEEN: No Jimmie Sue, don't start actin' like White Boy again. When you started kissin' me, didn't it mean anything when I did't push you away? ... Cause I kept on kissin' you.

JIMMIE SUE: So sorry, Madeleen. I wasn't for certain sure, you liked my kiss. I keep fergettin' that we different color.

MADELEEN: I can't nevah forget ... I think we'd better get outta the water an' talk, if you've a mind to.

JIMMIE SUE: I'll go get my clothes on.

MADELEEN: Yeah, an' on the way you'll wanna get all

that black tar off ... I've already got the 'baccer gum off me, but I won't nevah be able to wash all my black away.

*Jimmie Sue starts to move toward her again, but reverses and wades up stream instead and starts scrubbing.*

SLOW FADE.

## EXT. AT CREEK 30 MINUTES LATER

*Madeleen and Jimmie Sue sit on the footbridge upstream from the swimming hole. They face the swimming hole, quietly watching a water snake slither across the water.*

**JIMMIE SUE:** Mamma said befoah I came down to the creek, thet with the 'baccer gum bein' all ovah me  thet I look like I belong to yoah fambly.

**MADELEEN:** Why yoah mamma bein' throwin' off on my fambly,thet away? Thet don't sound like Aunt Sue atall.

**JIMMIE SUE:** She didn't mean nothin' bad 'bout what she said.

**MADELEEN:** Well I tell ya right now.  I seen lotsa things in my time, but I ain't nevah seen no colored boy nur white boy nur high-yaller boy with the colorin' ya got. Whut with them black arms an' head, speckeldy spots colorin' on yah face an' streakedy stripes down yoah back. Ya look moah like a dominecker chicken than a boy of any color. You'd look moah like a dominecker roostah, if I could see some of yoah red roostah comb through the black gum on yoah head.

**JIMMIE SUE:** Ya think you be the black Cornish hen?

**MADELEEN:** Jimmie Sue don't ya be belittlin' me, an' don't you be fergettin', One of the reasons I like you so much is because you have so much fun. . .

*Jimmie Sue tries to interrupt her, but she continues.*

**MADELEEN:** An' you want other folks to have fun too. But it'd be nice if you could be serious sometime.

**JIMMIE SUE:** Madeleen, I've never been more serious in my life.

**MADELEEN:** About me?

**JIMMIE SUE:** About you an' me. In fact, I'm so serious I skeer myself.

**MADELEEN:** Jimmie Sue, (choking up with emotion) I think we bettah get on home,'cause if I stay any longer I won't ever be able to get home.

**JIMMIE SUE:** A quick kiss, maybe?

**MADELEEN:** It can't evah be a quick kiss any more.

**JIMMIE SUE:** Let it be whatever it may be.

*Madeleen puts her hand over his on the edge of the footbridge. Nothing more is said, as they look deeply into each others' eyes.*

FADE OUT.

*EXT. HILTONS' BARNYARD*

*No audible dialogue ACTION ONLY.*

*The boys are seen pitching hay off two hay wagons. They're in a hurry because of an impending summer shower.*

*Jimmie Sue and Madeleen are tramping while the others are throwing the hay off the wagons. When the haystack is about half finished, we see Jimmie Sue grab onto the stack pole for balance. He clasps his right hand over Madeleen's left hand on the haystack pole. Jimmie Sue pulls himself to the haystack pole then grabs her right hand, pulling her tight to the pole. They are so close to each other that they can speak with each other without anyone else knowing what they're saying.*

*The other workers have taken a break to get some good cool spring water. As the camera begins to zoom in for a close-up, the other boys jump up on the hay wagons to commence pitchforking the hay again. Just as they re-enter Jimmie Sue and Madeleen disengage and begin tromping again.*

*THERE'S A BREAK IN THE ACTION*

*Jimmie Sue and Madeleen are finishing at the top of the haystack. Madeleen takes off her scarf and attaches it to end of the pole. Two of the boys are finishing thatching the outside of the hay to prevent water from seeping into the hay.*

*Madeleen and Jimmie Sue are high on top of the hay stack. Only the top of the pole is now sticking out. Madeleen takes off her scarf from around her neck and ties it to the tip-top of the pole.*

**JIMMIE SUE:** Why'd you do that?

**MADELEEN:** I don't know ... Kind Of a sign I s'pose.

**JIMMIE SUE:** What kinda sign?

**MADELEEN:** Mebbe jest a sign we be finished.

*Jimmie Sue looks worried.*

**JIMMIE SUE:** Finished with what?

**MADELEEN:** Finished with the haystackin', silly.

**JIMMIE SUE:** Oh, yeah! Silly me!

*RAIN drizzles, George Dow, Clyde and Simon run for the house. Cletus and the GIRLS are already gone. Madeleen and Jimmie Sue plop down on top of the haystack and slide down the newly thatched sides. They then run to the barn shed, but get soaked on the way.*

CROSS FADE.


*INT. HILTON'S BARN SHED - MOMENTS LATER*


*When they get under the shelter of the shed roof, Madeleen and Jimmie Sue turn around to look at the clouds.*

**MADELEEN:** The rain cometh.

*Jimmie Sue and Madeleen stand under the roof, drenched from the rain.*

*Jimmie Sue has his shirt off, and he drips wet from his chest. Madeleen's overalls and shirt are soaked.*

*They look at each other in renewed amazement.*

*Madeleen laughs.*

**MADELEEN:** Ha ha ...

**JIMMIE SUE:** What you laughin' 'bout?

**MADELEEN:** The watah drippin' off yoah nose makes out like you got a real bad cold with a runny nose.

**JIMMIE SUE:** Why you always pokin' fun of me? What things I do or what I might look like?

**MADELEEN:** You like to do the laughin'. Some times someone else likes to laugh.

JIMMIE SUE: You right. But it be more better when we laugh together. Why don't we climb up to the loft?

MADELEEN: You don't s'pose anyone will see or hear us up there?

JIMMIE SUE: We could wait out the storm theah. An' have some time to ourselves.

> *Jimmie Sue looks back at the haystack.*

JIMMIE SUE: An' the rain cometh an' droopeth yoah hangin' flag sign on the top of the stack pole.

MADELEEN: Waal now it jest be a soggy sign of finishin'.

JIMMIE SUE: Maybe it means there's gotta be a dryin' out time? The barn loft could be a dryin' out time an' place.

MADELEEN: Maybe so. But it be too much dangerous.

JIMMIE SUE: What be the danger, 'cept maybe a rat or two?

MADELEEN: The danger be us.

JIMMIE SUE: Well, I'll promise not to hurt you, if you promise not to hurt me ... Just follow me up the ladder.

> *Jimmie Sue leads the way up the ladder. They each find a comfortable spot to sit and lean back on piles of loose hay, not too far from each other.*

JIMMIE SUE: See? No danger so far.

MADELEEN: Jimmie Sue, do you evah get serious? (pause) Papa told me 'bout Mr. Goins' threat to kick us off his property, because of you an' me.

JIMMIE SUE: Let's give 'em somethin' to talk 'bout.

MADELEEN: There you go again. Just when we need to talk serious. Bein' funny.

JIMMIE SUE: Tryin' to be funny.

MADELEEN: I mean my whole family. No one's gonna do anything to your family.

JIMMIE SUE: 'Cause nobody let me, let us get serious, talk serious. (pause) We could run away, an' no one could do a damn, darn ... thing about it. Would you wanna do thet?

**MADELEEN:** I already found out 'bout that.

**JIMMIE SUE:** You got train tickets?

**MADELEEN:** I didn't have money for that. I wrote to Richmond to find out if we could marry. And found out we couldn't.

**JIMMIE SUE:** Of course not. We not quite 16 yet. Maybe in six months ...

**MADELEEN:** I'm black an' you white.

**JIMMIE SUE:** You remindin' me of that again?

**MADELEEN:** The legal people reminded me of that, as if I hadn't noticed it. Because we different racial colors. The word they used was mis-ce-gen-a-tion.

**JIMMIE SUE:** Madeleen, I don't know what that means, but I'm sure that Mr. Bowen and Mr. Goins won't know what we promise to each other. Even if we hafta wait a while ... until we reach 16.

**MADELEEN:** We'll have to keep it a little secret, an' just mind what we do an' say in front of other people.

**JIMMIE SUE:** 'Specially our own family. Thelma Lou would just love to know that we have a secret an' even more so to know what that little secret might be ... OUR little secret.

*Jimmie Sue rolls over to Madeleen and leans over her to kiss her. Madeleen pushes him away.*

**JIMMIE SUE:** What the hell? We just promised to run away together, an' I can't hsve one little kiss.

**MADELEEN:** Jimmie Sue if I know you, an' I do know me, we can't have a LITTLE kiss.

*Jimmie Sue laughs at that.*

**MADELEEN:** Jimmie Sue, I'm not bein' funny.

**JIMMIE SUE:** I'm sorry Madeleen. I know you're not bein' funny, an' I know you're right 'bout our kisses.

**MADELEEN:** We can't be makin' babies befoah we be legal.

**JIMMIE SUE:** Now that's somethin' else.

**MADELEEN:** What you mean somethin' else?

**JIMMIE SUE:** The somethin' else is that legal stuff. I'm already legal, an' aftah that war an' President Lincoln, you're just as legal as me.

**MADELEEN:** You know, Jimmie Sue, what I mean.

**JIMMMIE SUE:** That's just a little piece of paper.

**MADELEEN:** I don't care for the little piece of paper
any more that you do. But the paper just lets the world
and you and me know that our bein' togetha is blessed of
the Lord.

**JIMMIE SUE:** I s'pose you're right.

**MADELEEN:** Jimmie Sue, Brothah Hiatt be so nice in
the spring as to invite us to yoah church Association Day
meetin' an' dinner on the grounds. You like to visit our
church fer revival meetin'?

**JIMMIE SUE:** Maybe.

*They are silent for a moment. Madeleen HUMS the tune:*
*ShallWe Gather at the River. They stand and go to the ladder*
*while she is still humming.*

FADE OUT.

*INT. GENERAL STORE*

*Bowen and Goins sit by a potbellied stove with no fire in it.*
*It's the local zone for the gathering of men and boys.*

**GOINS:** You sure he's comin'?

**BOWEN:** How can a body ever be for sure what
somebody else might do. Hell I can't really be for sure
thet I'll do or even be able to do what I've promised.

**GOINS:** Hadn't you tole him 'bout it yet?

**BOWEN:** Well, not in so many words.

**GOIN:** What in the Hell does thet mean?. It surely don't
take many words.

**BOWEN:** The Bennetts are awful good customers.
Whenever there's a new product on the market, they're
usually the first to try it.

**GOINS:** Like what?

**BOWEN:** Those new fangled clothespins with a little
spring in them ... Jimmie Sue was in here just a few days
ago to order three dozen for his Mama. You know what
thet fool boy did?

**GOINS:** Thet fool boy bettah be carful what he gonna do. What he already done is caution enough to pay 'tention.

**BOWEN:** He come in to buy new clothespins for the ones he lost. He lost the damn things in the Sapling Ridge creek.

**GOINS:** How'd he do that?

**BOWEN:** By putting them on his nose when he went swimmin'. Can you imagine?

**GOINS:** When he went skinny-dippin'?

**BOWEN:** That stands to reason.

**GOINS:** He bettah start thinkin' 'bout reason when he goes skinny-dippin'.

**BOWEN:** Why boys 'round here ... Even you an' me back in ...

**GOINS:** What about skinny-dippin' with colored girls?

**BOWEN:** Whatcha talkin' 'bout?

**GOINS:** I see what I see an' I know what I know.

**BOWEN:** Does what you know bear repeatin'?

**GOINS:** Sure ... when the time comes. I look aftah what belongs to me.

**BOWEN:** If you talkin' 'bout the baptizin' hole ... That belongs to me.

**GOINS:** The sharecroppers belong to me.

**BOWEN:** Now when they were slaves, yeah they belonged to whoevah bought them or inherited 'em. But now they be sharecroppers you can't ...

**GOINS:** What I can't do now is sell 'em at auction.

**BOWEN:** So what can ...

**GOINS:** I suely can move 'em. You know what happened to my last sharecroppers?

**BOWEN:** It seems that somethin' happened with that colored boy.

**GOINS:** Thet boy was lucky he didn't get strung up.

**BOWEN:** I guess you notified the boy's folks.

**GOINS:** I gave them 24 hours. (THUNDER rumbling in the background.) You know down to Pierson, there's talk of the Klan.

**BOWEN:** Not here in the hills. That's down in the flatlands, here they ...

**GOINS:** I guess we'll know when ...
*(interrupted by LOUDER THUNDER)*

**BOWEN:** It's likely we'll get a big one.

**GOINS:** Not no summer shower this time ... I'd better get on to home.

**BOWEN:** Bennett musta seen this one comin'.

**GOINS:** He bettah think of a considerably bigger one, if things don't change. I can't change the world to my likin', but I can Godfer-sure keep a handle on where my arms can reach.

*THUNDER CONTINUES*


*EXT. BENNETT FARM - BARN – EVENING*


*Piles of unshucked corn are seen in front of Barn.*
*The Bennetts have a neighborhood corn-shucking party.*
*The Bennet family and OTHER NEIGHBORS shuck corn. ALL DO THE SAME ACTION: shuck ears of corn, throw the ears into a nearby basket. ONE MAN passes a jug of hard cider shared by all.*
*Lige finds a red ear, jumps up and down excited.*

**LIGE:** Now I get fer rewards to kiss a girl. Thelma Lou, Thelma Lou! I getta kiss my Thelma Lou.

He holds up the red ear and runs to chase Thelma Lou. She runs, and makes him chase her. He catches and kisses her.

All the FOLKS clap and are excited for him. Jimmie Sue jumps up, claps at Lige's success. Lige throws the red corn away.

**FOLKS:** Yay! Go, Lige!

*Jimmie Sue runs to the discarded red corn and sneaks it into his overalls pocket.*
*The Hilton's mule-pulled wagon comes down the road.*
*Uncle Levi and Aunt Lily sit on the wagon seat.*
*All the FOLKS look surprised at COLOREDS coming to a corn shucking like this. They stop their work and watch.*

**ROBERT:** Levi, I sure 'preciate you comin' like I said. The boys will need a hand with gettin' all these shucks into the barn stalls. An' it's awful good of you, Lily, to come and help Sue and Thelma Lou with the fixin's fer a little after-work dinnah.

*The WHITE FOLKS look uneasy at each other.*

*Jimmie Sue looks at the Hilton wagon, and notices no children are on. He feels into his overall pocket to make sure his red corn is secure.*

*During the shucking, Emmett finds a jar of moonshine, hands it to his DADDY. All the MEN share it. The BOYS sip some moonshine behind the ADULTS' backs.*

*They all eat the evening snack, while Uncle Levi helps with getting the corn shucks into the barn stalls.*

FADE OUT.

*INT. BENNETT FARM - KITCHEN - NIGHT*

*Aunt Lily, Sue and other WOMEN clean up in the kitchen.*

CUT TO:

*EXT. BENNETT FARM - CORN CRIB – NIGHT*

*Jimmie Sue totes the last baskets of corn to the corn crib.*

CUT TO:

*EXT. BENNETT FARM - PORCH – NIGHT*

*Jimmie Sue walks to the porch, sits down on the porch steps. He takes the red corn out of his pocket, admires it closely.*

*Aunt Lily steps out onto the porch, and sees Jimmie Sue in a dazed stupor. She eases herself down next to him.*

**LILY:** Thet's a mighty nice year of corn, Jimmie Sue. Did you get to kiss a purty girl tonight? Who might thet be?

**JIMMIE SUE:** Aunt Lily, if you was to have to tell what

color this year of corn might be, what color would you say it is?

LILY: I'd say it's lotsa colors-red, yellow, even kinda purplish.

JIMMIE SUE: Thet'd make it colored, wouldn't it?

LILY: Jimmie Sue, I see you ask a lotta oncomfortable questions.

JIMMIE SUE: I didn't go to make you oneasy, Aunt Lily.

LILY: Not oneasy atall ... Course you right, but folks can't always see whut some others-like yoahself see. About colors I mean.

JIMMIE SUE: Aunt Lily, if you be a conjure woman, what do you do to find out things?

LILY: You just let things come to you.

JIMMIE SUE: Huh

LILY: In Proverbs it says, 'But wait on the Lord.' When He come, he be acomin' in many shapes. At times He be a unexpected person, an' then maybe jest a voice, an' sometimes a idea 'bout somethin' mighty important.

JIMMIE SUE: Aunt Lily, how do you figure church things an' conjurin' an healin' go together?

LILY: All things on God's green earth goes together. As you gets older and keep lookin' an' listenin' an' askin', then more of it starts comin' together.

JIMMIE SUE: Well if all things come together on God's green earth, why cain't folks on God's green earth come together? Aunt Lily, you know what I think? Well, I wonder if all God's green earth come togethah, why can't Madeleen and me be togethah? Madeleen is a good person an' a lovin' person!

LILY: Yes, Child, but sometimes I be skeered.

JIMMIE SUE: Skeered of what?

LILY: I sometimes be skeered if my children may know too much. An' then it be dangerous like thet dynamite stuff they use in the mines. Thet power might 'splode.

JIMMIE SUE: Aunt Lily, would you min' doin' somethin' for me?

**LILY:** Why, no, Child, what would it be?

**JIMMIE SUE:** Would it be awright if you took this year of corn to Madeleen?

**LILY:** Acourse, thet'd jest tickle her to death.

**JIMMIE SUE:** Oh! I certainly wouldn't want her to die over it!

**LILY:** (chuckles): Oh I don't think there's no fear of thet. But I was put on notice by Madeleen to remin' you 'bout our revival next week. S'pose you could come?

*Jimmie Sue's face lights up, eyes happy.*

**JIMMIE SUE:** I'd be much obliged to come to the revival. Should I bring my folks?

**LILY:** Bring whoever you've a min' to.

*Lily stands up slowly. She notices Levi coming back from the barn with Robert.*

**LILY:** We better be goin' now, Jimmie Sue.

**JIMMIE SUE:** Don't forget the colored corn.

*Jimmie Sue hands her the corn.*

**LILY:** Colored corn for Madeleen. Take keer of yoahself, Jimmie Sue. An' we'll maybe see you nex' week at the revival meetin'?

**JIMMIE SUE:** Yeah. . . The Lord willin'.

*Aunt Lily chuckles.*

FADE OUT.


*INT. COLORED CHURCH - EVENING - REVIVAL MEETING*


*PREACHER CONNERS is standing behind the pulpit and PREACHER PEEPLES is sitting in the pulpit chair. PIANO PLAYER plays softly. Jimmie Sue appears in church door and after an awkward pause, sits at the closest open seat. It happens to be right next to Madeleen, who is sitting there with her MOTHER and Ruthie. Madeleen is startled by his sitting there, as it's the women's side of the church.*

**MADELEEN:** Jimmie Sue, yoah on the wrong side.

**JIMMIE SUE:** Why am I always in the wrong place?

**MADELEEN:** (pointing to other side) You belong on thet side with the other men.

*EVERYONE stares at him as he crosses the aisle and tries to find a place to sit. The only place is up front on the mourners' bench where RUFUS JONES, the annual drunk convert is already sitting. Rufus is swaying back and forth, but not from religious fervor. During all of the dialogue and action above, "AMENS," "HALLELUJAHS," AND "TOE TAPS" fill the church, along with the MUSIC of the PIANO and general hubbub of the congregants.*

**PREACHER CONNERS:** Brothah Peeples, I call now upon you and yoah people to look forward to thet Promised Land, an' prepare the way of the Lawd. Thar still be deserts ahead of us. Deserts as hot as the furnaces of hell. An' thar still be mountains we gotta climb. Mountains so high with wild beasts so fierce and storms so harmful we cain't get our minds around it. But, we be assured that the steady arms of the Lord swim us acrost thet ocean-sea. We been promised thet the comforting hand of Jesus cool ouah furrowed brow in thet hellish desert. An' the very wings of the Holy Ghost carry us ovah them high mountains whut block our gates to ouah own Promised Land.

*Preacher Conners wipes the heavy sweat from his brow with a white hanky, loosens his tie.*

*Brother Peeples Rises.*

**BROTHER PEEPLES:** Sistah Hilton, would you be so kind as to have Madeleen come forward agin an' lead us in this altar call hymn?

*"AMENS," "HALLELUJAHS," AND "TOE TAPS" ring out.*

*Sister Foster plays the piano while Madeleen comes up and stands beside the piano to lead the song.*

*EVERYONE sways in unison.*

**MADELEEN:** (leading the song)

Just as I am without one plea.

But that Thy blood was shed for me.

*PEOPLE dance in the center aisle. Several PEOPLE come forward to shake the PREACHER's hand.*

**MADELEEN:**

Because Thy promise I believe,

Oh, Lamb of God, I come, I come.

*Rufus rises from the mourner's bench and makes his way down to the front of the communion table where he sways back and forth and shakes the hand of Brother Peeples.*

*SINGING continues.*

**BROTHER PEEPLES:** Rufus, hit's good to see you back at this altar ... once again.

*Rufus collapses onto his knees, he prays with passion.*

*Several PEOPLE come to shake the PREACHER's hand while Madeleen sings.*

**MADELEEN:** Because Thy promise I believe, O'Lamb of God, I come, I come.

*Jimmie Sue sways and taps his foot as everyone sings.*

*YOUNG WOMAN dances down the aisle. She "SHOUTS" and "AMENS," and grabs PREACHER CONNER's hand.*

*As if a sudden bolt of lightning strikes her down, she swoons backwards, right in the arms of a YOUNG FELLOW who is right behind her. He kneels and administers mouth-to-mouth resuscitation.*

*CROWD, stunned, scared, all chatter amongst themselves.*

*OLDER WOMAN opens her purse, takes out a bottle of digitalis.*

*YOUNG WOMAN regains consciousness, gets up, jumps to sing and shout again. Jimmie Sue is impressed with this energy.*

*PIANO continues throughout.*

*Brother Peeples preaches loudly and looks around to whom he will call on next.*

**BROTHER PEEPLES:** Almost persuaded! Thet's whut it is almost persuaded to heed thet inner voice in yoah heart an' answer the comfortin' voice of Jesus, callin' to you from the heavenly heights.

*Brother Peeples looks to Sister Foster at the piano.*

**BROTHER PEEPLES:** Sista Foster, would you strike the chord for Almost Persuaded while Madeleen lead us in the singin' of thet glorious revival hymn?

*Madeleen stands next to the piano, not far from Jimmie Sue's seat. Jimmie Sue looks at Madeleen in awe.*

*Sister Foster plays the piano, as Madeleen leads singing.*

**MADELEEN:** Almost persuaded, now to believe. Almost persuaded, Christ to receive; Seems now some soul to say, 'Go, Spirit, go Thy way, Some more convenient day, On Thee I'll call.

*Jimmie Sue sits on the mourner's bench and sways with a huge smile to Madeleen's voice.*

*Brother Peeples calls on CHURCH GOER #1. Motions him to come forward.*

**BROTHER PEEPLES:** Come forward now, afore it's too late to avoid the eternal grip of the devil nor be enclosed in the grasp of the death angel's arms. That ol' reaper be acomin' fer each of us, but why don't you come forth before the reaper gets to you, an' it be too late?

**CHURCH GOER #1:** Yes, brother, here I come.

*He comes up to Brother Peeples and joins the OTHER CHURCH GOERS in rejoicing, waves arms, sings and shouts.*

*Madeleen finishes the third stanza.*

**MADELEEN:** Almost cannot avail; Almost is but to fail! Sad, sad that bitter wail.

*Before Madeleen sings the last word, Jimmie Sue springs up from his seat, onto his feet.*

**MADELEEN:** Almost, but lost.

*Jimmie Sue, is in the midst of the NEW CONVERTS, who SHOUT and WHIRL around him. OTHERS toe-tap to their rejoicing with dance.*

*All the CHURCH GOERS reach out to Jimmie Sue, arms open to embrace him.*

**CHURCH GOER #2:** We extend our hand of fellowship.

**CHURCH GOER #3:** Come into the arms of the family of Goda'mighty.

**CHURCH GOER #4:** Welcome to yoah light of Jesus! Come out of yoah darkness. It's not too late.

*All CHURCH GOERS sweat from the heat, and dance on the wooden floor, with their holy shouts.*

*Jimmie Sue stands in the middle of the circle of REVIVALISTS as they surround him, and circle him in rejoicing chants.*

*He makes his way toward the PREACHER then suddenly his feet turn toward the front door.*

*He exits the church.*

CUT TO:

*EXT. CHURCH - FRONT STEPS - NIGHT*

*All is suddenly quiet.*

*Jimmie Sue steps outside the door. He looks around, and hears silence. He looks back toward the church and watches DARK SILHOUETTES against the inside lamp light.*

*Jimmie Sue and OL' PETE, his mule, turn towards home in the light of the full moon.*

*Jimmie Sue listens to the faint sounds in his head of Madeleen's singing voice.*

**JIMMIE SUE:** But ... she's colored.

FADE OUT.

*EXT. JIMMIE SUE'S HOME - BARN - NIGHT*

*Jimmie Sue arrives home on his mule. Ol' Pete stops suddenly at the barn door.*

*Jimmie Sue jumps off and leads him inside the barn.*

*INT. BENNETT FARM - BARN - NIGHT (CONTINUOUS)*

*Jimmie Sue lights a barn lantern and unbridles his mule. He hangs up his bridle on a hook. He scoops some oats from a large burlap sack and dumps it into the feed trough.*

*The mule eats.*

*Jimmie Sue pulls out an old saddle quilt blanket.*

CUT TO:

INT. BENNETT FARM - BARN LOFT - NIGHT

*Jimmie Sue climbs up with the lantern to the top of the barn loft filled with hay. His besmirched shirt hangs off one of the rafters.*

*He pulls off his brogan shoes, opens the loft door for air and moonlight. He hangs the lantern on a nail, but doesn't blow it out.*

*He lays down his blanket on top of a hay pile, and gets under, wraps himself, falls asleep.*

BEGIN JIMMIE SUE'S DREAM SEQUENCE

EXT. RIVER - DAY

*Jimmie Sue floats down a small creek into the river, without a boat, he floats toward the waterfall.*

*He sees Madeleen, who seems older. He tries to call to her. No sounds come out of his mouth. He tries harder, still no sound. Madeleen sees him now, and turns from him deliberately.*

*He floats farther down river, comes closer to the waterfall, tries to call her. She ages fast, gets older and older.*

*The mighty waterfall roars. He feels like he is falling in.*

*Jimmie Sue tries to scream out, looks up at her facing down at him.*

*Her face looks down the rock edge. She is much older now. She points downstream to warn him. He floats in the rough waters, out of control, in circles. He floats around a large boulder, and sees Madeleen lower her hands, her tears fall into* her cupped hands. He finds his voice and screams, which wakens the farm animals.

END OF JIMMIE SUE'S DREAM SEQUENCE

*INT. BENNETT FARM - BARN LOFT - NIGHT*

A leak from the roof drips on Jimmie Sue's face while he is sleeping. The water awakens him suddenly.

**JIMMIE SUE:** Ahhhh. No ...

*Jimmie Sue jumps to his feet, confused. He wakes up the barn animals. He shakes his head.*

*The mule brays, chickens cluck, pigs scuffle, goats and sheep whine with baa's. The barn owl screeches.*

*He notices his face is wet. By the light of the lantern he sees water dripping on his bloodied shirt, hanging from the rafter.*

*Jimmie Sue calms down, listens to the RAT-A-TATTING of the rain on the metal barn roof.*

*The barn cat, RASCAL, rubs against him. He lies down, fades to sleep.*

*The rain taps like a drumbeat to the music and Madeleen sings.*

**MADELEEN (O.S.):** Shall we gather at the river. Where bright angel feet have trod. With its crystal tide forever, Floating by the Throne of God? Yes, we'll gather at the river ...

*The song FADES away as Jimmie Sue falls asleep.*

FADE OUT.

*EXT. BOWEN'S GENERAL STORE*

*PEOPLE are seen coming in wagons and going into store.*

FADE TO:

*INT. BOWEN'S GENERAL STORE*

*Bennetts are inside.*

*Three MUSICIANS are tuning up: GUITARIST,*

*FIDDLER and JUG PLAYER.*

*PEOPLE are still coming in.*

*Hiltons arrive and stand together behind the pot-bellied stove.*

**MR. BOWEN:** Come on in an' pay 'tention to my hat here on the counter, an' write out yoah family name on a slip of papah an' put it in fer the chance of winnnin' a basket of groceries. Be sure an' write it so's I can read it.

*PEOPLE respond by laughing and some writing and some putting in their ticket.*

**MR. BOWEN:** An' welcome to the musicians, the Fulcher boys, from ovah to Pierson.

*PEOPLE clap and MUSICIANS start playing. As the music gets faster and faster, everyone starts looking toward Jimmie Sue, who usually dances to the fast tunes.*

*His toes start tapping and rather soon he jumps out right in front of the musicians and starts dancing the "buck and wing".*

*Madeleen starts moving her hands to the beat of the music, then tapping her toes as she looks toward Jimmie Sue.*

*She takes a step toward him, but Aunt Lily stops her by grabbing her elbow.*

**LILY:** No Honey, we can't do thet. We gotta keep 'memberin' who we be.

*Mr. Bowen calls for attention and the MUSICIANS pause.*

**MR. BOWEN:** Now thet ever'body in the hereabouts seems to be here we'll draw a name fer those groceries I was talkin' 'bout. We'll let the littlest one here come an' pick out a name. I b'lieve thet might be the Little Bennett girl.

*Everyone could see that Ruthie Hilton was the smallest child, but Mr. Bowen proceeds anyway.*

**MR. BOWEN:** Missus Bennett, would you send ovah yoah little girl?

*Mrs. Bennett gives Rosie a little shove.*

*She goes up to Mr. Bowen who stoops forward with the hat and lets her pull out a name.*

*He gives Rosie a gum drop and with a big grin unfurls the paper. Just as quickly he frowns broadly.*

**MR. BOWEN:** This name is much too scribbly. We'll jest hafta pick another.

*He crumples up the paper and throws it on the floor then stoops again with the hat for Rosie to pick another name.*

*Jimmie Sue picks up the crumpled paper and sees HILTON written in plain letters.*

**MR. BOWEN:** Pulling another name out of the hat. I can read this one ... Bennett.

*MUSICIANS strike up again, a general hullaballoo of people gabbing, as Jimmie Sue shows his DADDY the first slip of paper.*

**ROBERT:** (After seeing the Hiltons' name) Well, we'll hafta get our basket full an' jest give it to the Hiltons as a special Christmas gift from one of the wise men.

*The Bennetts start filling a bushel basket.*

FADE OUT.


*INT. HILTON KITCHEN*


**LILY:** (while taking groceries out of box) Jimmie Sue, it is real nice for you to share yoah grocery winnin's.

**MADELEEN:** Jimmie Sue, it looks like you sent the whole passel of groceries.

**JIMMIE SUE:** 'Cause you won 'em all.

**LILY:** Whut you mean by ...

**JIMMIE SUE:** At Mr. Bowen's store! He pulled yoah name at first, but claimed he couldn't read it. So, you recall, he threw it on the floor.

**MADELEEN:** I knew thet, because I wrote the name HILTON on real big letters. An'I got good handwritin'.

**JIMMIE SUE:** So I picked it up and showed it to Papa. He said we ought to take the the groceries to the rightful owners.

**MADELEEN:** I don't like the way Mr. Bowen treats us when we go to buy somethin'.

**LILY:** Madeleen, don't go makin' things up.

**MADELEEN:** He looks at me in a strange way.

**LILY:** Don't say nothin' like thet to yoah daddy.

**MADELEEN:** Don't need to.  I can look aftah myself.

BLACKOUT.

### EXT. OLD FIELD CREEK AREA - DAY

*Jimmie Sue and Rosie are down by the creek with a sled.*

**JIMMIE SUE:** Well, Little One, we better get home. Mamma'll start worryin', an' hit'll soon be suppah time.

**ROSIE:** But I left Hildy on Rosie's kitchen table.

**JIMMIE SUE:** Hildy?

**ROSIE:** My doll baby!

**JIMMIE SUE:** Why don't we plan to come back tomorrow? We can get her then.

*They leave the sled on the creek bank.*

*Jimmie Sue carries Rosie across the creek, carefully on the little bridge foot-log.*

**JIMMIE SUE:** We can get the sled tomorrow when we go back to Ruthie's fer yoah doll and with a big surprise.

**ROSIE:** Oh what'll the surprise be?

*Rosie's eyes get tired. Jimmie Sue picks her up into his arms, and carries her up the slope. Rosie drifts off to sleep.*

**JIMMIE SUE:** (SINGS) Good night, good night, beloved mine, good night, sleep well, my dear ...

SLOW FADE.

### INT. BENNETT'S HOME - KITCHEN - MORNING

*Jimmie Sue, Rosie and their other FAMILY members sit at the breakfast table.*

*Rosie bugs Jimmie Sue while he eats breakfast: pancakes, jelly, grits, milk, bacon and eggs and biscuits.*

**ROSIE:** What's the surprise we're takin', Jimmie Sue? Can we start right now? Can we make snow angels?

**JIMMIE SUE:** Maybe we'll be fergettin' th' snow angels this mornin'. We can start as soon as Thelma Lou can get yoah wraps on. I'll tell you 'bout the s'prise, jest as soon as we get to the footbridge acrost the creek.

**SUE:** Rosie, did they like the Cris'mas cookies, what I sent with you yesterday?

*Rosie stuffs her mouth with pancakes and drips syrup down her chin. She talks with her mouth full, chews fast to get the words out.*

**ROSIE:** Oh, ever'body liked them real good. I used mine to dip inta the snow cream.

*Sue smiles, and pours coffee for herself.*

**THELMA LOU:** Did Aunt Lily make some snow cream?

**ROSIE:** Yeah, an' with canned peaches.

**SUE:** Thet sounds like a real tasty idea. We'll have to try it our own self sometimes.

*TIME PASSES*

*Jimmie Sue picks up Rosie who is dressed for cold, wrapped up in layers, and puts her onto a chair, looks her over, backs up to her.*

**JIMMIE SUE:** Okay, now, Little One, grab aholt on my back.

**ROSIE:** Oh, we gonna play horsey?

**JIMMIE SUE:** Yep, at least as far as the footbridge. You might have to save yoah strength fer crawlin' up Saplin' Ridge.

**ROSIE:** We gonna have to crawl?

**JIMMIE SUE:** Nauw, but there'll be places, you know, like yesterday, where we hadda go on all fours fer a ways, acrost some of them big rocks.

CUT TO:

*EXT. BENNETT'S HOME - PORCH - MORNING*

*Jimmie Sue and Rosie come out the door, and go down the porch steps.*

*Jimmie Sue walks over to the chop block and picks up an ax embedded there. He and Rosie trek through the snow.*

ROSIE: Do you know yet what the s'prise gonna be?

JIMME SUE: I've got a real good notion.

ROSIE: Well, I wanna know, right now.

JIMMIE SUE: When we get acrost the footbridge, I'll tell you fer certain.

FADE TO:

*EXT. SLEDDING AND CREEK AREA - SAPLING RIDGE - DAY*

*Jimmie Sue steps off the footbridge, and Rosie speaks up.*

ROSIE: Well, we are hyar now.

JIMMIE SUE: Yep, we's hyar.

ROSIE: Well?

JIMMIE SUE: Well, what?

ROSIE: The s'prise! You promised!

JIMMIE SUE: I'm sorry, Little One, fer keepin' on teasin' you. You see the sled yonder we left hyar las' night? Well, we gonna get a Christmas present so big fer Ruthie, thet we'll hafta tote it on the sled.

ROSIE: Where we gonna get somethin' thet big down hyar at the creek?

JIMMIE SUE: You see thet big stand of pine trees up the creek thar?

ROSIE: Yeah.

JIMMIE SUE: Thet farm b'long to Mr. Bowen down to the general store.

ROSIE: He give me gumdrops.

JIMMIE SUE: Yeah, an' I think he wants us to take one of his pine trees as a special Christmas present to Ruthie.

ROSIE: Oh, goodie! That one.

*Rosie picks a fully branched tree about 6 ft. tall. Jimmie Sue chops hard at the tree trunk and pulls Rosie aside as it falls away from them.*

*He takes some twine out of his pocket, ties the tree secure to the sled. Rosie jumps up and down, circles the sled, tries to help him.*

> *Jimmie Sue points to her to let her hold the twine down with her finger, while he ties it tight.*

**ROSIE:** Jimmie Sue, why does the pine tree smell like Chris'mas?

**JIMMIE SUE:** Maybe 'cause we always put up a fresh pine tree, that smells like this in our house ever' Chris'mas.

**ROSIE:** An' what's this sticky stuff hyar where you cut?

**JIMMIE SUE:** Thet's jest pine rosin, but you oughten not touch it, 'cause hit'll stick to yoah fingers.

> *Rosie touches the rosin with her pointer finger before Jimmie Sue finishes speaking, and when she touched that finger to her thumb, they stick together. She cries.*

**ROSIE:** Jimmie Sue, my fingers're stuck togetha. Kin I evah get 'em unstuck?

> *Jimmie Sue laughs.*

**JIMMIE SUE:** They'll come unstuck with a lil'l bit of hot water and some lye soap.

> *The two climb up the Sapling Ridge slope, lugging the sled with its cargo.*
>
> *Halfway up the ridge they stop and catch their breath. They both sit down on a rock.*
>
> *Jimmie Sue looks up at a white oak tree and sees a large growth of mistletoe with lots of white berries.*

**JIMMIE SUE:** Now, Little One, set real still right hyar, while I go climb thet tree.

**ROSIE:** Why?

**JIMMIE SUE:** I'm gonna get some of the mistletoe up thar.

**ROSIE:** Is it good to eat?

**JIMMIE SUE:** Nauw, they's poisonous, but they be good fer other things.

**ROSIE:** Like what?

**JIMMIE SUE:** Like a kinda magic.

**ROSIE:** Oh, I wanna see thet.

**JIMMIE SUE:** You need ta set real still hyar on this rock ledge, jest like a pretty little flowerpot.

**ROSIE:** Okay!

*Jimmie Sue shinnies up the tree like a squirrel and breaks off a huge sprig of mistletoe loaded with white berries. Then he climbs down. He lodges the sprig under the tied-up pine Christmas tree, and he and Rosie head up to the Hiltons.*

CUT TO:

*EXT. HILTONS' HOME - DAY*

*Dogs welcome Rosie and Jimmie Sue as they arrive.*
*Madeleen comes out onto the porch.*
*Ruthie hides behind Madeleen's skirt.*

**MADELEEN:** What'cha got there?

*Ruthie peeks out around Madeleen's skirt.*

**RUTHIE:** It looks like a tree to me.

*Jimmie Sue looks at Ruthie.*

**JIMMIE SUE:** Sistah, this hyar is a special Chris'mas tree 'specially fer you.

**ROSIE:** Mr. Bowen wanted us to bring it fer you.

*Madeleen smiles.*

**MADELEEN:** Why, Jimmie Sue, thet's the most thoughty thing I evah 'member 'bout Chris'mas gifts ... from unexpected places ... ike white neighbors. Hit's a whole lot like the gifts of the wise men, don't you think? How nice of Mr. Bowen, 'cause he's never showed thet kind of neighborliness twarge us afore.

**JIMMIE SUE:** Oh, we didn't wanna bother Mr. Bowen directly. So hit was jest like his piney woods contributed the Chris'mas tree fer Ruthie.

*Madeleen looks appreciatively at Jimmie Sue.*

**RUTHIE:** I thank you, Rosie an' Jimmie Sue an' Mr. Bowen.

FADE OUT.

*INT. HILTON'S HOME - LIVING ROOM - DAY*

*Jimmie Sue fastens the tree onto a cross-planked stand. Aunt Lily shows Jimmie Sue and Madeleen where to put the tree. They carry it to a corner of the room, away from the fireplace. Uncle Levi and the boys, Cletus and Clyde, come in. They both shake off their coats and hang them up. Aunt Lily waves her husband and boys to come over to the tree area.*

**RUTHIE:** Look, Papa, whut Rosie an' Jimmie Sue brung ovah fer Chris'mas.

*EVERYONE stands back to admire the tree.*

**LEVI:** Thet sure is a thoughty thang to do.

**LILY:** Hit smells up the house real good. I always liked the fresh scent of a new-cut pine.

*Rosie and Ruthie, both under the tree playing, giggle.*

*EVERYONE looks to see what the girls are giggling about.*

*Aunt Lily peeks under the tree.*

**LILY:** Now, what're you girls doin' down there?

*The GIRLS come out from under the tree, their hands stuck together with the pine sap.*

**ROSIE:** I showed Ruthie 'bout thet pine juice. It stuck our hands togetha. Does thet mean we be sisters now we stuck togetha?

*EVERYONE ignores the question.*

*Madeleen takes Rosie and Ruthie into the kitchen.*

*Jimmie Sue walks over to the front door, sees a little nail that sticks out over the door.*

**JIMMIE SUE:** I'll be back in a minute.

*Jimmie Sue runs out the door, comes back in the next minute with his mistletoe.*

*He reaches above the door, balances a fork of mistletoe sprig onto the nail head.*

**JIMMIE SUE:** Now, thet's jest a little more Chris'mas decoration.

*Madeleen, Rosie and Ruthie return to the living room. They look over at the mistletoe.*

**CLETUS:** But Jimmie Sue, whut's it fer? Whut does it mean?

**JIMMIE SUE:** Well, I jest think it's kinda pretty with little white berries an' leaves still green in the middle of a snowy winter.

*Madeleen looks at Jimmie Sue, smiles.*

**MADELEEN:** Didn't it usta mean somethin'in the old country?

**JIMMIE SUE:** Well, hit's supposed to bring real good luck an' lots of love to ever' one in the house where it be hangin'.

*Madeleen smiles at Jimmie Sue and walks over to the mistletoe.*

**MADELEEN:** "Faith is for things hoped for, the evidence of things not seen."

*Jimmie Sue wanders under the mistletoe, next to Madeleen.*

*Madeleen startles him by reaching up, and with her hands on his arms, kisses him passionately.*

*EVERYONE gasps, watches Jimmie Sue and Madeleen with mixed emotions.*

**LEVI:** Was thar any call fer you to go an' do thet?

**MADELEEN:** I was jest follerin' what it said in a book 'bout Chris'mas things, 'specially mistletoe.

*Jimmie Sue blushes.*

**JIMMIE SUE:** Jest 'cause hit's the usual thing to do when a body might be under the Mistletoe?

**MADELEEN:** It might also mean to bring thankfulness an' gratitude fer Chris'mas kindnesses.

*Jimmie Sue smiles.*

*Madeleen looks up at Jimmie Sue with fearful eyes, full of wonder. She hurries off into the kitchen, leaves EVERYONE in a daze.*

**JIMMIE SUE:** Well, it's time fer Rosie and me to go 'on home.

**LILY:** You'll wanna stay fer dinnah?

**JIMMIE SUE:** Nah. Like to. We s'posed ta go on home. They're spectin' us soon. Mama worries 'bout Rosie, if we be gone too long.

*EVERYONE waves to Jimmie Sue and Rosie as they walk out, grab their coats, put them on.*

**CLETUS and RUTHIE:** Bye. Bye, ya'll.

**JIMMIE SUE:** Bye.

*Jimmie Sue and Rosie walk out the door.*

FADE OUT.


*EXT. HILTONS' HOME - DAY*


*Jimmie Sue and Rosie walk down the porch steps. He brushes the snow off the sled and lifts it up, pulls it by its rope through the snow.*

**ROSIE:** Jimmie Sue, why didn't anyone answer my question?

**JIMMIE SUE:** What question was thet, Little one?

*Rosie skips through the snow. Picks up some and forms a snowball while she walks.*

**ROSIE:** Bout me an' Ruthie bein' sisters if we be stuck together with pine juice.

**JIMMIE SUE:** Well, now, maybe the pine rosin 'mind us what the scriptures say thet we s'posed to be like brothahs to each othah, an' I'm sure it means also sistahs too.

**ROSIE:** Then me an' Ruthie be sistahs whetha nobody likes it or not.

FADE OUT.


*INT. HILTONS' KITCHEN LEVI AND LILY SITTING AT THE TABLE. LATE SPRING.*


**LEVI:** I don't know how Mr. Bowen heard about the pine tree, but he somehow got wind of it from some of the men who buy stuff theah.

**LILY:** But it was awful little to take much notice of. Jimmie Sue was just doin' somthin' nice for Madeleen and Sistah. Thet was moah than three months ago.

**LEVI:** Well I don't know how he found out about it. But I wuz tole, thet thet wuz the least of it. Mr. Goins saw me at the store yesterday. He had heard about the pine tree thing with Mr. Bowen. He wants to talk with us next week before we put the 'baccer plantbed in. He an' some othah men are plannin' somethin' like they heard was goin'on in Richmon'. It's called a klang or somethin' like thet.

**LILY:** Just cause Madeleen an' Jimmie Sue likes ...

**LEVI:** They plannin' a big meetin' next week.

**LILY:** Well, we gotta do somethin'

**LEVI:** An' pretty quick!

**LILY:** Maybe instead of bein' pushed off the place, we can make our own choices. Sister Rachel has long waited for us to come to Baltimore. She says we can find jobs theah, an' won't hafta keep workin' that devil weed.

**LEVI:** There's no need for the whole family to move. The contention seems to be Jimmie Sue and Madeleen. If Madeleen goes to Sistah Rachel, Jimmie Sue can go later when they can get married, an' in that state whites an' blacks can be married.

BLACKOUT.

## INT. BENNETTS' KITCHEN

*Sue and Robert sit at the kitchen table.*

**ROBERT:** I knew no good would come of it. Jimmie Sue ...

**SUE:** But it's been just an innocent ...

**ROBERT:** It's not so innocent when neighbors start totin' their guns.

**SUE:** We'd bettah talk with Jimmie Sue.

BLACKOUT.

## INT. OF BENNETT'S BARN

*Jimmie Sue is milking the cow.*
*Robert is feeding the stock.*

**ROBERT:** Jimmie Sue, Mamma said you wanted to talk with me.

**JIMMIE SUE:** Yeah. Let me put this milk bucket aside

for a minute. The drummin' on the bottom makes it well nigh impossible to hear anything else.

**ROBERT:** Have you got Madeleen in trouble?

**JIMMIE SUE:** No! Why would you say that?

**ROBERT:** You must know that there's talk.

**JIMMIE SUE:** What I wanted to talk with you about is how our family is so beholden to the Hilton's.

**ROBERT:** How would you know anything 'bout that?

**JIMMIE SUE:** I just put two and two together, an' kinda figured out what the mystery was really all about.

**ROBERT:** There's a mystery here; no doubt about that. But you tell me what mystery you talkin' about?

**JIMMIE SUE:** Eveybody's been curious 'bout yoah limp.

**ROBERT:** You know very well I don't want any talk about that.

**JIMMIE SUE:** I know that you don't want folks talkin' about it. But surely you know that just makes them talk more about it. That may be the mystery is some skullduggery.

**ROBERT:** That's no such thing.

**JIMMIE SUE:** Papa, you know that. Mamma knows that an' now I know that. An' I know what it means for our families. Mamma told me that in the war a colored man helped you into your saddle, after you were shot.

**ROBERT:** That's what I don't wanta talk about.

**JIMMIE SUE:** You don't wanta talk about a black man saving you?

**ROBERT:** Course that's not it. It's what happened next.

**JIMMIE SUE:** What was that?

**ROBERT:** I saw him shot an' killed with a shot right in his heart.

**JIMMIE SUE:** You know his name?

**ROBERT:** It was told at the time that it was Luke.

**JIMMIE SUE:** Madeleen said that her Uncle Lucas was a cook and was killed after he helped a white soldier ride away on his horse ... I figure that soldier was you, Papa.
*A Moment of Silence.*

**ROBERT:** I somehow knew that there was a bond

between our fameleis, but I didn't even suspect that.

**JIMMIE SUE:** Mamma also felt we owed them something, which she couldn't explain. Do you s'pose Uncle Levi knew the connection?

**ROBERT:** I doubt it. He also didn't want to talk about the past ... But now we must talk about the future.

**JIMMIE SUE:** Well the way I figure it, the future is gonna happen, one way or another.

**ROBERT:** Jimmie Sue this is no time to be your usual smartass way.

**JIMMIE SUE:** Papa, that sounds kinda scary.

**ROBERT:** You better believe it ... Bowen found out about the Christmas tree you chopped on his place.

**JIMMIE SUE:** How did he know about that? How did you know about it?

**ROBERT:** Rosie told us about the Christmas tree you took to Madeleen and Ruth. There was nowhere else to get it except from Bowen's plot of land down by the creek. And, as you know, the word gets around.

**JIMMIE SUE:** We could always pay for the damn tree.

**ROBERT:** Whatta you gonna use for money? Play money won't work in this little game.

**JIMMIE SUE:** I could always work it off.

**ROBERT:** That is now the least of it. Ol' Man Goins is in on the game. It seems he's about to join with some Klan members or at least kick the Hiltons from this farm. It seems he's workin' in both directions at the same time, but you can bet on it that he'll take at least one of those choices ... By the way, did you an' Madeleen go skinny dippin' back in the summer?

**JIMMIE SUE:** How did anyone know anything ...

**ROBERT:** Did you or didn't you?

**JIMMIE SUE:** It was just by accident.

**ROBERT:** Now, Jimmie Sue, I may be a gulibble old man, but I could not for a second be persuaded that a pretty colored girl and a rovin' white boy would be skinny dippin' by accident.

**JIMMIE SUE:** It was by accident, on her part. After I had to work in the t'bacer that day alone, I went to the creek to wash off the t'baccer gum. Madeleen was already in the creek washin' herself.  She wasn' expectin' me and I wasn't really expectin' her. I was the one skinny dippin' as usual with the boys. She had on a kind of bathin' outfit.

**ROBERT:** But you ... ?

**JIMMIE SUE:** Jumped in any way ... I had no idea anyone would ...

**ROBERT:** Well Goins knew or someone told Goins, an' he's been on the warpath ever since.

**JIMMIE SUE:** Why did he wait unitl now to ...

**ROBERT:** Think. Jimmie Sue. It was in the middle of the summer, and a crop could be lost if he had made a fuss an' kicked them off this farm. An' you surely know that he wouldn't want to lose a penny of this world's goods.

**JIMMIE SUE:** So what do I ...

**ROBERT:** Finish  the milkin' an' come on to the house.
BLACKOUT.

*HILTONS' HOME - PORCH - SPRING EVENING*

*Madeleen sits on the PORCH SWING, SINGING.*

**MADELEEN:**
Shall we gather at the river
The beautiful, beautiful river Gather with the saints at
the river That flows by the throne of God.
*Madeleen starts singing the chorus.*
*Jimmie Sue stands just off the porch behind her and sings the chorus with her.*

**MADELEEN and JIMMIE SUE:** Yes, we'll gather at the river
*Madeleen quits singing and greets Jimmie Sue. He sits on the porch floor, and leans on the porch post facing her.*

**MADELEEN:** Why Jimmie Sue, it seems forever since I seen you. Course we were snowed in for a long time.

**JIMMIE SUE:** Yeah it's been a real bad wintah. I

sometimes wondered if spring was evah gonna come this year.

*Madeleen is in quiet contemplation for a moment.*

*Jimmie Sue sits by her on the swing.*

MADELEEN: Jimmie Sue, did yoah Daddy tell you 'bout Mr. Bowen? An' what he's plannin'?

JIMMIE SUE: Yeah, but I didn't think too much of it. Why can't they jest leave you an' me alone?

MADELEEN: But thet cain't nevah be. Not us togethah.

JIMMIE SUE: Whatta you mean thet cain't nevah be? Hit's jest you an' me. We's hyar ain't we?

MADELEEN: We's hyar, but there be a fence atween us ... We got a fence song. (sings) So high we can't get ovah it. So wide we can't get 'round it. So deep we can't get under it.

*Jimmie Sue sings last line with her.*

MADELEEN and JIMMIE SUE: We gotta come in at the door.

*They are both silent for a moment.*

MADELEEN: Thet door be locked.

JIMMIE SUE: A lock kin be unlocked.

MADELEEN: Not this lock. Yoah folks ... white folks locked it an' threw away the key 'long time ago. An' the lock be rusted tight shut, 'til Judgement Day ... Thet Great Getting up Mornin'.

JIMMIE SUE: Madeleen, when you reckon thet'll be?

MADELEEN: Judgement Day be hyar ever'day.

JIMMIE SUE: You mean like Mr. Bowen an' Mr. Goins ...

MADELEEN: In one way or 'nother we be judgin' ourselves.

JIMMIE SUE: I be judgin' thet you an' me belong ...

MADELEEN: We both belong to the Lawd ... But we can't belong to each otha, not in this life time ... 'cept in our dreams, maybe.

*Jimmie Sue slides over closer to her until their bodies touch.*

JIMMIE SUE: You remember the snow angels we made?

MADELEEN: For ouah little sistahs.

**JIMMIE SUE:** I made my snow angel for Ruthie's big sistah.

*Madeleen jumps up on swing, looking away from Jimmie Sue.*

**MADELEEN:** At times I feel like bein' a real angel an' flyin'.

*She turns toward Jimmie Sue and spreads her arms like wings.*

*Madeleen starts singing "I'll fly away O Glory"*

*Jimmie Sue spreads his arms like wings.*

**JIMMIE SUE:** It's Hallelluia by an' by ...

*Madeleen begins to teeter on the uneven swing and is about to tip over backward, when Jimmie Sue wraps his arms around her knees to steady her.*

*She gasps as though trying to catch her breath. Now, rather than pushing him away, she gratefully helps in steadying herself by putting her hands on his shoulders. Lowering her off the swing, becomes a duo effort.*

*He holds her more tightly than necessary for balance. Gradually, she is lowered until her feet touch the floor, and the hem of her flimsy dress has gathered at her waist.*

*The descent continues all the way to the porch floor until both of them are prone, facing each other. She is no longer resisting any amorous moves from Jimmie Sue.*

*His lips approach hers, as she holds his face in her hands, then a long passionate kiss. Time seems to stand still. Madeleen jumps up and retreats into the house.*

FADE OUT.

*INT. KITCHEN - CONTINUOUS*

*Aunt Lily is kneading bread dough to be ready for baking.*
*Madeleen bursts into kitchen crying. She runs into her mother's embracing arms.*

**AUNT LILY:** What be the matter, Child? I know you both care fer each othah. But you're gonna have to listen to Mamma this time.

**MADELEEN:** Awhile ago ... On the porch ...

LILY: What 'bout 'while ago ... On the porch?

MADELEEN: Jimmie Sue kissed me. I mean, really kissed me. An it wadn't no mistletoe friendly kiss.

LILY: Uh-huh, an' did you kiss him?

MADELEEN: I did kiss him, an' Mamma it seemed like the most natchel thing to do, an' nothin' else in the world seemed to mattah, an' I didn't consider what nobody nowhere would say ner care.

LILY: Then you run inta the house?

MADELEEN: Thah wuz nowhere else to run.

LILY: Why you be runnin'?

MADELEEN: If theah's one moah minute with Jimmie Sue, there'd be no runnin' back from where we be headin'.

LILY: Do you love him, Madeleen?

MADELEEN: If I understand love, I know I love him, but I know it nevah can be. Why did the Good Lawd put these burdens on us, Mamma?

LILY: Yoah Aunt Lucy in Richmon' wrote thet theah might be a job carin' fer some white folks' chilren. Me an' yoah papa hev saved up enough money fer you to take the train to Sistah's. We'll pack tonight an' go first thing in the mawnin' down to the train depot.
                         FADE OUT.


                 *NEXT MORNING EXT. TRAIN DEPOT*


*Madeleen is seen getting on the train with a fabric bag. She stops at top of steps and waves goodbye to her parents. The train starts out of the station.*
                         FADE OUT.


                 *INT. TRAIN*


*Madeleen is sitting in a quiet spot in the train. She pulls her bag of clothes up close to her. Suddenly, she is startled by a LARGE BLACK MAN who sits down next to her. He*

*seems to take an unusual interest in her. Then an OLDER
BLACK WOMAN approaches.*

**OLD WOMAN:** (to man) I'm sorry, Mistah, but I needs to
set nex' to my granddaughtah.

*The man stands and walks away.*

**MADELEEN:** Thanks ... Grandma.

**OLD WOMAN:** (patting Madeleen's arm.) It's awright,
Honey. It's just ouah liddle secret.

**MADELEEN:** I 'preciate it.

*Madeleen takes out Bible and starts silently reading.*

**OLD WOMAN:** Would you be so kind as to read
somethin' to me? I nevah had the chance to learn to read.

**MADELEEN:** I'll start readin' Psalms.

**OLD WOMAN:** All the Good Book is nice to hear, but I
likes them songs.

**MADELEEN:** And he shall be like a tree planted by the
rivers of water, that bringeth forth his fruit in his season;
his leaf also shall not wither; and whatsoever he doeth
shall prosper.

**OLD WOMAN:** Now ain't thet the gospel truth.

*Madeleen stares off in distance, meditating on those words*

**MADELEEN:** (quietly praying) I do pray dear Lawd that
whatsoeveh he doeth shall prosper ... even though I not
be a part of his whatsoevah.

*She looks at the old woman, who motions her to put her
head on the old woman's shoulder.*

FADE OUT.

*EXT. HILTON'S HOME - FRONT - TWO DAYS
LATER*

*Jimmie Sue walks into the yard toward the house.
Ruthie comes running out of the house.*

**RUTHIE:** Oh, Jimmie Sue, Jimmie Sue. Madeleen be
gone.

**JIMMIE SUE:** Gone? Gone where? What you mean she
be gone?

**RUTHIE:** Better talk with Mamma.

*Aunt Lily and Cletus joins Jimmie Sue and Ruthie on the porch.*

**AUNT LILY**: Cletus you take Ruthie in the kitchen and find a cookie fer her. You might want one too. Me an' Jimmie Sue needs to talk.

*Lily sits on the swing and pats the swing for Jimmie Sue to sit; the very spot where he had sat two nights before with Madeleen.*

**JIMMIE SUE**: Why Madeleen gone? Gone where? Why didn't she say nothin'?

**LILY**: Slow down, Jimmie Sue. I kin answer only one question at a time. She took the train to my sistah's in Richmon' to help take care of her children.

**JIMMIE SUE**: But why didn't she say nothin' to me? She didn't say ...

**LILY**: I thought she tole ...

**JIMMIE SUE**: Well she didn't.

**LILY**: I know she be afeared of how you might take it.

**JIMMIE SUE**: But ...

**AUNT LILY**: We — me an' her — felt she might be carin' too much.

**JIMMIE**: Carin' too ...

**LILY**: An' we both know you be carin' fer her.

**JIMMIE**: What's wrong with carin'?

**LILY**: Well the way you two be carin' fer each other needs to be blessed of the Lord, an' she find out that the legal law here in Virginia won't let thet happen, no matter what the Lord may think 'bout it.

**JIMMIE SUE**: You mean she tried to find out if a white boy an' a colored girl could get married here in Virginia, even in the mountains?

**LILY**: An' she find out you can't.

**JIMMIE**: What we need a ol' piece of papah to love each othah? Couldn't the Lord bless us even if a county jedge didn't sign fer it?

**LILY**: The law in Richmond don't think so. Surely you know what's goin' on at Mr. Bowen's Store?

**JIMMIE SUE**: Yeah. He sent Henry Beasley up to the

house to tell my folks thet they'd bettah talk with me
'bout ...

**LILY:** Then you know!

**JIMMIE SUE:** I can take care of ...

**LILY:** Her daddy an' me didn't wanna put you in thet
kinda danger ... Nor Madleen neither.

**JIMMIE SUE:** You s'pose I could write to her?

**AUNT LILY:** If you can write it she can read it. But don't
write no sweet stuff. She past thet now.

**JIMMIE SUE:** But where would I send a lettah?

**LILY:** I got the address right here in my apron pocket. It's
my sistah's place in Richmon'.

*Lilly hands a paper to Jimmie Sue, who unfurls it and
looks at the address almost as though he's looking at
Madeleen's picture.*

*They stand in silence; Jimmie Sue looks at the letter and
Aunt Lily looks at him.*

SLOW FADE OUT.


*INT. BENNETT FARM - BARN LOFT*


*Jimmie Sue writes with a pencil in a school tablet.*

*Several sheets of wadded up paper are on floor next to
Jimmie Sue.*

*He starts several times to write. He puts the pencil point to
his tongue to make the lettering darker.*

*Jimmie Sue wads up another sheet of paper before he slowly
writes again. He WRITES, "Dear Madeleen, I miss you.
Love, Jimmie Sue." He carefully folds it.*

FADE OUT.


*EXT. BENNETT FARM - MAILBOX*


*Jimmie Sue paces nervously waiting for Mailman, who
arrives after a short wait.*

**MAILMAN:** I have a letter here fer James Lafayette
Bennett, but I have no notion who thet might be.

*Jimmie Sue snatches letter, thanks mailman and runs.*

FADE OUT.

*INT. BENNETT FARM - BARN LOFT*

*Jimmie Sue opens the letter and reads aloud.*

**JIMMIE SUE:** Dear Jimmie Sue, Taking pen and paper in hand I begin this epistle to you. I miss you too. I would have written sooner, but lots of things be happening. I'm working for a white family now. They have a boy who looks a lot like you, but he is not like you at all by what he says and what he does. He scares me some times. I think of the times you and I had together. Tell your folks hello for me and especially say hello to Rosie. I hope she and Ruthie still get a chance to play together. Goodbye in the name of the Lord. Madeleen

FADE OUT.

*INT. DINING ROOM OF THE FAMILY WHERE MADELEEN IS SERVING BREAKFAST.*

*MR. and MRS. TAYLOR (in their 50s) and PERCY (17) their son*
*As Madeleen serves biscuits to Percy, he teases her by untying her apron.*

**MRS. TAYLOR:** Now Percy, leave the colored girl alone.

**PERCY:** Aw, Mother, I'm just a funnin'.

**MRS. TAYLOR:** I know, Honey, but you know the colored help could so easily get ideas that you're innerested in 'em. I mean in a more social way than just havin' a little innocent fun.

*They ignore Madeleen's presence. When she passes by Percy again, he pinches her on her buttocks.*

**MADELEEN:** Ouch!

*As she grabs her bottom.*

**MR. TAYLOR:** (laughing uproariously) Percy, you better be careful or you'll have her followin' you to bed like a little black puppy dog. (laughing at his own witticism)

**MADELEEN:** Mrs. Taylor, may I go to my room and come back a little later to clean up an' wash the dishes?

**MRS. TAYLOR:** Are you sick or somethin? ... (no answer) I suppose that'll be ok. But don't be spreadin' around no sickness.

*Madeleen leaves and goes to her room which is right off the kitchen pantry.*

*She sits at a little table and picks up a pencil and paper and begins to write, "Dear Jimmy Sue ..."*

SOUND OF HER DOOR OPEN AND SLAM SHUT

*We hear Percy's voice but do not see him.*

**PERCY:** How many times do I hafta tell you to undress?

*MADELEEN sits frozen in fear.*

**PERCY:** Do I hafta do ever'thing?

BLACKOUT.


*BEGIN MONTAGE*


*Several cameo scenes of Jimmie Sue waiting by the mailbox over several months.*

Super: MONTHS LATER


*EXT. BENNETT FARM - HOME - FRONT - DAY*


*Cletus walks onto Bennett's porch and knocks.*

*Thelma Lou points him toward Jimmie Sue out at the barn.*

*Jimmie Sue meets up with Cletus in the yard.*

**JIMMIE SUE:** Cletus, hit's been a month of Sundays since you been ovah hyar. Hev you come with some news?

**CLETUS:** Yeah ...

**JIMMIE SUE:** Is Madeleen comin' home?

**CLETUS:** Thet's what I come to tell 'bout ...

**JIMMIE SUE:** Well, thet's real good news ...

**CLETUS:** Thet's not the whole story, whut I come to tell you. Mamma wanted me to special tell you.

**JIMMIE SUE:** Cletus, thet be wonderful good news, but why you look so downtrodden?

**CLETUS:** When I say she be comin' home, I mean to say Madeleen's body be comin' home.

**JIMMIE SUE:** What'cha mean by thet?

**CLETUS:** Jimmie Sue, Madeleen died! Mamma wanted you to know right away, 'cause she felt she gave you some wrongful hope 'bout Madeleen.

*(An awkward pause between the two)*
*Jimmie Sue chokes up, and holds back tears.*

**CLETUS:** Mamma say the funeral be this Saturday an' she' want particular for you to come.

*Jimmie Sue, in shock, answers.*

**JIMMIE SUE:** What she die of, Cletus?

*Cletus is uncomfortable, not wanting to share any more details, but answers after a pause.*

**CLETUS:** She be dyin' of childbearin'.

**JIMMIE SUE:** What? I didn't even know she's married, Cletus.

*Jimmie Sue gets angry.*

**JIMMIE SUE:** Why didn't you all tell me she was married?!

**CLETUS:** Thet be the trouble, Jimmie Sue.

*Jimmie Sue calms down.*

**JIMMIE SUE:** Oh, I see. But they still gonna bury her in the church graveyard?

**CLETUS:** Yeah. Preacher Peeples say we can't turn nobody away what needs a final restin' place. But we'd have to bury her way back at the back corner right next to the woods an' acrost the fence from the white folks' graveyard. You welcome to come to the funeral, Jimmie Sue, if you likes. They won't be many folks there, 'cause we ain't tellin' many folks.

**JIMMIE SUE:** What 'bout the baby?

**CLETUS:** He died too. His name be Moses.

FADE TO:
BEGIN FLASHBACK

## INT. CHURCH - REVIVAL MEETING

*Jimmie Sue sits near Madeleen.*
*She gets up to sing while CHURCH GOERS sway back and forth to piano music and hymns.*

**MADELEEN:** (sings) Shall we gather at the river. Where bright angel feet have trod. With its crystal tide forever, Floating by the Throne of God? Yes, we'll gather at the river ...

*The CHURCH GOERS sway and hold up their hands, sway to her voice.*

FADE OUT.


## EXT. SWIMMING HOLE – DAY

*Jimmie Sue and Madeleen are in the water. They splash each other.*

**MADELEEN:** Yo! White Boy!

*A snake slithers by them.*
*Madeleen, startled, paddles off and screams.*

**MADELEEN:** Ahhh! The Devil's chasin' me!

*The snake slithers under the diving rock where it came from.*
*Jimmie Sue watches helplessly.*

END FLASHBACK
FADE TO:


## EXT. BENNETT'S HOME - FRONT - DAY

*Cletus shuffles back and forth, uncomfortable.*
*Jimmie Sue collects himself, starts to shake Cletus's hand, stops suddenly, pulls back.*

**JIMMIE SUE:** Much obliged, Cletus. I 'preciate you comin' ovah hyar to tell me. Tell yoah mama and daddy I'm real sorry 'bout Madeleen, an' I be grievin' too.

*Jimmie Sue holds back his tears, but is shaken.*

*There is an uncomfortable silence for a moment between Jimmie Sue and Cletus.*

*Jimmie Sue moves deliberately toward Cletus, startles him as Jimmie Sue takes him into his arms, embraces him like a long lost brother. Jimmie Sue and Cletus sob, and console each other.*

FADE OUT.

*EXT. BLACK CHURCH - FRONT STEPS - DAY*

*MOURNERS walk into the church, dressed in black with WOMEN's heads covered in black veils. All cry and walk in somberly.*

*Jimmie Sue is the last one to go in, the only white person attending the funeral.*

CUT TO:

*INT. CHURCH - DAY*

*The church is dressed with some wild flowers.*

*Jimmie Sue stands at the back door, and watches from behind.*

*He walks to the back pew.*

*Lily Hilton waves Jimmie Sue down to the front where the casket is. He shakes his head, and just sits at his seat.*

*The casket with Madeleen and the baby is in front of the pulpit. PIANO PLAYER sits and plays SOMBER SPIRITUAL MUSIC.*

*MOURNERS weep and softly chatter among themselves.*

*All the MOURNERS take their turn to line up and view Madeleen in her open casket. They all cry and give last good-byes softly or silently to her.*

*Jimmie Sue has his turn to say his goodbye. He looks down at Madeleen and the baby.*

*Madeleen's face is more mature, a face with an expression of peace, calm and acceptance on it.*

*She holds something in her right hand. He looks down at*

*her hand closer. It holds a red ear of corn - that same ear of corn he'd sent to her by Aunt Lily. Jimmie Sue looks over at Aunt Lily. She nods to him.*

*He turns back and views Madeleen.*

FADE TO:<br>BEGIN FLASHBACK

### INT. HILTON'S HOME — LIVING ROOM — DAY

*Jimmie Sue wanders under the mistletoe, next to Madeleen. He turns to the others, who admire the mistletoe.*

*Madeleen startles him, reaches up, and with her hands on his arms, kisses him on the cheek.*

*Everyone gasps, watch Jimmie Sue and Madeleen with mixed emotions.*

END FLASHBACK<br>FADE TO:

### INT. CHURCH – DAY - CONTINUOUS

*Jimmie Sue stands over Madeleen's casket. He gently kisses his own fingers and reaches towards her cold full lips and touches her mouth. He turns around and notices the baby.*

**JIMMIE SUE:** Was this the baby the hateful ways of the world have denied me an' Madeleen?

*The MOURNERS walk out after they view Madeleen and her baby.*

*Jimmie Sue watches all leave and leaves after them.*

FADE OUT.

### EXT. CEMETERY — DAY

*MOURNERS stand in the Colored Folks' side of the cemetery.*

*Jimmie Sue walks to the white cemetery where he watches from there. He leans across the rusty iron fence from where they'd dug the grave for Madeleen.*

*Jimmie Sue sits on an old tree stump, he listens to the singing Mourners, prayers and blessings.*

*Later ...*

TIME GOES BY.

*Everyone leaves the cemetery while Jimmie Sue watches. He puts his head down to pray.*

*Aunt Lily walks up the hill to the front gate of the colored's cemetery over to the white folks' cemetery gate, and down the hill. She walks toward Jimmie Sue. He doesn't notice her coming over to him. She startles him.*

**LILY:** Jimmie Sue. I's so sorry. I knowed how you cared for her. An' you must know how she cared for you ... I s'pose you prob'ly want your grave dug right ovah hyar.

*Lily points to a spot.*

**JIMMIE SUE:** Why you think thet, Miz' Hilton?

*She cocks her head, smiles.*

**JIMMIE SUE:** Yes, Aunt Lily, I thought I'd be put to rest right hyar, planted by this ol' oak stump. Maybe if they plant me real close here, then I be rooted by this tree an' in this mountain fer sure.

*Both Lily and Jimmie Sue chuckle.*

**JIMMIE SUE:** Bye, Aunt Lily.

**LILY:** Bye, Jimmie Sue. Come by an' visit us soon, ya' hear?

*Jimmie Sue nods okay. They smile at each other.*

*Lily turns and walks through the "white folks" cemetery. He watches her walk away, smiles. As he watches, Lily stops at each white folk's marker. She says a silent prayer to each one as she heads away.*

FADE OUT.

*EXT. CEMETERY — NEXT DAY*

*Jimmie Sue sits on the tree stump, looks through the rusty fence at a small fieldstone, Madeleen's gravestone.*

## FOLLOWING DAY - CONTINUOUS

*Jimmie Sue again sits on the old tree stump honoring
Madeleen.*
*Insert: Madeleen's marker*
*On the stone: MADELEEN HILTON, written in
black paint, made from tobacco tar.*
*Insert: Baby's marker*
*This small stone rests beside Madeleen's stone with just the
name MOSES inscribed on it with tobacco tar.*
FADE OUT.

## EXT. CEMETERY — DAY

*Super: Fifteen Years later*
*Jimmie Sue sits on the old tree stump, looks at the two
graves. He kisses his fingers and gently blows the kiss toward
Madeleen's gravestone. Jimmie Sue turns to walk away. Takes
a few steps. He stops, digs into his pocket and pulls out
mistletoe. He walks to Madeleen's grave. He gently lays the
mistletoe on Madeleen's gravestone.*
**JIMMIE SUE:** Merry Christmas, Madeleen.
*He heads home.*
FADE TO:
BEGIN MONTAGE

*SEVERAL CAMEO SCENES OF JIMMIE SUE
COMING TO THE WHITE CEMETERY AND
SITTING FOR AWHILE AS HE LOOKS OVER AT
MADELEEN'S GRAVE. IN EACH SCENE HE
SHOULD BE GETTING A LITTLE OLDER AS
THE YEARS PASS BY.*
END MONTAGE
FADE OUT.

## EXT. WHITES' CHURCH

*Super: 1949*

*A HEARSE is parked in front of the open church door.*

*A NEW GRAVE has been dug right across the fence from Madeleen's grave in the colored cemetary.*

*Inside the church we can hear AMAZING GRACE being sung, led by a preacher with a BOOMING VOICE. The SONG IS LINED, which means the PREACHER recites a line and then the assembled congregation sings the line:*

**PREACHER:** Amazing Grace how sweet the sound.

**CONGREGATION:** (singing) Amazing Grace how sweet the sound.

**PREACHER:** That saved a wretch like me.

**CONGREGATION:** (singing) That saved a wretch like me.

**PREACHER:** I once was lost but now am found.

**CONGREGATION:** (singing): I once was lost but now am found.

**PREACHER:** Was blind but now I see.

**CONGREGATION:** (singing) Was blind but now I see.

*The song can continue as long as desired, but no one should be seen before the whole scene fades out.*

FADE OUT.

END — STORY FLASHBACK

*EXT. CEMETERY - VIRGINIA - HIGH COUNTRY*

*FRANK (AGE 14) and NOEL (AGE 18) BENNETT, Grand-nephews of Jimmie Sue, stand downhill from Jimmie Sue's headstone.*

*A LONG SHOT FROM THEIR POV, ENCOMPASSING HEADSTONE IN FOREGROUND, GATE BETWEEN CEMETERIES TO THE LEFT AND CHURCH UP THE HILL.*

**NOEL:** Well Frank, Uncle Jimmie Sue's headstone is in place. It looks real nice here across the gate from Madeleen's gravestone.

*They walk up the hill to look across the gate into the coloreds' cemetery.*

**FRANK:** (looks at Madeleen's memorial stone.)

*That's a real nice headstone. I thought the Hiltons were sharecroppers.*

**NOEL:** They were.

**FRANK:** How could they afford a real headstone?

**NOEL:** Oh, Uncle Jimmie Sue put that stone there, years ago by saving up money from odd jobs.

*They look at her headstone.*

*CAMERA CLOSEUP OF HER HEADSTONE AND THAT OF THE BABY'S.*

**NOEL:** (reading) Madeleen Hilton, born September 29, 1860, died March 15, 1877 ... Moses born and died on the same day, March 15, 1877 ... They never gave him a last name.

**FRANK:** I guess Moses didn't need a last name.

*CAMERA FOCUSES ON THE BABY'S HEADSTONE. "SUFFER THE LITTLE CHILDREN."*

*CAMERA FOCUSES ON MADELEEN'S HEADSTONE INSCRIPTION, "SHALL WE GATHER AT THE RIVER." AND HER DATES.*

**FRANK:** Was it that long ago that she died?

**NOEL:** Yeah, Uncle Jimmie Sue lived moah than seventy years after that. But he tended their graves till he got so feeble, he couldn't walk up here any longer.

**FRANK:** (as they look at Jimmie Sue's memorial stone.) What about Uncle Jimmie Sue's headstone? It must have cost quite a bit.

**NOEL:** You know, most of the kinfolks up here didn't ordinarily carry life insurance ... didn't believe in it. Except for burial insurance! Uncle Jimmie Sue wanted to make sure he was put away proper.

**FRANK:** "James Lafayette Bennett, born December 24,1860, died March 15, 1949." I see that he added to Madeleen's question: "Where bright angel feet have trod."

**NOEL:** They seemed to think a lot about angels.

*CAMERA SHOTS OF ANGELS ETCHED INTO EACH OF THE THREE HEADSTONES AND THE DOUBLE LATCH WROUGHT IRON ANGELS ON THE DOUBLE GATE, WHICH IS OPENED SLIGHTLY.*

*One of those angels is painted white and the other black, though both are badly weathered and their colors barely noticeable.*

**NOEL:** When snow storms would come they loved making snow angels with their little sisters.

**FRANK:** Well now that Uncle Jimmie Sue's headstone is in place, there won't be much need to come up the mountain any more.

**NOEL:** I'll be back for sure - particularly when I need to meditate on the meaning of "Love that passeth understanding."

*RAIN BEGINS to fall.*

*Frank and Noel open their umbrellas and watch the rain trickle off the graves and commingle under the gate then begin to flow downhill.*

CAMEOS OF EARLIER SCENES ARE SHOWN.


**EPILOGUE (V.O.):** The rain falling on the sarvisberry bloom

Also nurtures the roots of the oak. The commingling water

Gurgles happily down the hillside

Toward an old swimming hole,

Where rejoicing souls

Were once refreshed

In the spiritual baptism

Of childhood romps.

FADE TO BLACK.

THE END

# Part II: Multi Acts

# 'Twixt Heaven and Hell

In 1980 I was invited by Davis and Elkins College in West Virginia to direct Inherit the Wind. While still serving as Adjunct Professor at the college, I was asked to write a script with a theme pertinent to the current time and place of the college.

Only a few years prior I had researched on a Fulbright Grant, the theatre training in India. My dissertation focused a great deal on the clash between classical training, which was described in detail in the Natyasastra, and current European training, usually ascribed as Stanislavski Method.

The culture of the Appalachians at that time was experiencing a similar clash, as the young mountain men returned from World War II with quite different values than those held by their parents and grandparents. Thus the dramatic setting of 'Twixt Heaven and Hell. Michael Pedretti directed the premiere production.

Brother Jarrell didn't understand why his grandson, Moyer, couldn't or wouldn't, accept the way of life, he had experienced before his European experience in war and otherwise. Without some significant compromise mutual annihilation is inevitable.

# 'TWIXT HEAVEN AND HELL

*by E. Reid Gilbert*

Cast

| | |
|---|---|
| **BROTHER JARRELL** | .grandfather |
| **MOYER JARRELL** | ....grandson recently discharged from the army |
| **LIZZIE JARRELL** | ....grandmother |
| **SAL PICKINS** | ........14-year-old girl |
| **BROTHER WHITE** | ...a preacher |
| **SISTER WHITE** | ......the preacher's wife |
| **BROTHER REECE** | ...a preacher |
| **SISTER REECE** | ......the preacher's wife |
| **BROTHER HIATT** | ....a preacher |
| **SISTER HIATT** | ......the preacher's wife |
| **GLENN CONWAY** | ....the Jarrell's neighbor |
| **GILL DALTON** | .......Moyer's friend |
| **NED WALKER** | ......bootlegger |
| **NATE** | ...............one of the boys |
| **TOM** | ................one of the boys |
| **EZRA** | ...............one of the boys often bullied |
| **POL** | ................a friend of Sals |
| **BETZ** | ..............a friend of Sals |
| **GRACE** | ..............a friend of Sals |
| **EIGHT CHILDREN** | ..neighborhood flock |
| **PEOPLE IN CHURCH** | parishioners |

## Note from the playwright:

I have attempted in this script to capture some of the authentic speech patterns of the Southern Appalachians. To aid any directors I would say that the value of the dialect will best be fulfilled by the rhythm of the phrasing rather than by strained pronunciation. Despite the realism of the dialect and presumably the costuming, the staging is envisioned as open platforms with acting areas and levels. The church house should be a platform about a foot above the church yard level. The mountain could be a series of platforms behind and to one side of the church and Brother Jarrell's house, represented by a small platform. All three specific acting areas would share a common performing area — downstage center.

Although there is a great deal of music in the play, it is not intended to be a musical. It is simply impossible to write of the Southern Appalachians without including music which pervades its culture. Therefore operatic voices are not of primary concern, but the singing should capture the clarity of the tone of the Appalachian folk singer.

However Moyer's singing should have the nasality of the "hillbilly" Grand Ol' Opry voice.

These general suggestions are not meant to suppress in any way the dramatic imagination of the director or actors, as I value highly their creative input into this story. In fact, I am willing to make revisions of the script at the reasoned suggestion of an astute director.

**NARRATOR:**

> There is a place twixt heaven and hell,
> Which is the burden of my tale.
> Folks fer years had lived in the hills;
> They lived by the church and lived with the stills.
> Many things changed, but some of them ain't
> Some folks have too, but some of them can't.

## ACT I

### SCENE 1: CHURCH HOUSE AT NIGHT IN LATE JULY, 1945.

*A thunderstorm is raging outside. The house lights dim as the storm sounds begin and increase. Moyer enters with an army duffel bag and dressed in a soldier's uniform. We see him only when the lightning flashes as he makes his way toward the church, walking quite confidently, in fact somewhat cockily, during and right after a flash of lightning. (The clothes he is wearing and those in the duffel bag are gradually given to the children during the course of the play.) Moyer is seen at the back We see a barn lantern carried by Brother Jarrell coming from a distance. He enters the church and shakes the rainwater off the old raincoat he has over his head. He at first does not see Moyer, who has been watching the approaching light.*

**JARRELL:** Beejeebers. Who in tarnation? Moyer! You nearly skeered the liver outen me. I thought shorely it was the old boy hisself.

**MOYER:** Hello Papa. Now I don't understand why you would think the devil would be standing around in a place like this. Why if anything I would imagine that you would have right off expected anyone unusual here to be the Lord himself.

*Moyer's speech pattern at the beginning has obviously been influenced by the outside. He reverts to the mountain dialect as the play proceeds.*

**JARRELL:** Are we gonna start right in a-arguin' about them things which I consider sacred and them which you had just as soon fergit about. You can think what you think and say what you say but you're not gonna make light of the Lord-not in this place nor in my hearin'. (Silence) Now that we got some things straightened out maybe we can be civil with each other....at least as long as we gotta share this haven of rest midst the 8torms of life.

**MOYER:** Papa you've started preachin' now....and there ain't nobody here but just the two of us. Preachin' ain't assigned until tomorrow, cause I understand that then is Association Day.

**JARRELL:** Yeah. 'sociation Day tomorrow. Hit shore is good having you home for such an occasion. There's likely to be lots of folks here we ain' t seen fer a spell.

**MOYER:** I was hopin' I'd get my discharge to get home in time. I been wonderin' what altl them ol' boys have been up to.

**JARRELL:** I guess hit don't never mind what they been up to ... Hit matters what they gonna be up to.

**MOYER:** What you mean by that Papa?

**JARRELL:** Oh I reckin hit don't differ none. Hit ain't in my hands to do nothin' and ain't in my mind to say nothin'. (obviously changing the subject) What I wanta know is how · you got here so quick. I thought from your letter you was gonna get into Patrick later on in the evenin', so I was sure I had plenty of time to get there and fetch you on back home.

**MOYER:** Well, the bus was early, so I just started in walkin', 'cause I knew I'd meet you somewhere along the way. And then when the storm came up I just temporarily ducked in here to keep from gettin' drenched.

**JARRELL:** What I don't understand is how you got in here ... the church house been' locked an' all.

**MOYER:** Yeah I wondered about that. I don't ever remember anyone lockin' the church before.

**JARRELL:** Like I been a'sayin'. Some things 're different 'round here now...real different. You can't trust folks nowadays to treat the church house like the house of the Lord ... You still ain't told me how ...

**MOYER:** Oh I jimmied the back door.In the army I was assigned to demolition you know so I've had experience at undoin' things.

**JARRELL:** Son, don't go to undoin' things around here.

**MOYER:** Aw don't worry Papa. I just undo those things that're about to explode.

**JARRELL:** Well the church weren't about to explode.

**MOYER:** (chuckles) Yeah, I see what you mean. (pause while listening to the rain and thunder) Damn, if that thunder don't sound just like all them German shells bustin' all around us there in France.

**JARRELL:** You musta heard a lot and seen a-lot off there in that foreign land.

**MOYER:** Papa you wouldn't hardly believe all those people, the cities, the planes, the tanks, the ... everything. (pause, as he relives some of those scenes). But there's one particular thing what sticks in my craw. (pause) Hit was that god ... awful sergeant.

**JARRELL:** Well, I allus heard that sergeants was supposed to be mean and tough.

**MOYER:** Oh hit weren't just that. I'm sure I peeled more taters and cleaned more latrines.

**JARRELL:** La ... what.

**MOYER:** La-trines ... but you wouldn't understand ... But they didn't give awards fer that sort of thing. I did get a ribbon fer shootin'; they called it RIFLE MARKS-MAN-SHIP. There won't nobody in the whole outfit what could outshoot me. But that turkey-necked sergeant didn't keer fer that atall. He thought I was too dumb even shoot a rifle straight.

**JARRELL:** That don't seem like ...

**MOYER:** When I first got assigned to my unit I hadn't hardly opened my mouth before that scrawney bastard was callin' me "the Hillbilly."And ever'time he wanted a quick laff from the boys he'd just say somethin' to or about "The Hillbilly"... Hit's a good thing the Germans got him or I would shot him a new one my own self.

JARRELL: Moyer, sometimes you care too much (Moyer tries to protest) and sometimes you aim too high.(Moyer again tries to interrupt). Here in this life we dwell somewhere 'twixt heaven and hell. (Moyer tries to counter, but Jarrell counters himself). I know the church concerns hitslf about carin'. That's true enough, but there's only so much we can do and the rest is up to God A'Mighty.

MOYER: Papa you don't need to tell me no more about heaven and hell, 'cause I been through enough hell fer one lifetime and now I aim fer a little bit of heaven, an' I can't hardly wait to git started.

JARRELL: (sharply) Moyer! I don't like the tone of your voice. (changing the subject)

MOYER: (while Jarrell continues to stare) Hit's a real gully washer this time.

JARRELL: (after a short silence) Yep, sure is.

MOYER: (after another silence and a thunder clap) Papa, you know hit's all always been a mystery to me why folks hereabouts git so all fired skittish when summer storms come up.

JARRELL: Only when they're here at church.

MOYER: Yeah.That's even wierder somehow.You'd think if folks really believed in the providence of the Lord they'd go runnin' to the church instead of away from it when a storm come up.I mean you're all the time singing about firm foundations, refuge from the storm and such like as that.Amazing Grace ain't so amazing if you're running from the church house just 'cause a storm's abrewing.

JARRELL: (a little peevish) That's enough of that kinda talk, Moyer. It ain't becoming to blaspheme about the Lord's ways right here in the church house.

MOYER: But now just give it some thought, Papa. Don't hit seem like ...

JARRELL: (greatly agitated) Hit mostly seems that you've fergotten yourraisin'. (short pause) You know well's I do why folks get scared of these storms.

**MOYER:** Yeh, I know, but you ain't told that to me in a long time. I don't recollect the details. I know hit's got something to do with old man White's grandaddy getting lightning struck during services.

**JARRELL:** (looking across the church yard as if to visualize the whole scene again) He was setting right by this very window. He'd brung in a straight chair from out in the yard when the dinner was over and set it right by the window where he could see the young'uns playing, watch the rains a-comin' and listen to the preaching and singing all at the same time.

*Moyer has hunkered down by the window to listen to this tale of his grandfather's.*

**JARRELL:** He was awful short of breath, too. He was getting on toward ninety and would get these awful wheezing spells. And I reckon he figured he could breathe better next to the window here. The air being so close and all, the way it does before such a storm.

**MOYER:** Did you know him, Papa?

**JARRELL:** Not too well. (pause) Acourse ever'one started runnin'.

**MOYER:** Did you run, Papa?

**JARRELL:** No. I figured even then as only a small boy, if hit's the Lord's will to take me, no amount of running will do any good.

**MOYER:** It sure appears that those other folks didn't understand that. Maybe they think they can thwart the will of the Lord by runnin' away from his storms.

**JARRELL:** You got no call to go a-faultin' the other folks that way. They got their own reasons.

**MOYER:** Papa, do you really believe all that stuff about predestination and all?

**JARRELL:** I got no reason to disbelieve it.

**MOYER:** What is gonna be is gonna be?

**JARRELL:** What is to be, will be, whether it ever happens or not.

**MOYER:** There's something awful funny about that.

JARRELL: Ain't nothin' funny but a contrary head that can't believe and a contentious heart that won't believe.

MOYER: Come on Papa, let's git on in home. I bet Gramma's already fell asleep in her rockin' chair.

JARRELL: Yeah. Hit does look like the storm has let up a little. And tomorrow will soon be upon us.

*Jarrell exits.*

MOYER: Hey Papa there's somethin' here I wanta show you. Somethin' I brought back fer Gramma.

*He reaches into duffle bag and pulls out garishly colored pillowcase with "mother" embroidered across it.*

JARRELL: But thet says ...

MOYER: I know it says "Mother" but Gramma's been my only mamma for a long time. And you ... Come on now whatta you think of it?

JARRELL: Well. I must say ... hit shore is colorful. I know she'll be right pleased with it. Just knowin' thet you were thinkin' about her an' about home while you wuz there in them foxholes. She'll be tickled to death with it.

BLACKOUT.

*SCENE 2: A SUMMER SUNDAY AFTERNOON. AN OLD TIME BAPTIST CHURCH ON ASSOCIATION DAY.*

*The preachers and congregation of older people are inside the church. The younger people and children are outside the church. The preachers are quite informal as they discuss aloud who will preach next. The boys outside can be heard and seen as they take occasional nips from a half-gallon fruit jar and as they make comments about the girls who walk by time after time in order to catch the boys' eyes.*

*Children on jump board before scene begins. Fighting over whose turn it is. During scene, the children have to abandon jump board because of the young folks and old folks getting in their way. The children keep trying to jump on the board during the scene and when they are not doing this they are running into the church to nag their mammas for some goodies or running outside giggling at the young folks.*

*The congregation is singing as the scene opens:*

On Jordan's stormy banks I stand, And cast a wistful eye
  To Canaan's fair and happy land, Where my possessions
  lie.
I am bound for the promised land I am bound for the
  promised land, O who will come and go with me?
I am bound for the promised land.

The following dialogue while the boys are drinking:

**BROTHER JARRELL:** Brother Reece, how's folks up
yore way?

**BROTHER REECE:** Oh, fair to middlin'. No cause to
complain, I reckon.

**BROTHER JARRELL:** How about folks up yore neck of
the branch, Brother Hiatt?

**BROTHER HIATT:** The Lord's been awful good to us,
Brother Jarrell. Howsomever, we might remember Sister
Wilson in our prayer this morning.

**BROTHER JARRELL:** How's ever'thing down toward
Little Gap, Brother White? I heard you had a real gully
washer last week.

**BROTHER WH!TE:** A little hail with it too, but them
terbaccer plants shore needed the rain. How're yore
folks? They say that Moyer come back from the war
today.

**BROTHER JARRELL:** Yep, the Lord sent him back
home. I hope he can stay this time. I just don't feel right
bout him traipsin' all over the world and creation.

  *Takes a drink of water from pitcher and passes it to the
  other preachers.*

  *The following dialogue, takes place OUTSIDE, while the
  preachers are drinking:*

**TOM:** Heidy, Moyer. I didn't know you was back.

**MOYER:** Yep, got back from France, yesterday.

**EZ:** I thought you was in Paris. Nate said you was in Paris.

**NATE:** Shut Up, Ez, if you ain't got no better sense than
that. Paris is in France. You oughta know that ... Tell us,
Moyer, tell us what was ever'thing like?

**MOYER:** Well now, the war, itself was like Hell on earth.

**TOM:** We know 'bout the war. We listened to the radio ever' night. But you weren't fightn' all the time.

**MOYER:** It was when we were in Paris that evah'thing was different.

**EZ:** How you mean? Diffurnt?

**MOYER:** It was like the state fair every night. But that happened only after the war was nearly over. Then It was lit up all the time, and the nighttime just as bright as day.

**TOM:** But what about the girls?

**MOYER:** You ain't never seen so many girls in yore life, they was a dime a dozen.

**EZRA:** Did you have to pay fer 'em?

**MOYER:** No, Ez, not exactly. They was cheap like I tole you but you never really paid fer 'em, you just kept puttin' up down payments on 'em.

*All laugh and continue to talk inaudibly, while INSIDE:*

**BROTHER JARRELL:** Brother Hiatt, do you feel called upon by the Lord to say a few words this afternoon?

**BROTHER HIATT:** Brother Jarrell, I don't feel led right at this time to speak. Maybe Brother Reece could lead us in a word of prayer.

*A boy whistles.*

**BROTHER JARRELL:** Brother Reece, could we commence this afternoon by calling upon the Lord?

*OUTSIDE the girls giggle*

**BROTHER REECE:** (building in tempo, rhythm and pitch)

A'mighty God

Thou who set the sun on its course Thou who put the stars in their places

Thou who hast ordained thy children to heed thy voice

We call upon thee from the mire of our sins

We look to thee from the sin in our hearts

But we know that those whom thou hast called

Are saved from their sin,

Because thou has predestined it

And we have been baptized with the Holy Ghost.
A'mighty God, hear our prayer
A'mighty God, Sister Wilson is lying on her bed of pain
A'mighty God, Brother Jenkins is turning to the devil
   instead of to thee
A'mighty God, we know that this old mortal body is
   weak
But Oh Lord
We know that the spirit is strong
Don't forget us
O God in our time of need
Don't neglect us
When the devil begins to call us
Don't forget us
O God when the way seems dark
And the burden of this old world
Seems too heavy for our shoulders to bear.
And when, 0 God,
Thou hast finished with us
In this mortal life
Take us to thee
Take us to our loved ones
Take us to see Jesus, face to face.
Bless all these brethren and sisters, 0 God.
Bless Brother Jarrell and his good wife.
Bless Brother White and his family.
Bless Brother Hiatt this afternoon ·
And lay the burden of thy message upon his heart
That we may be blessed with thy word during this
   association meetin'.
In the name of Jesus we pray.
   Amen.

*During this prayer, the other preachers are amening, one of
the women squeals with the spirit occasionally, the boys outside
have been sampling a fruitjar of moonshine. At the end, all
the preachers amen together.*

*The two (INSIDE and OUTSIDE) are performed
simultaneously. The light and sound designs and the actors*

*must lead the audience to the appropriate scene.*

*Just as the boys let out a loud whoop, the preachers confer together inaudibly for a while.*

**TOM:** Moyer, you 'member Ned Walker?

**MOYER:** Oh yeh. Is he back from the reformatory yet?

**NATE:** Be back two weeks ago next Sattidy.

**EZRA:** But the reformatory never re-formed him none.

**MOYER:** What's he up to now?

**NATE:** He's workin' in a cafe down to Patrick, an' doin' a little extra business on the side.

**MOYER:** Maybe I'll go down some day this week an' drop in on him.

*Boys talk excitely but inaudibly to others*

**BROTHER HIATT:** Brother White, has the Lord laid on your heart a scripture for this afternoon? Why don't you go ahead and preach, and maybe the spirit will speak to me later.

*The audience is guided back to the boys, as the girls are sashaying around.*

*One of the girls walks by Moyer.*

**MOYER:** Hot dingies'. Look at that one.

*The girls go running and the boys give chase.*

*Meanwhile INSIDE:*

**BROTHER WHITE:** I'd like to say that it is awful good to see so many of our friends here. Some from down near Spray. The good folks from Rocky Creek Church are here. And the dinner which we just enjoyed. We ought to thank the sisters of the meetin'. A good dinner together always sets things right. I want to take for my text Romans 8:29: "For those whom he foreknew he also predestined to be conformed to the image of his Son, in order that he might be the firstborn among many brethren."

*The boys push Moyer after girl who vanishes and Moyer returns.*

**BROTHER WHITE:** I was talking with a preacher from another church last week over at Patrick And he was

saying that he believed in a mighty God and a mighty
devil but that man could choose between the two. What
he was really saying was that he believed in a mighty God
and a mighty devil, but an almighty man who could
choose. If God is Almighty, He is Almighty.

*Boys drink and talk during following lines:*

**BROTHER WHITE:** (delivered in a strongly rhythmic
pattern that drops decidedly at the end of each line with
the last line dropping back into a conversational tone)

> "For those whom he foreknew he predestined"
> For God A'mighty did the choosing
> Some he chose for heaven
> And some he chose for hell
> And what a glorious time that will be
> When we who he chose for heaven
> Get to that promised land
> The promised land that is filled with milk and honey
> The promised land where the streets are paved with
>   gold
> That promised land where there'll be no more tears
> That promised land where there'll be no more sorrow
> That promised land where we'll meet our Savoir face
>   to face
> Where God A'mighty himself will say
> "Well done, thou good and faithful servant."

*The following passage should begin in a low conversational
tone and build in rhythm just as the prior passage.*

*Three girls go by arm in arm; boys mock them by doing
same. Boys talk and laugh during next lines.*

**BROTHER WHITE:**

> I had a dream the other night
> Two weeks ago last Friday.
> I was standing on the mountain
> And the sun was about to come up
> I heard: a low moaning sound toward the east
> As it got louder it was singing I heard

And a young man was leading the singing
When the sun came up
I could see that it was a funeral march coming right
   up the mountain toward the church
When they come closer I stopped the young man and
   said
"Young man, whose funeral is it?"
He turned to me
   And I could see his eyes swollen with tears of sorrow
And he said, "Brother White, don't you know?
Ain't you heard?"
"Heard what," I says.
"I killed him ... I killed him."
I still couldn't make out who the young man was.
He looked awful familiar.
But he had a distressed countenance somehow.
So I opened the casket lid and there laid Brother Jarrell.
Brother Jarrell was in that casket.
Brother Jarrell had gone to his reward.
But what will we do
What will we do when
Brother Jarrell is gone?
   *More girls come by and boys make remarks at them.*

**BROTHER WHITE:**

When Brother Jarrell goes to his predestination.
What will we do?
He's walked with us
He's talked with us
He's lifted us up when we were near falling.
He's kept us going when we felt like stopping.
He's been preaching longer than most of us have been
   breathing.
He's been singing longer than any of us have been
   preaching.
But he won't always be here to listen to our troubles.
And then we will be on our own
We will stand before God without the support of

Brother Jarrell
For Brother Jarrell will be gone.
Brother Jarrell will be in his father's house of many
   mansions.
   *Girls walk closer to boys, who try to flip up their skirts,*
*but girls jump teasingly away.*
**BROTHER WHITE:** I remember years ago just as if it
was yesterday.
I had been under godly conviction for some time but I
was young, and I was troubled. So I talked with Brother
Jarrell And I said,
   "Brother Jarrell, I've been under conviction for nearly
      a year now.
   And I want to be baptized.
   I want to join the church.
   I want to preach.
   But I'm not even twenty-five."
   Brother Jarrell said, "George,
   Most young men have to sow their wild oats;
   Most young men have to go to their frolics;
Most have to chase their girls;
Most have to taste their liquor.
But God A'mighty has a work for you.
And you must be about it.
If anyone is contentious about it,
You have to remember that
You must stand approved before God
And God only."
It's remembrances like that
That we all have of Brother Jarrell
But we know that someday we will
Have to bid goodbye to Brother Jarrell.
   *Girls are daringly closer to the boys.*
**BROTHER WHITE:**
   But when our loved ones bid us goodbye,
   Can they say that we are going to the house of many
      mansions? Can they say that we are going to meet our

loved ones?

Can they say that we are going to meet Jesus?

Can they say we are going to be with Brother Jarrell?

*Moyer catches one of the girls by the skirt, instead of flipping it. They get acquainted during the following lines and other boys and girls begin coupling and running a set.*

**BROTHER WHITE:**

For most of us they'll have to say, "No."

Cause too many of us been a-sinnin'

We been thinkin' about wordly things

An' we been doin' an' likin' wordly  things.

(a male amen)

We been thinkin' about carnal things

An' a-doin'carnal things.

(a female squeal)

An' them what ain't been a-doin' the sinnin',

been a-pattin' their foot a-keepin' time fer

Them what was a doin' it ...

Fer sin ain't no respecter of persons ...

Sin ain't somethin' you can hide from ...

Sin ain't somethin' you cah talk about ...

Sin ain't somethin' you can lie about ...

Sin ain't somethin' you can live with ...

Cause when you're sinnin'

It's the sin what's livin'

An' you're done dead ...

Sin ain't somethin' outside you ....

It's somethin' inside you ...

An' what's inside you Gotta come out ...

An' it's the comin' out what makes all the fuss ...

It's the comin' out what does all the damage ...

It's the comin' out what stirs things up ...

Fer it's the comin' out of sin

That makes men go a-whorin' ...

It's the comin' out that makes women fergit their

homes

An' throw their skirts over their heads ...

It's the comin' out what leads our young men up the
    hollers to the stills ...
It's the comin' out what leads our young girls up the
    mountain to the Lord knows all ...
An' it's the comin' out of sin what makes us all fergit ...
Fergit the Lord Jesus Christ ....
Fergit the Holy Ghost ...
Fergit the Lord God A'mighty ...
Fergit the things of the spirit ...
An' set our minds on things of this old world ...
Will we be ready
When God A'mighty sends his death angel from the
    sky
Will we be ready
When it comes our time to lay aside this old carnal
    flesh?
Will we be ready
To put on the robes of white and walk the streets that
    are paved with gold?
*(back into conversational tone)*
"We will not know the day nor the hour."
Brother White shakes hands again with all the preachers,
who commend him for the fine sermon.

*The boys and girls are clapping their hands for running the
set and whooping and hollering. The noise subsides from the
boys and girls but the action does not.*

**BROTHER WHITE:** Brother Jarrell, could you line out a
song?

*Lining up and singing, everyone shakes hands during the
song.*

**BROTHER JARRELL:**
    There's a land that is fairer than day
    And they say you can see it afar,
    For my father waits over the way
    To prepare us a dwelling place there.
    In the sweet bye and bye,
    We shall meet on that beautiful shore

In the sweet bye and bye
We shall meet on that beautiful shore.

*By the time the hymn is half over, Moyer has begun picking the tune on the guitar. When the congregation finishes the first stanza they continue singing and shaking hands, but the words are now indistinguishable. Tom and his banjo join Moyer and his guitar, and they jazz the hymn tune until all the young people are fairly rocking with the rhythm.*

*The noise of the music and yelling and whooping of the young folks is gradually superseded by the growing sounds of a summer thunderstorm. As the sky blackens and the thunder increases the lightning flashes grow in intensity. The young folks become more and more frantic. The old folks become agitated and begin to gather their belongings and dinner baskets and young'uns. The old folks and young folks evolve from their age groupings into family groupings as they become increasingly anxious to leave the premises. Jarrell is attempting to calm down his followers and Moyer is trying to hang on to his audience. Finally, as the rains descend, Moyer and Jarrell are the only two people left. They stand at the back of the church side by side looking out the window across the church yard. They stare for a while and Moyer breaks the silence.*

**MOYER:** Hot damn, the old man up there is really pouring it on.

*Jarrell glares at Moyer and starts to speak but turns and exits across the churchyard.*

**MOYER:** Now what'd I say wrong this time? But Papa, you ain't benedicted yet. You can't leave meeting without any blessun' at all.

*His grandfather doesn't hear him or ignores him. Moyer looks uneasily toward the front of the church, tries to think of an appropriate benediction, lowers his head slightly, his eyes still open.*

**MOYER:** Amen.

*Moyer leaves the church quickly, stops in the middle of the churchyard and goes in the opposite direction from his grandfather's as the two exit.*

# BLACKOUT.

## SCENE 3: THE JARRELL HOME.

*The scene is set in the Jarrell home. Elder Jarrell and his wife are in the living room which also serves as their bedroom. They are alone as the scene opens, but we can see and hear Moyer in his room playing his radio (a ballad singer) and accompanying it with his new steel string guitar to which he has attached an electric pickup. Jarrell is whittling and spitting in the fireplace, as lizzie, his wife, comes from the kitchen where she has just finished the supper dishes.she is wiping her hands on her apron. A jumpboard and firecrackers are heard in background.*

**LIZZIE:** John, what's all that infernal racket?

**JARRELL:** Why you know Moyer got that caterwauling' guitar fixed up.

**LIZZIE:** I'm not talking about the guitar.I mean them explosions. Hit sounds like the Fourth of July or somethin'.

**JARRELL:** Oh, I guess some of the boys has been up to the highway at Big Gap and got some firecrackers at that roadside place up there. (louder explosion) Things sure are different nowadays. (silence) Did Moyer bring in the kindling?

**LIZZIE:** What kindling?

**JARRELL:** You mean he ain't even split it up yet?

**LIZZIE:** Now, John, you know that there ain't been a stick of light'ard at the woodpile for a week and a half.

**JARRELL:** That don't make no never mind as long as there's some dry laurel. He knows that he's supposed to keep the kindlin' box filled. You're just not fitten to do it yourself.

**LIZZIE:** John, he was plum tuckered out from those two years in that ol' nasty war, and that job down to Patrick is taking a lot out of the boy.

JARRELL: It sure is.And it's putting a lot in him too, — rot-gut likker. You didn't see him stagger in last Friday night, but I seen him. I seen him and I nearly puked; he was that sorry looking.

LIZZIE: Now John don't go faultin' him, cause somethin' inside the boy has died. Things ain't in the right place for him ...

JARRELL: There you go taking up for him again. I know he's our own flesh and blood and I know he can't help cause his maw is dead anymore than we can help it cause his paw run off. But landsakes, woman, he's growed up and it's high time he started acting like it.I know there ain't any harm in taking a little nip once in awhile.Why I always feel I can preach a little better if I have just a little toddy before I get in the pulpit.But his contrariness and sorriness I just can't abide.

LIZZIE: But John, you've always said that what is to be will be and...

JARRELL: Of course I believe that, but I'm not going out to the railroad track and lay my head on it. I know the Lord will work in his own way in his own time; but what Moyer has been up to ... it ... well ... it just ain't natural.It's tempting the God Amighty, that's what it's doing.

LIZZIE: John, is there something you ain't telling me?

JARRELL: I hear things. I hear a heap of things. But I don't blabber everything I hear.

*The children are heard coming from the distance, some girls are jumping rope and chanting jumping rhymes such as follows:*
Fudge, fudge, tell the judge Mary's havin' a baby
Wrap it up in old corn shucks
Throw it into a coal mining truck
How many more will she have?
One, two, three, ....

*Although these are unholy chants, their delivery in this scene should be rather neutral and even naive. One of the boys will be playing with a homemade explosive contraption made of two bolts end to end held together by one nut. Placed between the two ends will be a match head which will fire when the bolts are thrown against a hard object. During the scene he will periodically fire this by throwing it against the stone hearth, reloading it after each explosion.*

JARRELL: I'd better punch up the fire a little. The night air's already getting a little nippy, and the young'uns will probably want to warm up after walking across the gap.

LIZZIE: Yes, summer's almost gone, and I wonder where it went so fast.

*The children come in running and laughing, and go immediately to Jarrell,*

JARRELL: Well, Howdy, young'uns. I never expected to see you tonight.

CHILD 1: Uncle John, you're fibbing again. Why you and me fixed it up just yesterday that I was going to bring everybody up here tonight so's you could sing some of your devilish songs and tell some of those old tales.

LIZZIE: Why John, so you put these young'uns up to this traipsing around at all hours of the night, and just to hear you carry on with those wicked ditties and tales.

JARRELL: Now, Lizzie, don't go getting so riled.I just thought it would be good for the young'uns to remember some of the old ways before they get their heads crammed full with so much of the trash that they see in those magazines from the city and hear on that infernel radio. Howdy Jeems, how's cousin Delly?

CHILD 2: Oh she's fine.You know she warn't really sick at all.She just had another baby, that's all.

JARRELL: Well, what was it this time?

CHILD 2: Another boy. Called it Sam.

JARRELL: Even' Sal. Are your sister and Aubrey's boy still talkin'?

CHILD 3: No, Cousin John. They quit talking last week.You know he got drafted into the army, didn't you?

JARRELL: No. When did that happen?

CHILD 3: Just afore they quit talking. That's why she huffed up so.

**JARRELL:** Why that shore seems funny. He couldn't he'p it if he wuz drafted could he?

**CHILD 3:** No but he didn't seem to mind too bad and that sorta made her mad so she just huffed up and quit talking. You know she's awful feisty.

**JARRELL:** I reckon I do; and her maw never help her much.

**CHILD 1:** Uncle John riddle them that riddle you riddled me last time I was up here.

**JARRELL:** Which one was that? I don't rightly recollect.

**CHILD 1:** Aw, you know the one about goin' to the bushes...

**JARRELL:** (quickly) You mean:

I went to the woods to get it.
I brought it home because I couldn't find it.
The more I looked for it the more I hated it.
When I did find it I threw it away.
What is it?

**CHILDREN:** I don't know. I give up. Tell us. Come on, tell us.

**JARRELL:** Have you ever been to the woods barefoot?

*Moyer enter unnoticed except by Child 3.*

**JARRELL:** (looking at Moyer) Last week I seen someone go to the woods barefoot. But I seen four feet. How many feet you got, Moyer?

*Everyone turns and sees Moyer and children greet him and run to him.*

**JARRELL:** Hey, you ain't unriddled that riddle for me yet.

**CHILD 3:** Aw, I know it's supposed to be a briar. But Moyer tells it diffrunt. I went to the bushes to get it. The more I looked for it the more I liked it. When I did find it, I couldn't bring it home.

*All the children giggle*

**JARRELL:** (Sharply) Sal, that's enough of that tomfoolery. (Saucily) Where've you been hearing such trash, Moyer?

**MOYER:** I keep my ears open.

**CHILD 2:** How about that one about the croakers?

JARRELL: Two lookers, two crookers, four down
  hangers, one long switcher trail along behind?

CHILDREN: What does croakers mean?Is the switcher a
  tail?Tell us Uncle John.

MOYER: It's a cow. What about this one? Two lookers,
  two knockers, one little twitch-a-tail bouncing along
  behind?

JARRELL: Moyer, shut yore trap. That's about all I'm
  gonna take off'a yore foolishness.

MOYER: Okay Papa I just thought they'd like them a little
  more up to date. People don't ...

JARRELL: Never you mind up to date.

CHILD 2: Are you gonna sing fer us, Elder Jarrell ...The
  Riddle Song?

MOYER: That's the one about "giving my love a cherry"
  ain't it?

JARRELL: I ain't got no notion of playing the riddle
  song.
  *Strums a chord of wayfaring stranger and sings:*

JARRELL: I'm just a poor wayfarin' stranger
  A travellin' through this world of woe
  But there's no heartaches, toils, nor dangers
  In that bright land to which I go.
  I'm going there to see my Father
  I'm going there no more to roam
  I'm just a-going over Jordan
  I'm just a-going over home.
  *Moyer picks up the tune on his guitar and jazzes the
  rhythm after Jarrell has finished singing. Jarrell attempts to
  ignore him.*

CHILD 3: Cousin John, how come all of your songs are
  always so sad? Why don't you sing something like "I
  picked her up in a pickup truck and she broke this heart
  of mine."? You know that one don't you Moyer?

MOYER: Yep. (singing and playing) I picked her up in a
  pickup truck and she broke this heart of mine. I know I
  hadn't oughter

Fer she's his only daughter
And we got married on the Tennessee border.

**JARRELL:** (interrupts moyer's singing) We ain't gonna
have that kind of carryin' on in here as long as I got
anything to say about it.

**LIZZIE:** John there ain't no harm atall in that song that
Moyer sung. Hit's just a play-party song. Hit don't lead to
no bad thoughts atall.

**JARRELL:** I ain't worryin' about bad thoughts, that just
ain't the kind of music one oughter go in fer. I mean just
unthoughtedly, so to speak.

**MOYER:** Whatta you mean Papa?

**JARRELL:** I mean fer one thing that that confounded
guitar is so dadburned loud you can't even hear yourself
think and that song, who ever heard of that song before?

**MOYER:** What you mean is that this is a new guitar and
that was a new song and you don't like nothing' that's
new. Ain't that it?

**JARRELL:** Now that ain't it atall. Hit's just that ... well
nobody ain't never sung music like this afore and ...

**MOYER:** Ain't that just what I said. Hit's new and if it's
new you're agin it.

**LIZZIE:** (trying to change the subject) John, why don't
you tell them that tale about the Old King and the
stranger.

**CHILDREN:** Yeh. Yeh, tell it, Uncle John. I ain't heard
that one. Everybody quiet now.

**JARRELL:** (apprehensively and haltingly at first) Well,
once upon a time there lived in a country across the
ocean an old king and his beautiful daughter.

**MOYER:** You mean three daughters, don't you, Papa?

**CHILD 3:** What kind of trial was it they had? Was it like
that one they had at Patrick last month?

**CHILD 4:** I never heard about that. What was it?

**JARRELL:** No, it wasn't like that. They didn't have that
kind of trials back then. Folks then knowed how to
behave themselves.

**CHILD 2:** Why did they have any trials atall then Uncle

John, if everyone behaved themselves?

**JARRELL:** Now you gone and plumb interrupted my story. You got me so flustered and discombobulated I clean fergit where I was.

**CHILD 5:** The old king saw a bunch of people in the courthouse yard.

**JARRELL:** Oh. yes: So he seen this crowd and thought he was in a pow'ful big hurry to get into the courtroom, he didn't want to miss out on any big excitement. Why this might be some enemy there a making all these people listen to him, and the king felt it wasn't nothing but his duty to investigate the matter a little further. And besides,: it might be one of those evangelist type preachers coming through the country, and the king sure didn't want to miss out on any good preaching. It never hurt nobody to hear some good preaching once in awhile.

**CHILD 1:** Would that have been Ol' Baptist preaching, Uncle John?

**JARRELL:** Wal, now, no it warn't. What it was, was a total stranger. Nobody there what had ever seen a pow'ful good talker. And ever'body was taking notice of him instead of going into the courthouse. Wal, the king seen what was going on and all and he decided as how nobody didn't know this stranger, so maybe he better stick around a little longer just in case things got out of hand and they needed somebody to handle matters.

**CHILD 5:** Elder Jarrell, where was the stranger from?

**JARRELL:** That's just it. Nobody knowed fer sure. But the · king had a notion he was from across the mountain, and so that's why he stuck around a little longer. Now, this stranger had a box that he was a showing off and ever'body was a-oohing and a-aahing over it. You see it was made of gold and just plumb covered with diamonds and other jewels. And when the old king seen that box he sorta whispered under his breath, "What I wouldn't give fer that purty little box. Sure would like to give it to Bessie. That was his beautiful daughter, Bessie."

**MOYER:** She must of not been very purty with a name like that.

**JARRELL:** (ignoring Moyer) Now the stranger had just been a-waiting fer the king to get into earshot, cause he had the notion of selling that box to the old king. Now the king thought he had walked in there with the crowd unbeknownst to the stranger, but the stranger seen him out of one corner of his eye. He was a sly one, he was. Then that stranger started telling what all thar little box could do. He'd already appointed some of his fellow rogues to be in the crowd and tell the box what one n'all to do. One feller said real loud, so's ever body could hear, especially the king, "Let it make music." And there come from the box an awful loud sound, a pigpen full of shoats, and a passle of youn'uns thrown in to boot. Then the stranger said (still keeping the old king in the corner of his eye), "Ain't that the most beautiful sim-funny you ever heard?" And it sure was agreed that nobody hadn't never heard music like that before.

**CHILD 2:** What kind of music was it?

**JARRELL:** Well, it sure wasn't like the music that the old king was used to. It was like maybe several hundred dulcimers, and fiddles, and pump organs. Now, the old king was getting' mighty interested. So he said he wanted to know if the box could give advice. "Give advice?" the stranger said, "Why this little box can give you all the advice any man would need to run even this fine country. Why you wouldn't need no more judges you wouldn' t need no more high sheriffs; you wouldn't ever need no more preachers a-telling you what to do." "How about showing us?" says the king. "Ask it a question", said the stranger. "If it can answer this riddle with two words, I will buy it and let you name the price. What is newer than new and older than old, stronger than stone and purer than gold? Wal, I want you to know that box just squawked out the answer quicker than the old king could say "Jack Robinson". It said "Woman's love."

**CHILD 4:** Was the box really doing those things, Cousin John?

**JARRELL:** Now you're getting ahead of the story. The old king thought all of these things were for real, but this stranger was a real sly rogue. For all that music the rogue had one of those new Victrolas, and the king hadn't ever seen one of those things. The rogue had learned to throw his voice without moving his mouth and it seemed just like the answer to the king's riddle come right out of that little box. That box weren't even gold. Hit was just painted and the diamonds was just pieces of glass. But the old king didn't know all that yet. He had made a bargain with the stranger and as he was a honorable man he intended to keep his end of the bargain, so he said he would buy the box if the stranger would just name his price. Well, the stranger said he wanted to marry the king's daughter and he wanted half of the kingdom. Now this sorta saddened the old king. He didn't want his daughter marrying just any old thing, leastwise a stranger that nobody knowed a thing about. But he had made a deal and he had to keep his word. So the king appointed the time for the wedding, and, after the marrying ceremony; he was going to give the stranger half his kingdom. Just before the king was supposed to leave the castle to go to the church for the wedding, he thought he would ask his little expensive box fer some advice. So he said to the box, "Now that I'm about to lose my daughter to a stranger, what should I oughter do?" Now we know the box couldn't do all the wonderful things, but the old king didn't know it. There was a good fairy who lived in the castle and she couldn't stand to see the good old king come out on the short end of the horn on such a rotten deal so she witched the box, so it said, "Old King you've been tricked. I can't really do all those wonderful things, why if you open my lid you will see that I am not gold but wood painted gold. My advice to you is to catch the rogue and throw him in the dungeon."

**CHILD 5:** Did he do it Elder Jarrell? Did he do it?

**JARRELL:** Yep that's exactly what he done and he married his daughter off to one of the town boys, and everyone lived happily ever after and folks didn't listen to no more strangers about outlandish new gadgets that warn't worth the breath to talk about them.

**MOYER:** Papa, you got the wrong ending to that story.

**JARRELL:** What do you mean the wrong ending? That's the only ending there is.

**MOYER:** Nope. What really happened was that the box really worked and the stranger married the beautiful daughter. But the old king was so sure that he had been wronged that he went completely batty and his daughter and new son-in-law had to ship him off to the insane asylum. Then the daughter and new king lived happily ever after and made all the people happy cause they made a lot of big changes in the way everything had been run in the kingdom.

*The children giggle and a couple of them sidle up to Moyer.*

**JARRELL:** Moyer Jarrell, that's about all the foolishness and sass I'm about to take for one night. You're always so all fired sure that you know everything about everything. Well, let me tell you a thing or two. You're so green you ain't even dry behind the ears yet and .

**LIZZIE:** Now John quit carryin' on so. What'll the young'uns think? And besides it ain't fitten fer an elder of the church to be behaving like ...

**JARRELL:** Now just keep yore tongue in yore head, woman. It's high time someone told this boy the facts of life and I'm a'gonna do it.

**MOYER:** Aw Papa, don't carry on so. I wuz just a funning, I didn't mean no harm by nothing I said. I wuz just a teasing you that's all. I'm sorry if I hurt your feelin's.

**JARRELL:** Now boy don't go trying to sweet-talk me. You've been needing a tongue lashing for a long time. Do you think I don't know what you been up to? Just because you've got a cafe job down at Patrick don't give you no call to carrying on the way you been doing. I don't mean just with that confounded radio and that infernal guitar. I know you're thinking about buying a worn out trap of a car, and if you do, you'll break yore fool neck in the thing.

MOYER: If I wanta git a car that oughter be my business and besides...

JARRELL: But that other business ain't yore business.

MOYER: What business you talking about now?

JARRELL: I heard who you been hanging around with down there at Patrick, and there ain't no good atall comin' of it. That boy's daddy has been in the federal pen three times and the boy's gonna land there too if he lives long enough.

*Moyer starts playing his guitar and continues until end of scene, getting increasingly louder and more children gather around Moyer until by the end of the scene they are all standing close by him.*

LIZZIE: Now John take it easy. The boy oughter know how to pick his own friends, and besides all this you been asaying is just hearsay.

JARRELL: There's hearsay and there's hearsay, and now I'm asayin and I'm asaying that Moyer, I intend fer you to promise me before you go to bed tonight that you ain't gonna have nothing more to do with Ned Walker and that gang of convicts.

MOYER: Is that the way it's gotta be?

JARRELL: That's the way it's gonna be.

MOYER: Ain't I gonna have no say?

JARRELL: Your say is what I say.

MOYER: And if I don't ... ?

JARRELL: There ain't no ifs.

MOYER: Papa, that's the way it allus ends.

JARRELL: There ain't no other way.

MOYER: Sometimes there's new ways.

JARRELL: There's nothin' new under the sun.

MOYER: I guess your God Almighty told you that.

**JARRELL:** If you spent as much time with the scriptures as you ...

**MOYER:** Sal, do you reckon yore maw could make a pallet on the floor fer me to stay the night?

**CHILD 3:** Why I reckon so.

**MOYER:** I'd sure be much obliged

**LIZZIE:** Moyer ...

**MOYER:** Come on, young'uns. Night folks.

*The children follow him out as he picks guitar, almost like the pied piper.*

*He exits. The guitar and the children's laughter can be heard as the old couple are left standing at the door, quite obviously defeated in the first round of their battle with Moyer.*

*Lots of fireworks and hooting and hollering.*

FADEOUT.

CURTAIN

ACT II

SCENE 1:AUTUMN: OUTSIDE THE JARRELL
CABIN.

*Brother Jarrell is splitting kindling and has stacked up quite a nice little pile of wood beside the chop block. He seems preoccupied and does not seem to notice the children's voices in the background. Particularly interesting is the sound of a homemade bullroarer which one of the boys keeps swinging at regular rhythms throughout the scene. When the children first appear. Moyer is with them and is swinging the bullroarer and demonstrating its qualities and construction to the children. Several of the children have various kinds of noise making and weapon toys, such as slingshots, whistles, plain sticks for poking, clubs and homemade crude banjoes and guitars. The noise of the children continues throughout the scene. the sounds of jarrell's axe seem orchestrated with the sounds of the children. When Moyer sees his grandfather he gives the bullroarer to one of the boys and walks nonchalantly over to his grandfather who does not yet see him or at least does not notice him. Moyer stands for awhile looking at his grandfather.*

**MOYER:** I reckon it's gonna be a rough winter.

**JARRELL:** (stiffening but not looking at Moyer and as nonchalantly as possible) What gives you that notion?

**MOYER:** I allus heard tell that when the squirrels start storing the hickory nuts early and when old men commence to splitting a month's supply of kindling wood then you better expect a bitter cold winter.

**JARRELL:** They ain't no sech saying as that.

**MOYER:** Well, I just added a little wisdom of my own.

**JARRELL:** I don't really figger the world's waitin' for your wisdom.

**MOYER:** Papa (STRAINED PAUSE) there you go again.

**JARRELL:** There who goes again?

**MOYER:** You, Papa. I s'pose you have about a thousand ways of giving me a put-down.

**JARRELL:** A what?

**MOYER:** A put-down. Why that's what folks outside would call a way of knocking a person down to size.

**JARRELL:** If that's what you meant, why didn't you say it? (a pause and jarrell has now sat down on the chopblock) I reckon you heard a lot of things and saw a lot of things and done a lot of things there in service that warn't like around here.

**MOYER:** Yep. Papa, you ought to a seen what'n all ...

**JARRWLL:** Iffen I ought to a seen it I woulda seen it. I've heard tell of ...

**MOYER:** But Papa it ain't all like what you heard, away from the mountains.

**JARRELL:** I heard enough.

**MOYER:** I know what you heard. You heard all the bad stuff. 'Cause you talked with Brother Hiatt about all that trouble his boy got into up in Cincinnati. An' with the Appersons and all the problems they had when they first got up there. If things had been so bad away from these hills, they wouldn't have stayed away so long. When times was good, they was makin' good money.

JARRELL: But they come back howsomever. If they was making such big money, they didn't scatter too much of it around here when they come back and settled up on that old ridge farm that's washed full of gullies and can't grow even poke sallet in wet weather.

MOYER: That was because they got in trouble with the law, then there was that dispute with the welfare folks, and the mill laid him off.

JARRELL: That don't sound like good times to me. They lived up there in what they called apartment buildings with as many as ten young'uns sleeping in one room.

MOYER: There're folks living right around here with nearly that many living in such close quarters.

JARRELL: But they got ground to stretch on, and they got air to breathe, and they got woods to hunt, and they got land for foodstuffs.. It just ain't natural to keep folks cooped up in chicken coops stacked on top of each other like them big trucks full of white leghorns chickens, hauling them over the Fancy Gap Road down to the towns to slaughter.

MOYER: Yeh, and you ought to a seen them streets, and buses, and cars. Why it was more people that I'd see in one day than you'd likely see in a full month of church Association Days. And it was just big cement buildings just everywhere you turned. You're right about not having any mountains or woods. (abruptly realizing he is agreeing too much with his grandfather) But they was also other things.

JARRELL: What kinda things.

MOYER: Well, first off there was ... there was some parks.

JARRELL: What were they for?

MOYER: They had some trees and picnic tables and places for playing.

JARRELL: Did they have brush arbors for preaching?

MOYER: Oh, no. They didn't allow preaching out in the parks that away without a special permit. That was done only in the churches.

JARRELL: What was they like?

MOYER: They was awful big and had real pretty windows that lighted up with all kinds of colors when the sun was shining outside.

*Moyer stares off into space in a kind of daydream.*

JARRELL: What were the folks like?

MOYER: What folks?

JARRELL: The folks at the church. Didn't you see no folks there?

MOYER: Oh, no, I didn't go for regular services. I tried once but the people was all so dressed up and didn't seem to take no notice of me atall, 'cept some of them stared funny when the greeters spoke to me and they heard me talk. No, I just went into the churches and set down and looked at them windows during the weekdays when nobody was around 'cept some janitors, and they didn't seem to bother none. You know, it was just them church windows and them bright lights at night that I just can't seem to fergit. They just keep flashing in my head, when I'm a kind a studying things, you know.

JARRELL: Studying what kinda things?

MOYER: Oh, you know, like what's out yonder ahead of me. That kinda thing?

JARRELL: What is out yonder for you, Moyer?

MOYER: (defiantly): The world and everything in it'.

JARRELL: How much of it can be yours? To keep and own and hold.

MOYER: Just whatever I can grab, and I'll tell you one thing, Papa, I aim to grab and I aim to grab high and I aim to grab tight, cause this old world goes around just once fer everybody.

JARRELL: What kinda talk is that

MOYER: It's the kinda talk you gonna hear quite a bit from now on, if you see much of this big boy. I'm sick and tired of being a hick from the sticks. Whenever any of us leaves and goes into the mill towns we're allus that funny talking hillbilly. I heard tell they got organizations in Chicago just to help take care of the hillbillies what come in there to work, and try to live. They figger we're so strange that we need some special care. And when them fat ass politicians come in from the state capitol they stay just long enough to promise a few drams of liquor on election day in exchange for some measly votes. Even the Washington politicians come by here and have their pictures taken with a few snotty nose kids an' nothin' more is heard from them except them courthouse officials seem to drive newer cars after the federal boys come through. There ain't a soul on God's green earth outside these hills what gives a diddly damn what happens to us here, 'cept to poke fun of us on radio and shed imitation crocodile tears near election time at the plight of the mountain folks.

JARRELL: You're all het up, Moyer. Why I just met a couple of nice young college fellas only last summer that seemed to take an uncommonly nice interest in the folks in these parts and the old ways what we still practice. I only wish our own young folks took as much interest in the old ways.

MOYER: It was old ways alright. I met them boys too, and they seemed to me to ask an awful lot of questions.

JARRELL: 'Bout what?

MOYER: 'Bout everything. But the questions wasn't the end of it.

JARRELL: What you mean by that?

MOYER: I seen what they wrote in their fine college paper when they got back. "Tar paper shacks, Bible thumping preachers, crooked officials, moonshining men, whoring girls, black water creeks, fly covered babies setting on their own dung heaps." Oh, they closed off by saying they had learned a lot about human ways while they was here and only hoped they were able to teach us some things. I guarantee for my part they taught me not to put no store atall in sweet talking strangers from the flatland.

JARRELL: Moyer, I been meaning a long time to talk

with you about a particular stranger who come in here from off yonder sommers. (pause) You know, these strangers nowadays ain't the first strangers to come into these parts and take advantage of folks.

**MOYER:** What you mean by that?

**JARRELL:** There was timbering men come in · here and for nigh on to nothing they wheedled their way into cutting off all the fine timber. Why you shoulda seen the fine stand of oaks and maples and even walnuts on the back ridge before my daddy lost it to the lumber mills. And over in Monroe County where they's so many coal mines, them coal companies come in here and bought up the coal rights at fifty cents to the acre and they been ruinin' the hillsides and crops and creeks ever since.

**MOYER:** What you tryin' to tell me, Papa?

**JARRELL:** You 'member what your mamma told you 'fore she died about your daddy? Well, he was a stranger from off yonders.

**MOYER:** Papa, you don't have to beat around the bush with me. I know mamma lied to me, and you and Grandma been lying to me ever since 'bout my daddy. He was a horse trader who come through these parts one time, and that was enough to give me a special little push into this great big beautiful world.

**JARRELL:** Moyer, nothing worthwhile comes from a bitter heart.

**MOYER:** I ain't interested in "worthwhile". I'm interested in grabbing what I can for number one — Moyer. I'll have what fun I can. I'll be as lazy as I wanna be or I'll be as busy as I want to and if ever I get my hands on some real money I'll ride in fine cars with fat cigars and buy my mansion on the ridge and not have to wait for my mansion in the sky.

**JARRELL:** Son, I know you've a mind of your own and growed up enough to go in your own direction, but you ought ...

**MOYER:** I don't want to hear nothing about ought. That's the same as naught and you know as well as me that that means zero — just a big fat zero. So don't talk with me about no zero — ought.

**JARRELL:** Hit don't seem like you atall to be so serious about all this business, when you've allus been so fun loving, so full of mischief.

**MOYER:** And I aim to have my fun. But let me help you recollect what you said awhile back. You said, "The world ain't waiting for your wisdom." And that's what I know and that's what jams tight inside my craw. I may not be better than other people but by God I'm just as good as any other man that walks on the face of this earth. And somebody's gonna know I'm around. I just passed 21 and for all anybody cares I might as well be ten. But someday somebody somewhere is gonna know I'm alive for something.

**JARRELL:** Speaking of twenty-first birthdays. We got you a little something for growing up and coming back home. You know, the prodigal son come home to a rejoicing father who heaped fine clothes and jewels on him and I kinda think of you a little like that. 'Course I don't have fine things to give you, but ... Lizzie, hey Lizzie, why don't you bring Moyer's birthday present out to him.

**LIZZIE:** (appears with gun) John, do you think it's the right time now?

**JARRELL:** Of course it's the right time. It's the perfect time. (takes gun and gives it to moyer) Here Moyer is a grown up gun for a grown up man.

**MOYER:** (almost like a little boy with a new toy) God ... bless it'. That's the purtiest gun I ever seen. A double-barrel 12 gauge.

*He opens it, inspects the inside of the barrels, closes it, inspects the sight, and the children gather around.*

**JARRELL:** (trying to get moyer's attention again from the gun and the children) Moyer, hit's a awful powerful gun. It's got a mighty strong kick to it.

**MOYER:** Oh, hit's a fine gun, Papa. I sure am much obliged to you.

**JARRELL:** Hit's nothing to make a fuss over.

MOYER: Why this baby is really something to shout about. I can't hardly wait to show it to Ned. He's just gonna go ape over this piece of equipment.

JARRELL: Is that Ned Walker you talking about?

MOYER: Yep!

JARRELL: Moyer, I'm kinda troubled about all them things you been a-talking about. I don't understand why you can't be satisfied with things around here the way they are and why you can't be content to let the Lord work things his own way. We talked before about Ned Walker and that gang and I don't think it fitten for you to keep ...

MOYER: Are we gonna fight over that again, Papa? I done said ...

*They stand facing each other as if to square off for a fight.*

MOYER: Besides, if hit's the will of the Lord ...

*Jarrell starts really glowering.*

MOYER: Aw, Papa, maybe both of us been too serious. I'm getting to bed early tonight to take this baby hunting in the morning. Why I'll get there even before they start a-cutting the hickory nuts.

*Moyer exits into house. The children start leaving. Jarrell stares after Moyer, then bends to get some kindling.*

BLACKOUT.


SCENE 2: AN AUTUMN AFTERNOON ON THE MOUNTAIN.

*Moyer is hunkering with his shotgun waiting for a squirrel to show itself. while he is waiting, he hears something in the bushes. he starts to shoot, but then decides to try to catch whatever it is moving in the bushes. he slowly stalks the bush that is moving, then he pounces and tumbles from behind the bush with sal.*

MOYER: Why, Sal. I didn't go fer to knock you down like that. I thought sure it was some varmint a-thrashing around out here in the underbresh.

SAL: O pshaw. I don't reckon it'll kill me. I ain't exactly made of glass.

**MOYER:** You know this is the first time I laid eyes on you since that night you young'uns was up at our place and I left with you'all and spent the night at yore folks.

**SAL:** Yep, I know.

**MOYER:** You young'uns was shore in a devilish mood that night ...

**SAL:** Moyer, I ain't a young 'un no more.

**MOYER:** (wanting to change the subject) Yeh ...Well ... What in nation you a-doin' way up here on the mountain by yoreself? I allow that you're old enough to know better than that.

**SAL:** I left the house after breakfast to pick chink-a-pins. I kept goin' from one bush to another and afore I knew what was happenin', here I was.

**MOYER:** When I was in Detroit, you know there was folks there that ain't ever heard of chink-a-pins. And when I told them it was some kind of a nut, they'd say, "You're the only kind of a nut that we know anything about." They was all the time sayin' things like that to me, cause I was all time cuttin' up an' all. They like to hear me talk, too, cause they said it was awful funny the way I talked. Course I laughed at hearin' them talk too. They talked real fast, an' you couldn't hardly understand a word they said unless you just paid point-blank attention to ever' little thing.

**SAL:** Did you like it, Moyer?

**MOYER:** Waal, I never really considered much whether I liked it or didn't like it. Folks was pretty stand-offish.

**SAL:** Was you lonesome, Moyer?

**MOYER:** A feller can git lonesome most any place, but I guess you're right. It's lonesomer than bein' the only critter up yore fork of the branch.

**SAL:** You ain't lonesome now are you, Moyer?

**MOYER:** No, not just this minute, but ... (changing subject) Say, how many chink a-pins did you pick afore you had to pick yoreself off'n the ground?

**SAL:** Enough.

**MOYER:** Enough fer what?

**SAL:** Enough to get here.

**MOYER:** Let me look in that there bucket.

**SAL:** Why, there ain't no call fer doin' that.

**MOYER:** Come on let me look in yore bucket. (grabs bucket) Yep, just like I thought there ain't a smidgin of chink-a-pins in here. I bet you knowed all the time just where them chink-a-pin bushes was a leadin' you as you flitted from one bush to the other and just sorta happened to land up here.

**SAL:** Yeah.

**MOYER:** Just why did you come up here, anyway?

**SAL:** I dunno. I always heerd tales about the mountain and what-n all goes on up here an' I just thought I'd take a peek. But it ain't atall like them tales. It's just as quiet and peaceful. Even more so than down in the hollow ... Now that you know why I'm here, you gotta tell me why you come up here all alone. Don't you know it's pow'ful dangerous to be up here all alone?

**MOYER:** It's different fer a man to be up here alone.

**SAL:** Why?

**MOYER:** I don't know. It's just diffrunt, that's all.

**SAL:** Are the panthers that they all talk about more partial to woman vittles than man vittles?

**MOYER:** No it ain't that.

**SAL:** Might a woman get lost up here quicker'n a man?

**MOYER:** Yeh, yeh that's partly it ...

**SAL:** That's partly it?

**MOYER:** What I mean is other things than gettin' lost might happen.

**SAL:** Could these ... other things happen to men too?

**MOYER:** (chuckling) Oh yeh, but ...

**SAL:** Well, then ...?

**MOYER:** Well, then but it's all diffrunt for men

**SAL:** You know, Moyer, I sometimes think you're awful twisted around in your (pause). You never did tell me what you was a-doin' up here ... all alone.

**MOYER:** I was squirrel huntin', if you gotta know.

**SAL:** No, I ain't gotta know, but there is somethin' I'd like to know.

**MOYER:** Yeh, what's that? I thought you already knew ever'thing.

**SAL:** How do you hunt squirrels without a gun? Do you catch them with your hands? Or do you just run up behind them and yell boo at 'em? ... Skeer 'em to death? ... Or maybe you sneak up from around a bush and knock 'em over?

**MOYER:** I got a gun.

**SAL:** Where?

**MOYER:** Right over there where I laid it when I seen some varmint a sneakin' around out here in the bresh.

**SAL:** (looking around for the gun) Where is it? I don't see it.

**MOYER:** It's layin' there in the leaves, somewheres.

**SAL:** (finding it) Yeh. Hey that's some gun. What kind is it?

**MOYER:** It's a shot-gun.

**SAL:** Silly, I know that. What gauge is it?

**MOYER:** Twelve.

**SAL:** That's the biggest kind ain't it?

**MOYER:** Yep.

**SAL:** Why this is the biggest gun I ever seen and the prettiest, too.

**MOYER:** You really like it, eh?

**SAL:** Yep. If I was a man I would have a big pow'ful gun just like this and if anybody invaded my territory I'd just blast them betwixt the eyes or in the middle of the rear, depend on which end was the most handy at the time.

**MOYER:** Iffen you was a man. Iffen a bullfrog had wings it wouldn't keep bumping his tail all the time. But you ain't a man, an' you're a-handlin' that gun awful dangerous-like.

**SAL:** Let me shoot it, Moyer.

**MOYER:** Nope.

**SAL:** Aw come on, let me shoot it.

**MOYER:** No. Now put it down. It's dangerous, it might go off.

**SAL:** Let me just hold it then.

**MOYER:** If you're so all-fired taken with it, I guess I can let you hold it but not until I unload it. I reckon if you was a man you wouldn't follow nothing but shootin'.

**SAL:** (while moyer unloads gun) You're as right as a Junebug in July. Where'd you get this gun? Did you buy it with all that money you made?

**MOYER:** Are you kiddin'? I didn't hardly have enough money to thumb a ride back home. Papa give me the gun fer my birthday.

**SAL:** That sure was awful nice of him to do a thing like that.

**MOYER:** Yep.

**SAL:** Yore grandpap's pretty good to you ain't he, Moyer?

**MOYER:** Oh, I reckon he's good enough.

**SAL:** He sure was touchy that night you run off.

**MOYER:** He's an old man.

**SAL:** I know he's old, but he's stubborn too.

**MOYER:** Us Jarrell's ain't called mules fer nothin'.

**SAL:** Just cause you're mules don't mean you gotta be jackass too.

**MOYER:** What you mean by sayin' a thing like that?

**SAL:** I mean sometimes you can't tell a mule from a jackass an' then sometimes the same is true with Jarrells.

**MOYER:** Now look-a-here Sally Pickins. I ain't gonna take ... Sal, who has been playing with the gun all this time wheels and pokes the gun barrel in Moyer's stomach.

**SAL:** You men ain't always so brave on the business end of this firearm ... (laughing) Thay law, you done plum fergot that this thing ain't loaded. I believe you thought I'd use it on you. That sure took the starch out of your britches.

**MOYER:** I oughter tan yore britches.

**SAL:** You oughter what my britches?

**MOYER:** Tan.

**SAL:** Oh ... I just heard the britches part.

**MOYER:** Sal, you ought'nt play with a gun that away.

**SAL:** But it ain't loaded.

**MOYER:** That don't differ none. You shouldn't oughter touch a gun till you know how to use it.

**SAL:** (laughing heartily) You are silly, Moyer. How in nation can I learn to use a gun iffen. I don't touch it afore I know just exactly how to use it? The ignorance of some folks is amazing.

**MOYER:** Here, gimme that gun.

*Moyer snatches the gun.*

**SAL:** Aw, Moyer, just let me hold it.

**MOYER:** Don't you go pointin' it at nobody.

*Moyer hands the gun back to Sal, who holds it and croons to it like a doll baby.*

**SAL:** (singing)

Bye-low, baby bunting

Daddy's gone a-hunting

To get a rabbit skin

To wrap the baby bunting in.

Sal wraps the gun up in her skirt.

**MOYER:** Sal, you're a pure fool.

**SAL:** What makes you say that?

**MOYER:** Iffen you ain't careful, you gonna get yourself into a passle of trouble.

**SAL:** I'm big enough to take care of myself.

**MOYER:** Big enough, Ha. You're still wearin' didies.

**SAL:** Who's wearing didies? I'll just show ...

*Sal stands up to show Moyer what she is wearing.*

**MOYER:** All right, all right. You got no call to git so all fired feisty.

**SAL:** But you said ...

**MOYER:** I know what I said. How old are you anyway?

**SAL:** Young enough to enjoy it an' old enough to know better.

**MOYER:** You don't even know what that means ...

**SAL:** Well, what does it mean?

**MOYER:** I don't know. Where'd you hear it?

**SAL:** From Vicey Dawson.

**MOYER:** Yep, that figgers. Have you been talkin' to her lately?

**SAL:** Oh, yeah. She's a real good talker.

**MOYER:** What does she talk about?

**SAL:** Now she talks just mostly about that widdy of her'n. It can't even hold it's head up yet. I've heard tell that it's a waterhead. But she takes awful good care of it. She just sets aroun' now holdin' that there young'un.

**MOYER:** An' you go just to hear her talk about that young'un? Don't she ever tell you who it's daddy is?

SAL: Oh, no, she don't ever talk about things like that.But it was last year when I really liked to talk with her.

**MOYER:** Why?

**SALLY:** I jest wanted to talk fer a spell.

**MOYER:** There ain't no harm to it, as I know of.

**SAL:** I'd been a'wonderin'.

**MOYER:** Wonderin'?

**SAL:** About growin' up and crossin' the mountain.

**MOYER:** Law, I reckin I know what you got on yore mind.

**SAL:** Vicey told me often enough before what ever'thing was like. Vicey said that she'd spent most of her natcherel childhood dreamin' about out yonder. When you come from a family like Vicey's, she thought those things seem so much more important somehow. An' just cause I got a regular family ... at least with a daddy and ever'thing. She thought yonder wouldn't mean so much to me.

**MOYER:** But it still does, huh?

**SAL:** She didn't have to draw no pitchers fer me. I know what hit's like waitin'' fer over yonder to happen. Sometimes I would think that over yonder was a place, and then I'd think it was some distant time, and then I'd think "Why no, over yonder is both time and place and again I'd think hit had nothin' to do with any time nor any place ... " I'd hear them church folks singin' and even talkin' about over yonder. Now I never had in mind exactly what they meant when they said it, but I figgered hit had somethin' to do ... after you was old and some place that had nothin' to do on this earth. I weren't willin' to settle fer no sech over yonder that was so far away. I 'llowed I'd take my chances 'bout yonder bein' a little closer, in time anyways, than all that. So I been bidin' my time for over yonder. Just the way she said she'd been biding her tme. I said, "Vicey, iffen you wuz me ..."

*She answered that real quick.*

**VICEY'S VOICE:** There hain't no call atall fer me to be supposin' I wuz you or you to be figgerin' what an' all I might do iffen I wuz you. I do what I do and you gotta do what you gotta do. There ain't nobody whut kin tell you, not me not yore folks, not even some boy. We live our own lives an' we can't fault nobody else fer what we done or gonna do.

**SAL:** She then told me that about a year ago how she had always wondered what was up on the mountain and over on the other side. So one day she just took off and traipsed up here maki n' out like she was lookin' fer light'ard knots. It took her half a day to get up the mountain an' she went plum over the top, an' down the other side.

**MOYER:** What'd she find there?

**SAL:** The world and ever'thing in it.

**MOYER:** What?

**SAL:** Yeh, that's what she said.

**MOYER:** Do you know what's on the other side of this mountain?

**SAL:** Yeh. The world an' ...

**MOYER:** No, I mean what is really on the other side.

**SAL:** What?

**MOYER:** Squealem Holler.

**SAL:** What?

**MOYER:** Squealem Holler is on the other side of the mountain.

**SAL:** Who ever heard of such a crazy name?

**MOYER:** It's a crazy place. Folks there don't even live in houses, their heads're set on back'ards and them what can see atall ain't got but one eye right in the middle of the forehead.

**SAL:** They ain't no sech thing.

**MOYER:** Ain't you never heard of Squealem Holler?

**SAL:** Yeh, but ...

**MOYER:** You 'member Rob's uncle, what was killed last year?

**SAL:** Yeh.

**MOYER:** He was killed up in Squealem Holler, cause them folks don't let nobody come in there. Why Rob's uncle was tore up so bad by them Squealem Holler folks that you couldn't hardly rekanize his body atall.

**SAL:** I don't believe a word of it, cause you're just sayin' that to skeer me.

**MOYER:** All right. Can you tell me what you think's on the other side of the mountain?

**SAL:** I can't tell you ever'thing about it.

**MOYER:** Naw, you don't have to tell me ever'thing about it. Jest enough to give me a good notion what it's like.

**SAL:** Waal, first of all it's awful pretty, and it's magical, an' it's like music (even prettier than church music). It s like all them fairy tales folks tell about kings and princes and lords an' ladies. An' when folks go there they grow up real sudden-like. An' young'uns what was young'uns ain't young'uns no more.

**MOYER:** You still ain't told me how old you are.

**SAL:** Sixteen going on seventeen.

**MOYER:** You still in the notion of huntin' for chink-a-pins?

**SAL:** I don't know.

**MOYER:** If you don't know, who does?

**SAL:** You, maybe.

**MOYER:** Well, I'm in the notion.

**SAL:** You mean, you'll go up the mountain and hunt chink-a-pins with me?

**MOYER:** Yeh, but I ain't gonna be responsible. Mind now, I don't fault you none fer wantin' to go, but I'm just a-warnin' you that it's yoah care and not mine.

**SAL:** Why, sure. That's the only way I'd have it.

**MOYER:** An' if you get lost huntin' chink-a-pins or somethin' else happens to you up there, it ain't no skin offen my nose.

**SAL:** My nose carried me up here and if any skin's to be taken, I reckon it'll be mine.

*Sal picks up gun and starts off.*

**SAL:** Come on, slowpoke. I declare yore gonna be late fer yore own funeral.

**MOYER:** (picking up the bucket) Hit might not be my funeral that I'm attendin'.

**SAL:** Shut up and come on, afore I go on without you.

*Moyer, laughing, follows as both exit.*

BLACKOUT.

## SCENE 3: AUTUMN EVENING IN THE CHURCH GRAVEYARD

*Hunting horns can be heard in distance, calling the opposum dogs. The horns continue throughout scene, getting closer and closer. Outside cars can be heard coming toward the church, then lights from one car shines directly on church but it turned off just after car motors are turned off. Total darkness. Much yelling and confusion is heard while tumbling over tombstones.*

**NED:** God-Damn it Moyer, turn them headlights on. It's blacker than hell out here.

**NATE:** (laughing) Maybe it is hell, Ned.

**MOYER:** (also laughing) Yeh, that's it. Ned's done gone and led us straight to hell, and we can't see a gold-durn thing.

**NED:** Ha-ha so you're both real funny. Now turn them mully headlights on before I remember how to use this.

**JOSH:** Aw, come on Ned. Don't take on so. Why this is what you been a-planning the whole time. (much laughter) You brung us right to hell, and you're the ol' devil hisself.

**NED:** Okay. If that's the way you want it, that's the way it's gonna be. Now hear this, Now hear this ... I, the Ol' Devil do here and now pronounce you dead and guilty and condemned to roast in the fires of hell. You, convicted Moyer Jarrell turn some lights on so's I can see what in hell I'm doin'. (Lights of car come on and project ned's shadow on church.)

**NED:** Them light's ain't red enough. Make them redder.

**MOYER:** How?

**NED:** That's yore worry. Now, don't anger me none. Sinner Josh find a throne fer the devil.

**JOSH:** (laughing) Just set down on yore fist and rar back on yore thum.

**NED:** I'll have no more back-talk from any of you sinners. Josh, go into the church house and bring out the preacher's big chair.

**TOM:** Ned, it don't hardly seem right to break into the church house that away.

**NED:** This is hell where nothing ain't right except what's wrong and nothing ain't wrong except what's right.

**TOM:** Ned. I don't feel ...

**NED:** It don't differ what you feel. This is hell and you feel what I make you feel. While you're at it, bring out the pulpit too.

*Josh and Tom go into the church through window.*

**EZRA:** Ned, I'm tired a-playin' this game. I druther play "Tag on the Mountain".

**NED:** This ain't no game we're a-playin', Ez. But I tell you iffen you'll just do what I tell you, we'll sure 'nuff play "Tag on the Mountain" in jest a little while.

**EZRA:** With real girls!

**NED:** With honest to gosh real live female-type women.

**EZRA:** Hot-jiggedy'.

**NED:** But you gotta do like I say.

**EZRA:** What I gotta do, huh, what I gotta do?

**NED:** Just simmer down now. You gotta go round the.church house an' look to see if anybody's comin'.

*Ezra runs off.*

**NED:** Sinner Moyer, ain't you fixed my red fires yet?

**MOYER:** Ned, I don't know how to make them headlights red.

**NED:** I really picked a ignerrant one this time. Use that red bandanna of yourn.

*Moyer takes the red handkerchief out of his pocket and advances to the headlights off-stage with one light wrapped in the handkerchief the light looks much redder as the headlights are still the only source of light.*

**NED:** Sinner Nate, yore first requirement here in hell is to go to the car and get our refreshments and bring them here where we can all look at them.

**NATE:** You don't mean all them ...

**NED:** Who you think you talkin' to, man? If yore gonna talk to the devil you gotta show more respect. Now, address me proper like.

**NATE:** (somewhat intimidated and frightened by this change in Ned) Ned, your honor, sir, you don't mean you want me to bring that whole box of jars out ...

**NED:** That's what I said, warn't it?

**NATE:** Yes ... sir, your honor, Ned.

*Josh and Tom bring out both a chair and a pulpit.*
*Ezra runs in.*

**NATE:** I don't see nothin' Ned.

**NED:** Run back quick, so's you don't miss nothin'.

*Ezra exits.*

**NED:** Okay boys, you can bring out the table.

**TOM:** Waal, Ned, we already got the pulpit so I don't reckon it'd do no more harm to go ahead and bring out the communion table.

**NED:** Yeh, that's the spirit.

*Ned sets the chair in a prominent place for his throne and places the pulpit near it.*

*Nate comes in with a box of quart and half-gallon fruit jars filled with moonshine. Tom and Josh poke the table through the window to Moyer and Ned who place it beside the chair and put the moonshine on it, lining the jars around the edge. The boys have already been drinking a little and they*

*begin to join in wholeheartedly with ned and his sacrilege.*
*Ned sits in his throne and surveys his new domain.*

**NED:** Hey, Sinner Moyer. Where's all that female talent you been talking about? I thought you told us there was some women up here.

**MOYER:** They ain'y exactly women ...

**NED:** Don't tell me they're part man and part woman. Moyer you ain't gonna show us some moffydites are you?

**EZRA:** (poking his head around the church) Nothin' yet, Ned.

**MOYER:** Naw. What I mean is that they ain't really old enough to be called women.

**NED:** Who is it you supposed to meet here?

**MOYER:** You know Sal Pickins, don't you?

**NED:** Ain't that Pickins' baby sister?

**MOYER:** Yep, but she ain't exactly a baby.

**NATE:** I reckon Moyer could tell you about that.

**TOM:** Why, yeh. I hear he stayed the night there a couple months ago. Anything to that there Moyer:?

**MOYER:** What if I did. That don't mean .

**JOSH:** Did her Paw put yawll on different sides of the sheet?

**TOM:** What happened, Moyer? Come on, tell us what happened.

*Ezra enters a little frightened.*

**EZRA:** (speaking quietly) Ned.

**NED:** That's enough clamoring out of you infidels now. I gotta keep remindin' you that you're in hell and you gotta pay a mind to the devil and that's me.

**TOM, JOSH, NATE and MOYER:** Yes, your Honor, Ned.

**NED:** Sinner Moyer, you know we can get into real trouble.

**EZRA:** Messin' around with girl too young.

**MOYER:** I didn't think the devil was partial to age.

**NED:** You got a point, infidel. You got a point. But we can't get these hell fires started till the skirts come. You sure they're comin'?

**TOM:** Maybe if we tooted the car horn, it'd hurry them up a little.

**EZRA:** Ned!

**NED:** Yeah that's a good idea.

*Moyer runs over to a car and honks three small blasts then one long one.*

**SAL:** (yelling from off stage) Is that you, Moyer?

**MOYER:** Yeah! Where the hell you been? We been waitin'.

**SAL:** We been right here.

**MOYER:** Come on out, where we can see you.

*Sal and three other girls appear from around the church.*

**MOYER:** What you all doin' back there?

**BETH:** We seen the red lights and heard all sorts of things, an' we weren't sure it was you.

**NED:** (in sepulchral tones, frightening the girls) Moyer, I thought you said there was gonna be five girls.

**MOYER:** That was the way it was s'posed to be. What happened Sal? You said Vicey was gonna come.

**SAL:** Wall you know how she is when she's got a notion in her head.

**NED:** Nate, you fergot to bring them two dozen store bought doughnuts we picked up down at Patrick.

*Nate runs to car to get doughnuts. Moyer chords and sings the following song and the others join in.*

**MOYER:**

Come, Thou Fount of every blessing,
Tune my heart to sing thy grace.
Streams of mercy n'er ceasing,
Call for songs of loudest praise.
Teach me some melodious sonnet,
Sung by flaming tongues above.
Praise the mount, I'm fixed upon it'.
Mount of thy redeeming love.

*During the song the boys pantomime the words with imaginative double meanings and the girls begin to squeal by the last line.*

**NED:** Brother devils, you can now take the vittles to the good sistern.

*Each boy takes a doughnut and a jar to a girl, Moyer to Sal, etc. The boys mumble inaudibly as they feed the girls. The whiskey has immediate effect on the girls and is also beginning to have a greater effect on the boys.*

**NED:** Sister Grace, you got a awful pretty name. Let's see if you can act as pretty. If I told you them lights wasn't red enough, what would you do?

**GRACE:** Why I'd just go an' straddle it with this red dress.

*She goes to light and stands just in front of it with feet wide apart, with much yelling especially from boys.*

**NATE:** Thay Lordy, that's a jaybird if ever I seen one. Why woman, I can see plum' ...

**MOYER:** (singing) Amazing Grace, how sweet you stand and strain a wrench with me.

**NATE:** With me, you mean.

*Nate runs toward Grace who runs off-stage behind the car.*

**MOYER:** (still singing) It once was lost but now it's found...

*Grace squeals*

**MOYER:** and everything now I see.

**NED:** Moyer, how's about pickin' us a tune on that thar guitar? Something sad and religious-like.

*Moyer plays a mournful dirge. Tom joins him with his banjo and sings the first stanza with exaggerated religiosity.*

**TOM:**

Come, come angel band Come and around me stand
O bear me away on your snowy wings To my eternal
  home
O bear me away on your snowy wings to my eternal
  home.

*Tom and Moyer then begin to jazz the song until it becomes danceable. Nate and grace come slowly back on stage with leaves falling off their clothes and clinging to their hair. Everyone but the musicians begin to run a set and Moyer does the calling. Opposum horns are heard closer.*

**MOYER:**

> Head couple out and sashay the hall
> Right back up and you give a squall
> *They yell.*

**MOYER:**

> Swing 'em high an' swing 'em low
> Gals lift up them calicos
> *The girls lift skirts and squeal as boys yell.*

**MOYER:** Next couple out an' you give 'er a swing

> *Ezra and a Girl couple out.*

**MOYER:** Hold him tight to ever' little thing

> *Girl holds Ezra tight and they nearly topple.*

**MOYER:**

> Now the next an' you give 'er a twirl
> Give a swig to yore little girl
> *A boy grabs a jar and pours from it into the Girl's*
> *upturned mouth.*

**MOYER:**

> Now the last as quick as yer able
> Put that gal up on the table
> *He puts Sal up.*

**MOYER:**

> Little foot up an' little foot down
> Throw that shawl down to the ground
> First the one and then the two
> Throw away them pretty little shoes
> Kick the pint and then the quart
> Then you drop that pretty little skirt
> Around and around and around and around
> Take that little blouse and throw it down.

> *Sal begins unbuttoning her blouse. Brother Jarrell and*
> *friends appear out of the shadows. The lights from the car had*
> *been getting dimmer all this time. The whole party had worked*
> *up to a real frenzy. A hush falls over the party at the*
> *appearance of Brother Jarrell, who is carrying a kerosene*
> *lantern.*

> *Jarrell stands gazing in horror and distress.*

> *Sal faints limply. Brother Jarrell catches her as she topples*

*off table. There is much confusion of movement as in early part of scene, but there is a deadly silence as the young folks revive Sal and all of them pile into cars and roar away, leaving Jarrell standing behind the pulpit. His friends start taking furniture inside, but dare not disturb the pulpit and the old man who has stood silently gazing in the direction of Moyer's exit.*

**BROTHER JARRELL:** "Train up a child in the way he should go and when he is old, he will not depart from it."
FADEOUT.
CURTAIN

## ACT III

### SCENE 1: TWO DAYS LATER. IN THE CHURCH
*Moyer is starting a fire in the pot-bellied stove.*

**MOYER:** I don't see no sense atall in it. Us a-comin' in here like this. Folks won't like it when there ain't no meetin' appointed.

**SAL:** We shorely couldn't talk down to my house. An' Brother John wouldn't like it much if I come to see you at his house, would he?

**MOYER:** Well, you know his house ain't exactly my house no more. Now that we're here, what do you wanta talk about? It must be pow'ful important.

**SAL:** (hesitatingly) Moyer, I don't hardly ever see you no more.

**MOYER:** You mean you drug me in here to tell me you don't see me much no more?

**SAL:** No, that ain't it.

**MOYER:** That ain't what you brung me in here to tell me?

**SAL:** No, what I mean is it ain't jest that what I wanted to talk to you about. But it has been a long time since we seen each other long enough to talk any.

**MOYER:** You already said that once.

**SAL:** Yeah, I know it.

**MOYER:** But you jest said that ain't what you brung me in

here to talk about. Now you tell me fer the second time
what you didn't bring me in here to tell me in the first
place ... Make up your mind; do you or don't you have
somethin' to talk to me about?

SAL: Yeah.

> *Sal begins to sob.*

MOYER: There ain't no call to go gettin' hysterical.

SAL: I ain't, Moyer.

MOYER: Okay, so you ain't gettin' hysterical. Now what is
it you wanta talk about? An' quit beatin' aroun' the bush.

SAL: I wasn't beatin' around the bush, Moyer, I jest
wanted you to know it's been mighty lonesome not seein'
you much an' all.

MOYER: Okay, okay, okay so it's three times you told me
already. You think I'm that dumb that it takes a tellin'
three times fer it to soak into my brain?

SAL: No, it ain't that.

MOYER: Well, what is it then?

SAL: Did you have a good time that day back in
September we went chink-a-pin huntin' up on the
mountain?

MOYER: Yeh, I reckon. Don't tell me you brung me in
here to talk about chink-a-pin huntin'.

SAL: Well, sort of. We did pick a lot of chink-a-pins, once
we got to goin'.

MOYER: Yeh.

SAL: Wouldn't that be nice to do again? Wouldn't it be
nice if we was a'climbin' the mountain now, lookin' fer
chink-a-pins?

MOYER: Have you gone plum daffy? It's colder'n a
witch's titty up on that mountain now, an' besides there
ain't no chink-a-pins up there now.

SAL: Wonder what happened to 'em.

MOYER: Wonder what happened to what?

SAL: The chink-a-pins! Do you suppose someone picked
ever' last one of 'em? ... Don't you want to go again?

MOYER: Do you mean go up on the mountain in this kind
of weather?

**SAL:** No, that ain't exactly what I'm f!ltalkin' about ... Hit is awful bad weather we been ahavin' ain't it?

**MOYER:** Yeh.

**SAL:** Paw sez hit's the worst winter since yore maw died.

**MOYER:** What's he talkin' about my maw fer?

**SAL:** He ain't, Moyer.

**MOYER:** You jest now said that he said this is the worst winter since the winter my maw died.

**SAL:** Hit is a awful bad winter.

**MOYER:** What's that got to do with my maw? You never knowed her.

**SAL:** (Ignoring his protest) You know, hit's such a bad winter that I sometimes wonder if spring will come this year. At times I don't think spring is ever gonna come agin. Do you suppose it will?

**MOYER:** Why I reckon so, iffen we live long enough.

**SAL:** Moyer, has there ever been days that you wanted to live over an' over agin?

**MOYER:** Yeh, I reckon.

**SAL:** Is there times when you jest wisht the clock would stop an' the calendar would stop, an' things would stay jest exactly like they was at that particular time?

**MOYER:** Don't tell me that you're enjoyin' my company so much that you wisht time would jest stop right now.

**SAL:** Nope, this ain't the time I was athinkin' about. But I was thinkin' about a time when we was together.

**MOYER:** What time was that?

**SAL:** Up on the mountain.

**MOYER:** I thought we jest got through all that.

**SAL:** Nope, we ain't jest got through all that. We ain't never gonna get through all that.

**MOYER:** What you mean by that?

**SAL:** I seen your grandpap the other day ...

**MOYER:** What has that to do ... my grandpap the other day ... What has that to do ...

**SAL:** He said I was gettin' so big, he didn't hardly reckanize me ...

**MOYER:** So?

**SAL:** Ain't you noticed? It seems ever'body noticed but you.

**MOYER:** I told you last fall that I reckon you was gettin' to be a big girl now an' I still reckon it. Maybe even now biggern then.

**SAL:** That ain't what I mean, Moyer ... I'm a gettin' big.

**MOYER:** You mean you been knocked up? (SAL NODS WITH LOWERED EYES) Am I supposed to congratulate you or give you my sympathy?

**SAL:** Moyer, don't you see what I'm atellin' you? You done it. Up there on the mountain that day last September. (pause) Ain't you gonna say nothin'?

**MOYER:** What you want me to say?

**SAL:** Like how I'm feel in' or somethin'.

**MOYER: How you feelin' ?**

**SAL:** Oh, I feel purty good now. It was at first when it was so bad. I didn't have no notion what was wrong. I thought fer sure a cold bug had done bit me, but Vicey told me right away what it was. An' ever' mornin' I had them awful spells with my stomach, an' I started geetin' peakeder an' peakeder. But I didn't let on atall to Ma and Pa what was wrong, until Granny Amos come by one day acallin' an' she took one look at me, then she looked at Ma an' said, "That gal is mighty po'ly lookin ... What's ailin' her?" Ma said she hadn't taken notice to me bein' sick, so Granny said, "Course she ain't said nothin' cause she's in a family way." An' acourse Granny Amos knew cause she likely birthed more babies than any granny woman between here an' Patrick. Well, I want you to know, when she said that you coulda knocked Ma over with a feather, but it warn't long afore she was on her feet an' abeatin' time acrost the room where I was asettin' ...

**MOYER:** Shut up, fer God's sake.

**SAL:** What's wrong, Moyer , did I say somethin' wrong?

**MOYER:** You said plenty wrong.

**SAL:** I didn't go to rile you up that away.

**MOYER:** What makes you think I got any time fer this kinda talk?

**SAL:** What kinda talk?

**MOYER:** This kinda talk about havin' babies an' Granny Amos tellin' yore Maw ...

**SAL:** Why, I jest thought you'd be a little innerested.

**MOYER:** An' give me jest one good reason, why I oughter be innerested.

**SAL:** Moyer, the baby's gotta have a daddy.

**MOYER:** Why pick on me?

**SAL:** Cause you're already its daddy.

**MOYER:** What gives you that notion?

**SAL:** Surely you remember that day last fall when we went up on the mountain an' picked that bucket full of chink-a-pins.

**MOYER:** I remember all right. But how many more buckets of chink-a-pins did you pick last fall?

**SAL:** Moyer!

**MOYER:** I mean I ain't got no guarantee that that young'un you're a-carryin' is mine, an' I ain't buyin' no pig in a poke.

**SAL:** I reckon you'll jest have to take my word fer it.

**MOYER:** I reckon I don't have to take yore word fer nothin'.

**SAL:** But I gotta do somethin'. When Paw found out I was gettin' big, he was so mad he was fit to be tied. Ma told him tonight at supper. He ... uh. he ... kicked me out. He said if I was startin' my own family now, I'd need a house of my own an' that his'n wasn't big enough fer two families. An' he also allowed that I was another man's care now, so I figgered as how you was the daddy an' all that it was only fitten that you help out now. We could walk across the gap to yore grandpa's, an' he could marry us up tonight.

**MOYER:** You're gettin' a little ahead of yoreself now. I ain't got no notion in the world of gettin' married. Not jest now leastwise. Don't you remember that jest afore we went chink-a-pin huntin-thet I said somethin' might happen and that it wasn't gonna be no care of mine, an' you said that you didn't expect it to be no care but yourn? You remember that?

**SAL:** Yeh, but I didn't know ...

**MOYER:** You didn't know. You didn't care. I tried to warn you, but you wouldn't have nothin' but goin' to the top of the mountain cause that's where Vicey Dawson had so many purty tales about.

**SAL:** Her tales didn't say nothin' about anyt hing like this.

**MOYER:** If you like her tales so good, why didn't you go to her to hear some more of them purty tales? Yeh, why don't you go now an' have her tell you a tale about what you do now?

**SAL:** Where can I spend the night?

**MOYER:** I don't know bout you, but I gotta go back into Patrick. Me an' Ned's got a big load to carry acrost the state line tonight, an' I can't be bothered with no girl hangin' roun' my neck.

**SAL:** You mean you ain't gonna take me with you tonight?

**MOYER:** Not tonight nor any other night.

**SAL:** (strongly) Do you want yore own natcheral child to be borned a bastard like ...

**MOYER:** (glaring) Like what?

**SAL:** Moyer, I know hit was a lot fer me to expect. But I kinda wanted you to want me an' I was sure you'd take me even if you didn't want me, cause hit's yore baby I'm acarryin'. I thought sure you'd do things right fer the sake of the baby. (pause) I bet it'll be a boy ... an' I bet hit'll look jest like hit's daddy with faraway blue eyes an' coal black hair. He'll probably allus be funnin' around and, why the way he's been kickin' ...

**MOYER:** Now don't go to change my mind. Ned's awaitin' fer me now down to Patrick ... But I tell you what I'll do. I'll poke up the fire fer you, so's you can spend the night here, then tomorrow mornin' when I git back I'll come by to pick you up.

**SAL:** I knowed you'd think of somethin', Moyer.

**MOYER:** Don't go reachin' fer the stars yet.

*Moyer exits abruptly. The sound of a car starting and roaring away leaving only the sounds of winter. Sal sits at window and stares.*

BLACKOUT.

## SCENE 2: FIVE DAYS LATER IN THE GRAVEYARD BESIDE THE CHURCH.

*Moyer is standing a long way from the others and is never noticed. Brothers Jarrell, Reece, White and Hiatt and two women stand at an open grave singing.*

**BROTHERS JARRELL, REECE, WHITE and HIATT and TWO WOMEN:**

I have heard of a land on the faraway strand,

'Tis a beautiful home of the soul

Built by Jesus on high, there we never shall die.

'Tis a land where we never grow old.

Never grow old, never grow old,

In a land where we'll never grow old;

Never grow old, never grow old,

In a land where we'll never grow old.

**JARRELL:**

Let us go to the Lord in prayer:

O Almighty God,

Lord of all mountains and all valleys

Master of all men and all creatures

We come to thee with heavy hearts and tear-stained eyes

For a daughter gone wrong

An' a daughter done wrong.

A'mighty God

Look with pity on all thy creatures

But especially

Look with loving kindness

Upon the soul of this child

And upon that unborn soul

She carried 'neath her heart.

O God we know she sinned

An' she knowed she sinned
An' you know she sinned,
But you're the only one
Who can do anything about it.
If it be her time to go, so be it.
If it be thy will to take her, so be it.
An' we accept what we know has got to be.
But, A'mighty God open the eyes of others
As they think on this pore child
An' convict their heart
With the fear of the everlasting flame
And the terror of the Day of Judgement.
An' A'mighty God
The boy what got her in trouble
May his soul rot in hell, this night.
(others act startled)
In the name of Jesus, we pray. Amen.
Earth to earth, ashes to ashes, dust to dust.

> *Moyer and the women exit.*
>
> *The other preachers leave the grave and begin talking.*

**REECE:** What a shame!

**WHITE:** What a pity!

**HIATT:** What do you reckon she was adoin' in the church house, Brother Jarrell?

**JARRELL:** I don't know. Hit's a real puzzlement that's what it is. Doc Tuttle said she musta been there at least three days. There'd been a fire in the stove, but she warn't nowhere near it. She was asettin' at the window farthest from the stove, the window what looks down toward the public road. She wouldn't afroze if she'd jest kept the fire agoin' an' stayed clost to it. Hit was like she was awaitin' fer somethin' or somebody. But what I'm awonderin' now is who got her in that fix.

**WHITE:** Don't you know?

**JARRELL:** I ain't got no notion.

**HIATT:** It seems ever'body else knows but you, then.

**JARRELL:** You ain't athinkin' who I'm afraid you're athinkin'.

**HIATT:** I'm afraid I am.

**JARRELL:** Come on.

**REECE:** Where're you go'in'?

**JARRELL:** I got some business to 'ten to, an' you're agonna help me. Brother Hiatt, you run up the branch and fetch Gill Dalton, an' you, Brother Reece, get Glenn Conway, an' Brother White you come home with me. We'll all meet at the store in 'bout a hour, then do what we gotta do.

### SCENE 3: ON THE MOUNTAIN ABOUT TWO HOURS LATER.

*Ned's coming down mountain carrying rifle. Moyer enters carrying double barreled shot gun.*

**NED:** Where in the hell you been? I been lookin' all over hell an' creation fer you.

**MOYER:** You know very well where I been. They caught my ass an' put me away for a few days. I thought for sure you'd come make bail.

**NED:** You know I can't afford that. It's not just the money ... which I don' have ... but hey also out lookin' for me. But where you been today? I was told you got out earlier today.

**MOYER:** I've been down to the church house.

**NED:** What in the sam hill's goin' on down there that's so all-fired important?

**MOYER:** Jest a funeral.

**NED:** Do you think we ain't got no goddamn more to do than to jest be traipsin' aroun' payin' courtesy calls on the dead? Now git yore ass up there an' stand guard.

**MOYER:** Stand guard? But I'm supposed to carry a load.

**NED:** Shut yore goddamn mouth, you bastard, an' listen to me. Someone down at the store jest heard that they're makin' a raid on the still today, an' we gotta have all the men here.

**MOYER:** Ned, let me carry a load. The way I feel today I could carry it to hell an' back an' there ain't a state cop in three states what could stop me. Why if ...

**NED:** I done tole you to shut yore goddamn trap. Now ... Hey is that shotgun the only gun you got with you?

**MOYER:** Yeh, what's wrong with it?

**NED:** What's wrong with it? You don't have the brains God gave a muley billy goat. You can't git no goddamn range with a shotgun. You'll have to hide up here clost to the trail where you can't hardly see a thing. I got a rifle you can use today, then you buy a rifle tomorrow, an' them's orders from headquarters.

**MOYER:** I ain't gonna use no rifle neither. Papa give me this shotgun, an' it's good enough fer me.

**NED:** Well, listen to that. He ain't only goddamn stubborn, he's Papa's boy.

**MOYER:** (pointing gun at Ned) Now, listen ...

**NED:** Now you listen to me buddy. Don't you go gettin' so goddamn riled or I'll show you how to really use a gun ... You didn't see nobody when you come up here, did you?

**MOYER:** Nope. Who you expectin'?

**NED:** I ain't got no idea. Nate jest come up from the store and he heard somebody talkin' about some men comin' up here to the still, an' we ain't takin' no chances on who it might be.

**MOYER:** That oughter give us a little excitement. I'll blow the brains outa the first man I see.

**NED:** Don't go gettin' too damn excited or you'll get us all shot to Hell. Now git yore ass up there above the trail.

*Moyer and Ned exit. Brother Jarrell and five other men enter.*

**WHITE:** But Brother Jarrell you cautioned us not to poke our nose into this moonshinin' fuss.

**JARRELL:** This is diffrunt. They ain't runnin' this jest fer their own enjoyment, which is one thing. But they're acarryin' it acrost the state line an' doctorin' it besides.

**REECE:** What jou mean doctorin' it?

JARRELL: They're puttin' red devil lye in it to flavor it, an' if they ain't careful they'll put in too much an' kill some pore soul.

HIATT: But Brother Jarrell, this is a job fer the revenooers.

JARRELL: Yep that part of it is, but the revenooers can't do what we come to do.

HIATT: What be that, Brother Jarrell?

JARRELL: We come to save Moyer afore he gets any deeper in sin, an' ...

WHITE: How you 'tendin' to do that?

JARRELL: First we gotta git to the still an' find Moyer an' then ...

GLENN CONWAY: Now wait, Brother Jarrell. I know what that boy means to you an' all, but it's pow'ful dangerous, jest walkin' up on a still thataway.

GILL DALTON: Yeah, we'll git shot fer sure.

WHITE: Brother Jarrell, why don't we wait till Moyer comes home or some of us see him down at the store or ...

JARRELL: No, hit'll be too late then.

REECE: What makes you think it'll be too late?

JARRELL: I reckon you fergit that prayer I prayed today at that pore girl's funral.

REECE: Bout the boy's soul gain' to hell tonight?

JARRELL: Yeah. So I've gotta see him afore nightfall, an' there ain't but one way to do that an' that's by gain' to where he's at ... Are any of you going with me? ... Well, I can't fault you none fer that, but if you'll wait fer me at the foot of the mountain I'd be much obliged.

*The men exit slowly left and Brother Jarrell starts climbing onto first ledge. when he reaches the ledge he stands upright and just as he does, Moyer shoots him with his shotgun.*

MOYER:

I got one.

I shot one.

I got me a son-uv-a-bitch.

*Moyer appears at top of mountain.*

**MOYER:** The bastard thought he could sneak by me. Not me, Moyer Jarrell.

*Moyer climbs down toward Brother Jarrell and yells and babbles all the way. When he sees who it is he stands stunned until the elders enter and climb up to the ledge and the moonshiners climb down to the ledge. Moyer drops his gun and kneels by Brother Jarrell and holds his head in his lap.*

**MOYER:** Papa, speak to me. Hit's Moyer, Papa. Hit's me. I didn't go to do it, Papa.

*Moyer rocks Brother Jarrell now like a baby.*

**MOYER:** Why I thought hit was some goddamn federal man. I couldn't hardly see a dad-blasted thing from them bushes where I was a-hiding. (pause) That gun you give me, I told you it was the most beautiful ever in the world. Hit's the shootingest ... (pause) Don't leave now, Papa. Things'll be different now. Things'll be all different now.

*Moyer pulls the bottom of Brother Jarrell's coat up under his head like a pillow, and continues to cradle him.*

**MOYER:** Now, Papa, when we get home, we're gonna have that talk all over again. (pause) We'll have time now, Papa, you and me. We'll have time now, Papa.

*Church people start toward Moyer. His eyes warn them back. He starts very quietly humming "That Lonesome Valley", letting the volume of his voice build slowly.*

*The moonshiners start toward Moyer. He abruptly drops the body of Brother Jarrell, quits humming, stands up and belligerently faces his friends who back away.*

*Church people pick up the body and look at Moyer as though to ask him if he is going with them. He slowly looks away and stares at the ground. They proceed down the mountain. The moonshiners start up mountain. Moyer stands still until everyone exits. He then picks up gun, climbs to top of mountain. He disappears over the mountain. There is another shotgun blast. The sound of the gun covers the sound of the first few words of "Lonesome Valley" sung by church people, from offstage.*

**CHURCH PEOPLE:**

... that lonesome valley.

You gotta walk it by yoreself.

There's nobody here can walk it for you.

You gotta walk it by yourself.

Jesus walked that lonesome valley.

He had to walk it by himself.  There was nobody else
  could walk it for him.

He had to walk it by himself.

You gotta go and stand yore trial.

You gotta stand there by yourself.

You gotta  walk that lonesome valley.

You gotta go there by yourself.

  *The words grow fainter and fainter.*

  *The children were in background of the cemetery scene.*
*During this scene they follow Moyer to mountain but he does*
*not allow them to cross the footbridge where he encounters Ned.*
*They drift over to side of stage and sit quietly until church*
*people come.*

  *When Brother Jarrell is shot they scamper across footbridge*
*to the body and almost attack the body except that Moyer's*
*sudden appearance pushes them again to one side. They again*
*hover to one side while Moyer tries to revive his grandfather.*
*When they hear the second gun blast they seem to fly over the*
*mountain and very indecorously drag Moyer's body back into*
*view. They hunker around the crumpled body stoically looking*
*at it or at the distance or each other, expressing no emotion.*
*They wear heavy hand-me-downs, coats probably too big for*
*them. Winter gives the children a rather peaked look for lack*
*of sunshine and wholesome food. Their make-up gives the eyes*
*a rather black hollow look. With their sunken eyes, hunkered*
*positions, and heavy coats, they should have the appearance of*
*a flock of birds, something between vultures and sparrows or*
*maybe a combination of both.*

  *At curtain close, the children are quietly sitting and the*
*song of the church elders is slowly dying out in the distance.*

FADEOUT.

CURTAIN

# Coming of Age

From 1995 to 2005, my wife, Robin, and I developed and produced summer theatre in our building in Thomas, WV. Prior to that, Chuck Nichols, Cleta Long and I developed a revue, Tucker Tales, based on stories of Tucker County, the home of Thomas. We performed at various times and places around the county.

As the 20th century rolled into West Virginia, Tucker County was coming of age into maturity of work, play, school and home life, just prior to the first world war. In many ways this script also celebrates the writers of Tucker County in revealing its history and way of life. One of the first explorers and the first writer in the area was Porte Crayon. His assessment of the geography of the area is contained in some of the early dialogue in the script. Although set in the Appalachian Mountains where the population was sparse, the county attracted international migrants. People from 32 different countries were naturalized there. The playwright, was resident of Thomas and Red Creek for several years, and wrote this play to commemorate the centennial of

the Cottrill's Opera House and Miners and
Merchants Bank in Thomas in 1902. Feaster
Wolford in his book of poems, Mountain
Memories, describes various activities of
town and farm in the area. Cleta Long,
another noted Tucker County poet, releases
the audience with her poem The Closing,
published in her collection of poems in Dry
Fork's Daughter.

However, I wanted to honor the local
history somewhat more seriously. I wrote
Coming of Age, containing tales and
history of the county. The man characters
are fictional, but they convey the music,
poetry and local culture of the county.
Thirty-two nationalities were naturalized in
the county. At Ellis Island, new immigrants
were told, "Go to Thomas, West Virginia,
where there are plenty of jobs digging coal
from the bowels of the earth."

# COMING OF AGE

*by E. Reid Gilbert*

Cast

**NARRATOR**
**BUSTER FOSTER** . . . . . . . .Son of Mr. and Mrs. Foster
**ROXIE FOSTER** . . . . . . . . .Buster's little sister
**UNCLE JIMMY**
    **JACK WRIGHT** . . . . . . .Buster's and Roxie's Uncle
**MR. HINEBAUGH** . . . . . . .Banker
**GUARD** . . . . . . . . . . . . . . . . . .In the bank
**MR. FOSTER.** . . . . . . . . . . .Father of Buster and Roxie
**MRS. FOSTER** . . . . . . . . . . .Mother of Buster and Roxie
**SEROFINA MAZZONI** . . . .Roxie's friend
**MRS. MAZZONI** . . . . . . . . .Serofina's mother
**BETSY** . . . . . . . . . . . . . . . . . .School teacher
**FRED GILLEY** . . . . . . . . . .School teacher
**MR. EVANS** . . . . . . . . . . . . .School teacher
**SALLY AND TOM** . . . . . . . .Students at the Ball
**WILLIAM FOSTER** . . . . . .Buster's son

# ACT I

## SCENE 1: MARCH, 1902, IN BUSTER FOSTER'S ATTIC BEDROOM

**NARRATOR:** This play commemorates the history of Tucker County, WV at the time of the beginning of the 20th century. Feaster Wolford in his poem, Remembered Towns of Yore, sets the tone of life in town and farm. (recited or sung)

> As I sit here by the fireside
> And watch the embers glow
> I think of all the places
> I knew so long ago.
> As I think of all the people
> In towns that used to be
> A host of precious memories
> Come flowing back to me.
> I long to hear the whistles
> Of the many busy mills
> And the zest they brought to living
> For folks among the hills.
> Even though this way of living,
> I may never hope to see,
> I can cherish still the memories
> Of the days that used to be.

It's March,1902, in Buster Foster's attic bedroom.
*Buster is stretched out reading beside an oil lamp.*

**BUSTER:** (calling downstairs to his little sister, Roxie.) Crawl up here Roxie and listen to-what I found in this book.

**ROXIE:** (from below) You better be quiet, Buster, or Mama will hear. You know I'm supposed to be asleep.

**BUSTER:** Oh Mama won't hear and 'sides you know she likes for us to read, an' I've found something that happened a long time ago right here. It might be kinda like a history lesson.

**ROXIE:** I don't want no history lesson. 'sides that's for school.

*Roxie pokes her head up through floor of attic.*

**BUSTER:** You're always sayin' "I wonder what around here looked like before they cut all the trees."

**ROXIE:** Don't you ever wonder what it was like when there were lots of trees?

**BUSTER:** Oh yes, you know there was a big celebration in town, when they cut the last tree in Canaan. Uncle Jimmy Jack said that if trees could cuss this wouldn't be a fitten place for a Sunday School picnic Apparently this fellow was writing out what it all looked like along the Blackwater in 1851.

**ROXIE:** (crawling up beside him) All right. Go ahead and read, but I don't aim to take no test on it.

**BUSTER:** You know there won't be a test. I'm not your teacher.

**ROXIE:** You may not be my real teacher, but you sure try to teach me all the time.

**BUSTER:** That's what big brothers are meant to do. Just lay still an' listen to this.

*Buster reads a Chronicle passage, p. 171.*

**BUSTER:** "On either side, the mountains rise up, almost a perpendicular ascent, to a height of some 600 feet." He's talking here about the Blackwater canyon.

**ROXIE:** I could figure that out.

**BUSTER:** "They are covered down their sides, to the very edge of the river, with the noblest of firs and hemlocks, and as far as the eye can see, with the laurel in all its most luxuriant growth — befitting undergrowth to such noble growth of forest, where every here and there some more towering and vast Balsam fir."

**ROXIE:** Do you suppose it will ever look like that again?

**BUSTER:** The mountains are always with us, and the Indian would say "Mother Earth will grow her hair again."

**ROXIE:** When did you say that fellow wrote about the Blackwater?

**BUSTER:** Well, he explored it fifty years ago in 1851 and put it in a book in 1853.

**ROXIE:** What did you say his name was?

**BUSTER:** I didn't say, but it was Strother. That was his real name, but his pen name ...

**ROXIE:** What do you mean his real name? An' what's a pen name?

**BUSTER:** It's like your real name is Roxie, but ...

**ROXIE:** No, my real name is Roseanne. People just call me Roxie. Is that my pen name?

**BUSTER:** No, that's your nickname.

**ROXIE:** Well what's my pen name?

**BUSTER:** You don't have one.

**ROXIE:** Why don't I have one? ... Do you have a pen name?

**BUSTER:** No, I don't have one either.

**ROXIE:** Why can't we have pen names?

**BUSTER:** We could, but ...

**ROXIE:** Then let's get us some pen names.

**BUSTER:** You can't get a pen name until you've written something.

**ROXIE:** You remember I wrote that Christmas ...

**BUSTER:** No, I mean when what you've written gets put in a book. Like Samuel Clemens' pen name was Mark Twain.

**ROXIE:** Well I think it's plum silly. 'sides you didn't tell me what that writer's pen name was.

**BUSTER:** It was Porte Crayon.

**ROXIE:** (She gets a case of the giggles.) Why that's even sillier.

**BUSTER:** Things won't seem so all fired silly when you've come of age.

**ROXIE:** Now what does that mean?

**BUSTER:** What does what mean?

**ROXIE:** "When you've come of age."

**BUSTER:** It means when you're old enough to know things, an' you no longer have to ask so many questions.

**ROXIE:** Uncle Jimmy Jack said that that's the only way you can learn anything ... to ask questions.

**BUSTER:** But you won't have to pester a body to death asking so many questions, one right on top of each other before waitin' for an answer.

**ROXIE:** So when I "COME OF AGE" I'll have all the answers an' won't have to ask any more questions?

**BUSTER:** Well now, it won't be exactly that way ... But you'll probably keep your questions to yourself.

**ROXIE:** How do you do that? ... If I have a question, I just gotta ask somebody or I don't get the answer.

**BUSTER:** You could try journaling; that's what I've started doing.

**ROXIE:** What's journaling? Is it like taking a trip?

**BUSTER:** It is like taking a trip, but not on a horse or a train. It's like travelling on paper in your own mind. Like that BLACKWATER CHRONICLE I read to you. That was a journal Porte Crayon kept of his journey into this region.

**ROXIE:** That seems like keeping a diary. Sue Sloan has been keeping a diary, an' she let me read it. I now know all about what she feels about Johnny Brown. She writes down everything she does or whatever happens to her and what'-n all she thinks about.

**BUSTER:** Well that's a little different from a journal.

**ROXIE:** Oh I understand now. A diary is what happens to you and how you feel and a journal is where you ask your questions.

**BUSTER:** I guess that kind of sums it up.

**ROXIE:** What was the question he was trying to find an answer for when he journaled?

**BUSTER:** You're asking an awful lot of questions again.

**ROXIE:** But that ought to be all right, 'cause I haven't come of age yet.

**BUSTER:** Oh yeah ... Now what was that question again?
*Roxie starts to repeat the question.*

**BUSTER:** You want to know what was his question?
*Roxie nods in agreement with Buster.*

**BUSTER:** His question was, "What is the fishing like in

that river called the Blackwater, which he thought ought to be called the Amberwater, on the western slope of the Backbone Mountain?"

ROXIE: Did he get his question answered?

BUSTER: Yep. He and his friends caught five hundred trout one afternoon, right above the Falls.

ROXIE: Now that you're writin' your own journal, have you come of age?

BUSTER: (laughing) No, Not hardly, but maybe it will help me in my growing up.

ROXIE: Do you think it will help me to grow up?

BUSTER: Oh yes, but you have to grow bigger and taller and older at the same time. You better get back to bed.

ROXIE: Read me just one short thing he wrote about the Falls.

BUSTER: He gets poetic sometimes. I'm reading from p. 167 "And it seems to me now, when I revert my thoughts to that morning's exploration of the Blackwater that all the divinities of old fables must have had their dwelling-place out there with all the beautiful creations of old poesy, the spirits or gods that now 'No longer live in the faith of reason,' all were around me in the unknown wild — Sometimes the fancy has possessed me that I saw Undine sitting in all her beauty by the foam of the little Niagara." He goes on and on, poetically, about the river and the falls.

ROXIE: (crawling backwards toward ladder) I really liked that.

BUSTER: You really and truly liked it?

ROXIE: Now you're asking questions. Yeah, I'll think about what that Crayon fellow wrote next time we go to the falls. I liked your advice too.

BUSTER: Gee, thanks!

BLACKOUT.

## SCENE 2: LUMBER JACK SCENE JUNE 9, 1902

BUSTER: Uncle Jimmy Jack, does your coffee suit you?

**UNCLE JIMMY JACK:** Does my coffee fit me?

**BUSTER:** Is it ok?

**ROXIE:** Uncle Jimmy Jack, how long did you work in the lumbering?

**UNCLE JIMMY WRIGHT:** Why, Honey Pet, I worked thar all my public working life. An' I'll tell you right now it sure warn't no Sunday School social.

**BUSTER:** But you didn't have to worry about what you'd have to eat or a place to sleep did you?

**UNCLE JIMMY WRIGHT:** Oh no, Buster Boy, we had good eatin's. No doubt about that. Now fer breakfast at about 5:30 in the a.m. we'd always have plenty of good strong coffee right off the bat. That'd kinda give everbody a good jump start. We had one cook who just couldn't catch on to how.to make good wakin' up coffee like this here'n. So one mornin' when I took a sip of that feeble coffee, I set the cup down right on the floor.

**ROXIE:** What'd you do that for?

**UNCLE JIMMY WRIGHT:** That's exactly what he asked, so I just told him it was so weak I wuz afraid it might fall off the table.

**BUSTER:** But, surely you had more than just coffee.

**UNCLE JIMMY WRIGHT:** I was just getting' to that part. Oh yes we had fried potatoes, prunes, fried eggs, oatmeal, donuts, steak and of course plenty of hot biscuits. We allus had plenty. of meat. Every camp would keep 30 to 40 head of cattle an' 'bout as many hogs. An' the cook an' his helpers'd butcher ever day. You know with that many men eatin' ever day, it would take a lot of meat. An' I tell you it wouldn't take them very long to devour a whole cow or pig.

**ROXIE:** Who did all that cookin'?

**UNCLE JIMMY WRIGHT:** Oh thar warn't very much lookin' goin' on.

**ROXIE:** Cookin', Uncle Jimmy Jack, who did all ... ?

**UNCLE JIMMY WRIGHT:** Oh, all that cookin'. Why hit was diffent fellas. Fer a short spell I did the cookin' in one of the camps, until I played a trick on the boys.

**BUSTER:** What kinda trick Uncle Jimmy?

**ROXIE:** Why would you want to play a trick on them?

**UNCLE JIMMY WRIGHT:** Well the reason I done it was that a whole gang of them had played a awful mean trick on me back in the summer when I had gone to take a bath in the river. Of course that was the only bathin' we'd do. To try that in the winter would be like suicide.

**BUSTER:** Weren't the other fellows in the river too?

**UNCLE JIMMY WRIGHT:** They was, but they got out before I was ready to go, an' I suspicioned somethin' when they made a lot of noise in the underbrush.

**BUSTER:** I can pretty much imagine what they did.

**UNCLE JIMMY WRIGHT:** Yep, they took all my clothes and shoes back to camp with them, an' when I come out of the river I found out real soon what they'd done ... I had to walk all the way back barefooted and buck naked, over rough rocks an' through a briar patch. When I come back to camp, they was all laughin' an' yellin' all sorts of things, an' me all scratched up from them rocks an' briars. Well I didn't give them the satisfaction of thinkin' they had bothered me in the least. I just howdied them an' walked just as directly as you please to the bunkhouse. I made out like it was just a ever'day thing for me to walk around barefoot and nekkid.

**BUSTER:** You didn't do anything to them then.

**UNCLE JIMMY WRIGHT:** Naw, I just bided my time 'til a real cold mornin' next winter, when ever'one would be wantin' their coffee right off, first thing when they got up. So that mornin' I got up real early and brewed up a strong pot of coffee. I didn't even start cookin' anythin' else.

**BUSTER:** Why not?

**UNCLE JIMMY WRIGHT:** I figured, fer certain, that they wouldn't be wantin' no breakfast that mornin' after their fust big cup of coffee ... what I had fixed up with Prince Albert smokin' tobacco. An' I tell you' them boys headed fer the woods; not fer lumberin', but fer throwin' up their entire innards. Yes, yes an' 'tis a fact.

**BUSTER:** What about the sleepin' accommodations?

**UNCLE JIMMY WRIGHT:** The sleepin' what?

**BUSTER:** Accommodation?

**UNCLE JIMMY WRIGHT:** Now I know what you're gettin' at. It would be stretchin' things a bit to call them accommodations. Why, it shore warn't very accommodatin' to be asleepin' 16 men to a bed an' a hundred men to a room, but hit was sometimes so cold we didn't mind the scrimpy arrangements.

**ROXIE:** Really; they would be that crowded?

**UNCLE JIMMY WRIGHT:** Yes, yes an' 'tis a fact.

**ROXIE:** How'd you sleep?

**UNCLE JIMMY WRIGHT:** Not much, an' in one camp the bedbugs was so bad, that we'd set the bed legs in buckets of kerosene to keep the bedbugs from crawlin' up in the bed. But anyways when we blew out the lamps the bedbugs would've been waitin' fer us on the ceiling an' then jump off right on our facesAn' usually wherever there was bedbugs there was an awful lot of lice.

**BUSTER:** Where would they come from?

**UNCLE JIMMY WRIGHT:** Why they'd come from other men what hadn't took care of theirselves. Now to accommodate them lice in my winter longjohns, I'd take them longjohns off real quick an' turn them inside out so the lice'd all be on the outside. Then I'd put em back on real quick an' jump in bed an' go to sleep as quick as possible 'fore the lice had time to make their way from the outside of those longjohns into the inside.

**ROXIE:** Now, Uncle Jimmy Jack, you're fibbin'.

**UNCLE JIMMY WRIGHT:** No, no, 'tis a fact.

**BUSTER:** I guess if you didn't take baths in the winter, you probably didn't shave then neither.

**UNCLE JIMMY WRIGHT:** Nor in the summer as a usual thing. Oh once in awhile a fellow'd take a double bitted axe ...

ROXIE: What's a double bitted axe?

UNCLE JIMMY WRIGHT: Why, honey pet. It's a axe what has two blades instead of one blade an' a hammer head.

ROXIE: Why would it have two blades?

UNCLE JIMMY WRIGHT: Well when one would get dull, you'd just flip it to other side an' use the other blade an' thataway you wouldn't have to stop so much and sharpen them up. Now thet double bitted axe come in real handy when I was a knotter.

ROXIE: What's a knotter?

UNCLE JIMMY WRIGHT: That's the feller what'd chop off the tree limbs. You know clean off the trunk of the tree.

ROXIE: But wouldn't that double bitted axe be awful dangerous, Uncle Jimmy Jack?

UNCLE JIMMY WRIGHT: You sure do ask a lot of questions for such a little girl.

BUSTER: That's what I keep tellin' her.

ROXIE: You still didn't answer my question about it seeming to be so dangerous.

UNCLE JIMMY WRIGHT: You know that's exactly what a fellow said when them axes was first brung down from Pennsylvania. This fellow over in Sugarlands said it sure looked dangerous as a fellow might liabley cut out his brains with one of those things. Another fellow answered him right back, "Well if you're gonna hit yourself in the head with a axe you might as well cut 'em out as to knock 'em out with the mail side of the axe.."

ROXIE: What'd that have to do with shavin'?

UNCLE JIMMY WRIGHT: I was about to tell you about thet, when you got me to explainin' what a doublebitted axe was. A fellow'd take a whetstone to a double-bitted axe and then a leather strop, just like they done in the barber shops. He'd then lather up his whiskers real good with some of that homemade lye soap, an' shave his self, real good. Ordinarily it would be a young fellow what'd want to do this, who had been talkin' to some pretty girl nearby.

**ROXIE:** Did you ever shave that way?

**UNCLE JIMMY WRIGHT:** Oh no, Roxie. Shavin' in any form was looked down on by most of the boys. Why it was practically as dandified as carryin' a pocket-handkerchief.

**BUSTER:** After you cut the trees down, did you float the logs down the river?

**UNCLE JIMMY WRIGHT:** Oh, before the railroads come in, that's what we done. But when they come, we mostly shipped t'em off on flatbed cars.

**BUSTER:** Is that mostly what the Shay engines did?

**UNCLE JIMMY WRIGHT:** Now I'll tell you they were real lifesavers, 'cause they can handle the curves a whole lot better than them other trains from the flatlands. A fellow by the name of Shay invented that engine with pistons just for the mountain narrow gauge roads.

**BUSTER:** Even then those downhill curves must've been pretty dangerous.

**UNCLE JIMMY WRIGHT:** You better believe that. One feller even sung about them curves.

*Uncle Jimmy Wright begins to sing Cabin Mountain Wreck:*

**UNCLE JIMMY WRIGHT:**

It was Feb. fifth on a cold winter night
And the ground all covered with snow
When Old Number Four sped down Cabin Mountain
You should've seen Old Number Four roll.
Fred Viering called to his coal-blackened fireman,
"Just shovel in a little more coal'
And when we cross that Cabin Mountain
You can watch Old Number Four roll."
He called his wife from the top of the mountain'
And said, "The weather's awful mean,
But turn up the fire and get my supper ready,
And I'11 be there at seven-fifteen."
Fireman Kline said, "You can't make it Fred,
The weather's much too bad."
Viering roared, "The truth of the matter,

I aim not to tell,
I'll eat my supper with my woman in Davis,
Or I'll eat with the devil in hell!"
It's a mighty rough road from down Cabin Mountain
And a road with many a turn;
It was on this road that he picked up speed,
And his brakes all begun to burn.
He was going down grade at fifty miles an hour
When his whistle began to scream;
He was found in the wreck with his engine in reverse,
And was scalded to death by the steam.
Come all you ladies and heed my warning,
When your lover leaves your board,
Pray that he slows down on the mountain
So the devil can't take him at his word.

**UNCLE JIMMIE JACK:** Hit's fer certain those trains was dangerous.

**BUSTER:** You never worked on the railroad did you?

**UNCLE JIMMY WRIGHT:** Nope, never did. But now there was a fellow who worked on the railroad I knowed who was played a mean trick on.

**ROXIE:** What kind of trick, Uncle Jimmy Jack?

**UNCLE JIMMY WRIGHT:** Well it was a trick played on him when he had passed out from drinkin'. He was a Cherokee fellow by the name of Boonie Young, an' was awful bad to drink, don't you know.

**BUSTER:** I didn't know there were American Indians here then.

**UNCLE JIMMY WRIGHT:** Oh, yes an' they still have plenty of family round here. Now this fellow, what I'm fixin' to tell you 'nout had passed out while on the job, an' the boys he was working with decided to take him to a graveyard down in Parsons, an' they hid where he couldn't see them an' waited for him to come to. When he did wake up an' seen hisself in a graveyard, he looked around but didn't see nobody else an' declared right out loud, "Well hit shore looks like hit's Jedgement Day an'

I'm the first fellow up."

**ROXIE:** Uncle Jimmy Jack, did that really happen?

**UNCLE JIMMY WRIGHT:** Yes, yes, an' 'tis a fact..

**BUSTER:** Well if you didn't work on the railroad, you did do some farmin' didn't you..

**UNCLE JIMMY WRIGHT:** Yes, Buster Boy 'tis a fact I did some farmin' from time to time. Mostly, just some garden farmin' an' raisin' some hogs, an' a milk cow.

**ROXIE:** Did you have pastures to fence them in for grazin'?

**UNCLE JIMMY WRIGHT:** No, we didn't need to do that. We'd just let them run free and forage for theirselves. The acorns, an' chestnuts, an' hickory nuts made awful good mash for farm brutes.

**BUSTER:** I thought mash was a part of makin' moonshine.

**UNCLE JIMMY WRIGHT:** Now you hesh up, boy. I don't fer the life of me know who come up with that name, "moonshine." I jest called it my "energizer" an' as the ol' feller would say, "What's good fer the patient was better fer the doctor." We wasn't even talkin' about that kind of thing atall. I wuz talkin' 'bout how we took keer of our stock. An' you interrupted the story what I wuz afixin' to norate.

**BUSTER:** Sorry, Uncle Jimmy Jack.

**UNCLE JIMMY WRIGHT:** It's alright. Now when it come time for hog butcherin', we'd just go out to the woods to find the hogs what belonged to us.

**BUSTER:** How'd you know which ones were yours?

**UNCLE JIMMY WRIGHT:** Oh we put a special mark on their ears when they was just piglets. Anyways there was one big boar what belonged to me that I was aimin' to butcher, an' the meat would've lasted us all year. He was that humongous. Well I found him sure enough, an' he was so big I mistook him at first fer a bear. Now as luck would have it, he had been benastied by a ...

**ROXIE:** He had what?

**UNCLE JIMMY WRIGHT:** Been benastied by a polecat. You know when a polecat jumps onto his front legs …

**BUSTER:** Oh, I know what that means.

**UNCLE JIMMY WRIGHT:** Well even with the terrible stink, so help me Hannah I was bound and determined to get aholt of that big feller, but all I could do was catch him by the tail. Then he took off with me a hangin' on, an' I shore won't about to lose that ol' Bangus Boar.

**BUSTER:** How'd you get him to stop.

**UNCLE JIMMY WRIGHT:** That was just the heck of it. I didn't get him to stop. He got me to stop.

**ROXIE:** How'd he do that?

**UNCLE JIMMY WRIGHT:** Hit was 'cause he was much smarter than me. You see, in them days hogs was called razorbacks for a good reason. Their backs come up to a real sharp ridge, an' their noses was likewise sharp an' pointy like a sawlog peavy. Well that ornery critter was headed straight toward a big hickory, an' I was sure that timber tree would stop him. But, don't you know he hit that tree with that sharp nose an' split the blame tree right half in two an' then ran right through that split with me stilla hangin' on. But by time I was pulled through that tree, hit sprung back together an' caught my coattail.

**ROXIE:** Oh, Uncle Jimmy, what'd you do then?

**UNCLE JIMMY WRIGHT:** Why, I had to let go and hung there in that tree for three days until someone come an' cut my coat loose. Yes. Yes, an' ' tis a fact.

**ROXIE:** Why didn't you just squirm outta your coat?

**UNCLE JIMMY WRIGHT:** I do declare you sure do ask a lot of questions fer such a little girl.(stands up to leave) I better be goin' anyways.

**BUSTER:** Tomorrow we'll be goin' to that new bank in Thomas. You wanna go along?

**UNCLE JIMMY WRIGHT:** No, I'm goin' down to the Dry Fork to go fishin'. By the by, what're they callin' that new bank?

**BUSTER:** Oh, it's named the Miners and Merchants Bank.

**UNCLE JIMMY WRIGHT:** Why wouldn' t it be the Huntin' and Fishin' Bank? I might be innerested in goin' if it was the Hunters and Fishers Bank.

**BUSTER:** I guess it's because miners and merchants have more money to deposit than hunters and fishermen. A person probably wouldn't need or want a place where you'd deposit old bearskins and salted down trout.

**UNCLE JIMMY WRIGHT:** Buster Boy, iffen you're not careful you gonna put me to shame fer tellin' tales.

**BUSTER:** Nobody's ever gonna beat you fer tellin' tales. Now Uncle Jimmy Jack, don't let 01' Scratch catch you on your way home.

**UNCLE JIMMY WRIGHT:** Now that'll never happen. Did I ever tell you 'bout the time 01' Scratch took off after me when I come across ...

**BUSTER:** About a dozen times. I might be able to tell it better then you can.

**UNCLE JIMMY WRIGHT:** Let's not try that ... Goodnight younguns, an' get to bed an' don't let the bedbugs bite.

*Uncle Jimmy Wright exits through the door yet is still audible.*

**UNCLE JIMMY WRIGHT:** I declare, my forgetter keeps workin' overtime.

BLACKOUT.

BANK SCENE 3: MINERS & MERCHANTS BANK IN THOMAS, JUNE 10, 1902.

**MR. HINEBAUGH:** Well, well young man, what can I do for you?

**BUSTER:** Are you Mr. Hinebaugh?

**MR. HINEBAUGH:** Yes, I am.

**BUSTER:** Are you the man in charge?

**MR. HINEBAUGH:** I suppose you could say that.

**BUSTER:** Do you own this whole building?

**MR. HINEBAUGH:** Actually stockholders own the building and the bank business, and I am one of the stockholders, along with Mrs. Geisberger, Mr. Stallings, and Mr. Weber.

**BUSTER:** Could I be a stockholder?

**MR. HINEBAUGH:** That would take a great deal of money.

**BUSTER:** I have 12 silver dollars.

**MR. HINEBAUGH:** That wouldn't be quite enough. You see, each of the stockholders invested $5,000 to begin the bank.

**BUSTER:** So how rich is the bank?

**MR. HINEBAUGH:** Well, one wouldn't exactly measure the richness of a bank, but would assess the assets, which this morning were $50,000, but since then we have some deposits amounting to $691.71, which added to the stockholders' investments comes to $50,691.71.

**BUSTER:** I guess I don't have enough money to become a stockholder. I have only twelve silver dollars.

**MR. HINEBAUGH:** How did you get that much money?

**BUSTER:** Daddy and I bring produce to town every week, and I get the egg money. Mr. Raese over in Davis paid me the twelve silver dollars for all the eggs I've brought him since last Christmas. He treats us real nice when we sell him produce. He doesn't just ignore us when someone else comes into his store. He said that I might like these silver dollars more than scrip or U. S. folding money.

**MR. HINEBAUGH:** What do you want to do with them?

**BUSTER:** I want to save them.

**MR. HINEBAUGH:** That's a grand idea. Are you planning to deposit them here in our new bank?

**BUSTER:** Would I be able to get them back whenever I need them; whenever I wanted to?

**MR. HINEBAUGH:** Of course, and with interest.

**BUSTER:** Are other people's money kept here?

**MR. HINEBAUGH:** Well, we certainly hope other people will deposit their money here in our new bank.

Receiving deposits is one of our purposes, as well as loaning money, owning land to build on to carry on banking ...

**BUSTER:** Can other things be done in your building?

**MR. HINEBAUGH:** Why yes, as a matter of fact in our building in addition to the banking business, we rent space for an insurance company, a dentist and of the central for the telephone company, and of course the U. S. Post Office.

**BUSTER:** Do you have to pay money to the Black Hand?

**MR. HINEBAUGH:** Why in the world would we want to do that?

**BUSTER:** I was told that businesses had to pay protection money to the Black Hand, and with all of the money you have to protect, I thought you would need to protect it, if the Black Hand is in that kind of business.

**MR. HINEBAUGH:** We have a substantial vault to protect our money, and we don't really talk around here about the Black Hand.

**BUSTER:** If I deposited these twelve silver dollars, would they be kept safe and protected in your vault?

**MR. HINEBAUGH:** Absolutely.

**BUSTER:** and ... when I came back to get them, you would give them back to me with "some interest".

**MR. HINEBAUGH:** Now I can't guarantee that we could give you back these exact silver dollars.

**BUSTER:** What would you give me then?

**MR. HINEBAUGH:** Twelve crisp new dollar bills.

*An armed guard enters.*

**GUARD:** Mr. Hinebaugh is the payroll ready?

**MR. HINEBAUGH:** Yes, it's right here behind the teller's window.

**BUSTER:** (looking at the large bag of money) You mean all that's your payroll? Why I just get ...

**GUARD:** No, this is the payroll for the men at the mines at Benbush, Douglas, Pierce,# 23. I'm just to deliver it and protect it.

**BUSTER:** Do you belong to the Black Hand?

**GUARD:** Of course not. They're just a bunch of ...

**MR. HINEBAUGH:** ... a group of men we don't like to talk about.

**BUSTER:** I heard that whenever they came to collect money from you they might slash ...

**MR. HINEBAUGH:** We don't know for sure what they would do, because you know they were a secret... uh.. sort of ...

**GUARD:** Yeah they were a kind of secret fraternity.

**BUSTER:** But I thought Mr. Silvestro ...

*Roxie enters running in as the Guard exits.*

**ROXIE:** Buster, haven't you put your money in the bank yet?

**BUSTER:** Not ... (interrupting himself to introduce Roxie) Mr. Hinebaugh this is Roxie ...

**MR. HINEBAUGH:** I take it that she's your little sister.

**ROXIE:** I'm not so little I'll be nine next month.

**BUSTER:** Yes, she's my sister, and Roxie, this is Mr. Hinebaugh. He runs the bank.

**ROXIE:** Did you give your silver dollars to him?

**MR. HINEBAUGH:** Yes, young man, have you decided if you're going to deposit those twelve silver dollars in my bank?

**BUSTER:** I just got them this morning, and I like to hear them jingle in my pocket. I have a bank at home that can keep them safe for awhile. I think Daddy's going to put some of his money in your bank, 'cause he has more than twelve dollars.

**MR. HINEBAUGH:** You tell him we are looking forward to meeting him.

**BUSTER:** But his dollars aren't silver.

**MR. HINEBAUGH:** That will be okay. We take folding money also.

**BUSTER:** (turning to go) Thank you, Mr. Hinbaugh for explaining how everything works here.

**MR. HINEBAUGH:** You're most welcome. We're always happy to welcome a new customer Or perhaps a future customer.

**BUSTER:** Oh, I'll be back.

**MR. HINEBAUGH:** I'll look forward to that. By the way, even though you're not depositing anything with us today, we would like to deposit some peppermint candy with you and your little sister.

**ROXIE:** (taking the candy) I'm not so little. I'll be ...

**MR. HINEBAUGH:** I haven't forgotten. You'll be nine next month. (as Buster is leaving) Oh and don't let the Black Hand know you're carrying that money. If I were you, I wouldn't want to jingle it too loudly ... especially in crowded places.

BLACKOUT.

**BUSTER:** They kept coming, or rather I should say, "We kept coming": the Pennsylvania Dutch into the Parsons and St. George area, from Virginia into Stringtown and Davis and from many of the old countries into Thomas, to harvest the timber, to farm the bottomlands, to mine the coal, to set up shops and banks in the towns and schools and churches in the neighborhoods.

*The song, "Going Dutch" is sung or heard.*

GOING DUTCH:

> When A Pennsylvania Dutchman from the thrify town of York
> Came to do some fishing on the waters of Dry Fork,
> He became so fascinated with the region's rustic charm
> That he moved to West Virginia, where he bought a mountain farm.
> As his life was drab and lonely, the expected came to pass
> When he married Molly Grady, a sweet Scotch-Irish lass.
> But the farmstead's only buildings were a pen for keeping hogs

And a tiny three room cabin, built of yellow poplar
    logs.
When the farm proved quite productive with its fertile
    sandy loam,
Molly started begging for a more attractive home,
Jacob said, "My daring Molly, have you never heard
    the yarn,
That good barns will build good houses, but a house
    won't build a barn."
"I'm sure the quickest method to impress our
    mountain friends
Is a new barn freshly painted with hex signs on the
    ends."
So he built this towering structure, which would be his
    joy and pride,
Plus a harness room with windows all the upper side.
When he thought that patient Molly was to all his
    whims inured,
He went looking for an agent and to get his barn
    insured.
When he came home that evening he thought that he
    have a stroke
When he saw his barn enveloped in a drifting cloud of
    smoke.
But his fear soon subsided and surprise replaced his
    gloom
When he saw that clever Molly had moved to the
    harness room.
With the stovepipe out the window and the table
    neatly spread,
She was busy getting supper in his nice new harness
    shed.
A smile replaced his anger when he found that he'd
    been hooked,
And he saw from Molly's standpoint how ridiculous it
    looked.
So he set about to please her and, as I complete this
    yarn

Molly has a brand new dwelling, that's much nicer
  than the barn.
**BUSTER:** Thus we ended our childhood in the
  industrious but innocent years before the first World War.
  Little did we know that those times of great activity and
  growing up would preview global international strife as
  well as personal losses. Uncle Jimmy Jack died out in the
  woods with his boots on; just as he would have wanted it.
  Many young men, including myself, were drafted or
  enlisted into the cause of the Great War. And each year
  could be marked on a yardstick of our COMING OF
  AGE.

BLACKOUT.
CURTAIN

**BUSTER:** After the war to end wars, Tucker County was
  coming of age, as we were in many ways living in a new
  world, - certainly a different world - a world of lost
  innocence, but with renewed energy to move ahead and
  turn our attention from war efforts to home and industry.
  Some of us returned from overseas, but some didn't and
  were sorrowfully missed and memorialized.
The lumbering, mines and coke ovens would be prospering
  for several more decades. The small hillside farmers had
  mostly sold their farms to the railroads or lumber mills or
  their mineral rights to the mining companies.
Anyways, we couldn't compete with those large level
  midwest farms, which after the war were beginning to
  mechanize with tractors and other motorized equipment.
  We couldn't quite figure how you could call yourself
  farming when you rode a vehicle around all day instead of
  following a plow an' a mule, particularly in the spring
  when you would shed your brogans and walk barefoot in
  the cool upturned earth. We fail to mechanize not for
  lack of entrepreneurship — we had plenty of that when
  you consider all of the entrepreneur risks we had always
  and continued to take — But we knew those tractors

wouldn't stay upright on our steep hillsides.

Oh in the bottomland maybe, but that acreage just couldn't stand a chance with the flat prairies of the midwest. So we had to  go to work for the railroads or mines or sawmills or just leave the state altogether to another state, which happened to me, but I kept in touch with home particularly with my letters to and from Roxie.

## ACT II

*At rise, we hear the song, JUST BEFORE THE BATTLE, playing on an old Victrola, with the sounds of scratches in the vinyl.*

*SCENE 1: THE FOSTER LIVING ROOM, 1918.*
*Roxie is now a young woman*

**MRS. FOSTER:** Buster has been gone so long and so far away that I fear that he may have changed.

**ROXIE:** Of course, Mamma, he' s changed. He's three years older, has travelled across the waters, fought a war. We're also three years older and have changed whether we've recognized it or not. Life is about change.

**MRS. FOSTER:** Of course it is, but you know what I mean. He's been through so much, I'm afraid he will be depressed or dissatisfied with living back here.

**ROXIE:** Mamma, I'm also concerned, but can hardly wait to see him and hear of all his adventures. His letters were always filled with great detail, both exciting and frightening. You know he often writes how you and Daddy have worked so hard to prepare us for the outside world and the challenges of growing up. He says that he's afraid that the outside world is no longer out there somewhere, but will be encroaching increasingly on all of us and our way of life. He would just as seriously look back at things as they were and events that had happened around here. It was almost as though he had to write about them to keep himself in touch with his roots.

**MRS. FOSTER:** I read those letters too, but what did he mean about his "roots?"

ROXIE: Where he came from, his family and neighbor folks, and school and church. That kind of thing. He even reminded me of how Baboon Hill got its name by that poor circus monkey accidentally hanging itself off the side of the circus wagon. Of course, I couldn't remember it and all he could remember of it was how you cried while everyone else was laughing at the plight of that poor animal.

MRS. FOSTER: Oh he would remember anything concerning animals being mistreated.

ROXIE: Where's Daddy?

MS. FOSTER: He left early with the wagon and a team to pick up Buster at the depot.

ROXIE: With the team? I hope Buster hasn't gained so much weight that two horses will have to pull the wagon back.

MRS. FOSTER: I told him that Buster wouldn't be hauling that much stuff that he needed a team of horses to pull the load. I think your daddy just wanted to show off his new horses to Buster and provide his own parade with them pulling our American hero all the way through town and back home. I suppose there will be celebrating in town tonight.

ROXIE: (a sudden change in attitude) Why?

MRS. FOSTER: Why ... celebrate the end of the war, of course.

ROXIE: (unenthusiastically) Of course, this was the war to end all wars.

MRS. FOSTER: I doubt that.

ROXIE: There has never been a war with such guns and ships and planes ... weapons never seen before. That should be enough power to keep anyone like Kaiser Wilhelm from invading other people again.

MRS. FOSTER: Well, we'll see.

ROXIE: What do you mean by that?

MRS. FOSTER: "There shall always be wars and rumors of wars."

ROXIE: But this was "he war to end all wars." That was what President Wilson and everyone else has said time and again.

MRS. FOSTER: One would hope ... but one mustn't contradict scripture.

ROXIE: What scripture do you mean?

MRS. FOSTER: Where it says, "There shall be wars and rumors of wars."

ROXIE: Where is that in the Bible?

MRS. FOSTER: I don't know exactly, but it's something your daddy quotes often enough. And you gotta admit he knows his scripture.

ROXIE: "His scriptures?"

MRS. FOSTER: Well the Lord's scriptures of course. But when we read and study and follow the scriptures, they become our own.

ROXIE: Where exactly is that saying found in the scriptures?

MRS. FOSTER: I don't know exactly, but I believe somewhere in the gospels. You might look it up.

ROXIE: I think I'll do that. (picking up the Bible) Somewhere in the gospels?

MRS. FOSTER: Somewhere in there ... Maybe in Matthew. I guess there'll be a lot of celebrating when the boys'll be marching home again. Why, just this morning your Dad was singing just as big as you please, WHEN JOHNNY COMES MARCHING HOME AGAIN, HURRAH, HURRAH except he changed the words.

ROXIE: To what?

MRS. FOSTER: "When Buster comes marching home, again hurrah hurrah, we'll give him a welcome home and then hurrah, hurrah."

ROXIE: Some will be marching on crutches and some will be carried and some will be wheezing from the mustard gas those Germans ...

MRS. FOSTER: Roxie, Honey, not all Germans are ...

ROXIE: No, Mamma. I know. The Schmidts, the Bioffs,

the Wolfords. They're as nice as you'd expect anyone to be. But it was the Germans under old Kaiser Bill that were so greedy and wanted all of Europe. And when they invaded Slovenia I couldn't persuade Tad not to go.

**MRS. FOSTER:** Well, he didn't have to go, 'cause coal miners were exempt from the draft.

**ROXIE:** Yeah, because coal was so important to the war effort. But Tad said he still had family over there, and it was not just his patriotic duty but his family duty to do what he could.

**MRS. FOSTER:** I knew you thought a lot of him, and it was terrible news when we heard about ... Your daddy and I thought you'd probably get married when he got back

**ROXIE:** Mamma, we hadn't told anyone, but we had planned to get married as soon as he came home. So, yes "We'll give them a hearty welcome then" when Johnny comes marching home. (reading)

> There'll be those who marched away,
> And will march back as a hero,
> And there'll be others who marched away,
> But to an early grave did go.

**MRS. FOSTER:** Roxie, honey, it sounds as though you're not happy that the war's over.

**ROXIE:** It's just as long as the war was going on, Tad's life and his death amounted to something. But now that it's over, his war is very likely to slip into the oblivion of history books with a paragraph or two. Of course, I'm very pleased that the war's over and simply delighted at the prospect of Buster's coming home., Oh here it is.

**MRS. FOSTER:** What is?

**ROXIE:** That quote about wars which you misquoted.

**MRS. FOSTER:** Well, where is it?

**ROXIE:** It's here in Matthew.

**MRS. FOSTER:** Well, if l misquoted read exactly how it goes.

**ROXIE:** Here in Matthew 24th chapter verse 6. "And ye

shall hear of wars and rumors of wars: see that ye be not troubled." It does not say that there will be wars. It says that ye shall hear of wars and rumors of ...

**MRS. FOSTER:** When St. Matthew used that word "rumors" the Lord must've been thinkin' ahead to Tucker County.

**ROXIE:** Yes, we do have our share of rumors. It doesn't say here that there will always be wars. It says people shall "hear of wars and rumors ... "

**MRS. FOSTER:** What's the difference, Honey?

**ROXIE:** People are always using scripture to prove their own notions and beliefs.

**MRS. FOSTER:** There have always been wars & rumors of war.

**ROXIE:** But this one has to be the last one, or else Tad and those other boys' deaths will go for naught.

**MRS. FOSTER:** Roxie, you've heard us say so often that time heals all ...

**ROXIE:** It may heal all wounds but the scar will be there forever. And as he would wait for me I'll wait for him until judgement.

**MRS. FOSTER:** Yes, he would. He was a good boy.

**ROXIE:** I have a letter here in my pocket which I've carried since the day I received it. The last letter the postman ever delivered from Tad. (reading from the letter)

"Dear Roxie, the war is worse than anything I could have imagined. Several of my buddies have already been killed and many others wounded. Some can hardly breathe due to the gas the Germans are spewing. The cold seeps down into your very soul. I suppose the reason I haven't suffered frostbite like so many have, is because of the warmth I carry in my heart of you and home. We don't get much sleep with the bombs and constant gunfire, both from them and from us. The sergeant says it will all be over soon. I pray that it will be so. There's a song the boys here sing; Just before the battle Mother, and as my mother died so long ago I sing the refrain, 'Farewell Roxie, you may never, Press me to your heart again, But oh you'll not forget me, Roxie, If I'm numbered with the slain.' But we must now not think of such things. We will think only of our future. All my love and counting the days. Your intended, Tad."

It was over soon for Tad and for our hopes, and yet it will never be over for the love and hurt I carry in my heart, though "he's numbered with the slain."

*Roxie begins to play SONG on phonograph, JUST BEFORE THE BATTLE MOTHER. We begin to hear a man singing outside, WHEN BUSTER COMES MARCHING HOME Then a second male voice joins in.*

**MRS. FOSTER:** Oh, I believe they're home. Let's go, Roxie, and join the parade.

**ROXIE:** I will Mamma, but I need a few minutes to get ready.

*Mrs. Foster exits, and we hear Buster and Mr. and Mrs. Foster outside greeting each other. Roxie attempts to get herself ready for a joyous reunion with Buster; however, she begins to cry softly, as she exits, hearing the others coming in.*

**MRS. FOSTER:** Roxie, you should just take a look at your brother. He's ... (turning back to address Buster and her husband.) She was right here when I came out a minute ago.

**BUSTER:** I'm anxious to see her. Is she okay? I know about Tad, and I'm sure she's ...

**MRS. FOSTER:** She just seemed to've become a different person, after we heard about Tad. You know, she was always so full of life and fun-loving. It seems that life has now become a burden for her, and she's too young to be that weighed down by worries.

**BUSTER:** How did she get the news? I'm sure the telegram went to his mother.

**MR. FOSTER:** Oh yes. Tad's little brother Tom came right over. He said both his father and mother were pretty broke up about the news, but they felt that Roxie ought to be told as soon as possible.

**MRS. FOSTER:** That's right. In fact she was sitting at the window, looking out and saw him riding up on Tad's horse. Here Buster you've got to have some of this pound cake, 'cause I made it just for you as I know you've always been crazy about it.

**BUSTER:** I believe I will and coffee too if it's ready. You say she was sitting at the window?

**MRS. FOSTER:** There's plenty of coffee. (serving coffee to Buster and Mr. Foster) She started looking out that window every evening about a week before she got the news. She'd finish the dishes as soon as she could and then would go to the window, sometimes with a book; but I don't think she would do much reading as she would keep glancing out the window and then she'd just gaze.

**MR. FOSTER:** It was almost that she knew some news would be coming, either good or bad and she might catch a glimpse beforehand of a messenger or Tad, himself.

*Roxie enters having composed herself a bit and dried her eyes. Everyone is a little tense, caught in a dilemma between Roxie's sorrow and their happiness with Buster's return. Roxie is the first to speak and break the silence.*

**ROXIE:** Well look at you. There must have been a bevy of beauties at the depot when they spied you in that uniform.

**BUSTER:** Roxie, I don't hardly know what to say. It's wonderful to be home and see you, but I'm terribly sorry to hear about Tad.

**ROXIE:** Yes, but we have to move on don't we? ... There'll be celebrating in town tomorrow, and you must go in uniform.

**BUSTER:** If it will attract a bevy of beauties, as you tend to believe, I'll probably wear it every day until it wears out. Will you be going with us?

**MRS. FOSTER:** Oh yes, Roxie will be going. I've just finished making her a new dress, just for the occasion of your homecoming.

**MR. FOSTER:** If the roads are not too muddy, that McClure boy will take all of us in the car he bought just before the war.

**ROXIE:** I'm not sure I'll be going. I've not been feeling too well.

**MRS. FOSTER:** Of course, you've got to go. And you'll look so pretty in that new dress.

**ROXIE:** That is a beautiful new dress, Mamma, and I do appreciate all the time and love you've put ...

**MRS. FOSTER:** Then there's no more talk about it. Of course you'll

**ROXIE:** I'11 sleep on it tonight and see how I feel in the morning.

*Mrs. F. starts to respond but is interrupted by Mr. Foster.*

**MR. FOSTER:** Come on down to the barn, Buster, and take a look at Old Dan. I don't believe he'll make it through another winter. I stopped working him over a year ago. I know how partial you've always been to him ever since we used to haul produce into town with him pulling the buckboard.

*Everyone looks at Roxie, who is straightening up the table and getting a cup of coffee for herself. She cuts a piece of cake as nonchalantly as possible. Mrs. Foster breaks the silence.*

**MRS. FOSTER:** (addressing no one in particular) You know that McClure boy ...

**BUSTER:** Dad, I would love to go visit Old Dan. You can't imagine how many times in my mind I've retraced that road and lounged in our barn midst the smells and sounds in the warmth of our put up hay.

*They start exiting as Mrs. moves to Roxie who has turned upstage. Mrs. Foster gently touches Roxie.*

FADEOUT.

## SCENE 2: SEROFINA'S APARTMENT IN THOMAS, 1925.

*The apartment exhibits lots of lace, color and chintz, religious icons.*

*Roxie, Serofina, and Mrs. Mazzoni are together.*

**SEROFINA:** Mamma, my friend, Roxie, is coming over for dinner, if you don't mind.

**MRS. MAZZONI:** Now, my child, why would I mind? You know I never say a word when all your uncles and brothers come by here after the ballgames. (laughing) Why I suppose they could eat a whole bushel of pasta apiece if the others hadn't finished it first.

**SEEROFINA:** But don't you mind all of them coming by together after every game ... even after every practice.

**MRS. MAZZONI:** I said that I've never said a word about that.

**SEOFINA:** I didn't ask if you'd never said a word. I asked if it didn't bother you; at least just a little bit?

**MRS. MAZZONI:** Has anyone ever heard me complain about ...

**SEROFINA:** No. No one has ever heard you complain about anything, and I think no one ever even thinks about it, except me. Sometimes it worries me ...

**MRS. MAZZONI:** If I need help I get Dr. Baker to come up from Parsons on train ...

**SEROFINA:** But Mamma, Dr. Baker has lost his medical license.

**MRS. MAZZONI:** But he is still good doctor like always.

**SEROFINA:** But, Mamma, Dr. Baker performed an illegal operation.

**MRS. MAZZONI:** That poor girl was in bad trouble, not just for reputation but for her life. What do you expect her to do? What you expect him to do?

**SEROFINA:** Mamma, of course, you're right but I thought you might not ...

**MRS. MAZZONI:** By the Blessed Mother, Serofina, the Dear Lord has been good to me and I have no complaints, ... so I don't complain.

**SEROFINA:** Mama I know, but ...

*There is a knock on the door.*

**SEROFINA:** That must be Roxie now.

*Serofina goes to answer the door.*

**SEROFINA:** Hello, Roxie. Do come in.

*Roxie enters.*

**ROXIE:** Hello, Serofina. (looking around) What a lovely apartment.

**MRS. MAZZONI:** You like?

**SEROFINA:** Oh I'm sorry, I should introduce you to my mother.

**ROXIE:** It's so nice to meet you Mrs. Mazzoni.

**MRS. MAZZONI:** If you are friend of Serofina you must call me Mama. Your Mama still living?

**ROXIE:** No, she passed away some time ago.

**MRS. MAZZONI:** Well then you must call me Mama. All Serofina's friends call me Mama.

**ROXIE:** I would be much more comfortable calling you Mrs. Mazzoni.

**MRS. MAZZONI:** Of course that is fine. So many difference people here with lots of different ways. It can be confusing to someone like me who come from old country. But also very interesting. It is like learning but not go to school. Me? I never go to school even in Italy. It was ...

*Serofina interrupts her.*

**SEROFINA:** Mama, should I start supper? The boys will be finishing their game before long.

**MRS. MAZZONI:** Oh, I can hear them up there across the river. You can put on the water in the big pot for boiling.

*Serafina exits toward the kitchen.*

**MRS. MAZZONI:** (yelling toward Serofina) You know I started the sauce hours ago. (to Roxie) My boys tell me that when I get my spaghetti sauce to cooking, they can smell it all the way up to the ball field, which must be at least a mile away ... They say even the boys, whose Mammas don't fix the old way spaghetti, why they say, "Tony, your mamma is fixing spaghetti tonight. She's already boilin' the tomatoes." Of course, I'm already boilin' the tomatoes. That's where I start. Child, does your mamma fix the pasta?

**ROXIE:** No, Mrs. Mazzoni, my mother ...

**MRS. MAZZONI:** Oh, by the Blessed Mother, my child, I am so sorry. You just told only two minutes ago. Please excuse an old woman who doesn't understand the language well and who forgets.

**ROXIE:** Why, of course Mrs. Mazzoni.

**MRS. MAZZONI:** I can't remember a thing from yesterday ... even five minutes ago.

**ROXIE:** I understand perfectly. It happens to me all the time. Sometimes, I start to give my students a test which I had given them the day before. A lot of soft giggling starts occurring, then it gets louder and finally a great crescendo like an Italian opera.

**MRS. MAZZONI:** Oh the Opera ...

**ROXIE:** Mrs. Mazzoni, I didn't mean to offend you.

**MES. MAZZONI:** No, my child the opera never offend. In fact I have opera phonograph of Caruso. You must hear.

**ROXIE:** I would love to. I bought a phonograph for myself last Christmas. I play mostly songs from the war.

**MRS. MAZZONI:** I heard those songs. They mostly sad songs. What that song, "Before the Battle".

**ROXIE:** Yes. That's the one I play over and over.

**MRS. MAZZONI:** It's about a boy thinkin' about his home and his mother?

**ROXIE:** Yes.

**MRS. MAZZONI:** And maybe too about sweetheart.

**ROXIE:** Oh. Perhaps.

**MRS. MAZZONI:** I may not remember five minutes, but I do remember the long past. I remember the old country, the war and I remember BEFORE THE BATTLE. It was almost like song sung just to me for one of my brothers died in one of those battles. I still pray to the Virgin for my understanding of such things ... He was young man and never have chance for life, for family ... You so quiet child. I old woman go on and on about past things, when you want to think about new things. modern things.

ROXIE: No, no, I want to hear.

MRS. MAZZONI: You maybe have someone, brother or father not return from war.

ROXIE: Yes, my fiancée.

MRS. MAZZONI: Oh, my child I am so sorry.

ROXIE: Thank you, but it's all right. (silence) It is all right that we talk about it, but it's not all right that I will not see him again in this life.

MRS. MAZZONI: Was he from here?

ROXIE: Yes. His name was Tad Sloviki.

MRS. MAZZONI: Oh, I know his Mamma well. She came from Czechoslovakia. She tell me about his girl friend from out in the county. He was a very good boy.

ROXIE: I certainly thought so.

MRS. MAZZONI: And now you teach in the same school as my Serofino.

ROXIE: Yes.

MRS. MAZZONJI: Everything so different now.

ROXIE: You mean when you were a young girl.

MRS. MAZZONI: Yes, I was born in the mountains of Italy and come to mountains of West Virginia.

ROXIE: With your parents?

MRS. MAZZONI: Oh, no. They stay in Italy. I come to be with my older sister who had married here.

ROXIE: What a long way to come all by yourself.

MRS. MAZZONI: And a long time. A month on the ship to New York and then the long train ride to Thomas.

ROXIE: How old were you?

MRS. MAZZONI: I was sixteen, and my sister had already found a husband for me. I was very excited.

ROXIE: You must have been a little frightened also.

MRS. MAZZONI: Why would I be scared? I was coming to exciting new country and be with my sister and to get married to a boy also from Italy. He had good job in the coal mines.

ROXIE: Oh, I'm sorry. I didn't mean to imply ...

MRS. MAZZONI: You are right about frighten, but not until train stop in Thomas.

**ROXIE:** Was something wrong with the train?

**MRS. MAZZONI:** No, child. Train was very fine, but we get to Thomas in October and rain was drizzle. Not too much but like drizzle and fog at same time and when I got out at the depot it was nighttime, but even as sky was black and filled with rain and fog, it was also filled with smoke. Across the river the mountain had a thousand mouths belching out fire. Later I find that those were coke ovens, That fire lighted up all that fog and smoke. The train engine was hissing with steam, and the other train cars were clanging against each other and clacking on the steel tracks. I had heard the Father describe the fires in bowels of Hades, and I was sure I would soon see the Devil himself with his pitchfork ready to throw me into those ovens.

**ROXIE:** Oh , Mrs. Mazzoni, wasn't your sister there?

**MRS. MAZZONI:** Yes, but I see the inferno first. And even when I see her, she couldn't stop me from crying.

**ROXIE:** Was your intended boyfriend there?

**MRS. MAZZONI:** I believe so, but I couldn't see him because of my tears. I had left my parents and the beautiful mountains of Italy. I was so frightened and disappointed that I cried for a month, it seems.

**ROXIE:** How terrible!

**MRS. MAZZONI:** I could have lost my chance for husband, when he see girl be so silly. How could she be bride here?

**ROXIE:** Is he the man you subsequently married?

**MRS. MAZZONI:** Yes.

**ROXIE:** Sometimes I feel sorry for myself, because of losing out on part of life. Then when I see other people's troubles, my ...

**MRS, MAZZONI:** No, Child, not really troubles. Sorrows, yes, this life has full store, but also much sunshine. (laughing) Not everything like those thousand coke ovens what greet me as young girl.

*Serofina returns.*

**SEROFINA:** Roxie, is Mamma telling you about her arrival in Thomas?

ROXIE: Yes, and it frightened me just hearing about it. Mrs. Mazzoni, what helped you to stop crying? Was it being introduced to your future husband?

MRS. MAZZONI: No, Roxie. It was the music. It is always the music that takes us away in our souls and brings us back into our hearts. My boys, they have band and play for all kinds of times like wakes and school and dances. Serofina knows and understands. She put the music not only in her heart but also in her feet. Is it not so, Serofina?

SEROFINA: Yes. All my brothers play musical instruments. I suppose my musical instruments are my feet, so I dance. You know Roxie that I dance with everything that I do.

ROXIE: Yes, I see this at school all the time, and the students thoroughly enjoy your dancing and the dances you teach them.

SEROFINA: I dance at the kitchen sink when I'm washing dishes, I dance when I'm ironing and even when I sweep the floor. I pretend that the broom is my dancing partner.

ROXIE: I never had the opportunity to study dance.

SEROFINA: I was lucky I guess.

MRS. MAZZONI: I like when she dance to Italian Opera music. Serofino, put on phonograph the AIDA.

*Serofina puts the record on and executes a few dance steps at the beginning. Each character makes random, improvisational remarks during the music. Mrs. Mazzoni may comment about favorite passages or singers. As the record is ending we hear boys voices.*

MRS. MAZZONI: The boys are here. Get out napkins tonight, Serofina.

*Serofina looks quizzically at her mother.*

MRS. MAZZONI: For our guest this evening.

*The opera recording continues to play through the transition.*

BLACKOUT.

## SCENE 3: AT THE BALL, 1929

*Betsy and Fred are standing at the Punch Bowl Table.*
*They are pouring punch into the bowl from a large metal*
*kettle.*

*Big Band music is playing, and we can hear general noises*
*of school children at a dance.*

**BETSY:** It'll just have to do, because it's all we have. The apple cider mixed with the store bought ginger ale should be just fine. (takes a sip) Yep it tastes great.

**FRED:** Do you think this is going to be enough for everybody?

**BETSY:** It's all we have, so it will just have to be enough.

**FRED:** I could mix something else with it to make it go a little further.

**BETSY:** Fred Gilley, I know what you're talkin' about, and if you spike this punch with some of that illegal hooch, I'll certainly make sure you go a little farther from out of my sight.

**FRED:** Oh, Betsy I was just afoolin' you.

**BETSY:** I know what your foolin' is like.

**FRED:** I thought you liked my "foolishness," as you call it.

**BETSY:** That was before I saw you eyein' Mary Jane. I certainly don't like you foolin' around that way at all. You might figure you're just foolin' when you tease around with her, but I know for a fact she's as serious as a revival preacher when she looks at you. And when she gets ready to make the altar call, it won't be to the mourner's bench for the Lord. She'll be listenin' for the "I do, I do."

**FRED:** You gotta be mistaken. She's not ready for that, an' I'm for sure not ready for that.

**BETSY:** You may be for sure that you're not ready, but I'm for sure she is ready whenever she can hogtie you an' drag you or some other "for sure not ready" fellow off to Preacher Long's.

**FRED:** You mean I'm not the only candidate for her altar call. Now that's real hurtful.

**BETSY:** (slapping him on the shoulder) Get outta here Fred Gilley. If you keep carryin' on like that I'm not gonna dance with you even once tonight, an' I'll find someone else to see me home.

FRED: (grabbing her to dance): Well I'd better grab aholt while I got the chance.

*They dance off stage, as we hear voices yelling at them. ""Hey Fred, did you doctor that punch up there?" "Betsy, show us that new dance you learned down at Elkins", etc. Roxie and Serfino enter and check over the table decorations and the punch.*

SEROFINA: Well, it looks as though the kiddos have done a swell job getting ready for the dance.

ROXIE: Yes, it looks rather nice.

SEROFINA: Roxie, do you ever wonder what goes through the minds of children this age?

ROXIE: I wonder, and I marvel; particularly; when I remember or attempt to remember when I was that age. What were you doing when you were in high school?

SEROFINA: Of course, you know that the school I attended would have had no more than three or four high school graduates each year. Buster was away teaching in Virginia, and he and I kept up a pretty constant correspondence.

*Betsy enters.*

BETSY: I know that he kept you fairly well informed of the going's on in the rest of the world. But what kind of activities did you have out there in the backwoods: what kind of dreams would light up your imagination?

ROXIE: We weren't really in the backwoods; the country yes; but the backwoods were Dolly Sods or Otter Creek. It would mean a fairly protracted trip to journey into town; but we came in every week or so.

SEROFINA: But what did you do? What did you dream?

ROXIE: No one has ever asked me those questions before, and I haven't, not recently anyway, thought about those days.

SEROFINA: But what did you do?

ROXIE: Those usual farm things with chickens and cows

and gardening and helping Mamma with the housework. Before the electric lines were put in Daddy bought a generator, which generated our own electricity. Then Mamma got herself a brand-new washer with a wringer on the top.

**BETSY:** How in the world did she do her laundry before that? Did she take them to the river and beat them out on the rocks?

**ROXIE:** No, silly. We did take them down to the spring and boil them in a big iron pot. It was my job to keep stirring them around with a big stick. I never figured out why they had to be stirred, as I wouldn't suppose they would have stuck to each other or burned fast to the bottom. Anyways, come to think of it, I imagine she had me do that to keep me out of mischief.

**BETSY:** What kind of mischief would you have been able to get yourself into out there away from anyone else?

**ROXIE:** I could have been wandering around too close to the creek or trying to catch crawfish in the spring. That would always get it muddied up when anyone would stir up the bottom.

**BETSY:** Was your clothesline down at the spring?

**ROXIE:** No, it was up near the house, but before we could hang them on the line, we had to rinse them, then put them in the bluing. Everybody's collars had to be starched, before we took anything to the clothesline. I wonder ... I almost forgot the worst part. That's probably why I forgot it. We had washboards and homemade lye soap, which had to be used to scrub every piece of garment we had. I'm surprised Mamma didn't wear out her fingers. As a matter of fact she would often say, I've wore my fingers down to the bone. Didn't your mamma have to do that?

**BETSY:** She told me about some of that, but I think she used store bought Octagon soap, but you didn't tell me about your dreams.

**ROXIE:** Well I had dreams just like every other youngster.

**SEROFINA:** What ... about the boys?

**ROXIE:** What about the boys?

**SEROFINA:** Didn't you have some dreams about the boys?

**ROXIE:** Why yes, and I imagine you did too.

**BETSY:** But any particular boy?

**ROXIE:** There was one boy, named Ralph Roy. I believe he was a second cousin. But of course all of that was before I met Tad.

**SEROFINA:** What was Ralph like?

**ROXIE:** He was a kind of prankster, a joker. If there was some fun to get into, he'd be right in the middle of it. It was rather exciting when he told me I was his girl. I shot right back, "Well, you're certainly not my boy," even though I did like him a lot and wrote about him in my diary. My answering him that way didn't seem to faze him a bit or shake his self-confidence at all. That was disappointing, though I admired him for it.

**BETSY:** What kind of mischief would he get into?

**ROXIE:** Well all sorts of things at Halloween like turning over toilets and scaring little children at the windows.

**SEROFINA:** All the boys did those things, and even some of us girls would lend a hand.

**ROXIE:** But one time in spring, he secretively brought a whole mess of ramps into the schoolroom, and when the teacher wasn't looking he put them on top of the potbellied stove which heated the room. When they started getting hot we knew someone was cooking ramps, but by time the teacher actually found them they had burned, and their own natural smell along with the burnt smell was too much, so we got to leave school early that day.

**BETSY:** Did he get in trouble?

**ROXIE:** No one would tell on him, although all of us knew, and of course we appreciated it because we got to leave school early ... Thinking back on it, I'm sure we appreciated it also because someone was able to pull something over on an authority figure.

**SEROFINA:** You're that authority figure now.

**ROXIE:** I'm aware of that, and I believe I'm easier on the mischief makers because I remember that incident so fondly.

**BETSY:** Did Ralph just fade away?

**ROXIE:** He moved with his family over to Kentucky. I believe his daddy got a job in the mines near Harlan. But before he left, right after that ramp episode he wrote me a cute little poem about ramps.

> I love the ramps of Dry Fork
> With beans & plenty of pork
> They're good, but they're smelly
> They heat up your belly
> But alas, they did in poor Yorick.

**BETSY:** Poor Yorick?

**ROXIE:** Well, we were studying Shakespeare at the time, and Ralph, whenever he would take the notion, would pick up a rock from in the road or wherever and while holding it high in the air, he would gaze at it mournfully and pronounce, "Alas, poor Yorick; I knew him well."

**SEROFINA:** That was a limerick he wrote about Poor Yorick.

**BETSY:** A limerick?

**ROXIE:** That was the form of a poem that the Irish brought with them to this country. There's a county in Ireland named Limerick. The form of the poem is so much fun that it's quite popular in the pubs.

**SEROFINA:** We sometimes had great fun with the limericks when we were supposed to be studying and writing poetry.

**ROXIE:** Like Ralph, the other boys liked to compete with limericks. I believe my favorite one was:

> In my class there is a special girl
> She has my heart all awhirl.
> At the school dance
> I'll take the chance,
> And ask her to give me a twirl.

**BETSY:** Why would you remember that special limerick?

(to Serofina) Were you that special girl?

**SEROFINA:** No. But a special friend of mine was.

**BETSY:** (to Roxie) I'm surprised that you would remember that.

**ROXIE:** Of course I did.

**BETSY:** So you were the special girl?

**ROXIE:** Yes.

**BETSY:** Was that limerick also from Ralph.

**ROXIE:** No. Ralph had moved away by then.

**BETSY:** Then it must have been ...

**ROXIE:** Yes that was Tad. That was when we began talking. (changing the subject) I sure do like that music, even if it is new and the old folks don't approve. You must be real proud of your brothers; they're such good musicians.

**SEROFINA:** Why, yes, ever since I was just real little I can remember them practicing their music, sometimes well into the night. It was so loud sometimes it would wake me up.

**BETSY:** Here comes that new teacher from Parsons, Mr. Evans. I believe he's going to ask you to dance.

**ROXIE:** Oh no!

**SEROFINA:** Why not? It would be good for you to ...

*Mr. Evans enters and interrupts Serofina.*

**MR. EVANS:** May I introduce myself? I am Bill ...

**SEROFINA:** We know who you are. We read all about you in the paper.

**MR. EVANS:** And you are?

**SEROFINA:** I'm Miss Mazzoni and this is Miss Foster.

**ROXIE:** Roxie.

**MR. EVANS:** Miss Foster ... eh ... Roxie, may I have this dance?

**ROXIE:** Oh it's been so long that ...

**EVAN:** Well, now it won't be so long will it?

*They exit to dance.*

*Serofino watches envyingly and hums the tune. She dips herself a drink from the punchbowl and returns her gaze to the dance floor. Sally and Tom, students, come to pour themselves some punch.*

**SALLY:** It looks as if Miss Foster has found herself a beau.

**TOM:** Well, what if she has?

**SEROFINA:** It does look that way doesn't it?

**SALLY:** Did you say something to me Miss Mazzoni?

**SEROFINA:** No, I believe I said something to me.

**SALLY:** Oh, I'm sorry.

**SEROFINA:** That's quite all right.

> *The music stops. General hubbub of noise between dances. Roxie and Bill appear from dance floor.*

**MR. EVANS:** It may have been for such a long time since you danced, but you certainly remembered quite well.

> *The band begins another number.*

**ROXIE:** Well, it was nice.

**BETSY:** You both looked very chic out there shaking a leg.

> *They all pour drinks and awkwardly offer the drinks to each other. During this time, it becomes obvious that Serofina is flirting with Evans. Roxie begins to recede to the sidelines.*

**MR. EVANS:** Well, now isn't it a coincidence that all of us are teachers?

**ROXIE:** As this is a school function, it would stand to reason that the adults here would have some function in the school system.

**MR. EVANS:** Why, yes how obtuse of me. It's not a coincidence at all, but certainly a convenience.

**SEROFINA:** Yes, convenience.

**BETSY:** Convenient for us to get to know each other.

**MR. EVANS:** And that's the convenience of the highest order, wouldn't you say?

**SEROFINA:** I would indeed say that it is of the highest order in some peoples' codes.

**MR. EVANS:** Miss Foster ... Roxie ... ! believe this is the last number. Would you care??

**ROXIE:** Oh, I'm so sorry, but that little bit of dancing has exhausted me. I'm afraid I am not used to such exertion as of late.

**MR. EVANS:** I'm terribly sorry. I must admit that I am no longer accustomed to such strenuous exercises as these new dances require.

**ROXIE:** I'm sure Miss Mazzoni would be happy..

**MR. EVANS:** Why yes of course ... Miss Mazzoni ... ?

**SEROFINA:** Serofina!!

**MR. EVANS:** Miss Serofina would you be so kind as to honor me with this last dance?

**SEROFINA:** I would be so kind and delighted, Mr. Bill.

*They exit to the dance floor. Roxie pours herself a drink, but as she looks toward the dance floor she spills the punch on her dress. She frantically wipes off as much as she can with several paper napkins, which she accidentally throws into the punch bowl. Betsy sees her predicament and comes to her rescue, helping to clean up the mess as well as she can.*

**ROXIE:** I don't know how I could have been so clumsy. (attempting to joke) I'm sure it must have been something I drank.

**BETSY:** Oh, Miss Foster. I'm sure none of the boys spiked the drink this evening. I saw to that.

**ROXIE:** Betsy, I didn't mean even to imply that. I was just trying to be a little funny in the middle of all this mess.

**BETSY:** Miss Foster, the mess can be cleaned up pretty easily.

**ROXIE:** I suppose I'm alluding to another mess.

**BETSY:** But Miss Foster this is the only mess.

**ROXIE:** My dear child, unfortunately you will learn through sad experience that there are messes that can be cleaned up readily with a few paper napkins and then there are other messes ...

**BETSY:** Other messes?

**ROXIE:** Other messes in our lives which take more attention and time and sometimes there is not enough time.

**BETSY:** I don't understand.

**ROXIE:** I know ... It seems that the dance is over. Would you have Miss Mazzoni come up and help clear up the punch table before we go home?

**BETSY:** (looking out at the dance floor) I believe Miss Mazzoni has left.

**ROXIE:** Left?

**BETSY:** Yes, with that new teacher from down at Parsons.

**ROXIE:** Oh, ... I see.

*Dance Music Continues through the transition to the next scene,*

## BLACKOUT

## SCENE 4: THE HOMEPLACE, SEPTEMBER, 1945

*Buster is going through some of the papers Roxie has deposited in an old desk. Buster's son, William, is helping.*

**BUSTER:** Bill, don't just throw the papers around. We don't have much time, and we need to find the deed to the place on this trip, if possible.

**WILLIAM:** Dad, when will you stop calling me Billy and not my proper name? I'm no longer your little boy.

**BUSTER:** All right, William ... I didn't call you Billy.

**WILLIAM:** Bill ... Billy whatever. Bill is right next to Billy.

**BUSTER:** I'll try to be more circumspect ...

**WILLIAM:** Don't worry about circumspect. Just quit ...

**BUSTER:** I understand, and I'll try not to embarrass you again like that. (still rifling through papers) There's something you need to understand no matter how old you get. As long as I'm alive and you're alive you'll still be my boy.

**WILLIAM:** OK Dad. I appreciate the honor I have of being your son, whether Bill or Billy or William.

**BUSTER:** Thanks, William!

**WILLIAM:** Why didn't Aunt Roxie ever marry and get away from here?

**BUSTER:** In the first place, she had no hankering of getting away. I would have stayed too if there had been opportunities for employment ... She had a chance to get married to a fine young fellow, Tad Sloviki, a coal miner.

**WILLIAM:** Tad?

**BUSTER:** His proper name was Theodore. Like Theodore Roosevelt. We ... everyone ... including myself, shortened it to Tad.

**WILLIAM:** So he had to endure a childish nickname, too! ... Like some others, who weren't allowed to grow up with a grown-up name?

**BUSTER:** I'm really sorry, William.

**WILLIAM:** It's really okay. I'm creating an issue when there is really no need. What happened to him?

**BUSTER:** To Tad ... Theodore?

**WILLIAM:** Yes.

**BUSTER:** He and Roxie became engaged just before the First World War. She was 22, and he was 25 when the war broke out. He felt pretty strong about the war, as Old Kaiser Bill had overrun his home country of Slovenia.

**WILLIAM:** Kaiser Bill? ... Not Kaiser William?

**BUSTER:** Cut it out, Bill ... er ... William. The Kaiser was the Hitler of his day and his war. Anyway, so Tad and several other local fellows signed up.

*William gives Buster an expression of confusion.*

**BUSTER:** Enlisted.

**WILLIAM:** You told me miners were exempt from the draft for some reason.

**BUSTER:** Yep and railroad men too. For the government figured they were doing essential work for the war effort, but Tad said it wasn't fair for him to stay here enjoying life when he had so many buddies enlisting or being drafted to be put in harm's way for us here in the mountains to continue our way of life.

**WILLIAM:** And he never returned?

**BUSTER:** No ... and Roxie remained true to him and his memory to her dying day. After going off to Teacher's College for a couple of years to get her teaching certificate, she came back here to teach in the old Willoughby one-room school.

**WILLAM:** How many grades were in the one room?

**BUSTER:** Thre was a pupil available for each grade level.

WILLIAM: How many pupils were there in all?

BUSTER: You're asking as many questions as she used to ask.

WILLIAM: Really?

BUSTER: Yes.

WILLIAM: How did you get her to quit asking questions?

BUSTER: I didn't. She just said that that was the only way she was ever going to learn anything.

WILLIAM: Did she teach all of her life in the one-room school?

BUSTER: There's another question.

WILLIAM: I'm just trying to learn something ... I'm trying to learn more about Aunt Roxie. There were several years I hadn't seen her before she died.

BUSTER: You're absolutely right. You and she both missed out on a lot for not having known each other better. That's what happens when folks have to move away to find work, while some of the family stay and make do. Sometimes, as in the case of Roxie, even looking after the home place. It's somewhat like a tree that when it grows it reaches its trunk toward the sky and spreads its branches to the horizon. But it's always good to have healthy roots planted in the earth ... Roxie took care of the roots. I always knew where home was, no matter what kind of roaming I did.

WILLIAM: But the one room schoolhouse.

BUSTER: Oh yes. After the one room school was closed down, she took a position at the consolidated school in Davis. It was then that she had to learn to drive.

WILLIAM: You mean she didn't have a car before that?

BUSTER: No, she didn't need a car. The neighborhood school was just next door. The church house was less than a mile, and the grocery store was even closer than that. She didn't then have to go to the doctor. If she needed medical attention, Miss Ellen, at the store, would call Ol' Doc Werner, and he'd make a house call. The first car she ever bought was a little A Model Ford.

**WILLIAM:** One of those neat old cars with a rumble seat and a let down top?

**BUSTER:** No, no, no. She said that would be too flapperish for her.

**WILLIAM:** Flapperish?

**BUSTER:** Well, that's a good word. It WAS a good word. It meant like the flappers, stylish girls, after the first Big War on into the 20's. They bobbed their hair and danced the Charleston. Their knees were bare, as their dresses that didn't come down over their knees, and their stockings didn't come up to their knees. The old folks were scandalized by such attire, although I can't remember what was so objectionable about exposed knees. Anyway Roxie, being a schoolteacher didn't think it would be appropriate for her to dress in such attire and motor around in a convertible roadster.

**WILLIAM:** Why did she get rid of it?

**BUSTER:** She did just as we do now. She traded it in for her second and last car, which was a '36 two-door gray Ford with a 60 horsepower motor. There was an emblem with a 60 on it attached to the front grill.

**WILLIAM:** That's the one parked out in the barn?

**BUSTER:** Yes, after she quit teaching, and the gasoline was rationed and so expensive, she just parked it in the barn. She said she didn't need to go anywhere, anyway.

**WILLIAM:** (holding up a piece of paper.) Dad, look at this. It looks like some kind of agreement.

**BUSTER:** (taking the paper) My heavens! She has saved everything, even the agreement Daddy wrote out with ol' Man Carter ... because he couldn't trust spoken agreements anymore, especially with Mr. Carter. There was never an agreement that he'd ever been involved in that didn't have some crack in it ... that he could crawl through. Here, you read it. It will give you a little appreciation and understanding how things were back then.

**WILLIAM:** (reading) "I, J.K. Carter do hereby and hereafter agree with my good and faithful neighbor, Melvin Foster. that I will no longer put pigs or any other

farm brutes in the aforementioned fenced in lot, what I
built right up the hill from the Foster springhouse and I,
Melvin Foster, likewise and simultaneously will now and
subsequently refrain from taking my honorable neighbor,
J.K. Carter, to Court for befouling the water supply for
the Foster family. Signed Melvin Foster and J.K Carter."
Did Mr. Carter squeeze through a crack in this written
agreement?

**BUSTER:** Not really. He did live up to the written
agreement.

**WILLIAM:** What do you mean by that?

**BUSTER:** It's true that he never put any more animals in
the pig lot. He just let the pigs run loose to root for
themselves in the woods on the mountainside as
everybody used to do. And of course they found our
spring. (still searching) That's what you might call
fulfilling the letter of the law and defiling — that's a good
word in this instance — defiling the spirit of the law. The
spring really got defiled, so we had to dig a well to get our
water.

**WILLIAM:** (while still searching through the old papers
and books) Dad, here's a whole stack of notebooks, each
one marked THE JOURNAL /DIARY OF
ROSEANNE FOSTER 1900.

**BUSTER:** (looking at the books and musing to himself) It
seems that Roxie started journaling right after I read her
some of Porte Crayon's journal of his journey to the
Blackwater. When we were both kids, I used to read to
her in the evenings, being her big brother. And when I
read her a paragraph from the BLACKWATER
CHRONICLE by Porte Crayon, she asked lots of
questions, and we ended up talking about JOURNALS
and diaries. She tried to get the two words separated but
seems never to have been able to. They're probably about
the same anyway.

**WILLIAM:** (looking at the oldest book) This must have
been her first entry. "Buster wants me to write to myself.

He thinks I ask him too many questions. So I'll ask my questions to myself in my own diary. When will school start again? Somebody ought to be able to answer that. I'll ask a different kind of question. Does Paul Furman like me? Does Paul Furman like me a little? Does Paul Furman ... I ...

**BUSTER:** (trying to distract him) This is her last book, and this must be the last thing she wrote in the journal. In fact, I suppose it's the last thing she ever wrote at all. (reading) June 1, 1945. "This will probably be the last entry in my journal as my eyesight is deteriorating drastically, and I have been told by Dr. Loomis that I need to go to the hospital in Elkins. I am afraid this extensive written account of my attempt over the years to "come of age" "will be too boring for anyone later opening these pages."

**WILLIAM:** What does she mean by "my attempt to come of age"?

**BUSTER:** It was just something we talked about when she kept asking so many questions. I told her that she would understand a whole lot more when she had "come of age".

    *Buster looks up and reminisces.*

**BUSTER:** I wonder that she never again mentioned to me anything about journaling or "coming of age".

**WILLIAM:** Did you mean growing up?

**BUSTER:** Yeah, something like that. Discovering her journal does shed some light on several otherwise strange actions of hers when she would try to put on airs and act grown-up or when I would see a quizzical look come over her face. Instead of her asking me or anyone else a relevant question she would rush to her room and stay for a spell.

    *Buster reads to himself.*

**WILLIAM:** What else does she write?

**BUSTER:** (reading aloud) I constantly have been berated for asking too many questions, but Uncle Jimmy Jack told me to keep asking questions as that was the only way I'd ever learn anything. So that's what I did, often asking my question right out loud, and that's what I've always encouraged my school pupils to do. I'm not sure I have even now "come of age" even though I've passed the half century mark, myself I still have a lot of questions that I would like to ask someone, not just about myself, but about my neighbors, my community, about Tucker County.

We have certainly grown a lot since the turn of the century. The old corduroy roads have been transformed into paved roads. The horse and buggy have been replaced by automobiles. The communication of hollering across the meadow or up the hollow to one's neighbor for news is now done by telephone and radio. The schools have been consolidated. We in bygone days could settle our differences over the barnyard fence or in the Magistrates Court, but have since then fought two World Wars, both of which were said to end all wars, if not all differences. We would entertain and be entertained at school and at church; currently we have movies and TV. Now that we have made such progress, have we "come of age?" Although the wars were terrible, Tucker County saw boom times with the coal and coke, and everyone who needed to work could find it.

However, when people would say how wonderful the war was for our economy, I asked myself what kind of price would that put on the life of my Dear Tad and others who didn't return home. I wonder with all the boom times, if Tucker County has COME OF AGE. But I have the nagging suspicion that all of our questions haven't been asked or at least they haven't been answered. If you haven't looked at the past, can you really view the future? I suppose someone else will have to answer that question another half century from now. Somehow I view this half century and the coming half century as a river, like the Dry Fork which has sometimes prompted fear as well as inspiration, as it has flowed around and into my life.

**WILLIAM:** She must have written some poetry too. Look at it.

*William hands a book to Buster. Roxie appears in a shaft of blue light and sings as William and Buster hold in a tableau.*

**ROXIE:** (singing)

>The book is finished, the work is done,
>And life like the river continues to run.
>Through seasons of calm or wild with elation
>Toward its ultimate destination.
>Its cardinal path is already set
>It's course according to plan,
>Though sometimes altered by circumstance,
>Just like the journey of man.
>A time to be born, a time to die,
>A time to laugh, and a time to cry.
>A time of darkness, and a time of light.
>With the rhythm of rivers, these rhymes I write.
>With the rhythm of rivers these rhymes I write.

*Roxie's light fades and as she disappears William and Buster resume their conversation.*

**WILLIAM:** (reading) Dear Diary ... "Goodnight and Goodbye"

**BUSTER:** I suppose it is appropriate for Roxie to have the last word.

FADEOUT.

CURTAIN

# No Admittance

This play is an account of cultural/racial events in West Tennessee just prior to the assassination of Rev. Dr. Martin Luther King, Jr. The writer changed all the names except that of a very special participant, Sister Willie Mae Tyger, the president of Fite's Bottom Improvement Association. There is an occasional touch of humor in the mix of severe racial and political confrontation. It was produced by the Tucson Community Players and St. Francis UM Church in collaboration with the Tucson Racial Reconciliation Community 33rd annual Conference. Although the setting was fifty years earlier and two thousand miles away, the message is still relevant here, today.

# NO ADMITTANCE
# A PLAY IN TWO ACTS

*By E. Reid Gilbert*

Cast

**TOM NICHOLS** . . . . . . . . A white student; age 20
**BILL BOWEN** . . . . . . . . . A black student; age 19
**MAGGIE** . . . . . . . . . . . . . A white waitress; age 35
**CECIL TUTTLE** . . . . . . . . Country fellow with a gun; age 50
**POLICE OFFICER OBRIEN** A police officer; age 40
**THOMAS NICHOLS** . . . . An attorney; age 48
**LISA ANN NICHOLS** . . . Thomas Nichols' wife; age 45
**WILLIAM B. TWINING** . A country lawyer; elderly
**JUDGE BENJAMIN J. WORTHY** A judge; age 55
**JESSE CONGER** . . . . . . . . A prosecuting attorney; age 35
**SISTER WILLIE MAE TYGER** African American woman; age 80
**ADDY BOWEN** . . . . . . . . Bill Bowen's mother; age 44
**PATRICIA** . . . . . . . . . . . . . A receptionist in her early; 20s; works at City Hall
**NARRATOR** . . . . . . . . . . . Any age

Scene
Various locations around Jackson, TN.
Time: October, 1967
ACT I


Scene 1
SETTING: *Jackson, TN The Woolworth Lunch*
*Counter; 6:00 am. October 27, 1967*
*AT RISE: TOM is seated alone at one end of the lunch*
counter.

**NARRATOR:** (reading from a newspaper) The
JACKSON SUN reports that Thurgood Marshall has
been appointed to the Supreme Court. (speaking to the
audience) While historic events, like the first African
American on the Supreme Court, were happening in the
rest of the world, life in Jackson TN was calm ... though
a bit tense. Life was rather normal ... normal for
Jackson.

**MAGGIE:** (enters with pot of coffee) I s'pose you'd like
some coffee.

**TOM:** Yep, but I oughta have a cup first.

**MAGGIE:** You used to bein' waited on back home ... I
s'pose.

**TOM:** Yep, again.

**MAGGIE:** (MAGGIE pulls a cup and saucer from under
the counter and starts pouring.) Who waited on ya' back
there?

**TOM:** We had a cook ... in Memphis.

**MAGGIE:** So she just did whatevah it wuz thet you
wanted her to do!?

**TOM:** Not always.

**MAGGIE:** (arranging things on the counter) What made
the difference?

**TOM:** (putting sugar and cream in his coffee) Well she
first came to work for us when I was about five.

**MAGGIE:** An' she's still there?

**TOM:** Yeah!

**MAGGIE:** She surely stayed a long time. (TOM pours a little coffee in the saucer) What'd you do thet for? Is thet what yoah mamma done for you down in Memphis?

**TOM:** (blowing on the coffee in the saucer) Nope I did it for myself ... but she said that was what the men did where she came from back home up in the mountains.

**MAGGIE:** Yep, thet's what we always did when the coffee came right off the hot cook stove ... (pantomiming it) Saucered and blowed. (TOM continues quietly to sip his coffee out of the saucer.) You didn't tell me what yoah cook done for you when you was five ... I s'pose she was Black.

**TOM:** (now drinking his coffee from the cup) Well of course. As I recall ... It was such a long time ago.

**MAGGIE:** I s'pose all of 12 yeahs ago.

**TOM:** (ignoring her implication that it wasn't a very long time ago) The first morning she was there she said, "Little white boy, what you wants to drink for breakfuss?" She musta thought I'd reached my "age of majority", a term that grown-ups usta like to use.

**MAGGIE:** Oh, I've heard it many a time.

**TOM:** So I just straightened myself up and said, "I'll have coffee, if you please."

**MAGGIE:** (leaning with her elbows on the counter and looking directly at Tom) So she just poured the LITTLE WHITE BOY some coffee 'cause it pleased him?

**TOM:** No it wasn't that ... She refused.

**MAGGIE:** What's that, you say?

**TOM:** She said, "Little white boy, thet don't please me atall. Iffen you drinks thet black stuff, you'll get as black as I is.

**MAGGIE:** (throwing her dishcloth on the counter and laughing at Tom's expense) Well, good for her. I s'pose then she wadn't gonna take no sass offen this little white boy.

**TOM:** Yeah, somethin' like that. She was a big woman with a lotta black. So I said. I think I'll have milk." She said "Thet's a mighty fine choice."

**MAGGIE:** (looking toward door) Speakin' of Blacks. Heah comes one.

**TOM:** One what? (also looking toward door) Oh, that's just Bill.

**MAGGIE:** So you know him?

**TOM:** Yeah he's a friend of mine. We planned to meet heah this mornin'.

**MAGGIE:** A friend?

**TOM:** We bunk in the same dorm.

**MAGGIE:** At Lambuth College?

**TOM:** Yeah. (Bill comes rushing in. He tries to hide behind a small table, where he hunkers down so as not to be seen from the door.) Bill what in the world is wrong with you?

**MAGGIE:** Seems to me he seen some kinda ghost.

**BILL:** Problem is, if that fellow finds me I might turn into a ghost.

**MAGGIE:** What fella you talkin' 'bout?

**BILL:** That man out there with a gun.

**MAGGIE:** O my Lord!

**TOM:** Would someone ... just any body ... tell me what's goin' on?

**MAGGIE:** (walking to door and looking out) It looks like they're doin' it.

**TOM:** (singing) Everybody's doin' it, doin' it.

**MAGGIE:** Can you be serious for a minute?

**TOM:** Serious 'bout what?

**BILL:** Tom, there's a redneck out there with a gun.

**TOM:** What's so serious 'bout that? Nothin' unusual. Probably just getting fixed to go huntin'.

**MAGGIE:** They huntin' awright.

**BILL:** I'm 'fraid they be huntin' for me.

**TOM:** Why they be huntin' for you? You don't have any feathers. Your drumsticks wouldn't be worth eatin' any ways.

**MAGGIE:** I heard through the grapevine they were gonna do it.

**TOM:** Do what an' why?

**MAGGIE:** Do some celebratin'.

**TOM:** Celebratin' what an' why an' where?

**BILL:** They prob'bly be rememberin'.

**TOM:** 'Memberin' what?

**MAGGIE:** There was a sit-in here seven years ago.

**TOM:** You mean a civil rights kind of thing?

**BILL:** Yeah, like she said. Seven year ago, today.

**TOM:** You both got things a little bamfoozled. That happened at a Woolworth's lunch counter over in Greensboro, NC ... 'bout that time I think.

**BILL:** Yeah, it happened here too, but the TV didn't take much notice of it. A cousin of mine was goin' to Lane College an' was one of the organizers.

**TOM:** Bill, why don't you hop up here to the counter?

**BILL:** Uh, Uh!

**TOM:** What you mean, Uh, Uh?

**BILL:** That's when we get in trouble tryin' to get served at a Woolworth's lunch counter.

**MAGGIE:** (looking directly at Bill) Aw, nobody's gonna pitch you out from here. Are you one of those Lane College fellows?

**TOM:** Didn't I tell you he was in the same dorm as me?

**MAGGIE:** At Lambuth College? I thought Lane College was set up a long time ago for his kind.

**TOM:** His kind of what?

**BILL:** My kind of skin ... An' all of my kin.

**TOM:** Oh, is that all?

**MAGGIE:** When did they start lettin' THEM inta a WHITE SCHOOL?

**TOM:** Maggie, it's not a white school. It's mostly red brick.

**MAGGIE:** (taking cup and saucer over to Bill's table) An' I s'pose Lane College built with colored bricks?

**TOM:** Maggie, you sure do a lotta s'posin'.

**MAGGIE:** (standing at Bill's table but directing her answer to Tom) I s'pose I do, but there ain't nothin'

stayin' in its place no more. There's nothin' you can
rightly say fer certain, so there gotta be a lot of s'posin'
goin' on' round heah. You boys up mighty early this
mornin'. I s'pose you goin' huntin'?

**TOM:** I s'pose not. I don't even know when huntin'
season sets in.

**MAGGIE:** Ya know this is West Tennessee ... It seems
that there ain't no accountin' fer the actual huntin'
season times.

**TOM:** Well we're not goin' huntin'. We headin' down to
Memphis where there's gonna be a big celebration.

**MAGGIE:** You ain't fixin' to do no celebratin' heah are
you?

**TOM:** No ... Why would we want to be celebratin' at
Woolworth's?

**MAGGIE:** I don't know ... but heah's where it happened.

**TOM:** Where what happened?

**BILL:** She done tole you 'bout that sit-in heah seven year
ago.

**MAGGIE:** I can see that yoah little friend can talk up too.

**TOM:** He ain't little, but he can talk. Not very pushy like
some folk 'round here.

**MAGGIE:** You wouldn't now be referrin' ... ?

**TOM:** If the shoe fits ...

**MAGGIE:** (heading to kitchen) I ain't gonna take that
kinda sass offen ...

**TOM:** You mean it happened right here ... at this very
same lunch counter?

**BILL:** Right here! My cousin was one of the ringleaders.

**MAGGIE:** (re-entering from kitchen) It be seven year ago
today.

**TOM:** Now that would be somethin' to celebrate wouldn't
it?

**MAGGIE:** Not heah boys ... not today nohow.

**TOM:** Seven years is a long time. I was only 13 then ...
way ovah in Memphis.

**MAGGIE:** Well evahthing just keep happenin; too fast

nowadays. But we were tole thet theah might be trouble heah today in mind of thet day.

**TOM:** Nauw! Not us! We just headin' ovah to Memphis to attend the celebration of one of our fraternity brother's weddin'.

**MAGGIE:** You mean yoah quiet friend heah is in yoah fraternity?

**TOM:** No, Maggie, they haven't gone quite that far yet. Oh no, but I can bring a friend.

**MAGGIE:** I kinda figgerred that a weddin' was kinda like a family affair. But he ...

**TOM:** Oh, I shoulda told you. This is Bill, my brother.

**MAGGIE:** But yoah daddy ...

**TOM:** Oh, yeah, we got the same daddy.

**MAGGIE:** What you mean the same daddy?

**BILL:** (picking up on the fun) Ouah Fathah is the Lord God A'mighty.

**MAGGIE:** (starting to the kitchen) I surely ain't gonna take that kinda sass off no colored ... (MAGGIE is interrupted by a man coming in with a hunting rifle. BILL hurries to the counter to sit beside Tom.)

**MAGGIE:** (to Cecil) Mawnin'. (Cecil looks around as though he's confused.) You can sit wheahevah you like.

**CECIL:** I wouldn't wanna set with no niggah. (CECIL continues to stand, holding the rifle, but in a casual way with the barrel pointing to the floor.)

**MAGGIE:** I ain't wantin' no trouble in heah this mawnin'. If you want some coffee, I'll be back with it an' a menu. (MAGGIE waits to see if there might be a confrontation.)

**CECIL:** Why would theah be any trouble? Trouble started quite a while ago, when I had to start settin' down with any darkies. (MAGGIE exits to kitchen.)

**TOM:** (to Bill) What's he talkin' about?

**BILL:** Don't be daft, Simple Simon. He's talkin' about me an' integration.

**TOM:** Oh, yeah I keep fergettin'. Things are a little different ovah in Memphis.

BILL: (whispering to TOM) But I can't afford evah to forget.

TOM: (to Cecil) You won't be needin' to set down with us. You can stand an' not be dirtyin' up your hind-end with sittin'. (waiting for a response) I believe they call that the vertical plan ... nobody sittin' an' evahbody standin'. Then evahbody be OK.

CECIL: I don't keer what kinda plan you be talkin' 'bout. I just aim to do a little huntin'.

TOM: What kinda game you be findin' in here?

CECIL: We be coon huntin' ... me an some fellers outside. I already got my firearm ready-loaded.

TOM: I thought coon huntin' was done at night.

CECIL: Oh, some kinda coons be roamin' 'round aftah the darkness be gone ... an' you can see 'em bettah then ... IN THE DAYLIGHT.

TOM: You can't be thinkin' what I think you ...

CECIL: If you be thinkin' 'bout coons an' coon-lovers like we been thinkin' fer yeahs. then yeah! We got huntin' right heah. You boys wanna have a little fun?

TOM: We're always up for a little fun, but we gotta get on the road to Memphis.

CECIL: Theah be othah roads, 'sides the road to Memphis.

TOM: To what other avenues would you be alluding?

CECIL: I ain't 'ludin' to nothin' but the road to perdition when my buddies get heah.

BILL: We not lookin' for any trouble this mawin', Mister ...

CECIL: Boy can you unnerstan' good English?

TOM: Now the operative word there is English.

CECIL: White Boy, are you just anotha niggah with a no-color skin?

TOM: It seems that we have here a matter of semantics.

CECIL: I got no notion of what Sammy you talkin' 'bout, but you don't wanna rile up a fight with me. Theah are others outside ... an' I'm the one in heah with the gun.

*The click of the gun being cocked can be heard. He picks a pistol out of his pocket and slams it on the table.*

**TOM:** Who the WE you be referrin' to?

**CECIL:** The Citizens' Counci! We ...

**TOM:** Would that be the WHITE Citizens' Council?

**CECIL:** It certainly wouldn't be no god-damned colored citizens' like that NAA somethin' or other.

**TOM:** You mean the NAACP!

**CECIL:** What we mean is thet we gonna have a little historical re-enactment heah on what took place seven yeah ago. An' you boys'll fit right inta the movie.

**TOM:** Oh you mean when those Lane College students staged a sit-in?

**CECIL:** Yeah thet niggah college on the othah side ...

**TOM:** I believe those fellows eventually won that little skirmish.

**CECIL:** They might've did. But this time we come prepared. (Police sirens can be heard approaching. Flashing red lights can be seen through the door.) The cops have got theirselves a hotrodder or some pore soul has broke outta the county pokey.

**MAGGIE:** (MAGGIE appears at door to the kitchen.) There're several police cars pullin' up out there.

**CECIL:** Some son-uv-a-bitch must've called the sheriff. (looking at MAGGIE) If you called the po-lice ...

**MAGGIE:** Didn't need to.

**CECIL:** Whatcha mean, "Didn't need to"? Somebody must've tipped –

**MAGGIE:** They already had a cop heah, maybe expectin' trouble from things the sheriff been hearin' 'bout from out in the county. (OFFICER O'BRIEN enters.)

**O'BRIEN:** Mr. Tuttle, I think it would be best if you come with me. (taking hold of Cecil's arm) They already got things under control out theah.

**CECIL:** You 'restin' me?

**O'BRIEN:** No, we're just tryin' to avert any trouble.

**CECIL:** If you ain't puttin' me under no arrest, you got no call to order me to leave ... An' let go my arm.

**O'BRIEN:** If you don't leave these premises, I will arrest you.

**CECIL:** Fer what?

**O'BRIEN:** For disturbin' the peace.

**CECIL:** I ain't disturbin' nobody's peace.

**MAGGIE:** He disturbin' my peace when he come bustin in heah with thet gun an' now the pistol.

**O'BRIEN:** Maggie, it be best if you don't say anything ... Or you may be called up as a witness.

**MAGGIE:** But the guns ....

**O'BRIEN:** Yeah! If you weren't disturbin' the peace, what is it with the guns?

**CECIL:** I missed the start of dove season, so I was gonna ...

**MAGGIE:** Theah ain't no doves in heah.

**O'BRIEN:** Maggie!

**MAGGIE:** Sorry!

**CECIL:** I brung my guns in heah to oil 'em whilst I wuz havin' my mawnin' coffee.

**O'BRIEN:** It be best for you to go on wheah you be goin'.

**CECIL:** Not had my coffee yet.

**O'BRIEN:** Maggie, would you please give this fellow some coffee? (MAGGIE puts a cup on counter and pours coffee.)

**MAGGIE:** You can take yoah coffee.

**CECIL:** But the cup?

**MAGGIE:** Compliments of the house! (O'BRIEN and CECIL exit.)

**BILL:** That was close.

**TOM:** I thought he was just foolin' around.

**BILL:** Tom, I know you're an upperclassman, but you got a lot to learn 'bout a man with a gun, 'specially walkin' into a café wheah they see a Black man. Maybe things are all different ovah to the big city of Memphis.

**TOM:** It takes a while for me to adjust ...

**BILL:** You gonna stop by to see your folks in Memphis?

**TOM:** Hell no!

BILL: Why not?

TOM: I've already told you that my dad and I don't get along very well.

BILL: Why not?

TOM: We have issues.

BILL: About what?

TOM: He doesn't like my major.

BILL: You mean English?

TOM: Yeah!

BILL: He does pay your tuition, doesn't he?

TOM: Yeah!

BILL: An' he bought a car for you, didn't he?

TOM: Yeah.

BILL: I wish my dad were still alive.

MAGGIE: You boys orderin' anything?

TOM: We just wanted a cup of coffee, but we'll be outta here before your real customers come in.

MAGGIE: That's fine by me. If you change yoah mind, just call me from the kitchen. (MAGGIE exits.)

TOM: (calling after her) OK! We better get goin' any way. (TOM lays some money on counter. Tom and Will put their cups down, gather their things and head for the door.)

BLACKOUT

END OF SCENE

ACT I

NARRATOR: (Reading in isolated spot before Act I, Scene 2, Reveal.) Carl Stokes, elected mayor of Cleveland. (to audience) The first Black mayor of a major American city in November 1967. That was an unacceptable surprise in the Nichols' Memphis living room.

SCENE 2

SETTING: The NICHOLS' well- furnished living Room in Memphis.

*AT RISE: THOMAS and LISA ANN are sitting in easy chairs and reading. THOMA is reading Time and LISA ANN is reading Southern Living. THOMAS is drinking scotch and LISA ANN is drinking wine.*

**LISA ANN:** These pictures of the Tennessee governor's mansion are just gorjus. I wonder if Buford and Helen could be a mite uncomfortable livin' in such a fish bowl ... ever'body oglin' them all the time.

**THOMAS:** Now wouldn't you love to be living in that mansion.

**LISA ANN:** Thomas, I've tole you a thousan' times, if I tole you once, you oughtta be runnin' fer public office, an I mean at the state level, not just hyar in Memphis, which is just a little minnow in the great fishbowl of Tennessee.

**THOMAS:** An' I've replied to you a thousand times that I'm doin' much better as an attorney than I would as an elected official.

**LISA ANN:** You mean much bettah off financially?

**THOMAS:** Yes!

**LISA ANN:** But what about community sehvice?

**THOMAS:** What kinda community service?

**LISA ANN:** You know good an' well that ever'thing is changin' so fast an' we need somebody who can help us preserve our cultcha.

**THOMAS:** Our culture?

**LISA ANN:** Ouah Southern way of life.

**THOMAS:** Oh I see what you mean. It must mean a lot to you to entice you to go to all those meetings.

**LISA ANN:** Well it's certainly worth what effort I ...

**THOMAS:** It would certainly not be worth my effort to seek ...

**LISA ANN:** (interrupting him and showing him a picture in her magazine) An' just look at this lovely silvah service at the mansion. It must be a bitch to keep it polished.

**THOMAS:** Lisa Ann, what would the ladies at your club think, if they heard that kinda language comin' from you?

**LISA ANN:** It just slips out evah now an' then. They know very well that I was not "to manor born" ... But now that I'm heah, I'm gonna make the most of it ... Thinkin' of all thet silvah 'minds me all ovah again how hard it is to get reliable help these days.

**THOMAS:** You might get one of your cousins from up Squealem Holler to polish the silvah ware for you.

**LISA ANN:** Thomas, you know good and well that I'm from Crossville and not from up some hog holler. An' don't start in on the financial circumstances of my fambly.

**THOMAS:** I agree that good loyal colored help is not easy to come by these days. There's an article here in TIME that Carl Stokes was recently sworn in as mayor of Cleveland.

**LISA ANN:** What's so unusual 'bout that? I knew a wonderful family back home by the name of Stokes. They were upstandin' citizens of the county.

**THOMAS:** Were they colored?

**LISA ANN:** Course not, stupid. I said they were upstandin' citizens.

**THOMAS:** Well, the new Mayor Stokes of Cleveland is a Nee-gro.

**LISA ANN:** Good Lord above! What is this country comin' to ... with folks leavin' the ol' ways an' marchin' down in Alabama an' disrespectin' even the guvment who is tryin' to finish that war ovah in Asia ... Even the coloreds are fergettin' their place.

**THOMAS:** It seems that their place might be changin'.

BLACKOUT

END OF SCENE

ACT I

**NARRATOR:** (Reading in isolated spot before Act I, Scene 3, Reveal) Miss Bronze West Tennessee (to audience) After Betty Friedan founded the N_O_W a couple of years ago, her members became agitated over the "white only" practice of the Miss America contest. So the good people of Jackson partially solved that problem by setting up a pageant for colored girls. Miss Bronze West Tennessee based just on talent. Of course the boys would talk about that in their dorm room.

## SCENE 3

*SETTING: TOM'S dorm room*

*AT RISE: A study table, two chairs and a bed are visible. TOM is at the study table as BILL enters.*

**BILL:** Tom, what was it you wanted to tell me?

**TOM:** (unfolding a much-abused letter) I got this nice letter from her.

**BILL:** A Dear John?

**TOM:** No, a course not. (showing him the letter) A Dear Tom.

**BILL:** You know what I mean?

**TOM:** Of course I know what a Dear John is. This isn't exactly that. She writes (reading) "It's not that there's someone else." You know in a Dear John there's usually someone else. (reading again) "It's just that I've got to move on."

**BILL:** Move on wheah ... to what?

**TOM:** Even last fall she was really upset 'bout that Miss America Pageant.

**BILL:** What in the name of Sam Hill does that have to do with a Dear John?

**TOM:** Not a Dear John.

**BILL:** No, 'course not ... a Dear Tom. Why was she so upset 'bout the beauty pageant? She wasn't a contestant was she? ... I 'member you sayin' she was beauty queen quality.

**TOM:** I never said that to her but one time.

**BILL:** Didn't like that, huh?

**TOM:** Nope. An' she wasn't a contestant. In fact she kept talkin' 'bout how those pageants put down women.

**BILL:** Put down? I thought it put them up on a pedestal.

**TOM:** I think she used the word "demeaned" women. You know she was mighty proud of gettin' involved with political stuff while she was still in high school up there in Baltimore.

**BILL:** Was that why she was majorin' in political science?

**TOM:** Yeah! An' she kept referrin' to NOW.

**BILL:** NOW? ... Whatta you mean NOW? What about WHEN and THEN? What's so special 'bout NOW?

**TOM:** N-O-W I think means some organization for women. The leader of that, whoever she is, said that the Miss America thing was racist and the contestants promoted the Vietnam War by entertainin' the troops.

**BILL:** What's racist 'bout that?

**TOM:** You know colored girls aren't allowed to enter.

**BILL:** That must be why they had a parallel contest here in Jackson ... Miss Bronze West Tennessee. What did all that have to do with Lillian?

**TOM:** She transferred to a northern Virginia college where the girls — women — Pardon me Diamond Lil. They were organizin' for Atlantic City later this year. She writes in the letter.

**BILL:** The Dear John ...

**TOM:** The Dear Tom letter that they're plannin' to march or boycott or somthin' at the Miss America Pageant.

**BILL:** That's not any time soon is it?

**TOM:** Here it is, (reading from the letter) "The pageant is in September but a lot of organizing has to happen. Northern Virginia College is the campus where a lot of the preliminaries are taking place, and it's not far from Arlantic City. I've already met Betty Friedan and that was so exciting. Maybe I'll see you some time in the summer."

**BILL:** Who the hell is Betty Free-dam? (TOM doesn't answer.) So you're upset with her.

**TOM:** Mad as hell. I don't give a good god-damn 'bout what happens in Atlantic City. But I figger that Lil could do her thing right here in Jackson. Let those yankee girls march an' parade or do whatevah they wanna.

**BILL:** You 'member that play, Look Back in Anger, that the theatre department did?

**TOM:** Yeah, so what?

**BILL:** There seems to be a whole category now that they call "Angry young men". You let Diamond Lil join her N-O-W an' you might join the A-Y-M.

**TOM:** The A-Y-M?

**TOM:** That's just the thing. Where do I sign up?

**BILL:** I think the way it goes is for women to SIGN UP an' for men to not sign up for anything, but just to ACT UP in disgust.

**TOM:** Not sign up ... to just act up? I like it. I'm all for it. Lil was always naggin' me 'bout my actin' up by drinkin'. You s'pose we could go down to Fite's Bottom where we can get some real moonshine from the hills?

**BILL:** Yeah I got a great aunt down there: Aunt (pronounce AHNT) Willie Mae Tyger.

**TOM:** Does she sell it?

**BILL:** Not anymore. But she always knows where ...

**TOM:** We could drive down there an' get us a half gallon. Then park the car on campus.

**BILL:** Someone's sure to see us drinkin', those religion majors ...

**TOM:** Yeah those pre-ministerial guys are tryin' to convert the whole world, an' pour all the booze in the river.

**BILL:** That's when all the church folk would sing (He sings) Shall we gather at the river, where ...

**TOM:** That's an old joke ... not funny anymore.

**BILL:** You seem a mite too serious 'bout all this'.

**TOM:** (Ignoring Bill's statement.) We can carry the moonshine down behind campus to the Jackson Memorial Garden.

**BILL:** Ain't that a graveyard?

**TOM:** They got benches an' shrubs an' stuff. Nobody need see us.

**TOM:** Now don't you be draggin' your superstitions inta ...

**BILL:** I reckon that missin' Miss Lillian so much is a good enough excuse for gettinr' soused.

**TOM:** Can you think of a better reason for getting' drunk than losin' the girl ...

**BILL:** Whose name you wanna change?

**TOM:** The girl you already lost your heart to.

**BILL:** I guess you're right. Let me run an' get my coat. Aunt Sister Willie Mae will surely be surprised to see us this time of night.

BLACKOUT<br>END OF SCENE

ACT I

**NARRATOR:** (reading in isolated spot before Act I, Scene 4, Reveal) Tennessee Remains Dry (to audience) The good church folk did it again. They seem to prefer getting their spirits in the hills or down in Fite's Bottom. It's rather ironic that one of the most successful enterprises in the state is the Jack Daniels Distillery. But it's a long ways away from West Tennessee and they do contribute to the state's economy. Too bad the bootleggers down in Fite's Bottom haven't been able to get their portion.

SCENE 4

*SETTING: Later that evening, Sister Willie Mae Tyger's front porch in Fite's Bottom.*

*AT RISE: There is only ambient light from the street lamps. While NARRATOR is finishing his lines and just prior to BILL and TOM entering, we hear voices from inside the house start to sing Love Lifted Me.*

**VOICES:** I was sinking deep in sin.

(BILL and TOM enter and go to the front steps.)

**TOM:** (obviously a little apprehensive.) You sure we at the right place? Far from the peaceful shore.

BILL: A'course it's the right place. I oughta know. I been here many a time. She's kinfolk fer godsake. Sinking to rise no more. But the master of the sea heard my despairing cry. I think I heard our "despairing cry." I believe we're interruptin' a prayer meeting. From the waters lifted me, now safe am I.

TOM: A damn prayer meetin'. What do they do in there? (people inside are heard singing) Love lifted me, Love lifted me ...

BILL: They usually pray ... It seems love didn't lift you. (singing continues) Love lifted me.

TOM: The whole thing just seems a little spooky down here in Fite's Bottom. When nothing else could help.

BILL: You prob'ly just call Fite's Bottom Niggah Town ... Remember you were the one wantin' ... Love lifted me.

TOM: Yeah, Yeah, Yeah. Let's get outta here.

SISTER WILLIE MAE: (voice from inside the house.) Who thet out theah?

BILL: (pronounced AHNT) Aunt Willie Mae. It's just me. Bill Bowen... Cousin Addy's ...

SISTER WILLIE MAE: Well bless my soul. (opening the screen door and coming out onto porch with a barn lantern, which throws some extra light on the scene) What in God's name are you boys doin' out heah at this time of ... The praya meetin' is just breakin' up.

BILL: (interrupting her) Aunt Willie Mae, don't you have a porch light?

SISTER WILLIE MAE: Law me honey (sits in rocking chair) Billy, acourse I got me a poach light. But this ol' lantern been with me for many a day (chuckling) an' night. The oil is far cheapah than the 'lectric an' there're times when the 'lectric don't work.

BILL: We didn't come down heah for the prayer meetin' ...

SISTER WILLIE MAE: Speakin' of this ol' lantern, 'minds me of somethin' right chere not so long ago.

BILL: What would that be Aunt Willie Mae.

SISTER WILLIE MAE: You boys know 'bout the Klang?

**TOM:** What's that ... the Klang?

**BILL:** Oh, Aunt Willie Mae, this is Tom, a friend of mine from over at the college.

**SISTER WILLIE MAE:** Please to meetcha, Tom. I'm awful glad Billy got some friends ovah theah.

**BILL:** Aunt Willie Mae, what's the Klang?

**SISTER WILLIE MAE:** Oh you know. Them white men what wear those white sheets with the pointy hats an' burn crosses ...

**TOM:** Do you mean the Ku Klux Klan?

**SISTER WILLIE MAE:** Yeah! As I was sayin' the Klang nearly skeers me to death. I was so afeared they was gonna burn a cross in front of my house.

**BILL:** Why would they wanna do that, Aunt Willie Mae?

**SISTER WILLIE MAE:** There ain't no accountin' what folks might do or why.

**TOM:** Sister Willie Mae, what happened?

**SISTER WILLIE MAE:** One evenin' I went to the stoah, an' I come back I went inta the house with my groceries. When I looked out twarj the street I seen it burnin' in my front yard.

**BILL:** Why ...

**SISTER WILLIE MAE:** So I goes out the back doah to the neighbors to use their phone. I ain't got no phone, don't cha know?

**BILL:** Yeah.

**SISTER WILLIE MAE:** I calls the po-lice, an' they come right away. Then they come to the doah, an' say, "Sister Willie Mae, does you have a lantern?" I says, "Acourse I got me a lantern. It's gotta be in hyar sommers." Then they say, "Would this be yoah lantern?" They held it up, an' I do declare I had left my lantern out in the yard an' fergot about it, an' when I'd looked out theah an' seen that light I was sure the Klang had done burnt a cross in my yard.

**TOM:** That musta been terrifyin'.

**SISTER WILLIE MAE:** Well yeah until I found out what it was ... Then I felt so silly, I could hardly wait to tell my neighbors.

**BILL:** They musta had a big laugh.

**SISTER WILLIE MAE:** I can usually take keer of myself, as ever'body round hyar can tell you.  But now that Klang thing in the middle of the night is somethin' else. (Brief pause) Is there somethin' I can do for you boys tonight? ... Or maybe you just come visitin'? You say you didn't come for the praya meetin' but what ...

**BILL:** We thought you could tell us where we might be able to pick up a fruit jar of white lightnin'.

**SISTER WILLIE MAE:** Now Billy, you know I don't carry that sruff no moah.

**TOM:** But we hoped you could tell us ...

**SISTER WILLIE MAE:** Well now, if yoah determined, I do wanna make sure you get some good stuff, an' not some laced with Red Devil lye.

**TOM:** We 'preciate that.

**SISTER WILLIE MAE:** You bring yoah half-gallon jar?

**BILL:** We never thought of that.

**SISTER WILLIE MAE:** I'll get you a jar left ovah from last summer's cannin'. Now if you go down hyar three houses (pointing). There's a light on the front porch. Just stand in the yard an' holler, "Sister Willie Mae sent ..." You won't hafta say no moah.

**TOM:** Thank you, Sister Willie Mae. It sure was nice meetin' you.

**SISTER WILLIE MAE:** An' the same heah ... Now Billy' I recommend you stand in front of yoah friend so they see you first, so's they realize they won't be thinkin' you be raidin'.

**BILL:** We'll be sure an' do that Aunt Willie Mae. Thanks so much, an' I'm sure Mamma would want to send her love.

**SISTER WILLIE MAE:** An' the same to her. Now you boys stand right hyar, whilst I fetch that fruit jar for you.

BLACKOUT

END OF SCENE

## ACT I

**NARRATOR:** (reading in isolated spot before Act I, Scene 5, Reveal) Rap Brown Organiazes S-N-C-C (to audience) That's not exactly good news in the Nichols' home.

## SCENE 5

*SETTING: The Nichols' Living Room*
*AT RISE: The scene as before but THOMAS is reading the New York Times and drinking a beer. LISA ANN is embroidering.*

**THOMAS:** It seems that even the students are organizing these days.

**LISA ANN:** Organizin' for what? The students today certainly have it much better than we evah did.

**THOMAS:** What're you talkin' about? You didn't go further than high school.

**LISA ANN:** But I was datin' college guys an' I knew what was goin' on.

**THOMAS:** This new complaining group is called Snick.

**LISA ANN:** What does SNICK mean?

**THOMAS:** The acronym is S-N-C-C, but they pronounce it SNICK.

**LISA ANN:** That doesn't make any sense at all. What does that S N so forth stand for?

**THOMAS:** Student Nonviolent Coordinating Committee

**LISA ANN:** Well it won't keep that name for long.

**THOMAS:** Why? What do you know 'bout it anyway?

**LISA ANN:** Like ever'thing else these days, they won't be able honestly to claim NONVIOLENT, 'cause evahthing nowadays explodes in violence sooner or later ... an' it's usually sooner.

**THOMAS:** What would it be then?

**LISA ANN:** S-N

**THOMAS:** C-C

**LISA ANN:** Let's see you take out the N and you have SCC. (pause) SILLY COMIC CONCLUSIONS.

**THOMAS:** Why that's plumb silly, itself.

**LISA ANN:** That's what I'm sayin'.

**THOMAS:** Saved by the bell. (LISA ANN picks up the phone.)

**LISA ANN:** Hello! The Nichols's residence ... Who ... Oh Tom, Honey. I didn't reckanize yoah voice. You're s so all grown-up now thet you're away from home ... in college ... Are you OK, Son? ... Well you certainly don't sound fine. Wheah are you? ... Wheah ... What in the world are you doin' in the Madison County FBI Office? Just this mawnin'? ... You must be doin' some hefty research to be invited to the FBI ... You weren't exactly invited? ... You were taken theah? ... Tom, I don't understand what ... I'm givin' the phone to yoah fatha. (She hands the phone to THOMAS Like a hot potato.)

**THOMAS:** Tom, what's all this mystery about? ... So you're in a bit of trouble? (lisa leaning over the phone and trying to eavesdrop)

**LISA ANN:** What kinda trouble?

**THOMAS:** (to LISA ANN) Please wait until I ... (attention back to phone and TOM) No, Tom, I didn't ask you to wait ... I was talkin' to your mother , who is terribly upset ...

**LISA ANN:** Of course I'm terribly upset. Our son ...

**THOMAS:** (to LISA ANN) If you will just give me time ... (into phone to Tom) No, Tom, I'm not asking you to give me the time. I can tell time for my own self ... What I want you to give me is the story – the whole story.

**LISA ANN:** What story?

**THOMAS:** (to LISA ANN) If you will just shut up. (to TOM) No, Tom I certainly don't want you to shut up. I just want your confession ... While I get your motha to control herself ...

**LISA ANN:** Confession? What in the world has he gone an' done now?

**THOMAS:** (over LISA ANN's line) You did a foolish thing? Why am I NOT surprised? ... Ok, Ok, I'm listenin' ... I'm not sure I wanna hear it ... but yes ... just start at the beginning ... NO it didn't start when you were born into this family. Obviously something ... Yes ... I'm listenin' ...

**LISA ANN:** (over THOMAS'S line) What What What

**THOMAS:** (cont'd) So you got drunk last Saturday. (hand over mouthpiece, to LISA ANN) I knew he couldn't keep his promise ...

**LISA ANN:** (over Thomas's line) Thomas now don't badger the poah boy. He only drinks heavily when he's stressed out 'bout somethin'. Did you send him that money I tole you ...

**THOMAS:** Yes and he seems to be stressed out all the time. It's his perpetual pastime.

**LISA ANN:** He must be under some kinda ... I know he takes his classes much too seriously. A college boy oughta have the rights to have a little fun.

**THOMAS:** (to LISA ANN) Will you just shut up? (to TOM) I'm talkin' to your motha. (back to LISA ANN) I suspect it was a little fun ... (back to phone and TOM) So you got drunk ... again ... and walked back to campus through the Jackson Memorial Garden.

**LISA ANN:** Isn't that a cemetery?

**THOMAS:** (to LISA ANN) Yes (to phone) Yes? You know there's no law about walking through a cemetery, unless you're desecrating a grave or vandalizing in some way ... Yes, I'm sure there were lots of little American flags there.

**LISA ANN:** Good Lord! What has he done to the American flag?

**THOMAS:** Yeah! So you took one of them and brought it to the Student Union on campus.

**LISA ANN:** Why would he do that?

**THOMAS:** So did you then get the attention you were looking for? ... Don't set into me with your constant complaining about the attention you DIDN'T get from us ... OK OK I'm listening.

**LISA ANN:** Is he sayin' we didn't ...

**THOMAS:** (with hand over the phone) If you'll just keep your damn mouth shut, I might be able ... (phone back to ear) No not you.

**LISA ANN:** Why that little ingrate (to herself) You carry them for nine months and your body getting' ... Moah an' moah out of shape ...

**THOMAS:** Yeah, I'm listenin' ... Oh, that's just Mother in the background.

**LISA ANN:** An' the mawnin' sickness was somethin' awful. I'd just like them to ...

**THOMAS:** So then after the crowd gathered ... Weren't there any college officials: a dean or professor or maybe a coach ... Of course I know you're all adults now, but some times it doesn't seem ... OK OK Not a sermon right now.

**LISA ANN:** (during THOMAS'S silences) What did he do with the American flag ... What in the hell ...

**THOMAS:** Then after a little speech by ... Oh, you gave a little speech about Vietnam? ... and also about the horror of flag desecration there ... What did you think was a flag's disrespect? ... What had happened to that flag? ... Yes, I remember your Boy Scout days.

**LISA ANN:** (during THOMAS'S silence) He was so good then.

**THOMAS:** Yes I remember those parades.

**LISA ANN:** I invited all the girls from the DAR ... an' also the children from my Sunday School class to watch Tom's patriotic ...

**THOMAS:** You still haven't told me anything particularly dastardly or unlawful, except the pickin' up a dirty little American flag off the ground ...

**LISA ANN:** That was bad enough but what else?

**THOMAS:** Yes, you've already introduced the Boy Scouts of America evidence ... I know that in the scouts you knew how to carry, display and dispose a flag.

**LISA ANN:** What in the world did he do with it? ... He

didn't flush it down the toilet, did he? ... Those beatniks an' hippies ...

**THOMAS:** If it is soiled or has touched the ground ...

**LISA ANN:** (greatly agitated) Oh my heaven ... he's just like all those others, marchin' ever'wheah, tearin' down ever'thing that we evah built up; ever'thing we've held sacred for yeahs.

**THOMAS:** So aftah your Saturday night drunken bash an' flag-burnin' party in the student union ... You had to wait until Monday for the FBI to pay any attention an' come to give you a ride to town?

**LISA ANN:** (screaming) Oh, my God ... the FBI ... What will all my friends think? ... I reckon there's no hope for my becomin' president of ... But if that bitch, Sally Scales ...

**THOMAS:** till there? (to LISA) He hung up on me. (Still holding on to the phone)

**LISA ANN:** Thomas. We gotta do somethin'

**THOMAS:** An' what do you propose we do?

**LISA ANN:** I'm sure I don't know ... I've nevah been drunk an' wavin' an American flag while streakin' through a sacred cemetery ... naked.

**THOMAS:** He didn't say anything about bein' nude.

**LISA ANN:** Well, he might as well have gone the whole way.

**THOMAS:** I believe the naked part was your contribution, Lady Godiva.

**LISA ANN:** You could call Buford. I'm sure he ...

**THOMAS:** Why would I call Governor Ellington?

**LISA ANN:** Aftah all, what are friendships for?

**THOMAS:** Lisa, if the FBI is involved, it's a federal matter an' not a state ...

**LISA ANN:** Why would a person give all thet campaign money to a politician, if you didn't expect a little help, now an' then? ... Now what do we ...

**THOMAS:** (putting phone in cradle) I know what I would really like to do, but it would be biologically impossible or surely illegal.

BLACKOUT
END OF SCENE

## ACT 1

**NARRATOR:** (reading in isolated spot before Act I, Scene 6, Reveal) 1968 Mass Movements (to audience) The various movements include, civil rights movement, student movement, Vietnam movement, Women's movement, gay rights and even environmental. The activities on the Lambuth College campus could hardly be categorized as part of a movement ... or ... could it? Tom gets a visit from his dad.

## SCENE 6

*SETTING: Tom's dorm room, January 25, 1968, 7:00 pm.*
*AT RISE: Study table, two chairs, single bed. Thomas is sitting with back to table and looking at Tom, who is lying on bed, throwing basketball up and catching it over and over.*

**THOMAS:** You must realize she's terribly upset about this little escapade of yours. (silence) She's fine. You know she's up for chairlady ...

**TOM:** Of what? ... This time?

**THOMAS:** You know how devoted she is to the DAR ...

**TOM:** What happened to that Confederate Women thingamabob?

**THOMAS:** She thought that was a lost cause.

**TOM:** A lost ... cause! Very clever Dad. I didn't think you had it in ya ... Why is she so upset, 'bout my behavior way ovah heah in Jackson? ... I would have thought she might enjoy tellin' her lady friends 'bout the recent activities of her only son, an' that it got federal attention.

**THOMAS:** She has no interest nor intention of talkin' anout it in public ... In fact, her fear is that she's sure ever'body is already talkin' about it ... behind her back ... She barely leaves the house any more ... Tom! Would you please stop that foolin' around with that basketball?

**TOM**: If you think this is foolin' 'round, I can show you what foolin' 'round ...

**THOMAS**: Oh, I know about your ability to fool around ... I believe that's why I'm here today instead over in Memphis where I OUGHT to be ... where I might have been able to make a buck or two.

**TOM**: (getting off the bed and shooting the basketball into the metal waste basket in the corner) Dad, I learned a long time ago that "ought" is a big fat zero and comes just before a one, if anyone's countin'. OUGHT, one , two, three ...

**THOMAS**: Tom, cut out the game playing.

**TOM**: But now a buck or two, that's a whole new kettle of fish. In her last letter, Mother assured me that the "buck or two" has reproduced ... into a humongous kettle of fish.

**THOMAS**: Do you realize how much I'm missin' by bein' here instead of ...

**TOM**: Do you realize what I been missin' for some time ... a visit from my folks ... Not even once ... to leave your glorious Memphis metropolis to come here an' see how I'm doin' in Podunk Jackson ... This is the first time in three years ... to drive only 80 miles to see your only son ... Maybe my "little escapade" was a subconscious attempt to see my folks.

**THOMAS**: Don't even think such rubbish. You know very well I had intended to come over when you won ...

**TOM**: I don't believe I saw you in the audience that day.

**THOMAS**: I'm sure you remember the big legal case that came up at the last minute ... in Memphis.

**TOM**: More bucks!

**THOMAS**: More than enough to pay for that Mustang ...

**TOM**: Used!

**THOMAS**: Collector's automobile!

**TOM**: I can't say I haven't enjoyed the car ... and I do appreciate it.

**THOMAS**: Thanks for saying so ... finally.

*BILL BOWEN walks in.*

**TOM:** Dad have you met Bill?

**THOMAS:** I don't think so.

**TOM:** Especially since you haven't been here.

*THOMAS and BILL shake hands.*

**THOMAS:** (to BILL) I've defended some of YOUR folks in the courts in Memphis.

**BILL:** I don't have any kin in Memphis.

**THOMAS:** Oh I mean your kind over there.

**TOM:** Dad, you know you're being ...

**THOMAS:** Bill, how're you doin' in your classes here?

**BILL:** Glad to meet you, Mr. Nichols ... Oh, I'm doin' pretty well in my classes ... Mostly A's an' B's last semester.

**THOMAS:** That's really surprisin'.

**TOM:** What's so surprisin' 'bout it. You think just because Bill ...

**THOMAS:** It has nothin' to do with his race. I'm not a racist. I figured that Bill musta gone to a segregated school ...

**TOM:** The same schools that the white politicians kept underfundin'.

**THOMAS:** Those schools ...

**TOM:** NIGGAH schools?

**THOMAS:** Tom, you musn't use that word.

**TOM:** We can't use that word but we can still treat them as what that word implies ...

**BILL:** Am I interruptin' something?

**TOM:** Well you know about that flag thing.

**BILL:** Oh, yeah, now that was a really ...

**THOMAS:** No, you're not interrupting. It's just that I'll hafta leave ...

**BILL:** Sure. Sorry. See ya later, Tom. Goodbye, Mr. Nichols. Nice to meet ya.

*Bill exits*

**TOM:** Bill doesn't have a Mustang ... or a car of any sort ...

**THOMAS:** But I bet he enjoys yours.

**TOM:** Yeah when I include him on any of my jaunts. You know his mom is a cleaning lady in Mississippi.

**THOMAS:** So?

**TOM:** Every time Bill is in a theatre production here at the college, his mom gets in her ol' Ford and drives up to see his performance.

**THOMAS:** That's nice ... but I suppose you could say in a few weeks, I'll be comin' over to Jackson to see your performance ...

**TOM:** My performance in what? ... Oh, you're being a comic again ... but my performance In court isn't gonna be very funny.

**THOMAS:** It will probably be a little different from Bill's performance. When his performance was over the curtain came down ... our performance probably won't have a final curtain anytime soon ... So Bill's mom comes up to see his ...

**TOM:** Somehow those visits by his mom, seem to have more value than a Mustang.

**THOMAS:** Well, as embarrassing as this whole thing has been, I will hire counsel for you.

**TOM:** One of your law partners in ...

**THOMAS:** No that's ...

**TOM:** Too expensive? ... Even in your own office?

**THOMAS:** Well there's so much overhead cost and ... there's no need to broadcast this all over Memphis. There's the reputation of my law firm and of course your mother ...

**TOM:** My goodness gracious, I hadn't thought about any of that.

**THOMAS:** Don't make an ass of yourself ... again.

**TOM:** Again? I've become a real pro at becoming an ass. Maybe they oughta put a harness on me an' hitch me up to a plow. At least the ass'd feel useful for somethin' then ... But if not a Memphis lawyer, who ...?

**THOMAS:** Attorney William Twining.

**TOM:** I never heard of him ... where from?

**THOMAS:** Humboldt'

**TOM:** Humboldt, Tennessee! Good God, Dad, that's a hellhole of a crossroads with only a handful of downfallen souls.

**THOMAS:** Don't be sacrilegious! It's just a few miles from Jackson, so it will be more convenient for any conferences we might need.

**TOM:** Do I get to meet him?

**THOMAS:** Of course ... in due time.

**TOM:** Is he a young lawyer, just gettin' his feet wet in our national pool of justice? ... and won't cost very much?

**THOMAS:** As a matter of fact, he's rather expensive ... considering ...

**TOM:** Here comes the fine print ... considerin' what?

**THOMAS:** Considering the total circumstances, which you should certainly be aware of ... He's known for his smarts, but prefers living in a small town like Humboldt. Actually he's not young ... only a few years younger that your grandpa.

**TOM:** (jumping back onto bed.) Oh, my God ... A damned old geezer. For sure they'll bury my butt under the jailhouse, an' throw away the key. (turns toward wall)

**THOMAS:** We're not tellin' your mother about this.

**TOM:** I thought she already knew 'bout ...

**THOMAS:** Of course she knows about your shenanigans and the court case.

**TOM:** Then what are we not tellin' her?

**THOMAS:** That your best friend ... is colored.

**TOM:** Oh' yes ... Let's keep it a little secret for a special surprise.

BLACKOUT
END OF SCENE


ACT I

**NARRATOR:** (in isolated spot before Act I, Scene 7, Reveal,) The court of the Honorable Benjamin J.

Worthy in Jackson would have to deal with the issue ...
to be convened in Jackson, TN March 29, 1968.

## SCENE 7

*SETTING: First Circuit Court, Jackson, TN, March
29, 1968*

*AT RISE: The Honorable BENJAMIN J. WORTHY,
presiding. TOM NICHOLS and Attorney JESSE
CONGER are seated at the Defense Table. Defense
Attorney JESSE CONGER is at the Plaintiff Table.
Seated at the front of the public area is THOMAS
NICHOLS and LISA ANN NICHOLS with a lacy
hanky which she constantly uses to wipe her eyes.*

**NARRATOR:** (to audience) The Jackson Sun Headline
(reading) Flag Burning Case in Circuit Court (speaking
to audience) Some student hooliganism, even in Jackson,
hits a certain level of notoriety.

**JUDGE:** The court will come to order. The Bench
recognizes Prosecuting Attorney Mr. Jesse Conger.

**CONGER:** Thank you, your Honor. It is charged that Mr.
Thomas M. Nichols, Jr., aka Tom Nichols of Memphis,
TN, a student at Lambuth College, did willfully and
maliciously on January 5, 1968 in Madison County, TN,
violate the Amendment 3044 of the Constitution of the
United States of America viz. the U. S. Flag Code, which
states in Provision III, Paragraph 8, "No disrespect
should be shown to the Flag of the United States of
America. " (He sits.)

**JUDGE:** (directed to the defense table) Mr. Nichols, how do
you plead? (Attorney Twining pokes Tom and pushes
him to a standing position.)

**JUDGE:** Mr. Nichols, must I repeat my question?

**TOM:** No ... Sir ... Your Honor. (promptly taking a seat
again at the table)

**JUDGE:** And your plea?

**TOM:** (jumping back up) Not guilty ... (starting to sit,
then straightens up) Your Honor! (sits quickly)

**JUDGE:** Attorney Twining, you may proceed.

**TWINING:** Thank you, your honor ... (shifting through a mass of papers) If you would bear with me for just a moment ... Please ... I must retrieve my notes ... It's been a long week for me, an' things are terribly unsettled up in Humboldt, since ...

**JUDGE:** We are well aware of the flooding, and the whole community has our sympathy ... Now, could we proceed with the matter at hand? Have you arranged a defense for Mr. Nichols?

**TWINING:** Yes, Your Honor. If you could just ... (rifling through more papers) Oh here it is. It states in this complaint that Mr. Thomas Nichols, Jr. did seriously malign the honor of the American flag and disrespected the heritage of the American people ... Is that correct?

**JUDGE:** Basically that is the charge as read earlier in this court.

**TWINING:** Thank you, Your Honor. Just a moment (searching through papers which are now scattered all over the table) Ah here is what I was looking for. (holding up paper then looking at it) And it states that the defendant accomplished this by burning the American flag ... Yes?

**JUDGE:** Yes, that is the crux of the matter.

**TWINING:** Your Honor and Prosecuting Attorney Conger, let me assure you and this court that neither I nor my young client would ever want to show disrespect to our Old Glory. In fact, my client is greatly chagrined that it would be thought of him that he would dishonor that sacred symbol in any way. May I remind the court that Mr. Nichols, as a mere boy, was a Boy Scout with many honors and a sash full of merit badges. If you could realize ...

**CONGER:** Objection! ... Irrelevant!

**JUDGE:** Sustained!

**CONGER:** Your Honor, it is completely irrelevant what this present-day miscreant did years ago.

**JUDGE:** (to CONGER) It is unncessary and unacceptable to be casting personal aspersions. Please refrain from referring to the defendant as a miscreant.

**CONGER:** Sorry, your honor, but as our country, including myself ...

**JUDGE:** Or personal vendettas ... Anything further?

**CONGER:** Not at the moment, your honor ... As long as the court records my objection of the defense counsel's irrelevant meandering and ...

**JUDGE:** Duly noted! Now Attorney Twining, are you going to present the defendant's defense or are you intending to deliver a eulogy?

**TWINING:** I beg your pardon, Your Honor ... Yes, Your Honor ... No, Your Honor.

**JUDGE:** If you continue to waste my time and the patience of this court, I WILL rule you in contempt.

**TWINING:** Oh, Your Honor ... and I would not blame you one but.

**JUDGE:** WHAT?

**TWINING:** Your Honor, I do beg your pardon (turning toward the court audience) and also the court (turning to CONGER) and Mr. Conger. (to JUDGE) but I have found the note that I had written to myself ... Could I share it at this time?

**JUDGE:** Pray do ... Yes, please share it with the court.

**TWINING:** Absolutely ... Your Honor ... It is my understanding that the complaint against my client is that he showed disrespect for the American flag.

**JUDGE:** That is correct ... As earlier detailed.

**TWINING:** Oh, yes, and according to my paper here, the language is included in Amendment 3044, Provision II, Paragraph 8 ... is that true?

**CONGER:** That is incorrect, if ...

**JUDGE:** If I have to warn you about such outbursts ...

**CONGER:** Sorry, your honor ... Objection!

**JUDGE:** Motion sustained. Now if you would like to clarify ...

**CONGER:** Yes, your honor ... It is stated thus ... But I believe it is in Provision III, not Provision II.

**TWINING:** Oh, yes. How sloppy of me.

**JUDGE:** Counsel!

**TWINING:** Thank you, Your Honor and Mr. Conger for that clarification ... Doesn't it also state in that Provision, Paragraph 6(a) that the flag must be flown only from sunrise to sunset?

**JUDGE:** Yes, except for special occasions.

**TWINING:** Your Honor ... would the prosecution please inform the court of what was the special occasion on January 5?

**CONGER:** (standing up and slamming papers down on his table) Objection! The special occasion had absolutely nothing ...

**JUDGE:** Attorney Conger, please be seated. I have not responded to your objection ... Would you like to apologize to the court for that outburst?

**CONGER:** Your honor, I do apologize. It's just that there is so much ...

**JUDGE:** Attorney!

**CONGER:** Sorry, your honor! (as he sits he bangs his fist on the table, which the Judge notes)

**JUDGE:** Counsel, it is indeed irrelevant at this point to establish that there was a special event at that time. However, you will have an opportunity to question the prosecution in due time.

**TWINING:** Oh yes ... That is the proper procedure, isn't it?

**JUDGE:** Do you have any further statements?

**TWINING:** I believe there's something else here that I would like to say ... If you'd be so kind ... Oh yes, but now that I think of it ... As Mr. Nichols brought the flag to the college campus after a bout of drinkin' that ...

**CONGER:** Objection! Irrelevant!

**JUDGE:** Sustained! Counsel, your client has not been charged with drunkenness, although as you very well know, this is a legally dry county. I do hope you're not intending to use his inebriated condition as a defense of his actions that evening.

**TWINING**: Oh, yes. I mean, oh no, Your Honor, we won't be usin' ... Sorry 'bout that. (turns to TOM) Sorry 'bout that Tom. I hadn't intended to publicize that drunk part. (TOM nods to him.) (to JUDGE) If I may continue ...

**JUDGE**: Yes, please do.

**TWINING**: As I was sayin'. I would assume that Mr. Nichols, after some ... uh ... uh ... evenin' celebration, brought the flag to the student union at the college, and that would be at night.

**CONGER**: Objection!

**JUDGE**: Overruled! ... Counsel, what was the question you intended to pose?

**TWINING**: At night? Your Honor, did it occur at night ... after sunset?

**JUDGE**: Mr. Twining, you do not need to state the obvious for the court. Of course it happened at night after, Mr. Nichols ... uh ... did what he did for his evening entertainment, took the flag after sunset.

**TWINING**: Thank you, Your Honor ... I felt it was important to get that established ... Ah, here's another note ... Do you suppose the flag may have been soiled?

**CONGER**: Objection!

**JUDGE**: Overruled! Do get on with it Mr. Twining,

**TWINING**: I would like to know if the flag may have been soiled in any way.

**CONGER**: Objection!

**JUDGE**: Overruled! How could one know now if it had been soiled?

**TWINING**: (chuckling) Exactly ... Any evidence unattainable ... It's burnt ... gone.

**JUDGE**: (addressing the courtroom) Order! Order! ... Any more such outbursts, and I will clear the courtroom. Please proceed, Counsel ... and get to the point.

**TWINING**: Yes, Your Honor ... Therefore no obtainable evidence! But as it was a small flag and only a few inches off the ground may we assume that it had gathered some of our red West Tennessee mud splashed on it from our recent rains? ... Ironically, the rains we had in Humboldt ...

**CONGER:** Objection! Irrelevant!

**JUDGE:** Sustained! What is your objection?

**CONGER:** The complaint does not address that issue. It's obvious that the defense is attempting to avoid ...

**JUDGE:** Attorney Conger. It is not your responsibility to state to the court your assessment of the defense attorney's plan. It is MY duty to rein in the defense, if it is necessary. (CONGER is fuming.) Counsel, would you restate your question?

**TWINING:** Yes, Your Honor ... I believe it is also stated in Amendment 3044, Provision III, Paragraph 8 (k) quote "The flag when it is in such condition that it is no longer a fitting symbol for display, should be destroyed or disposed of in some way." End of quote.

**CONGER:** Objection!

**JUDGE:** Sustained!

**CONGER:** Does the defendant claim to be respecting the flag by retrieving it from its undignified position?

**JUDGE:** Counsel, is that the point being made here?

**TWINING:** Basically that is the burden of this case. This upstanding American patriot, former Boy Scout, should be acclaimed by this court for upholding the dignity and honor of the flag, our glorious national banner. Not only did he rescue it from an after-sunset display on an unapproved flag staff, only a small stick, he discovered that it was soiled and rescued it from that lowly ...

**JUDGE:** Counsel, this is not an occasion for a Fourth of July oration. I must warn you again for disrupting the legal proceedings of this court.

**TWINING:** Yes, Your Honor. I beg your pardon and indulgence ... (rustling through a few papers and attempting to order them in a neat stack then turns back to the judge) Your Honor, in light of these charges of disrespect for our flag and in further evidence that the flag was not displayed properly on an appropriate staff and after the sun had set. Be it further assumed that the flag, having been left in this unprotected environment, was soiled from recent precipitation and that the defendant brought it to a public event and ceremoniously and patriotically ...

**JUDGE:** Must I warn you?

**TWINING:** Your Honor. Considering these aforementioned conditions and circumstances, I would like to add that the legal code of the flag further states and I quote: "When it is in such condition that it is no longer a fitting symbol for display ..."

**CONGER:** Objection!

**JUDGE:** Sustained!

**CONGER:** That statement has already been stated and admitted.

**TWINING:** If the prosecution will hear me out!

**JUDGE:** Please proceed.

**TWINING:** The last clause of the last sentence reads thusly, quote "should be destroyed in a dignified way, preferably by burning."

**CONGER:** But burning ...

**JUDGE:** Mr. Conger!

**TWINING:** (continuing) As Mr. Nichols has respected not only the spirit, but the letter of the law, by honoring the dignity of the flag according to the Flag Code in the American Constitution, there is no reason for proceeding in this issue of this non-crime. I therefore move that the case be dismissed. (A bit of flurry by JUDGE and CONGER and various sounds from the courtroom ensue. CONGER jumps up, waving a fistful of papers.)

**JUDGE:** Order! Order in the court. (quiet prevails) After all considerations brought to the attention of this court of the events on the evening of January 5, 1968, I am prepared to render my verdict. But before I do that I'd like to say that I am aware of the concern nationwide of marches and demonstrations with utter disrespect for our way of life and our flag. However our democracy honors the free speech of expression as well as commitment to the law. In the Bill of Rights of our Constitution, Amendment One, it states that no law shall abridge the rights of free speech. In our current excitable concerns we have often neglected to pay respect to a soiled flag and thus to forget the passages such as "preferably by burning". (long pause) Case dismissed! (strikes gavel on desk top)

(General hullabaloo in the room. CONGER is visibly upset and stands stuffing all his papers into his briefcase before stalking out of the courtroom. While that is happening, TOM shakes TWINING'S hand then turns to his folks who have walked up to stand beside him. He gives a peck on his mother's cheek. She gives him a mother's big embrace, as she smiles and dabs her eyes.)

LISA ANN: I knew you would nevah do anything to disgrace yoah mothah. (TOM then turns to his dad. They shake hands.)

TOM: Thanks, Dad! (They then embrace.) I knew YOU could do it.

THOMAS: Now ... there are some more things WE must attend to.

LISA ANN: Tom, honey, would you like to invite yoah friend, Bill, to have dinnah with us this evenin'? (THOMAS tries to intervene.) For a kind of celebration. (THOMAS tries to interrupt.) We already have reservations at the Ol' Hickory Suppah Club. (THOMAS tries, again, to interrupt.) Don't we Thomas?

THOMAS: Yes, but ...

LISA ANN: No ifs ands or buts about it ... Thet's all settled then.

TOM: Bill was gonna be here, but he had to wait for his mother to get to town.

LISA ANN: Why thet's just perfec'. We'll invite her too. Bill IS a close friend, isn't he Tom?

TOM: Yep ... My best friend. (BILL and his mother, ADDY BOWEN, arrive.) Here they are now.

**LISA ANN:** Dear Lord, above ... They're colored. Tom ... Why didn't you tell me? (THOMAS is busily greeting BILL and ADDY.)

**TOM:** (pause) Mother ... I didn't really see the point.

BLACKOUT

END OF SCENE

ACT II

SCENE 1

*SETTING: Sirianni's Pizza.*

*AT RISE: TOM, LISA ANN, THOMAS, ADDY and BILL are seated at a table. Pizza paraphernalia is covering the table.*

**NARRATOR:** 1968 was a leap year. March was leaping into events in Jackson as well as the rest of the nation. Hair would soon be opening on Broadway.

**TOM:** I still don't understand why you didn't go to the Old Hickory Supper Club.

**LISA ANN:** They weren't ready for us.

**TOM:** I thought you had made reservations.

**THOMAS:** We had reservations.

**LISA ANN:** But your father didn't have a jacket.

**TOM:** Is that all?

**LISA ANN:** They also informed us that they didn't serve colored clientele.

**THOMAS:** Your mother wants to organize a boycott of the Old Hickory Supper Club.

**TOM:** Really? I'm impressed Mother. What would your DAR ...

**LISA ANN:** No I wasn't about to start a boycott, but it would serve them right.

**TOM:** Maybe you could get the hippies to help.

**LISA ANN:** Tom, don't be daft. (turning to ADDY) Addy I suppose you have to put up with that kind of thing all the time.

**ADDY:** You get used to it.

**LISA ANN:** Well. It would certainly rankle my craw.

**TOM:** Oh, but we're integrated now?

**LISA ANN:** Well, not actually officially ...

**TOM:** It's like so many other things around here, it's just something we accept but don't really want to talk about.

**BILL:** Is that like a secret code, which we don't acknowledge, but we adhere to?

**THOMAS:** That about sums it up. Addy, that must be what your folks have dealt with for a long time.

**ADDY:** Yeah, for years, and if truth be told for centuries.

**LISA ANN:** But now that we're talkin' about them, what would those rules be?

**ADDY:** Oh there be many.

**BILL:** I can tell you one, which nobody seems to understand.

**TOM:** Whatta you mean?

**BILL:** (looking toward LISA ANN) Evah watch that Johnny Carson show?

**ADDY:** Now, Bill, what's that got to do with what we talkin' about?

**BILL:** Do you ever see Moms Mabley on theah?

**LISA:** You mean that large old colored woman?

**BILL:** Yeah!

**THOMAS:** She's from Brevard, NC, over on the other side of the Smokies.

**ADDY:** Son, what does Moms Mabley ...

**BILL:** You notice how she does that little backward shuffle an' ever'one laughs so hard?

**LISA ANN:** Yeah that's real funny. I laugh ever' time she does it.

**BILL:** She learnt that from the colored men folk.

**THOMAS:** What in the hell do you mean by that?

**BILL:** Here, let me show you. (He gets up to demonstrate.) When a black man finishes talkin' with a white man or woman, he wouldn't just turn on his heels, an' walk away.

**LISA ANN:** Why not?

**TOM:** It he did that, the white person would say, maybe to hisself, "That sure is a stuck-up niggah".

**BILL:** No! Not stuck up. Uppity. He' be an uppity niggah. (He demonstrates as he talks.) No, after the white man had his last say, the colored man would bend forward a little, then say "Yassuh" and shuffle slowly backward, while still bendin' forward, then just as slowly turn around to walk away. Ya learn to look toward the ground, when there's nothn' to see there, an' learn to have a little laugh even when there there's really nothing to laugh about. (He demonstrates a laugh.) But nobody evah admits to it.

**TOM:** I s'pose it was nevah written down in a catechism?

**LISA ANN:** Now, Tom, quite clownin'. This is a serious conversation, an' Bill is tryin' to teach us somethin'.

**TOM:** Bill's just puttin' into words what you already know. We've talked about this kind of thing a lot.

**LISA ANN:** Now that he's mentioned it, I guess I have to agree that that's the way it is. Mrs. Bowen, you must be mighty proud of Bill.

**ADDY:** Please call me Adeline or Addy, what most folks call me.

**LISA ANN:** I call my help by their first name.

**THOMAS:** How do you address your DAR friends? Miss or Mrs.?

**LISA ANN:** A'course not. I call them by their given name.

**TOM:** Well???

**LISA ANN:** This is somewhat awkward. I suppose there's a lot of meaning in every little thing that we do ... toward each other.

**TOM:** A whole heap of meanin's!

**ADDY:** Mrs. Nichols, what would you ...

**LISA ANN:** (interrupting her) What were we just talkin' about?

**TOM:** About Moms Mabley doing the shuffle ...

**LISA ANN:** Tom, don't be impertinent. We were earlier talkin' 'bout that, but also how we address each othah.

**TOM:** Oh ... what we call each other.

**THOMAS:** I don't care what you call me, just call me to supper.

**TOM:** Dad, if you keep up your comedy routines, maybe you'll be invited to the Johnny Carson Show, yoahself.

**LISA ANN:** Well maybe we'd better get home so that when Johnny calls, Thomas will be able to accept his invitation.

**THOMAS:** (picking up the tab and addressing Addy) I may be outnumbered by the clowns in my own family.

**ADDY:** I can't let you pay the whole tab.

**LISA ANN:** Now we invited you to dinnah, so it's only right an' propah for us to pay.

**THOMAS:** Unless Tom would like to pay, since it's really his celebration dinnah for bein' out of the hoosegow.

**TOM:** Dad!

**LISA ANN:** Of course he'd have to borrow the money from his fathah.

**ADDY:** We could agree to let you pay only if you'd give us the opportunity to return the favor an' treat you to a real Southern Sunday dinnah.

**LISA ANN:** How could you do that, since you live way down in Mississippi?

**ADDY:** On the last Sunday in March, my aunt, Sister Willie Mae Tyger will be celebratin' her 80th birthday, an' everybody in Fite's Bottom is throwing a big bash for her. That'll be March 31.

**LISA ANN:** But that's family ...

**ADDY:** When you get to know Sister Willie Mae, you'll understand that ever'body in Jackson is family to her.

**THOMAS:** But Memphis?

**ADDY:** As far as Aunt Willie Mae is concerned her Jackson family spreads all the way to the rivah.

**BILL:** Jackson didn't set up any city limits ... not for her anyways. When me an' Tom wuz down theah, you woulda thought Tom was as close kin as me.

**ADDY:** What were you an' Tom doin' down in Fite's Bottom?

**BILL:** (stuttering and stammering)

**TOM:** Oh I wanted to meet Sister Willie Mae Tyger. I'd heard so much about her.

**LISA ANN:** You sure her name's not Kyger? Our fambly ... had neighbors named Kyger?

**ADDY:** Here, in Madison County?

**LISA ANN:** No, on Harley Mountain in Roane County.

**ADDY:** That was where Aunt Willie Mae grew up.

**THOMAS:** Maybe your families knew each othah.

**LISA ANN:** Not likely.

**TOM:** Maybe our families are related by more than state citizenship.

**LISA ANN:** Unlikely! Tom, don't talk such rubbish. A'course we're not blood relatives. After all ...

**ADDY:** It's about time for me to get Bill back to campus and for me to get back down home.

**TOM:** Mrs. Bowen, I'll give Bill a ride. There're some things we might wanta talk about. You A-DULTS get on back to doin' what you been doin' before today.

**LISA ANN:** I'm not sure we'll be back to doin' things exactly the way we been doin' befoah today.

**ADDY:** Lisa Ann, why would that be?

**LISA ANN:** Oh I don't know. Things just seem to be a little diffrunt. Like we might have turned some kind of corner.

**ADDY:** Do you think you could come ovah to Jackson to celebrate with Aunt Willie Mae?

**THOMAS:** She sounds like a rather fascinating lady. It sure would be good to have a REAL southern cooked dinner.

**LISA ANN:** My cook is not the best in the South. But she is reliable an' that's somethin'. Addy, I'm sure we'll be able to make it. Maybe Bill could take Tom down theah to meet up with Sister Willie Mae befoah then.

**BILL:** Like we said before. We already been down there.

**ADDY:** How nice of you to visit kin folks like thet. How was Aunt Willie Mae doin'?

**TOM:** Oh she was real fine. I been thinkin' about goin' back to write an assigned paper for my sociology class.

**LISA ANN:** What sociology class would that be?

**TOM:** Sociology of the South.

**LISA ANN:** SOCIOLOGY OF THE SOUTH! That makes me feel like bein' under some kind of microscope.

**TOM:** Yeah we're just little planktons swimmin' around in a few drops of water an' bumpin' inta each other, then just movin' on in another direction, an' folks look at us through a set of lenses.

**LISA ANN:** Tom that sounds terrible.

**TOM:** Mother, do you have a better metaphor to describe our homo sapiens situation?

**LISA ANN:** I want no moah talk 'bout this homo stuff.

**THOMAS:** He's just trying to impress us now.

**LISA ANN:** It shore doesn't impress me his talkin' like that.

**THOMAS:** Homo sapiens just means human beings.

**LISA ANN:** Then why didn't he say human bein's?

**THOMAS:** I suppose he wants us to think he's learnin' somethin'.

**LISA ANN:** He could show us he's learned somethin' besides homo sappin's.

**THOMAS:** Not homo ...

**LISA:** Oh I know he's a highfalutin' college man now. Addy, does Bill do that to you?

**ADDY:** At times. Our time is now, to say our goodbyes, don't you think?

**THOMAS:** Thanks, Addy for jumpin' us off that merry-go-roun'. (They say goodbyes with handshakes and embraces.)

BLACKOUT

END OF SCENE

ACT II

## SCENE 2

*SETTING: late afternoon, SISTER WILLIE MAE TYGER'S front porch*

*AT RISE: BILL and TOM are there visiting with SISTER WILLIE MAE TYGER.*

**NARRATOR:** The war goes on ... worldwide I mean ... (reading) North Korea Seizes U.S. Ship (to audience) But that seems a long ways away. Meanwhile down in Fite's Bottom in Jackson on Sister Willie Mae's front porch.

**BILL:** Aunt Willie Mae, I 'preciate you takin' the time to visit with me an' Tom today.

**TOM:** Yeah, Sister Willie Mae, I've heard so much about you and Fite's Bottom Improvement Association. The last time we were here, we had somethin' else on our minds, an' didn't take time to really visit.

**SISTER WILLIE MAE:** You boys wuz heah befoah?

**TOM:** Back in January.

**SISTER WILLIE MAE:** Ah 'member now. How wuz the refreshments you got frum down the street? (TOM and BILL looking at each other, grinning)

**BILL:** Aunt Willie Mae, the hooch was fine ... But it got us inta a little trouble ... (TOM tries to shut him up) Actually it was Tom, who got inta some trouble.

**SISTER WILLIE MAE:** (looking at TOM and realizing he doesn't want to talk about it) You jus' as welcome heah as ya kin be.

**TOM:** I do appreciate the time you givin'.

**SISTER WILLIE MAE:** Law, Child, the only thing I have a lot of now is time. But I'll tell you boys somethin' now. I discovered longtime ago was thet you can't give someone time ... That's something you can'give away. An' the Good Lawd, ain't tole me how much of thet precious commodity I still have left.

**BILL:** But you do seem to have a lot of carin' still ...

**SISTER WILLIE MAE:** Yeah I hope the Good Lawd still have some carin' in my soul.

**TOM:** Sister Willie Mae, I'm tryin' to write a paper for my

college class about somethin' here in Jackson of a civic
nature.

**SISTER WILLIE MAE:** Of a civic ...?

**BILL:** What Tom means is a situation here in Jackson that
might be a problem for the city.

**TOM:** So I thought the housing here in Fite's Bottom
might be of some concern to the city fathers.

**SISTER WILLIE MAE:** The city motha's even moah so.

**BILL:** Aunt Willie Mae are you still president of the Fite's
Bottom Improvement Association?

**SISTER WILLIE MAE:** No, honey, I give thet up las'
year fer someone who was youngah an' had a bit moah
pep.

**TOM:** (taking out a pen and tablet) When you were
president, what sorts of things did you do?

**SISTER WILLIE MAE:** Oh, when theah wuz problems,
like po-lice botherin' people heah 'bout bootleggin' or
the streets gettin' too much tore up an' needin' fixin'.

**BILL:** Mamma tol' me somethin' 'bout you'd follow up
those complaints, but I don't understand how you could
do anything, since you don't have a car or telephone.

**SISTER WILLIE MAE:** (starts chuckling) Oh, I got two
good feets an' ah can walk, so long as I got some good
shoes.

**TOM:** So where would you walk?

**SISTER WILLIE MAE:** (still chuckling) Oh down to
city hall ... 'cause it was Mayor Congah or Chief of
Po-lice Blanton who'd need to tend to the problems.

FLASHBACK

*SETTING: Reception desk at Jackson City Hall.*
*PATRICIA is at the desk. Her phone rings.*

**PAT:** Hello! ... What ... Sister Willie Mae Tygah is comin'
up the front steps? ... Good Lord. I'll give the mayor a
quick call. (hangs up phone and makes a new call) Mayor
... I'm callin' 'cause Sister Willie Mae Tyger is headin' this
way ... Well I can't put her off indefinitely ... But Officer

Blanton always tries to get out of confrontin' her ... Oh I see her now. Better hang up.

**SISTER WILLIE MAE:** (entering) Mawnin' Miss Patricia, how ya this fine mawnin'?

**PAT:** I'm just great Sister Willie Mae. What can I do for you this fine Tennessee Monday morning?

**SISTER WILLIE MAE:** I come to see Mayah Congoh 'bout a little trouble ...

**PAT:** Yeah, I heard that Fite's Bottom ...

**SISTER WILLIE MAE:** Thet's what I come to talk 'bout with the mayah.

**PAT:** I'm just as sorry as I can be Sr. Willie Mae, but Mayor  Congah is tied up for a coupla hours ...

**SISTER WILLIE MAE:** Well, I wouldn't keer if maybe Chief of Po-lice Blanton could ...

**PAT:** Oh, but he's out on patrol, an' probably won't be back before this afternoon.

**SISTER WILLIE MAE:** Thet's jest all right, Honey, I got all day. So if you don' min' if I set down an' wait.

**PAT:** That's fine Sister Willie Mae. You're welcome to it.

**SISTER WILLIE MAE:** Take some burden off these weary bones. How's yoah Mamma, Honey?

BLACKOUT<br>END OF FLASHBACK

*MUSICAL INTERLUDE – Sister Willie Mae moves back to position for next scene.)*
(back to SISTER WILLIE MAE TYGER'S front porch)

**BILL:** Well, did they take care of yoah problem, after you'd waited so long?

**SISTER WILLIE MAE:** Oh they'd finally get aroun' ta talkin' 'bout it ... But they didn't do so much ... they were awful nice 'bout things and then they'd come down a couple weeks latah just to visit.

**TOM:** (now taking notes) Sister Willie Mae, do the folks here own their own homes?

**SISTER WILLIE MAE:** Oh no. Thet won't do.

**BILL:** I suppose they couldn't afford it, could they?

**SISTER WILLIE MAE:** Well now thet's true fer some folks ... sech as widows like me; then there'd be a few men who can't or don't or maybe won't work.

**TOM:** But what about the folks who could buy their homes?

**SISTER WILLIE MAE:** The houses are all owned by whites ovah on the othah side uv town. Somewheah near the country club, wheah they play that golf game ... chasin' thet little ball aroun' jest to put it in the groun'.

**BILL:** Well surely sometimes they might sell these houses.

**SISTER WILLIE MAE:** Yeah ... but not to the colored ... an' if they would sell, the coloreds couldn't get loans from any bank in town.

**TOM:** Even if the folks had good jobs?

**SISTER WILLIE MAE:** Who you s'pose give 'em thah work?

**TOM:** Surely the white folks ... But why wouldn't the white landlords fix up these houses a little?

**SISTER WILLIE MAE:** Oh, 'cause they been condemned.

**BILL:** They could at least paint 'em.

**SISTER WILLIE MAE:** Uh-uh. Once they be condemned they can't be fixed up no moah

**TOM:** Not even painted?

**SISTER WILLIE MAE:** Nor roof fixin's, nor weather-boardin' nor nothin'.

**TOM:** But they can rent 'em?

**SISTER WILLIE MAE:** Yeah, when the Jackson City Council condemned them, the owners made sure they could still rent 'em out.

**BILL:** That surely doesn't seem right to me ... not to be allowed to repair them, but could rent them.

**SISTER WILLIE MAE:** I discovered long time ago what is right fer some folks ain't right for some others. The trick is to get on the right side.

**BILL:** Or be born on the right side.

**SISTER WILLIE MAE:** (chuckling) Now if we could

jest 'range thet, wouldn't ouah troubles be ovah? But boys thet's 'nuther mystery thing. Yoah skin color cain't change, 'cept fer them college girls who lay out in the sun 'most nekkid, tryin' to get ouah color. Oh, theah be some colored girls try to lighten theah color by warshin' in Clorox ... It burned them a little but the darkness nevah left. The white girls get burned by the sun, tryin' to get colored, and the colored girls get burned by the Clorox tryin' to get white. It can be a crazy worl' some time ... It seems to some folks, the girls anyways, tryin' to get moah like each othah.

**BILL:** But they can't sit down together at a table to eat.

**TOM:** Why wouldn't those white girls then change their attitude about folks already with your color?

**SISTER WILLIE MAE:** Thet's 'nother life mystery. Some thinks they can change their color, but not theah heart. The truth is just the othah way 'round. You can't really change yoah color, but you can change youh heart ... that is if you've a mind to.

**TOM:** Sister Willie Mae, you said that the police come down here checking on liquor. When would ...

**SISTER WILLIE MAE:** Yeah, whenevah there's a ruckus of too much drinkin' an' stuff like thet.

**BILL:** I believe this is supposedly a dry county.

**SISTER WILLIE MAE:** But theah's always a lot uv wet 'round, even in summah dog days.

**TOM:** You helped us out a little some time back. At the college the frat boys figure they can always find some spirits down here in Fite's Bottom.

**SISTER WILLIE MAE:** Oh, yeah, theah's bootleggin' here from time to time.

**TOM:** Who'd be dealin' it here?

**SISTER WILLIE MAE:** No tellin' who it might be. Ever'body's gotta make some money somehow. But the po-lice come whether theah's bootleggin' goin' on or not. They come one time to my place when I won't even to home, an' they step up on my bed with theah muddy boots.

**BILL:** Aunt Willie Mae, why would they do thet?

**SISTER WILLIE MAE:** Lookin' fer some likker acourse, an they musta thought I had some in the attic ... So they tromped on my nice clean bed cover to open the attic to look up theah.

**TOM:** And?

**SISTER WILLIE MAE:** They nevah foun' nothing ... not right then any ways.

**TOM:** The next time they come down here, would you have someone call me? ... I would like to know how they go about it.

**SISTER WILLIE MAE:** You give me yoah phone number, an' I'll give you a call.

BLACKOUT<br>END OF SCENE

ACT II

SCENE 3

*SETTING: Two days later. Split screen, SISTER WILLIE MAE TYGER'S house and TOM'S dorm room. AT RISE: In blackout, Phone rings.*

**TOM:** Hello!

**SISTER WILLIE MAE:** They's heah. Even though it barely be daylight.

**TOM:** Who's there and where's here?

**SISTER WILLIE MAE:** The po-lice are heah. This is Sister Willie Mae down to Fite's Bottom.

**TOM:** Oh yeah.

**SISTER WILLIE MAE:** They goin' through a young man's stuff right 'crost the street from me.

**TOM:** Is he a bootlegger?

**SISTER WILLIE MAE:** Nauw! He ain't nevah done no bootleggin'. He just a young man with a young wife an' a baby not quite two month old. An' he ain't even to home. He's already at work.

**TOM:** How many police are there?

**SISTER WILLIE MAE:** Theah just two this time.

**TOM:** I'll be down there just as soon as I can get dressed, I'm on my way.

BLACKOUT
END OF SCENE

ACT II

**NARRATOR:** (Reading newspaper) Russia Invades Czechoslovakia. (to audience) That seems so much more important than the Jackson Police invading Fite's Bottom.

SCENE 4

*SETTING: 45 minutes later. SISTER WILLIE MAE TYGER'S front porch.*

*AT RISE: SISTER WILLIE MAE TYGER'S standing on porch leaning against a porch post and looking across the yard at neighbors and police, whom we don't see. TOM is standing on ground looking at SR WILLIE MAE TYGER and turning often to look at neighbors and police across the street. TOM has a camera and is taking photos of the action. Street noises and people talking can be heard. He turns to take a picture of SR WILLIE MAE TYGER.*

**SISTER WILLIE MAE:** Oh, Honey don' be takin' no picture of me. I ain't fixed myself up this mawnin'.

**TOM:** Sister Willie Mae, the way I see it and see you is that you're always pretty as any picture.

**SISTER WILLIE MAE:** Oh shucks! It's a caution how you young men likes to please the ladies. (POLICE OFFICER OBRIEN walks over to them.)

**O'BRIEN:** How you this mawnin', Sister Willie Mae?

**SISTER WILLIE MAE:** Oh , I be fine, thank ya.

**TOM:** (to SISTER WILLIE MAE TYGER) I see they know you.

**O'BRIEN:** Oh, ever'body in Jackson knows Sister Willie Mae Tyger.

**TOM:** (to POLICE OFFICER OBRIEN) Could I ask

what's goin' on' over there?

**O'BRIEN:** We just lookin' fer some alcohol.

**TOM:** Why would you be doin' that right now?

**O'BRIEN:** Oh we have to investigate whenever there's a complaint about sellin' or drinkin' alcohol. This is a dry county you know.

**TOM:** Who would've complained?

**O'BRIEN:** It's usually a wife or girlfriend who's gotten beaten up.

**TOM:** Who complained 'bout this fellow?

**O'BRIEN:** I can't divulge that.

**TOM:** Why not?

**O'BRIEN:** Confidential information ... invasion of privacy.

**TOM:** Looks like you already invaded his privacy. (Officer starts walking away) I see that you've opened the trunk of an old car and ripped some boards off the side of the house.

**O'BRIEN:** The boards were loose anyways, an' we have to look wherever the hooch might be stored.

**TOM:** It's my understandin' that this young fellow has never been involved in the liquor trade.

**O'BRIEN:** Well, we got him now.

**TOM:** Whatta you mean?

**O'BRIEN:** We found it out in the woodshed.

**TOM:** Found what?

**O'BRIEN:** A half a fruit jar of wine.

**TOM:** So whatta you do now?

**O'BRIEN:** Oh, we'll haul him in to the city jail for processing.

**TOM:** I understand he's not even at home.

**O'BRIEN:** Oh we know where he works.

**TOM:** You say this is legally a dry county. Does that include wine as well as the hard stuff?

**O'BRIEN:** Oh yes.

**TOM:** And champagne?

**O'BRIEN:** Any liquid with alcoholic content meant for drinkin'.

**TOM:** In the Jackson Sun last week there was an article in the society section about a brunch the local school superintendent had given in honor of our congressman.

**O'BRIEN:** Didn't read that.

**TOM:** And it was reported that champagne was served to all the guests. (pause) Did you raid that drunken bash?

**O'BRIEN:** No, we didn't.

**TOM:** Why not?

**O'BRIEN:** There were no complaints called in about it.

**TOM:** I wonder if the Jackson Sun would like to run a photo or two about our party down here in Fite's Bottom this mornin'.

**O'BRIEN:** I gotta go. I already said too much.

BLACKOUT

END OF SCENE

ACT II

**NARRATOR:** (reading) I Will Not Seek Nor Will I Accept ... (Interrupting himself) President Johnson's dilemma is much more complicated than the weather in Memphis.

SCENE 5

*SETTING: March 23, Saturday, The NICHOLS' living room*

    *AT RISE: LISA ANN and THOMAS are having their afternoon drinks. THOMAS is reading the Memphis Commercial Appeal.*

**LISA ANN:** What does the paper say about this ungodly snow storm?

**THOMAS:** It says the final depth was 17.3 inches.

**LISA ANN:** That's got to be the most snow this town has ever had.

**THOMAS:** No! It says here that there was a full 18 inches on March 17, 1892.

**LISA ANN:** Heah in Memphis?

**THOMAS:** No! It was in Tibet ... of course it was here in Memphis. Weren't we talking about the snowstorm here?

**LISA ANN:** Well, what happened bad back then with that snowstorm?

**THOMAS:** Like any snowstorm. People probably couldn't get around very well. (chuckling) But they didn't have any cars or trucks slidin' off the road or into each other.

**LISA ANN:** Thomas be serious. Why wouldn't there be any accidents?

**THOMAS:** I didn't say there weren't any accidents. There just weren't any automobile accidents, because it was before cars.

**LISA ANN:** Thomas I wasn't talkin' about road accidents.

**LISA ANN:** My grandmother would always warn about some drastic thing happening when there would be a bad weather storm of some sort.

**THOMAS:** Like a bad rainstorm or big snowfall?

**LISA ANN:** That's what I mean. But who would remember now about what happened way back then?

**THOMAS:** Oh there was an article in the unusual happenings section of the paper about the time of that snowstorm. It's right here. It doesn't say anything relating it to the snowstorm itself.

**LISA ANN:** Grandma would always warn about something more drastic than the storm, itself.

**THOMAS:** The writer does refer to a murder case in Memphis at that time.

**LISA ANN:** There are always murder cases.

**THOMAS:** But this one was different. It seems that two girls were in love with each other. (searching through the paper) Here it is. Their names were Frieda and Alice. They were classmates in an all-girl school. One of them was to dress as a man in order to marry the other one. But they were found out and prevented from ever seeing each other ever again. So they wrote letters instead. It seems that Frieda adjusted rather easily, apparently too easily for Alice, who stole her father's razor ...

**LISA ANN:** I don't need any more of the grisly details. I assume she used it to kill ...

**THOMAS:** Apparently! It was a national sensational story.

**LISA ANN:** At the time of the snowstorm?

**THOMAS:** It was about that time.

**LISA ANN:** That goes to prove that Grandma's predictions were right.

**THOMAS:** But there's no drastic news with this snowstorm. One reporter called it Snowmageddon.

**LISA ANN:** What in the world does that mean? I never heard of such a word.

**THOMAS:** There is no such word. Obviously he just invented the word based on the Bible warning. In Revelations, I believe, about the end of time there is predicted to be a great battle of Armageddon.

**LISA ANN:** Well let's hope the Good Lord's not preparing us for anything like that. But it'll be SOMETHING. You mark my word. It doesn't have to happen right now, but it's getting ready to happen. Just like those two poor girls in 1892. The snowstorm was just a warning.

**THOMAS:** Here's another item ... about this snowstorm. It seems that the snow made Martin Luther King, Jr. cancel his march here. He was scheduled to come here yesterday.

**LISA ANN:** Maybe he'll come back later.

**THOMAS:** Yeah! It seems that he's serious about supporting the sanitation workers' strike. I'm sure it will be going on for a while. (Pause) Aren't we supposed to go to Jackson next Sunday, March 31, and meet that interesting old colored lady?

**LISA ANN:** You trying to change the subject? ... Yes, we promised Addy that we'd do that. I certainly hope the weather will be better.

**THOMAS:** I don't think the weather will be concerned about our little jaunt over to Jackson.

**LISA ANN:** You know I kinda sympathize with Bill's Mama.

**THOMAS:** He seems to be doing OK. She has been able to send him to college.

**LISA ANN:** She had to beg and scrape to get what little

money she got to contribute to his education. But most of what he needed was earned by him and by scholarships.

**THOMAS:** I have a great idea.

**LISA ANN:** I'm always suspicious of your great ideas'.

**THOMAS:** Why don't you nominate Mrs. Bowen for membership in the DAR.

**LISA ANN:** Thomas, don't be so absolutely ridiculous.

**THOMAS:** Maybe that would be that earthshaking event your Grandma would predict in the aftermath of the Snowmageddon.

**LISA ANN:** But she wouldn't be eligible.

**THOMAS:** Why not? Because she's colored?

**LISA ANNE:** Exactly! It is a fascinating idea.

**THOMAS:** You might nominate Effie,

**LISA ANN:** My cleaning lady?

**THOMAS:** Yes! She once told me that her great-grandfather fought in the Revolutionary war in Alabama ... I believe that some of the white Alabama politicians have contributed to her family bloodline. (pause) You'd have to kiss goodbye to your hopes for being DAR president.

**LISA ANN:** I've already kissed that goodbye. It doesn't seem so important any more. I've been thinkin' that if we do go to Jackson next Sunday, I'll give Effie the day off.

**THOMAS:** Perhaps she could go to hear her grandson preach.

**LISA ANN:** His first sermon at the New Hope Baptist Church.

**THOMAS:** I am looking forward to a bona fide real southern Sunday dinner. Sister Willie Mae Tyger doth provide.

BLACKOUT
END OF SCENE

ACT II

NARRATOR: (reading) My Lai Massacre (March 16) War crimes ... our own war crimes in faraway places. (to audience) The battle ... uh ... misunderstanding in Fite's Bottom, continues more or less for years. Sister Willie Mae Tyger's front porch was often the command post.

## SCENE 6

SETTING: SISTER WILLIE MAE TYGER'S front porch.

*AT RISE: LISA ANNE and ADDY are sitting in straight back kitchen chairs. SISTER WILLIE MAE TYGER is in an old rocking chair. We can hear a lot of crowd noise in the background with gospel singing and musical instruments.*

LISA ANN: Addy I sure 'preciate you invitin' us down ... or ovah or ... up to Fite's Bottom to celebrate Sister Willie Mae's birthday.

ADDY: We actually should be thankin' Aunt Willie Mae.

SISTER WILLIE MAE: Fer what should I be thanked?

LISA ANN: For reachin' 80 an' invitin' us to this wonderful Southern cookin'.

SISTER WILLIE MAE: Theah ain't much I can still do, but I can cook up a meal fer a bunch of hungry farm hands, praise the Lawd.

LISA ANN: This is a mighty fine day, but as they say, "out like a lamb."

ADDY: I s'pose last week's big snowstorm over in Memphis was "in like a lion".

LISA ANN: Was the snow as deep over here in Jackson as it was in Memphis?

SISTER WILLIE MAE: It was might nigh as bad, but we lived through it just fine. Throwed a little moah wood on the fire an' just scrounged a little closer to one another.

LISA ANN: Did unusual, dire happenings occur?

SISTER WILLIE MAE: No. Why would that be?

LISA ANN: My grandma used to predict at such a time

what she called cataclysms of the body and tribulations of the soul.

**SISTER WILLIE MAE:** Oh Child, we got them all the time, but I recognize what you say. Yeah when the big earthly upheavals happen, you need to prepare for some godly messages ... your soul understanding.

**LISA ANN:** "Prepare ye, the way of the Lord."

**SISTER WILLIE MAE:** So you quote scripture too.

**LISA ANN:** Oh, occasionally. I wouldn't want my husband to know that about me.

**SISTER WILLIE MAE:** Oh no, Honey. It's not always the best thing to let our men folks know ... some special things about us.

**LISA ANN:** Where did you learn to cook for all those farm folks?

**SISTER WILLIE MAE:** Honey, where I was growin' up was in Roane County.

**ADDY:** Thet was up on Harley Mountain, wadn't it?

**SISTER WILLIE MAE:** It surely was, an' thet farm land was some hard scrabble farmin'. But we had us a good life, what with the fresh garden produce an' fresh milk an' eggs ever' day. An' good mountain spring watah. I still ain't got used to this city water what come outta the spigot, when you jest twist thet little handle, an' the watah just gush out ... Thet is if the pipes ain't busted from a big freeze ... or the city ain't cut off the watah.

**LISA ANN:** But back home you had to carry thet water from the spring, didn't you? ... an' most probably up a hill.

**SISTER WILLIE MAE:** (chuckling) Yeah, Honey, I surely did. When I was a young'un, I'd ask Mama, "Why did the Good Lord put the spring down the hill when he could just as easy have put it up the hill? ... Then you could tote the watah easier down the hill.

**ADDY:** What did she say to that?

**SISTER WILLIE MAE:** She say, "Though the Lord pervades the watah for free, you oughta have to work a little to get it home." (pause) She loved to tell about the preacher asking his congregation for some more money for the work of the lord. One of the brethren spoke right up and said, "But Preacha Tolliver, you said that the gospel is as free as the water that flows." The preacha answered right back, "Yes, Brother Tuttle, it's free all right, but it costs to pipe it to you." (BILL and TOM enter.)

**TOM:** Happy Birthday Sister Willie Mae. And a Good Day to you.

**SISTER WILLIE MAE:** I appreciate that. An' it has been a good day. But Tom you look so sad and so downtrodden.

**BILL:** Oh he's bein' morose because Diamond Lil didn't come back this semester.

**TOM:** Bill, I told you a hundred times to quit callin' her that. If you keep on referring to her as Diamond Lil, there's gonna be some bloody noses 'round here.

**SISTER WILLIE MAE:** Now if theah's gonna be some fightin' an' blood spurtin' , I bettah get in the house and fetch out some clean bed sheets fer bandages. (She exits into the house.)

**LISA ANN:** Did she really think the boys were gonna get inta a fight.

**ADDY:** Law me, no. She knew they were just joshin' with each othah. I figgah she went in to get some pound cake which she hadn't brought out yet. Aunt Willie Mae is famous all ovah Jackson for her pound cake. (SISTER WILLIE MAY TYGER comes onto porch with a freshly baked pound cake, already sliced.)

**SISTER WILLIE MAE:** Here you be. As good a cake as I evah baked. (She hands the cake to ADDY and then sits back in her rocker as ADDY passes around the pound cake which has already been sliced. She also passes out some paper napkins which are used in lieu of plates and forks.)

**TOM:** (takes a bite.) This is really delicious, but why do you call it a pound cake? It feels heavier than a pound.

**SISTER WILLIE MAE:** Oh, Tommy, it's called thet jest cause to make it we put in a pound uv this an' a pound uv that an' anothah pound of somethin' else; a half dozen eggs an' then we got some batter to mix up and pop inta a oven, an 'fore long we got us a pound cake. (The others have been eating their slices and commenting on the yumminess.)

**LISA ANN:** Sister Willie Mae, I've had pound cake before, and I've always doted on it, but this tastes a liddle diffrunt, somehow.

**SISTER WILLIE MAE:** Uh Huh!

**ADDY:** Lisa, I think what Aunt Willie Mae means to say without sayin' it, is that she has a secret ingredient she adds.

**LISA ANN:** I'd sure like to know what'nall that might be!

**TOM:** What does what'nall mean?

**ADDY:** If the words weren't so squeezed together. The jumbled-up word is "what in all".

**BILL:** Which basically means "everything".

**LISA ANN:** (leaning toward SISTER WILLIE MAE TYGER.) I'd still like to know what'nall is in it.

**SISTER WILLIE MAE:** (leaning toward LISA as if to blow in her ear.) It's a secret.

**TOM:** (trying to prevent his mother from being more aggressive) Sister Willie Mae, didn't you say you were from Roane County?

**SISTER WILLIE MAE:** Yeah I lived theah till I was sixteen an' 'loped.

**TOM:** What's "loped" mean?

**ADDY:** Eee-loped with a boy-friend. (to Willie Mae) Then you moved to Jackson?

**SISTER WILLIE MAE:** Yeah, my Henry, bless his soul, had a good job janitorin' down heah ovah to Lane College.

**TOM:** Mother, didn't you say you were from Roane County?

**LISA ANN:** Well, I was born theah, but I moved away shortly afterward.

**TOM:** How did you move away so quick, you just bein' born?

**BILL:** (to TOM) Maybe yoah motha eloped too.

**ADDY:** Hesh, yoah mouth, boy. Show some respect for ... yoah elders. Now you 'pologyze.

**BILL:** Sorry Missus Nichols.

**TOM:** But Mother, thet was a good question Bill asked. How ...

**LISA ANN:** Theah's some things we don't talk about.

**TOM:** Sister Willie Mae, it seems like we got secrets too.

**SISTER WILLIE MAE:** Why yes, ever' fambly I evah knowed anything 'bout had some secrets. Some things we don't wanna admit to.

**LISA ANN:** Did your family have secrets other than secret ingredients in your pound cake?

**SISTER WILLIE MAE:** (Chuckling) You know we had secrets that ever'body knew 'bout.

**ADDY:** Aunt Willie Mae, if ever'one knew, how would it be a secret?

**SISTER WILLIE MAE:** Well, it's like Missus Nichols said. There's some things we jest don't talk about.

**ADDY:** Oh I know now what you mean.

**BILL:** Well what does she mean?

**ADDY:** We're not talkin' 'bout it.

**SISTER WILLIE MAE:** Oh, it's all right, Addy Honey. Ain't no need to keep avoidin' talkin' 'bout what happened forty-five yeahs ago.

**BILL:** Well, then, Aunt Willie Mae, what was it that happened so long?

**ADDY:** Oh, I know now what you referrin' to. You mean that baby girl that Aunt Clara had by that white neighbor boy.

**LISA ANN:** What happened to the baby?

**SISTER WILLIE MAE:** Well the pretty little thing was mostly white, an even had blue eyes. As Clara wadn't married to the boy an' in those days the legal laws wouldn't let them get married, so the precious little thing was adopted by a white fambly. They had a law about thet kind of marriage back then. The law was called mis ... somethin' or other.

**TOM:** I believe it was miscegenation that they called mixed race marriages, that the law wouldn't allow.

**SISTER WILLIE MAE:** Somehow thet does sound like the right word.

**TOM:** Mother, I remember you saying that you were adopted a long time ago ... And aren't you forty-five years old?

**LISA ANN:** (avoiding the real question) No grown woman wants to talk about her actual age.

**TOM:** There seems to be a whole heap round heah of not talkin' 'bout. Things we don't wanna admit to.

**ADDY:** There's nothin' shameful 'bout bein' adopted.

**BILL:** Isn't that coincidental to have two different families meeting after adoptions?

**TOM:** Mother, maybe you been passin' all these years, an' never told us.

**LISA:** Tom, shut up about such nonsense.

**TOM:** You mean we not talkin about ...

**BILL:** Wouldn't it be awesome, Tom, for us to be cousins, somehow? Now that we're already good friends.

**TOM:** (laughing) Yeah maybe second, third or fourth cousins, but how many times removed? Twice removed, three times ... Moved from Roane County to Mississippi to Memphis to Jasckson. That's a lot of re-moveds.

**ADDY:** You boys cut out the joshin'. Yoah makin' Missus, makin' Lisa Ann nervous.

**SISTER WILLIE MAE:** We nevah knowed wheah the baby was adopted off to, but theah's certainly lots of folks have kin folks they don't evah know. (THOMAS and WILLIAM B. TWINING enter.)

**THOMAS:** (Standing in front of the porch and addressing SISTER WILLIE MAE.) Sr. Willie Mae, that was a mighty fine feast on your special day.

**SISTER WILLIE MAE:** An' the Lord's Day!

**THOMAS:** To be sure ... You certainly have a lot of

friends or at least a lot of nice kinfolks.

**TOM:** We were just talkin' about kinfolks. It seems that ever'body is kin to ever'body else.

**SISTER WILLIE MAE:** Now wadn't thet the gospel message?

**THOMAS:** Speaking of gospel, I feel I oughta introduce Attorney Twining.

**SISTER WILLIE MAE:** Is he a gospel man?

**THOMAS:** Well, kinda. He doesn't preach the gospel ... He practices the gospel.

**SISTER WILLIE MAE:** What ever'body oughta be doin'.

**THOMAS:** In the courtroom.

**SISTER WILLIE MAE:** In the name of Jesus, I would surely like to hear an' see thet.

**THOMAS:** Sister Willie Mae, you just might get the chance.

**SISTER WILLIE MAE:** Whatcha mean by thet?

**TWINING:** Sister Willie Mae, it's so nice meetin' you. Even up in Humboldt, folks have heard of you and your work here in Fite's Bottom.

**THOMAS:** Because Attorney Twining did such a terrific job at Tom's trial ...

**TOM:** We surely weren't gonna talk about that.

**THOMAS:** I thought he could help you here in Fite's Bottom to get the landlords to provide proper maintenance for their rental properties.

**SISTER WILLIE MAE:** You mean fix up our houses?

**THOMAS:** Hopefully.

**SISTER WILLIE MAE:** Even maybe paintin' 'em?

**TWINING:** Well whatever it is that the houses may need.

**THOMAS:** That'd mean changing some of the rules of the City Council about condemned properties.

**TOM:** I certainly saw what Attorney Twining did in that courtroom that day. He twisted the tail of the prosecuting attorney and even tweaked the judge's nose a little.

**TWINING:** I appreciate the compliment, if that's what it is, but I discovered a long time ago that there're many ways to skin a cat.

**LISA ANN:** I understand that theah are a lot of fat cats on this city council. But I don't reckon they'd appreciate bein' deprived of their hides.

**THOMAS:** Sister Willie Mae, after the celebratin' is over here today, Attorney Twining will sit down with you and discuss the situation here in Fite's Bottom.

**SISTER WILLIE MAE:** Oh, Law me. Lawyers can be pretty expensive.

**THOMAS:** I'm covering the cost.

**TWINING:** But I'm so impressed with Mr. Nichols' concern and you, Sister Willie Mae, you've done so much for this community.

**LISA ANN:** And for better understandin' of folks different from ourselves.

**TWINING:** So I'm willin' to contribute most of my services, pro bono.

**SISTER WILLIE MAE:** What's PROBONE mean?

**BILL:** Basically it means for free. (looking off right stage) Oh I see we got moah company comin'. (A police officer in full uniform enters.)

**O'BRIEN:** Aftahnoon, Sister Willie Mae.

**SISTER WILLIE MAE:** Hello Offisa O'Brien.

**TOM:** Sister Willie Mae, I believe you know everybody.

**SISTER WILLIE MAE:** Well, you know, I make it a point to 'member names of them folks who come to visit ... ever' once in a while.

**TOM:** I believe we've met, Officer ... O'Brien. (O'BRIEN looks Tom over.) How'd you like your pictures I submitted to the Jackson Sun?

**O'BRIEN:** Now I 'member you ... Well most ever'body like to see their likeness in the Sun, but next time I'd like a better angle ... My profile's not bad.

**TOM:** I'll remember that next time ... But what'nall brings you down to Fite's Bottom today ... aside from Sister

Willie Mae's birthday party?

O'BRIEN: Well there was a complaint about a lot of disturbance.

TOM: Were you invited to her birthday party?

O'BRIEN: Well kinda.

TOM: What kinda answer is that?

TWINING: Back off, Tom. Perhaps Officer O'Brien and I could engage in a little conversation.

O'BRIEN: (looking closely at TWINING) Uh Uh, not goin' theah. I saw what you did at the trial ' bout thet flag burnin' an' stuff. (pause) An' you gor a reputation in West Tennessee.

TWINING: Does my reputation include lyin'?

O'BRIEN: Don't believe it does. It's just that you have a way of twistin' what we have to say.

TWINING: I see ... Catchin' you up in your own hyperbole.

O'BRIEN: My high ... what?

TWINING: It just means that I try to sort out the truth hidin' somewhere in your own overstatements and hidden implications ... Do you remember what Judge Worthy said at the conclusion of the flag trial?

O'BRIEN: Yeah, a bit of it.

TWINING: He stated that in the Bill of Rights, First Amendment, that there can be "no abridgement of the freedom of speech".

O'BRIEN: Yeah, but thet's not what ...

TWINING: And I'm sure the good judge would recognize that in the same amendment of the Bill of Rights that there "will be no abridgment of the redress of grievances" ... That's why I'll be at the City Council meeting next month. We have some grievances we'd like to address.

O'BRIEN: Look Attorney Twining I got no rooster in this cockfight, not even a banty rooster ... I just try to do my job.

SISTER WILLIE MAE: An' we 'preciate that.

TWINING: So could you tell us in your own words and

as simply as possible, what brings you to the party this afternoon?

**O'BRIEN:** Well theah was a complaint lodged ...

**TOM:** From here in Fite's Bottom?

**O'BRIEN:** Well to quote the good lawyer we can't 'dress no bridges for griervin'.

**TWINING:** That's "abridgement of redress of grievances".

**O'BRIEN:** Yeah somthin' like thet. I believe it was one of those grievances I come to address. It was from some of the neighbors up on the ridge. It seems that they were disturbed from some loud noises.

**TWINING:** From fightin' an' riotin'?

**O'BRIEN:** To tell the gospel truth ...

**SISTER WILLIE MAE:** (interrupting him) What ever'body oughta be tellin' ... "the gospel truth".

**O'BRIEN:** Speakin' of gospel. I believe it was the loud singin'. The complaint was that the music was so loud the folks up on the ridge ...

**LISA ANN:** You mean the white folks?

**O'BRIEN:** Yes, Ma'am.

**SISTER WILLIE MAE:** Well I must admit, an' it's the God's own truth, that when my neighbors get to rejoicin', the little cherubs up yander get to blowin' their trumpets.

**O'BRIEN:** I was told that there was some horn blowin' down here in Fite's Bottom too.

**LISA ANN:** I thought the music was wonderful.

**O'BRIEN:** Of course you young people ... It was also brought to my attention that there may have been some imbibin' down heah too. (Both TWINING and THOMAS turn away from the O'BRIEN to hide their breaths.)

**SISTER WILLIE MAE:** Oh, Offisah O'Brien, theah was a lot of imbibin' right heah on my front poach.

**ADDY:** Some of the best lemoned, sweetened iced tea, I've had in a month of Sundays.

**O'BRIEN:** It seems that ever'thing is settled down now, so I'll just roll along.

**SISTER WILLIE MAE:** Officer O'Brien, won't you have a piece of pound cake afore you visit yoah next party?

**O'BRIEN:** I don't care if I do. It should be permissible. It's not like we public servants would be takin' a bribe or anything like that. (SISTER WILLIE MAE passes the cake dish to BILL who takes it to the officer.)

**TWINING:** Maybe I'll see you at the city council meetin' next month. (While everyone continues eating cake, drinking iced tea and visiting, SISTER WILLIE MAE starts singing softly.)

**SISTER WILLIE MAE:** When we all get together, What a wonderful feelin' that will be ... (The others, even O'BRIEN joins in, though a little timidly. It's obvious that SISTER WILLIE MAE is leading the singing.) Then we all see heaven, We'll sing an' dance the Jubilee. (Trombones and other singers join from offstage. The actors begin to hum the tune while the NARRATOR reads aloud from the paper.)

**NARRATOR:** (reading from the Memphis *Commercial Appeal*) Dr. Martin Luther King, Jr Returns to Memphis, next week (to audience) To continue his support of the sanitation workers.

**FULL CAST:** When we all sing together, What a wonderful meetin' that will be. (Lights begin to fade and the singing slowly subsides.) Then we'll all ride to Glory, On the train of Holy Jubilee.

BLACKOUT

END OF SCENE

# Ellen Craft: Running a Thousand Miles for Freedom

Acknowledging the contributions women have had in history, I became aware of the story of Ellen Craft. The story of how she and her husband escaped slavery in Georgia was extraordinary. As both her father and grandfather were white slave owners, she could and did, "pass" as white. By dressing as a white slave owner, traveling with her slave man servant (her husband) she was able to escape the economic institution of slavery. Truly a remarkable feat of human struggles for freedom! The theatre production of the script was sponsored by the 34th annual conference of the Racial Reconciliation Community.

# ELLEN CRAFT: RUNNING A THOUSAND MILES FOR FREEDOM

*written by E. Reid Gilbert*

Cast

| | |
|---|---|
| **NARRATOR** | Great Grand Daughter of Ellen Craft |
| **ETHEL SMITH** | Slave Owner, wife of James |
| **JAMES SMITH** | Slave Owner, husband of Ethel |
| **MARY SMITH** | Slave Owner, daughter of James and Ethel |
| **ELLEN CRAFT** | Slave hoping to escape to freedom, wife of William |
| **AUCTIONEER** | Male |
| **WILLIAM CRAFT** | Slave, husband of Ellen |
| **MINISTER** | Pastor of local Church |
| **CRAY** | Smith family friend |
| **CONDUCTOR** | Southern Conductor |
| **ROUGH SLAVE DEALER** | From Slave Auction |
| **MILITARY OFFICER** | Passenger at Train Depot with slave |
| **NATE** | Military Officer's Slave |
| **POMPEY** | Shoeshiner slave by trade |
| **TRANSIT AGENT** | Custom House Civil Servant |
| **TUTTLE** | Train passenger, an Abolitionist |
| **CAPTAIN** | Steamship Captain |
| **MR. WRIGHT** | A Gentleman train passenger |
| **ANN AND BETTY WRIGHT** | Mr. Wright's two spinster daughters in their 20s |
| **LADY** | Elder disgruntled slave owner |
| **GENTLEMAN MCWELCH** | Fellow train passenger |

OFFICER ...........Government civil servant
CONDUCTOR. .......Northern Conductor
ROBERT J. KNIGHT .Slave hunter
WILLIS HUGHES ....Slave hunter
RALPH BOWEN ......Freed slave
GUARD. .............Fellow passenger
ANOTHER MAN .....Fellow passenger
HENRY ............Boardinghouse owner
HELEN ............Wife to the Boarding house
                   owner (Landlord)

# ACT I

## SCENE 1: PLANTATION MANOR HOUSE PARLOR

*The stage is set up with various boxes, to be arranged for specific scenes.*

*The Narrator starts humming softly WADE IN THE WATER. The whole cast continues to hum during her narration. At the end of the narration the Narrator gives a cue for everyone to sing the first verse with STOMPS.*

*STOMP Wade in the water STOMP Wade in the water, children STOMP Wade in the water, STOMP God's gonna trouble the water STOMP. Humming continues until actors get in place.*

**NARRATOR:** I'd like to tell you about my great grandmother, Ellen Craft. She was born in 1826 near Macon, Georgia. Those were desperate times in our nation's history, especially so if your skin was dark. As a matter of fact, she was not so dark ... But that's part of the story, which my grandma told me about her mother ... as well as her father, William. He, of course, was my great grandfather. Ellen and William were anxious to escape the chains of slavery. I'll try to tell it as closely as possible to the way Grandma Craft told me. I'll start the story in Macon, Georgia, October, 1837 in the plantation house when Ellen was 11 years old.   The plantation owner, James Smith, and his wife, Ethel, had a bit of a misunderstanding.

**ETHEL:** James, we've got to do something about that child.

**JAMES:** What child you talkin' about?  There's surely a passel of children, runnin' 'round ...

**ETHEL:** You know very well what child I be referrin' to.

**JAMES:** I'm not gonna be playin' no games with you, Ethel. If you wanna talk about somethin', just blurt it out the way you always do.

**ETHEL:** That child, Ellen.

**JAMES:** Are we gonna dig all that up again?

**ETHEL:** There's nothin' to dig up. (pause) How you gonna dig up what's nevah been buried?

**JAMES:** I s'pose the game then you wanna play is Ring Around the Roses.

**ETHEL:** I think the game, you been playin' for years, is Beatin' Roun' the Bush. The bushes you been hidin' in for the Lord only knows how long.

**JAMES:** Ethel, we've gone over this time an' time again ... When you saw that baby that Black Nancy birthed ...

**ETHEL:** An' that child's been a thorn in my flesh ever since.

**JAMES:** That was nearly 10 year ago.

**ETHEL:** To be more precise, it's been 11 years ago, an' I'm tired of it.

**JAMES:** I don't see what's changed.

**ETHEL:** The change is that the problem keeps growin'.

**JAMES:** Of course the child is growin'.

**ETHEL:** The problem is not that she be growin'. It's just that she looks so much like our children, and like you ... that people keep regardin' her as our child ... MY child.

**JAMES:** Well, no wonder she looks white. Her mama was a mulatto. That means she is more white than black.

**ETHEL:** You know that according to legal law, one drop of black blood makes her a Negro; ALSO in the eyes of the Lord.

**JAMES:** If the gospel truth be known, she is ...

**ETHEL:** There's nothing gospel about it. She may be YOUR child, but she's certainly not mine. Folks continue to remind me how much she looks like you ... her daddy.

**JAMES:** Well what is it you propose?

**ETHEL:** I'm not proposin' anything. I'm tellin' you; you gotta sell her. There's gonna be the autumn auction comin' up .

**JAMES:** Ethel, how cruel can you be?

**ETHEL:** You shoulda thought 'bout the ramifications of your actions when you ...

**JAMES:** Even though she's born of a slave, she still ...

**ETHEL:** An' sired by the slave owner.

**JAMES:** So we can't just turn her out. She's now like one of the family. In fact our own children ...

**ETHEL:** Yes, they all play together like sisters. An' that's the problem. When we have company from somewhere else, they regard her as one of MY children. Then I have to explain the whole rotten mess all over again.

**JAMES:** Well, it's not like it's that unusual for a plantation owner ...

**ETHEL:** You're right. But speakin' of owning', she may not be my child, but she is my property, as much as she is yours. Don't forget as long as I'm married to you, and living on the land left to me by my parents, then what fruit the plantation trees drop belongs to me as much as to you. An' of course, I could've already consigned her to the auctioneer block without informin' you, until the deed was accomplished.

**JAMES:** You wouldn't dare. As the head of this family, I have the freedom to engage in whatever auction action or no sale action I please.

**ETHEL:** You should've demonstrated that 'bout 12 year ago. When you engaged in some unfortunate action ...

**JAMES:** An' I could engage again by preventin' the action you're suggestin'.

**ETHEL:** I'm not suggestin' anything. I'm tellin' you that if you don't listen to what I'm sayin', you might as well take all yoah family business to the slave shantys where you been oft times before.

**JAMES:** She's ours to do with as we please.

**ETHEL:** Oh yes, as someone else has put it, "The slaves are really only chattel property." But remember, I'm not your chattel property ... Now the question is, what do you hope to do with your ... our ... property?

**JAMES:** Rather than sell her. We could give her away.

**ETHEL:** Make a present of her?

**JAMES:** Now that Mary is married, she could probably use some help. She may already be pregnant.

**ETHEL:** But they been growin' up together, an' play together like sisters.

**JAMES:** Well they are.

**ETHEL:** Don't be remindin' me again. Yes I do think you may have a real good solution. On Mary's birthday ... comin' up soon.

**JAMES:** A sister given to a sister. Then they become master an' slave.

**ETHEL:** Mistress an' slave.

**JAMES:** Well, yeah. It's settled then ... That's what we'll do, come next month.

BLACKOUT

SCENE 2: MARY'S KITCHEN

(Mary is with Ellen. Ellen is preparing dinner.)

**NARRATOR:** Nine years later Ellen and Mary were in Mary's kitchen. Ellen, as usual, was preparing the next meal, dinner.

**MARY:** I believe you have a birthday approaching.

**ELLEN:** Yessum. In a couple of weeks.

**MARY:** I believe you'll be 20 then.

**ELLEN:** An' what ordinarily happens when a person turns 20?

**MARY:** When a WHITE girl turns 20, her mother and father give her things for her hope chest .

**ELLEN:** What if a person has no father nor a chest ... an' certainly no hope?

**MARY:** You know very well what I mean by person. It means of course a free person.

**ELLEN:** You mean a white person!

**MARY:** You know, very well that's the same thing.

**ELLEN:** Although I can't read nor write, I got ears, an' I listen to the white men when they talk politics. They count us slaves each as a part of a person, but not person enough to vote nor have any other rights.

**MARY:** You been listenin'?

**ELLEN:** That not all I be hearin'.

**MARY:** What else you be hearin'?

**ELLEN:** They also said that when your daddy ... also my

daddy ... coulda sold me on the auction block ... he instead decided to give me to you.

**MARY:** That's right ... An' that's the way it oughta be. When a person owns property, they can dispose of it in any way they see fit.

**ELLEN:** An' my daddy thought it wasn't fit for him to sell me, but to give me to my own sister.

**MARY:** Yes, and Ellen, you oughta be grateful to me and Robert. You know what it coulda been if Daddy had sold you to another planter. We treat you pretty decent, don't we?

**ELLEN:** Yessum, an' I be grateful for that, that our daddy didn't put me on the auction block. But it don't seem fitten to be owned by your own sister.

**MARY:** But as I was sayin' ...

**ELLEN:** An' you and Massa Robert could put me on the auction block, any time you please.

**MARY:** Ellen, that's enough. What Robert and I wanta do or hafta do is up to us, and we don't need to discuss it any furtha with nobody.

BLACKOUT

SCENE 3: AUCTION BLOCK

**NARRATOR:** That's' the way it started. Ellen and William were born in different townships in the state of Georgia. William's old master had the reputation of being a very caring Christian man, but he thought nothing of selling William's father and aged mother, at separate times, to different persons, to be dragged off never to behold each other again. The reason he had disposed of the parents in this way, was that they were getting old and would soon be of no value in the market. Therefore, he intended to sell off all of his old stock, and buy in a young lot. A most disgraceful conclusion for a man to come to, who made great professions of religion. William's old master, then, apprenticed William to a cabinet-maker. If a slave had a good trade, he would sell for more than another slave without a trade. Many slave holders would have their slaves take trade lessons on this account. But before William's time expired, his old master wanted money, so he had the auctioneer sell him and his sister.

*Auctioneer enters. Girl enters with a white woman guard.*

**AUCTIONEER**: (Starts auctioneer spiel, looking off stage) What am I bid for this young girl? Folks it'll be a good investment, Just look at her ... just comin' of age. Hale an' hardy for years of good labor, whether in the cotton fields or scrubbin' down yoah house hold or laborin' with birthin'. I believe she already be afine cook. An' boys I'm atellin' you, what a heifer she'd be. She's ready to drop a whole barn of new calves. What'll it be? Who'll start it off at twenty dollahs ... So ever'body can get in ... Do I hear ... (Off stage "TWENTY") I hear twenty who'll make it 25 ... I hear 22 ... someone wants in at 2 ...

**NARRATOR**: Of course, she was sold to the highest bidder. He was another planter, but lived quite a ways out in the country ... miles away from Macon. William was next to be sold.

**WILLIAM**: Massah, sir, could we wait for a liddle while? We've never been apart before. She's mah liddle sistah. I'm sure she's surely skeered ... They already sold off Mama and Papa to different folks. We usta be a fambly. Please let me just step down and say goodbye to my liddle sistah.

**AUCTIONEER**: Damn it! Get up! You can do the wench no good; therefore there is no use in your needing to see her.

**NARRATOR**: William saw the cart where she sat moving slowly off. (Pause) He never saw her again. William was knocked down to the cashier of the bank where they were mortgaged and ordered to the cabinet shop where he had previously worked. Well, they were only slaves and had no legal rights. (Reading from papers in hand)

In Louisiana: A slave is one who is in the power of a master to whom he belongs. The master may sell him, dispose of his person, his industry, and his labor; he can do nothing, possess nothing, nor acquire anything but what must belong to his master.

**NARRATOR:** As a cabinet maker, William was able to keep 10 percent of what was paid for his work. It was a common practice for white men to be the father of children by their slaves. They could and did sell them with the greatest impunity. The more pious and beautiful the girls, the greater the price and to use for whatever their owner's purposes were. The woman and the children, even those fathered by the white master were legally the property of the master. They were liable to be seized and sold for his debts. Some have been sold and separated for life. (Reading) It is unlawful for anyone of purely Europe descent to intermarry with a person of African extraction.

**NARRATOR:** (To audience) Though a white man may bed as many colored women as he pleases, there is no damage to his reputation in the white community or even in his church. Ellen and William's story was somewhat different. They were allowed to marry. She was back on the plantation which belonged to her father, as he had bought William at the auction.

## SCENE 4: PLANTATION HOME PORCH
*Minister, William, Ellen, James and Ethel enter.*

**NARRATOR:** Their wedding was a quiet and simple affair. It was early evening, just before dark, on the plantation manor house porch. James and Ethel and their pastor, Brother Hicks, were sitting on the porch.

**MINISTER:** James, didn't you say there was going to be a wedding here, this evening?

**JAMES:** Yes for a couple of our slaves. They should be here any minute. You can't always depend ... I believe I see them comin' now.

*Ellen and William appear on the edge of the porch.*

**MINISTER:** (Seeing them but addressing James.) James, I assume that these are the slaves you mentioned?

**JAMES:** Yes. Their names be William and Ellen.

**MINISTER:** Now we might as well get on with it. James, is it your wish that these two slaves get married in a Christian wedding?

**ETHEL:** It can't hardly be Christian, since they both be Negroes and slaves as well.

**MINISTER:** Why Sister Ethel, I neglected asking your permission for this ... marriage union.

**ETHEL:** That's all right Rev. Hicks. I get left out quite often when it comes to dealing with our chattel property. However I do agree that they should be married ... that way, there's less risk of one or both attempting to run away an' escape.

**JAMES:** But there's no point in readin' all that rigmarole 'bout Christ an' the Church an' such.

**MINISTER:** Of course, I do understand. By the way, Brother Smith, isn't this the girl, you ...

**ETHEL:** There be no cause to go into all that now.

**MINISTER:** Yes. I suppose you're right.

**JAMES:** What is it you hafta say?

**MINISTER:** Since it's not a christian wedding and there's no congregation, all I hafta do is sign the papers.

**ETHEL:** Why are the papers necessary?

**MINISTER:** It's for the purpose of keeping record of everyone in the county. The census will be coming up soon.

**ETHEL:** And that keeps a record that they belong to this plantation, right?

**MINISTER:** And to you, specifically.

**JAMES:** I have the papers right here, which Ethel and I have already signed as witnesses.

**MINISTER:** There's nothing yet to have witnessed.

**JAMES:** Of course. But that's just a formality.

*He produces the papers. The minister looks at them and*

*while holding them in his hand, turns toward the young couple, motioning them to come and stand in front of him.*

**MINISTER:** Under the Law of God and under the auspices of this church. I pronounce you man and wife. Now in the name of Christ our Savior, go in peace. O yes. I almost forgot about your signatures.

**JAMES:** That's all right. They're both illiterate. I'll sign for them and then they can X their names.

**MINISTER:** Well I suppose that finishes our ...

**ETHEL:** There is one more thing.

**MINISTER:** Yes? And what is that?

**ETHEL:** Even though I've given permission for this wedding for business purposes, they will not be allowed to live together and consummate this union.

**JAMES:** Why do you want to do that?

**ETHEL:** That's for business purposes also. It will be awhile before we'll be needing another litter of ...

**JAMES:** I know your real reason ... When these records are examined some time down the road of history, we'll be branches from the same ancestral tree.

**ETHEL:** That's not ...

**JAMES:** It's okay. As Brother Hicks has already blessed the couple and provided the benediction, we might as well go on in. Brother Hicks, I believe the kitchen help has some refreshments for you. And there's some business I have to attend to out back. (Crowd noise can be heard from around the house during the following dialogue. Whipping and screaming can be heard.) What kind of business is that?

**JAMES:** Oh, you know, the usual punishment for bein' too lazy in his work. They're gettin' ready now. I don't do the whippin'. I let one of the other slaves do it. One who is workin' up some merits.

**ETHEL:** You wouldn't want to be the one usin' the whip. It's almost too bloody and gory even to watch.

**MINISTER:** Would you like for me to pray over his soul?

**ETHEL:** His back side will probably welcome some Balm in Gilead.

*The three whites laugh and exit. William and Ellen are
left alone on the porch. They sit on a bench and hold hands.*

**WILLIAM**: That was a rough one. Glad it wan't me this
time ... You didn't seem to have much to say in the
weddin' ... He did say, "Go in peace."

**ELLEN**: (Laughing) Of course! You knew we wouldn't be
expected or even allowed to say anything. Now how and
when are we s'posed to go in peace? Especially after
listenin' to that whippin'.

**WILLIAM**: I believe we're s'posed to find it somewhere ...
out there ...

**ELLEN**: Maybe way out there. Somewhere outside of
Georgia. But how can we find peace in here in our
hearts, if out there our feet still be shackled in slavery
chains?

**WILLIAM**: Did you notice, they prattled an' carried on
like we weren't even there. The damn papers were more
important than we were.

**ELLEN**: An' she, my owner and step mother, was quite
honest about that. This ceremony wasn't for, or even
about us. It was for business purposes that we not live
together ... But I can live with that.

**WILLIAM**: Ellen. What in the world you talkin' 'bout?
That makes no sense at all. If we be married, but not ...

**ELLEN**: The reason I can live with that is because then
we won't be having babies.

**WILLIAM**: Ellen, you be completely daft ... ?

**ELLEN**: William, if we had babies, what would happen to
them?

**WILLIAM**: Why we'd raise them up ... our own flesh and
blood.

**ELLEN**: And what would THEY do with "OUR own
flesh and blood"?

**WILLIAM**: They'd sell ...

**ELLEN**: And when would they be auctioned? Maybe 6
weeks or 6 years. Or if they be a pretty girl at the age of
12, you know very well.

**WILLIAM:** Yeah, I do know. My sister was only 12.

**ELLEN:** I can't bear the thought of giving birth to a baby and having that child belong to someone else to do with as they've a mind to ... To whatever pleases ... (she starts to cry)

**WILLIAM:** Ellen, don't cry. We'll find a way to escape.

**ELLEN:** How we gonna do that?

**WILLIAM:** I don't know yet, but we'll find a way.

**ELLEN:** William, you know very well that they'd send out the bloodhounds and slave hunters ... no matter how far we go or how long we be gone ... and we'd be put into worse than what we already got here.

*James comes onto porch.*

**JAMES:** You two love birds still here?

*William shuffles up to him.*

**WILLIAM:** Yassuh

(He bows and looks toward floor, though not looking for anything there; then chuckling though nothing's funny.)

**JAMES:** You gotta disabuse yoahselves that you be a married couple. Just as my good wife patiently explained only minutes ago.

**WILLIAM:** Yassuh. She be good an' tellin' thet. But now thet we be married, where, we gonna live?

**JAMES:** Bein' married didn't change none of thet. Wheah you usually stay, William?

**WILLIAM:** More normal I live with the other ...

**JAMES:** (Interrupting him) Oh yeah, of course. You live with the other black bucks ... Them what's not married yet ...

**WILLIAM:** But ...

**JAMES:** BUT it makes no nevah mind to you, William. You'll still live as befoah.

**ELLEN:** But Daddy ...

**JAMES:** (Turning angrily toward her.) Ellen, I've warned you befoah ... nevah to call me thet in public nor elsewheah.

**ELLEN**: (Starting to cry.) Wheah will I ...

**JAMES**: Stop yoah snifflin'. Now thet you be married you'll have thet littlest cabin ... the one closest to the creek.

**ELLEN**: I thanks you.

**WILLIAM**: An' so do I.

**JAMES**: Thet be enough palaverin' ... But William, do as I told ... no married relationship ...

**WILLIAM**: I unnerstan' ... I surely unnerstan'.

**JAMES**: You bettah understan' ... cause I'm sure you know I have some of yoah black friends keep me constantly informed ...

**WILLIAM**: I know thet too.

(James glares at the couple, turns on his heels and exits.)

**NARRATOR**: The story then as Grandma told it,  two years later they were at Ellen's cabin.

BLACKOUT


SCENE 5:  ELLEN'S CABIN

*Ellen is inside her cabin and William stands outside Ellen's cabin door.*

**WILLIAM**:(From outside.) Ellen, I been waitin' all day ... The latch string is gone.

(Ellen holds the latch string and opens door)

**WILLIAM**: Waitin' just to get to see you for awhile.

**ELLEN**: It is an intolerable situation. But as long as we love each other, we can know that there'll come a day.

**WILLIAM**: Dear, Dear Ellen we can't wait for the day to come on its own accord.

**ELLEN**: William, let's sit an' talk this over.

**WILLIAM**: We talked this over an' over again 'n again. If we ever get away from this bein' married and' not bein' married ... We'll have to find some way.

**ELLEN**: You know there be a load of cotton leavin' for Macon on next weekend.

**WILLIAM**: I do know that, but how would that help? ...

**ELLEN**: I would be able to scrounge myself ....

**WILLIAM**: My dear Ellen, we can't afford to put you in such danger.

**ELLEN**: Do you have a better way for us ... ?

**WILLIAM**: I been thinkin'.

**ELLEN**: Yeah?

**WILLIAM**: You know, 'cause of you bein' so light complected, you can pass as white.

**ELLEN**: An' that's what got me in so much trouble ... even when I was just a tad.

**WILLIAM**: But instead of that bein' a problem for you, it might could be a blessin'.

**ELLEN**: I been prayin' for nigh on two years.

**WILLIAM**: There be times when the good Lord want us to make some choices.

**ELLEN**: A situation that slavery never really allows.

**WILLIAM**: Since we get so little time together in the evenin', I been makin' some plans. But first, we gotta get a pass to leave for three days at Christmas.

**ELLEN**: It does seem that every Christmas they let some slaves leave for three days to visit kin folks on another plantation. But what plantation we be visitin'?

**WILLIAM**: Nevah mind! We could make out thet we be visitin' yoah Mamma. Since Massah such a good Christian ...

**ELLEN**: What's bein' a good Christian got to do with it?

**WILLIAM**: No one need know what place. The main thing is to buy ourselves some time.

**ELLEN**: I'm not sure what you really got in mind, but I can get the pass, I'm sure.

**WILLIAM**: That'd be just fine. George is outside watchin' as usual. He's proved to be a good friend, but he reminds me often about Massuh as well as Benjamin, evah since Benjamin become overseer.

**ELLEN**: They nevah tell me anything, but I listen.

**WILLIAM**: You keep on doin' thet. I be goin' with Massuh to Savannah with that load of cotton. Thet'll be a good chance for me to notice how one can get to Savannah.

**ELLEN**: When'll you get back?

**WILLIAM**: In about a week. Maybe before I leave we might be able to spend ...

**ELLEN**: William, you know good and well that I love you more than life, itself, but we can't be takin' chances like ...

**WILLIAM**: There's no chance we'd get caught. I tol' you thet George be watchin' ...

**ELLEN**: You know that's not the chance I be ... WE can't be makin' no babies ... babies what would be taken ...

**WILLIAM**: Ellen, I know ...

*They look deeply into each other's eyes. They embrace and kiss. He exits after lifting latch on the door, as lights dim.*

FADE TO BLACK

SCENE 6:  A WEEK LATER

**NARRATOR**: About a week later Ellen had a visitor again. She was alone, and was getting ready for bed by turning down the top quilt. She heard footsteps on the porch, which frightened her considerably. Then she heard a soft knocking on the door.

*William pulled the latch string and opened the door and poked in his head. He was carrying over his shoulder a full burlap bag*

**WILLIAM**: Is it okay?

**ELLEN**: You know it's always okay ... A'course we see each other in the big house or out in the fields.

**WILLIAM**: But that's nevah enough.

**ELLEN**: The week you be gone I worried that somethin' may be happenin' to you. It could be that you get in a bad way with Daddy,

**WILLIAM**: Now Ellen you know thet I can handle Massuh to keep him mollified, as long as I bow an' scrape and lower my eyes and chuckle a little with his unfunny jokes.

**ELLEN**: I'm sick to my death of livin' ...

**WILLIAM**: Don't nevah say nothin' like thet, "Sick to my death" ... I got somethin' in mind.

**ELLEN**: What I mean to say is livin' like this ... sick an' tired of this sneakin' around to have a few minutes alone togethah. Tell me exactly what you got in mind.

**WILLIAM**: Let me show you what exactly I got in mind. (Goes to bag and lifts out a nice man's hat.)

**ELLEN**: I see what you got in hand, but I'm still not sure what you got in mind.

**WILLIAM**: You like it? (As he hands it to her to inspect.)

**ELLEN**: It looks okay, but it seems too small for you. (He takes it from her and puts it on her head.)

**WILLIAM**: It surely fits you.

**ELLEN**: An' to what purpose would I want to wear ...

**WILLIAM**: You do want to escape from here dontcha?

**ELLEN**: So I put on this fancy man's hat, an' while ever'one sittin' on front porch after Sunday dinner, I march by them ... all gazin' at me ...

**WILLIAM**: Why would you wanna do that?

**ELLEN**: How in the world could I use this man's hat to escape from here? (He tries to interrupt, but she continues.) An' another question. (He tries again to respond, but she continues.) Wheah did you get the money? (He tries again to respond, but she nearly stops him again. This time he persists.)

**WILLIAM**: Now if you just let me explain ...

**ELLEN**: Well, you certainly have some explainin' to do.

**WILLIAM**: Wheah you want me to start?

**ELLEN**: I don't care wheah you start. Just make sure you get it all covered.

**WILLIAM**: In the first place, I didn't hafta get the money. I been savin' the money what he let me keep my 10 percent part of the wages from my carpenter work ...

**ELLEN**: William, what in the name of the Lord do you mean to be takin' money from our escape hopes? This kind of frippery!

**WILLIAM**: You gonna let me finish?

**ELLEN**: I be fearin' that we both be really finished , if ...

**WILLIAM**: You know Ellen, with your light complected skin you can pass for bein' white.

**ELLEN**: I know that, but ...

**WILLIAM**: When we take our three-day leave of the place, they surely gonna stop us — twoslaves — somewheah. But a white man with a black slave goes wheahevah the white man wants to go.

**ELLEN**: It seems to be that you're figurin' I'm to be the white man.

**WILLIAM**: That's the idea.

**ELLEN**: I'm not so sure. Did anyone see you with this bag. What would we do for payin' for trains or boats? (He again tries to answer) I s'pose we just gonna waltz right outta here, then walk or maybe run all the way to Baltimore?

**WILLIAM**: Slow down again. I've put away enough money to last for quite awhile. Even though I didn't get to keep much of what I earned, but what they DID pay me, I was able to save.

**ELLEN**: Well, I'll think on it.

**WILLIAM**: We can't think too long, 'cause this three day pass gotta be used.

**ELLEN**: Not quite yet. Christmas is three days off and, as I remember it, we must leave on Christmas eve.

**WILLIAM**: Is that what's written?

**ELLEN**: William you know I can't read any more than you can. But I did ask for a Christmas pass.

**WILLIAM**: Yeah. If it wasn't Christmas time, we most surely would not have been given the pass.

**ELLEN**: That gives us two more days to get things arranged.

(Noises of dogs and men yelling can barely be heard in background.)

**ELLEN** (CONT'): I listened today and heard in the kitchen that they're 'specting some mischief afoot.

*He goes to door and looks out. When he turns away from her, she quickly pulls the quilt back in place on the bed. William, still looking out the door, listens for any unusual sounds. )*

**WILLIAM**: I know they be expectin' some after-dark shenanigans. But I'm of a mind to ignore any of that, 'cause this ain't the night for thet stuff ... Actually George is out there standin' watch.

**ELLEN**: But if he hears them ...

**WILLIAM**: We got a special whistle. If danger be lurkin'.

**ELLEN**: So ... what then?

**WILLIAM**: Why then I'll go out the back door and get to the creek and wade upstream a bit.

**ELLEN**: How long is George willin' to stand watch?

**WILLIAM**: He say he stay as long as we like.

**ELLEN**: I like ... forever.

**WILLIAM**: And we got forevah ... togetheah. But we not got forevah to do what we come to do tonight.

**ELLEN**: You got the papers?

**WILLIAM**: I got my walkin' round papers, what I carry always here in the bib of my overalls.

**ELLEN**: I know that. An' I'll be sure to carry mine when I'm away.

**WILLIAM**: That part may change some.

**ELLEN**: What you mean "change some"

**WILLIAM**: 'Bout yoah papers. Once we got ever'thing ready to go, I'll let Benjamin ... You know he's the overseer for the rest of the summer ... to let him know we'll be away for the 3 days. That way there won't be no hungry bloodhounds nor bloodthirsty white men chasin' through the night. I already got all the things you'll be needin'.

**ELLEN**: You sure, we doin' the right thing by this?

**WILLIAM**: Just as sure as I been 'bout anything befoah in this life time. Your Negro body be hidden by youah white skin, what make it possible to pull off this little play actin'.

**ELLEN**: Of course, I realized I pass for white even befoah Mrs. Smith got too nervous with me close to her children. I was 11 then ... when she gave me to my own sistah ... Even though she be only my half-sistah.

(We hear a whistle and dogs barking getting closer.)

**WILLIAM**: I don't know what thet's all about. I do know what I gotta be about.

**ELLEN**: It must mean that some slave musta escaped ... Always fearful of what might could happen, but there's no call fer you to be runnin'.

**WILLIAM**: We can't be takin' any chances at this point.

*He exits quickly. The sound gets louder of the dogs and men yelling.*

**ELLEN**: (Sitting on edge of bed.) Dear Lord above, don't let nothin' happen to William, my William , sweet William.

*The sounds of dogs and men continue. As Ellen sits and prays in her own silence Footsteps are heard on the porch.*

**JAMES**: (Yelling from outside.) William ... You in theah? (He tries to open door, but the latch string is on the inside. Ellen goes to door and opens it.) Wheah's William?

**ELLEN**: (Holding back her tears.) He ain't heah. See? (She motions toward the bed which still remains smooth.)

**JAMES**: I don't give a goddam 'bout thet. I need him. (Looks at bag by door.) What's in this bag by the door heah?

**ELLEN**: I been doin' some clothes washin' for ol' Aunt Mildred. She been awful po'ly lately. Whatcha need William for? Has he done somethin'?

**JAMES**: One of the Dalton's slaves has escaped. William knows these woods better'n anybody. He gotta help us fin'. ...

**ELLEN**: He stopped by here earlier.

*Lights dim slowly, as the dogs sound farther away.*

BLACKOUT

## SCENE 7: THE NEXT NIGHT

**NARRATOR**: It was the next night that Ellen waited for William ... twonights before Christmas.

**ELLEN**: Deah Lord, above, I've cried so many tears, I fear
my brain be dried up.

But my heart be sick with longing ... longing for
William ... and longing for freedom.

If it be thy will, dear Lord, let me perish from this life
of misery ... or if not ...

Interrupted by boots on the porch. William enters the
room. He is carrying a barn lantern.

**WILLIAM**: I'm so sorry, Ellen, I didn't intend to interrupt
your talkin' with the Lord.

**ELLEN**: I'm sure the good Lord don't mind at all, if we
be headin' ourselves toward Freedom and Glory or I'll
be dyin' for tryin'.

**WILLIAM**: Now, Sweet, Sweet Ellen, don't even be
thinkin' of dyin'.

**ELLEN**: Since you got here, tonight, the glory of death
not what I be thinkin'.

**WILLIAM**: I hope you be thinkin' the glory of freedom.

**ELLEN**: Yes, but after last night and all day today. Did he
find you last night?

**WILLIAM**: He did ... You musta tole him I was frog
giggin'.

**ELLEN**: Why you think I said that?

**WILLIAM**: He said, "Boy, how you be huntin' frogs down
heah in the creek with just yoah hands?" I sez, "Yassuh,
I comes down heah an' fergit all 'bout the frog gig. I also
be grabblin' for eels in the creek banks. " An' I laughs
my liddle laugh (he laughs) an' shuffle backwahds my
feets.

**ELLEN**: William, you surely didn't do that liddle dance
show for him.

**WILLIAM**: Of course, I did. I had to put him at ease as
quick as possible.

**ELLEN**: In the kitchen, they were talking about the chase.
And they said that the Dalton slave got clean away. That
doesn't usually happen if ...

**WILLIAM**: If they go the right way.

**ELLEN**: Why wouldn't they be going the right way?

**WILLIAM**: The right way depends on the right hunter.

**ELLEN**: You mean you ... Last night he said that you knew these woods better than anybody.

**WILLIAM**: I truly hated to have Massah Smith mistrust my judgement. But more important than that trust now was that that boy's escape and our pathway to freedom ourselves.

**ELLEN**: William we've not had the chance to talk 'bout what you started last night and about these men's clothes for me.

**WILLIAM**: Let's see if they fit.

**ELLEN**: I still don't understand how my dressin' in those clothes ...

**WILLIAM**: You know if we be able to get all the way to Savannah as two colored slaves, we then be `caught. But if you be dressed as a white man, travelin' with his black slave, there be no questions asked. I saw just the very thing this past week. A white slave owner was on his way to catch a train with his slave.

**ELLEN**: Where would they be going?

**WILLIAM**: To Charleston, S.C. Let's see if we can take the place of those two travelers.

**ELLEN**: And how ...

**WILLIAM**: You mean you not tried on these clothes yet?

**ELLEN**: I was waitin'.

**WILLIAM**: We don't need to wait no longer.

*He starts to help her get undressed, but she resists*

**WILLIAM**: What's the matter with you? Didn't the preacher pronounce us "man and wife?"

**ELLEN**: I know very well and long for the day.

**WILLIAM**: No need to long no longer.

**ELLEN**: If we get safely away from here, the time and place will come.

(She takes the bag of clothes behind a curtain that hangs across a corner of the room.)

**WILLIAM**: So what do I do?

ELLEN: You can wait.

WILLIAM: I been doin' that for ...

(She interrupts him.)

ELLEN: You can sing ... You can always sing.

WILLIAM: What should I ... What you want me to sing?

> Before she answers he starts humming BALM IN
> GILEAD. After a few seconds, she, in her hidden corner
> starts humming in harmony right along with him. We see the
> curtain moving back and forth as she undresses and dresses
> behind it.

ELLEN: Nearly ready.

WILLIAM: You know, they got a show like this in Atlanta.

ELLEN: What you mean, "A show like this?"

WILLIAM: I saw a show ovah there down near the river.
  Where a girl come out all dressed up from behind a
  curtain. When she comes out with the band playing
  music she struts around a bit then starts takin' clothes
  off. A little bit at a time, then she start thowin' them off
  to a fare-thee-well. Until there' weren't ...

(Ellen interrupts him by appearing partially clothed in the
  men's apparel, but without a shirt and tie.)

ELLEN: Now if you think you're gonna see a show here ...

WILLIAM: (Looking at her partially dressed with only her
  undergarments under her open coat.) I think there be
  possibilities here.

ELLEN: An' what kinda possibilities would you be
  thnkin'?

WILLIAM: The possibilities evah since Brotha Hicks
  married us up ... even before that ... But we got othah
  matters ...

ELLEN: William, I'm sorry we've had to live this way, but
  my faith in the Lord ...

WILLIAM: We now got other things we gotta work on.
  Actually, even without the full suit, you  gonna do just
  fine.

ELLEN: If this be the way we gotta go, we got no time to

lose. Now do you have all the things we need to pull off this little prank?

**WILLIAM**: I believe evahthing we need for the costume is in the bag. I even bought a pair of tinted glasses to hide your pretty woman's eyes.

**ELLEN**: I saw those and wondered.

**WILLIAM**: Now tomorrow we'll have to be finished, 'cause it's Christmas Eve an' they expect us to be gone on Christmas day,

**ELLEN**: Yes that's when they'll be planning the usual celebration.

**WILLIAM**: They won't hardly miss us.

**ELLEN**: It's getting' late. You better go before George gets tired watching.

**WILLIAM**: Just for tonight, then we be gone.

*They embrace. He goes to door and makes sure the latch string is on the inside.*

## FADEOUT

## SCENE 8: THE PLANTATION MANOR HOUSE
*James and Ethel meet on the front porch.*

**NARRATOR**: That same evening their owners met on the front porch of the manor house.

**JAMES**: I'm concerned about William and Ellen.

**ETHEL**: Why you so concerned 'bout them? You seem more interested in your bastard daughter than our legitimate children.

**JAMES**: You don't understand my concern. It's not my concern for her as a daughter ... It's my worry 'bout the two of them as my ... s our ... property.

**ETHEL**: Actually. I've been surprised how well, she's been performing her kitchen duties.

**JAMES**: And I can't complain about William's work ... here on the place ... but moah especially on the carpenterin' work he's been doing. Our part of the wages he earns from his cabinet makin' is makin' big difference in the expenses of runnin' this place.

ETHEL: What you mean OUR part of what he's paid? Don't we own him?

JAMES: Well, yes, of course.

ETHEL: Don't we feed him?

JAMES: We do.

ETHEL: An' pervide shelter.

JAMES: Such as it is.

ETHEL: Don't worry "'bout such as it is." He has no expenses. Why should he keep any of what his labor produces? His labor belongs to us. We paid good money in this investment.

JAMES: I feel it sets up a good faith situation for us to keep him mollified with his situation here

ETHEL: You think he's completely satisfied?

JAMES: I thought so until fairly recently ... Until that night the Dalton's slave got away.

ETHEL: What did that have to do with William?

JAMES: I went by Ellen's shack to find him, but she said he hadn't been there.

ETHEL: Was she lying?

JAMES: I think so, because I saw a man's hat on her bed. I'm sure I saw it, but while wewere talkin', the hat disappeared.

ETHEL: How can a hat just disappear?

JAMES: There're times when I suspect her of bein' a conjure woman like her mamma.

ETHEL: And her mamma?

JAMES: I'm sure you 'member her. I knew she was a conjure woman. How you think she got me in bed?

ETHEL: James, don't you dare ... Were all those other slave women conjurers?

JAMES: I sold her off you know.

ETHEL: Course I know ... But back to that hat. Was it a hat you'd seen him ...

JAMES: No. It was a real fancy hat ... the kind that I or my friends would wear to church or the courthouse.

ETHEL: You don't suppose Ellen been ...

JAMES: Course not, but both of them bear watchin'.

ETHEL: You know they have a three-day pass for visitin' ...

JAMES: They'll be comin' back from that. 'cause they wouldn't get far if they tryin' to escape. They'd have to show papers, which they wouldn't have. At least the proper ones.

ETHEL: We goin' to have to deal with that situation right after they get back.

JAMES: We both agree on that. Benjamin thinks he's workin' up points toward his freedom. I'll be able to count on him to help with that. He's sure to figure that if he helps me out thet way, he be getting' extra points he earnin' toward his freedom, and for an early release. When they think they got a good path to freedom, they'd sell out their own mother.

ETHEL: Would they auction off their own daughter?

He glares at her. Moment of silent face-off.

## BLACKOUT

## SCENE 9: ELLEN'S CABIN

NARRATOR: Come that Christmas in 1848, it was time for their foolhardy attempt to escape. They would be having two traveling bags: a fancy carpetbag for Mr. Johnson ... That was the name assumed by Ellen. For William a few things wrapped in an old quilt.

WILLIAM: I can't believe I could be married to this man, standin' in front of me.

ELLEN: I can't believe I be the man. Just hopin' thet everyone will recognize me as a man.

WILLIAM: An' not just any man. A plantation and slave owner. Pleased to meetcha, Mr. ... Ellen Johnson! It'll be Mr. Johnson from now on. Yassuh, Masta Johnson. (He bows, shuffles backwards, then laughs a nervous little laugh. He quickly shifts demeanor.) It won't be right, Mr. Johnson, for you bein' a self-respectin' man ... white man ... o have such long hair.

ELLEN: I hadn't taken that under consideration ... I got

some scissors here in my bag. I'll just sit in this chair, here, an' let you do the cuttin', if that was what you had in mind.

*During the ensuing dialogue, Ellen sits in chair and William cuts her hair.*

**WILLIAM**: We may be only playacting, but we gotta play this game as though it was for  real ... as though our lives depended on it.

**ELLEN**: In truth, our lives will depend on it.

**WILLIAM**: For the next days an' weeks, maybe months. It'll be the most real thing in our lives.

**ELLEN**: Except for the real love ...

**WILLIAM**: An' if I didn't have that reality, I certainly wouldn't be takin' this adventure.

**ELLEN**: `Nor would I. But you gotta act now as if you were my for real slave. Now when I sometimes feel I must show how obedient you can be, just don't be too surprised.

**WILLIAM**: You know how I bow and scrape for Massuh, I be happy to do thet fer you.

**ELLEN**: We gotta be careful how we talk ... You must start talkin' with me the way you talk with Massah and other whites. (He starts to protest, but she continues.) I know that you can speak better, and there'll come a day when we'll be able to talk like free people.

**WILLIAM**: An' you ... how'll you talk like white folks?

**ELLEN**: William, you know very well, that even though I can't read nor write, I listen carefully to all those white folks who come our way ... and you know there be some from the government and even some fancy writers. I may not set pen to paper, but I surely put word to mind. I particularly like the way they sound, when you say them right out loud.

**WILLIAM**: I be troubled 'bout somethin' else.

**ELLEN**: And what would that be?

**WILLIAM**: You know that even if we convince guards and slave chasers and sheriffs that you be a white slave

ownah an' me yoah slave. There still be a problem ...
(She waits for him to explain.) I been with Massuh to
Atlanta many a time when we'd be at the train depot or
other places an' the white man would have to sign
papahs , sayin' that ever'thing was in order.. . .How you
gonna sign?

**ELLEN:** I been thinkin' on that ... So I went and broke my
right arm.

**WILLIAM**: Ellen, some time I think you plumb crazy ...

**ELLEN**: I shouldn't tell it that way. I'm fixin' to break it.

**WILLIAM**: Well, quit fixin, an 'splain.

**ELLEN**: How could I sign any papers, if my arm be
broken?

**WILLIAM**: So you not ...

**ELLEN**: Course not. But I got a good piece of linen from
an old linen tablecloth that I saw down at the clothes
warshing place down by the creek.

**NARRATOR**: When Grandma Ellen made that
suggestion, Grandpa William helped her devise a sling
out of the piece of linen.

**WILLIAM**: We got ever'thing else we need? 'Sides from
clothes?

**ELLEN**: 'Course  we wear only one outfit at a time.
Celebration noises are heard from a distance away.

**WILLIAM**: It's time!

**ELLEN**: We may have some trouble gettin' past all the
partyin' at the big house.

**WILLIAM**: If we go behin' the  barn, we be okay.
*They kneel by the bed and pray silently. Then stand for a
couple minutes.*

**ELLEN:** You suppose someone may be watchin' ?

**WILLIAM**: I believe ever'body will be at the party. (Ellen
begins to cry) Come, Ellen. What's the matter?

**NARRATOR**: It must have been a strange picture to see
this small white man leaning on and sobbing on the
breast of a black slave.

**ELLEN**: (She raises her head.) I know we have miles to go before we find freedom ... not master and slave ... then we can live as the Lord intended ... wife and husband. Come, William, it's getting late. So let us set forth.

**WILLIAM**: You go by the piney woods an' I'll follow the creek. We'll meet up at the traindepot.

**ELLEN**: The full moon should be enough for us until the sun come up.

*They pick up their things and exit. Spot light on door latch, with the latch string on the outside. In a silent moment we see the latchstring pushed back inside, which means no one can enter now. We hear their footsteps across porch.*

FADE OUT

**NARRATOR**: They were on their way, hopefully from slavery to freedom. We'll take 15 minutes to prepare for the rest of the journey with Ellen and William.

INTERMISSION-
END ACT I

ACT II

SCENE 1: TRAIN DEPOT BOARDING DOCK

**NARRATOR**: Their journey then became more complicated and much more dangerous. They had managed to leave the plantation and Macon behind and had been able to buy a train ticket to Charleston, SC ... For a brief stop then on northward. They were on the depot loading dock with other travelers. Mr. Cray and a steward stood close by. Even though they were on their way, hopefully to freedom, their troubles were just beginning.

*Two passengers stand nearby watching them carefully.*

**WILLIAM**: Isn't that Mr. Cray? I believe I 'member him eatin' at the Master's house not very long ago. You 'member him?

**ELLEN**: I do remember him ... I just hope he doesn't remember or recognize me. He knew me when I was given to my half-sister, Mary. I was only 11 then.

*Mr. Cray walks toward them.*

**CRAY:** It is a very fine mornin', sir. I say, sir, it is a very fine mornin'. I will make him hear.

*William makes a motion with his hands toward his own ear, indicating that Ellen was deaf. William gets her attention and points to Cray.*

**ELLEN:** (Looking at Cray with downward shift of eyes.) Yes.

**CRAY:** For a moment there I thought I knew the young gentleman ... here's something about him. Well I have better things to do than attempting to engage in conversation with a deaf-mute.

*He stalks off and exits.*

**WILLIAM:** Massa, 'bout time for me to get our bags ready fir the train.

*He exits.*

**ELLEN:** That's right, William. Thanks for being so helpful.

William leaves just as the Military Officer enters ... The Military Officer and other passengers observe closely the movements of Ellen and William ... William. returns quickly with a small traveling bag.

**MILITARY OFFICER:** You have a very attentive boy, sir ... but you had better watch him like a hawk when you get on to the North. He seems all very well here, but he may act quite differently there. I've known several gentlemen who have lost their valuable Negroes among those damned cut throat abolitionists. I would not take a nigger to the North under no consideration. I've had a great deal to do with coloreds in my time, but I never saw one who ever had his heel upon free soil was ever worth a damn. Now stranger, if you had made up your mind to sell that there darkey, I'm your man; just name the price, and if it's not out of the way, I'll pay for him on this train with hard silver dollars. (Staring at Ellen) Whatta you say, stranger?

**ELLEN:** I don't wish to sell, sir; I cannot get on well without him.

**MILITARY OFFICER:** You'll have to get on without

him, if you take him up north, fer I can tell ye, stranger
as a friend, he will do you no good if you take him
across the Mason's and Dixon's line; he is a keen colored
man ...

**ELLEN**: I thank you for your advice, sir.

**MILITARY OFFICER**: (traveling with a man servant, to
Ellen) You will pardon me, Sir, for saying I think you're
very likely to spoil your boy by saying "Thank you" to
him. I assure you, Sir, nothing spoils a nigger so soon as
saying, "Thank you" and "if you please" to him. The
only way to make a Negro toe the mark, and to keep
him in his place, is to storm at him like thunder ... and
keep him trembling like a leaf.  Don't you see, when I
speak to my Nate, he darts like lightnin', and if he
didn't, I'd skin him.

   *Nate Enters.*

**MILITARY OFFICER**: Nate get the hell over here. The
Lord didn't give you the brains He give a billy goat.
Now get our things together for us to get on the train.

**NATE**: Yass uh.

   *He exits.*

**MILITARY OFFICER**: That's the way to speak to them.
If every Negro was drilled in this manner, they would
be as humble as a hound dog ... and never dare to run
away. (A long pause) Now you need to listen to what
we're saying. Don't take that Negro up North.

**ELLEN**: Well I need to go to Philadelphia where the air is
better for me.

**MILITARY OFFICER**: If it's for health reasons, you
oughta go to Warm Springs, Arkansas.

**ELLEN**: I've also been told that I can get better medical
attention in Philadelphia.

**MILITARY OFFICER**: Well, go where you damn well
please. But you'd be well-advised to sell for the deal that
fellow offered.

**ELLEN**: I appreciate all the free advice, but I certainly
need the boy to take care of my needs ... which he does
ever so well.

**MILITARY OFFICER:** Of course it's your call and your life. (We hear the train huff into the depot.) Well, we seem to be boarding. So Godspeed on your continued journey.

**ELLEN:** And the same to you, Sir.

*Pompey is on deck polishing boots.*

**POMPEY:** Your Massa give me new coin. He is big bug. He's the greatest gentleman dat has been dis way in six months.

**WILLIAM:** Yes, he is some pumpkins. I'm gonna have to polish boots for my Massa.

**POMPEY:** Say, Brudder, where you come from, and what side you on today, with dat dare little dressed up white man?

**WILLIAM:** I come from Georgia, but the side I goin' to is Philadelphia.

**POMPEY:** What! ... o Philamadelphy?

**WILLIAM:** Yes.

**POMPEY:** By squash! I wish I was goin' wid you! I hears um say dat dare's no slaves way over in dem parts; is um so?

**WILLIAM:** I've heard the same thing.

**POMPEY:** Well! (Throwing down the boot and brush and placing his hands in his pockets. He struts across the floor with an air of independence) Gorra Mighty, dem is de parts for Pompey ... an' I hope when you get dare you will stay, an' nebber follow dat buckra back to dis hot quarter no more; let him be eber so good.

**WILLIAM:** Thank you so much.

**POMPEY:** God bless you, Broder, and may de Lord be wid you. When you gets de freedom, and sit in under your own wine and fig tree, don't forget to pray for poor Pompey.

**WILLIAM:** I'm gonna have to polish my massuh's boots too.

**POMPEY:** If we nevah meet again, may de Lord look aftah you an' care for yoah independence.

*Sound of Train continues as the conductor's voice is heard off stage, "All aboard!"*

BLACKOUT

## SCENE 2: CHARLESTON - CUSTOM HOUSE

**NARRATOR**: In Charleston Ellen and William ran into a problem in the Custom House office.

*William helps Ellen into the office.*

**ELLEN**: William, you sure we at the right place?

**WILLIAM**: I believe the sign says something about Custom-house ...

**ELLEN**: How can you be sure what the words ...

**WILLIAM**: There was a fellow outside what could read and told me what the words were. I believe that mean-looking fellow behind the desk may be the very one we have to report to.

**ELLEN**: You stay right beside me ... We'll go and buy train tickets for Wilmington. (Ellen approaches the desk of the officer, who looks up suspiciously at them.) I'd like two tickets for Wilmington ... for me and my manservant.

*She pays for tickets. As they are being handed to her, the Officer looks suspiciously at William.*

**TRANSIT AGENT**: (Addressing William.) Boy, do you belong to this gentleman?

**WILLIAM**: Yassuh.

**TRANSIT AGENT**: I wish you to register your name here, sir, and also the name of your slave, and pay a dollar duty on him.

*Ellen paid the dollar with her left hand, which she used to point to the right hand in the sling.*

**ELLEN**: As you can see sir, my writing hand is indisposed and unable to sign the papers. Would you register his name for me?

*The officer indignantly jumps up, shaking his head vigorously and cramming his hands deep into his pockets with a slave-bullying attitude.*

**TRANSIT AGENT**: I shan't do it.

*Another passenger walks up*

**ELLEN**: Why hello Mr. Tuttle. It's good seeing you again. I thought Charleston was your destination.

**TUTTLE**: Oh no. Wilmington is my destination. I was born and reared in the old North State.

**ELLEN**: Perhaps we'll have another opportunity to visit on the train to Wilmington. That is if we can secure a seat.

**TUTTLE**: Is there a problem ... perhaps the cost?

**ELLEN**: Oh no nothing like that. The officer here won't register my manservant's name for me ... even though he can see I have a bit of a handicap.

**TUTTLE**: Could I be of help?

**ELLEN**: Perhaps if you could affirm who we really are.

**TUTTLE**: (To officer) Is there some misunderstanding here which I might be able to alleviate?

**TRANSIT AGENT**: I can't allow passengers on train who are not properly identified. If I allow passengers who do not have authentic papers, it could very well be that they could be runaway slaves ... That would be on my conscience forever. You know it's happening more and more with those damned abolitionists stealing our property from us. Sometimes from right under our nose.

**TUTTLE**: (Pointing to Ellen.) Does this fine gentleman look like a slave?

**TRANSIT AGENT**: No! But he won't file the papers to authenticate the Negro.

**TUTTLE**: Well there's a perfectly good explanation for that ... as you can see the result of a recent accident.

**TRANSIT AGENT**: Then you know them?

**TUTTLE**: (Looking at Ellen and smiling.) Why yes. I know him and his kin folk like a book.

**TRANSIT AGENT**: Very well!

**TUTTLE**: Shall we shake on it?

**TRANSIT AGENT**: Of course. (They shake.)

**CONDUCTOR GRAVES**: (Walks up.) Is there a problem here?

**TRANSIT AGENT**: Hello, Mr. Graves ... Well there has been a problem of late with slaves escaping. So I have to be real careful about letting people sign on to the steamer ... They may be slaves trying to slip through for those free states up north.

**CONDUCTOR GRAVES**: We're only going to Wilmington, and North Carolina is not a free state.

**TUTTLE**: I said I will take the responsibility upon myself. What is your name?

**ELLEN**: Johnson ... William Johnson!

(The officer puts down the names as he repeats them.)

**TRANSIT AGENT**: Mr. Johnson and slave. And the name of the boy?

*Ellen and William look confused. She can't use his real name, which is William.*

**ELLEN**: (Quickly regaining composure.) Of course, my manservant. I always call him Rastus, but his real name is Eurastus.

**TRANSIT AGENT**: And how do you spell that?

**ELLEN**: Spell?

**TRANSIT AGENT**: Yeah! How do you spell it?

**ELLEN**: Just the usual way.

**TRANSIT AGENT**: Do you mean E R A S T U S.

**ELLEN**: (Much relieved.) Yes.  Of course.

**TUTTLE**: It's all right now, Mr. Johnson.

*He exits.*

**TRANSIT AGENT**: Mr. Johnson, pardon my rudeness. But we have to be careful these days.

**ELLEN:** I quite understand.

**TRANSIT AGENT**: Now that the passenger list is complete, would you like to join me next door for a drink and a good cigar, before the train leaves?

*Ellen, not having been used to drinking or smoking, looks frantically at William. Ellen stands silent, while the Transit Agent waits for an answer and begins to look perturbed, then takes a couple of cigars out of his coat pocket. Hands her a cigar, which she reluctantly accepts. She watches him carefully, but tries hard to conceal her anxiety. The Transit Agent licks his cigar. She klicks hers as casually as possible. He bites the tip of his cigar and spits it on the floor. Nonchalantly he waits for a light. She bites the end off of her cigar, but before she has a chance to spit it out, she starts coughing. This forces the tip of the cigar out onto the floor.*

**WILLIAM**: (While talking to Ellen, he picks up the cigar tip.) Massah, I sorry for botherin' you and this gentleman, but I fear I must remin' you.

**ELLEN**: (With a sigh of relief.) Thank you Rastus. I was about to ferget what Dr. Baxter warned me about.

**TRANSIT AGENT**: Is there something amiss here?

**ELLEN**: It's just like Rastus say. The doctor took me off tobacco and likker, as long as this ailment persists.

**WLLIAM**: The Lawd knows how Massa like a good smoke.

**ELLEN**: That's enough Rastus. There'll come a time someday. (To Transit Agent) Thanks so much for your kind offer, an' I do apologize for my infirmity.

**TRANSIT AGENT**: Yes, of course!

*Officer exits*

**CONDUCTOR**: I must apologize for the Transit Officer. I realize it was rather sharp shooting there for a while, Mr. Johnson. It was not out of disrespect to you, sir, but they make it a rule to be very strict in Charleston. I have known families to be detained with their slaves till reliable information could be received respecting them. If they were not so careful, any damn abolitionist might take off a lot of valuable slaves.

**ELLEN**: I suppose so.

*Ellen and William exchange glances.*

BLACKOUT


## SCENE 3: ON A TRAIN TO RICHMOND

**NARRATOR**: From Charleston they had planned to take a

steamship all the way to Philadelphia. However, as the ships didn't sail into Philadelphia in the winter, they were forced to continue their journey by rail. After their stop in Wilmington, they then took the train to Richmond and ran increased risks, as there were other close passengers.

ELLEN: You know, dear William, that we still have to be extra cautious, because from what I've been told is that the slave-catchers work along these routes.

WILLIAM: I know! Ain't it terrible stealing the livestock property from the good Christian families? The next thing you know they'll be stealin' the cows an' horses.

ELLEN: William, it's not a laughable matter.

WILLIAM: (Ignoring her.) Before you know it they'll be auctionin' off their own bastard children birthed by their women slaves.

*This is too much for Ellen. Obviously William is forgetting, for the moment, Ellen's situation, as he is having fun by relaxing this close to freedom.*

ELLEN: (Quite upset, beating on William's chest and crying.) We've come this far, Praise the Lord, and I'll not have you ruin the whole thing by your little fun.

WILLIAM: Ellen, I'm sorry. I got carried away with the fun of the situation.

ELLEN: William, there's nothing funny about this whole trip. You know very well ...

WILLIAM: I'm sorry, but we're so close ...

ELLEN: That's why we gotta be 'specially cautious.

WILLIAM: I Know. I know.

ELLEN: What was it you were askin'?

WILLIAM: Folks wanta know 'bout your medical condition.

ELLEN: If anyone wants to know exactly what my situation is, simply tell them it's Inflammatory Rheumatism. That's what I heard the doctor telling my grandmother ... on my father's side.

WILLIAM: It's a useful ailment. I'll mention it next time,

when I'm asked 'bout your condition.

**ELLEN:** What more did they want to know?

**WILLIAM:** 'Acourse they ask all sorts of things about you bein' married or havin' children; that kinda thing.

**ELLEN:** It'd be nice if folks would mind their own business.

**WILLIAM:** I thought I'd bust a gut when thet feller invited you to have a drink and a GOOD cigar.

**ELLEN:** You know very well that although I've stolen some sips of hooch from those white men guests ... when they leave some in their glasses. But I've never even held a cigar. The idea of it is repulsive.

*As William exits, an elderly gentleman, Mr. Wright, enters and sees Ellen alone. He is followed by two pretty young daughters.*

**GENTLEMAN WRIGHT:** (to Ellen) Do you mind if we share this car with you?

**ELLEN:** Not at all. There's plenty of room ... so just have a seat

**GENTLEMAN WRIGHT:** I won't sit just yet. But I would appreciate it if you would protect my daughters until I return.

**ELLEN:** By all means!

**GENTLEMAN WRIGHT:** Now Ann and Betty be good and don't disturb the gentleman.

**ANN AND BETTY:** All right Papa. (He kisses each on the cheek and exits.)

**ELLEN:** I suppose you're Ann and Betty?

**ANN AND BETTY:** They giggle as they nod yes.

**ELLEN:** (After an awkward moment.) Tell me about yourselves.

**ANN AND BETTY:** (Answering at the same time.) I'm Ann. I'm Betty.

**ELLEN:** How am I to know the difference?

**ANN:** Well I'm Ann. My hair is a little lighter than Betty'.

**BETTY:** I'm Betty, and I'm a bit slimmer than Ann.

*Ann glowers at Betty.*

**ELLEN:** Why don't the two of you come sit by me? How nice it is for an injured gentleman to have the attention ... of course I mean the medical attention by two angels of mercy.

*They sit on each side of her.*

**ELLEN:** Now tell me about yourselves.

**ANN:** There's not much to tell. I've just returned home from New York where I earned a teacher's certificate to teach in elementary school.

**ELLEN:** (To Betty) And you Betty?

**BETTY:** Actually since Mother died, I've stayed home and looked after the household and of course, Papa.

**ELLEN:** Are you married?

*Wright enters.*

**GENTLEMAN WRIGHT:** Have you girls been bothering this young gentleman?

*He sits and they retreat from Ellen to sit next to him.*

**ELLEN:** No Mr. __?

**GENTLEMAN WRIGHT:** Wright

**ELLEN:** No. They've simply been entertaining an injured southern gentleman.

**GENTLEMAN WRIGHT:** I'm certainly glad to hear that. One can't be too careful with the behavior of their children ... particularly prior to their proper marriage. Now what can you do with grown children?

**ELLEN:** I was just inquiring about that.

**GENTLEMAN WRIGHT:** About that?

**ELLEN:** About their marriage status.

**GENTLEMAN WRIGHT:** Well tell me Mr.___?

**ELLEN:** Johnson.

**GENTLEMAN WRIGHT:** Mr ... Johnson, where are you from?

**ELLEN:** From Alabama.

**GENTLEMAN WRIGHT:** Your manservant ... The fellow leaving when we came in ... is your manservant, is he not?

**ELLEN:** Yes, he is.

**GENTLEMAN WRIGHT**: He said you were from Florida.

**ELLEN**: (Quite nervous.) Well, yes I suppose he would say that. You just can't depend on the Negroes to get the facts straight. He's right, in that I bought him at auction in Florida, but took him to my plantation in Alabama. He was so loyal as well as efficient that I chose him to accompany me on this trip.

**GENTLEMAN WRIGHT**:" Your trip to where? What is your destination?

**ELLEN**: Oh yes of course. I hope to get to Philadelphia.

**GENTLEMAN WRIGHT**: You have kin there?

**ELLEN**: Oh no! I was told that I could get excellent medical care there.

**GENTLEMAN WRIGHT**: Yes. You seem to be very much afflicted, sir.

**ELLEN**: Yes sir.

**GENTLEMAN WRIGHT**: What seems to be the matter with you, sir, may I be allowed to ask?

**ELLEN**: Inflammatory Rheumatism, sir.

**GENTLEMAN WRIGHT**: Oh that is very bad, sir. I can sympathize with you. I know from bitter experience what the rheumatism is. I feel you would begin to feel much better if you could lie down and rest yourself.

**ELLEN**: Thank you, sir. That's a good suggestion.

*Ellen lies down, as the ladies rise and cover Ellen with their shawls. They make a nice pillow for her head. Ellen feigns sleep immediately.*

**ANN**: Papa, he seems to be a very nice gentleman.

**BETTY**: Oh dear me. I never felt so much for a gentleman in all my life.

**NARRATOR**: Time passed for Ellen as she enjoyed the quiet sleep time.

*William enters and crosses to Gentleman Wright.*

**WILLIAM**: How is Massa doin'?

**GENTLEMAN WRIGHT**: He seems terribly debilitated.

**WILLIAM**: Yassah.

**GENTLEMAN WRIGHT:** He says he's seeking medical attention in Philadelphia?

**WILLIAM:** Yassah.

**GENTLEMAN WRIGHT:** You seem so devoted to him. Won't you be seeking your freedom in Philadelphia?

**WILLIAM:** O no suh.

**GENTLEMAN WRIGHT:** He must treat you uncommonly well.

**WILLIAM:** He treat me like family.

**ELLEN:** (Wakes up and struggles to get up) Boy!

**WILLIAM:** Yassah! I right here.

*He starts helping her to sit and so does Gentleman Wright. The girls help her get on her cloak. They all find places to sit, except for William, who sits on the floor near Ellen.)*

**GENTLEMAN WRIGHT:** We must get off the train soon. It has been a most pleasant journey. Thanks for sharing it. Good luck in your quest for medical assistance in Philadelphia.

**ELLEN:** I certainly am counting on it.

**GENTLEMAN WRIGHT:** My grandmother passed on to me a natural recipe for the cure of inflammatory rheumatism. (He hands her a piece of paper, which she puts into her pocket as quickly as possible.) Tell me young fellow, does your father have any more bright slaves like your boy?

**ELLEN:** Oh, yes sir. Lots of them.

**GENTLEMAN WRIGHT:** Before we depart, I'd like to invite you to visit us when you're in our area.

*He hands Ellen a business card. She avoids looking at it as she may regard it upside down, so she puts it in her cloak pocket immediately.*

**ELLEN:** We'll certainly ... I'll certainly do that.

**ANN AND BETTY:** Oh yes! Please do. We'll roll out the welcome carpet.

**GENTLEMAN WRIGHT:** I shall be pleased to see you again, and so will my daughters. Come girls, it's time to disembark.

*The train stops. They exit.*

**WILLIAM**: Mr. Johnson, I'll step out of the train for a minute, but I'll be right back.

**ELLEN**: Yes! Go get a little fresh air.

*He exits. A stout elderly lady enters and sits near Ellen. Gentleman McWelch and young man enter. Lady looks out the window and sees William. She jumps up and yells.*

**LADY**: Bless my soul. There goes my Negro, Ned!

**ELLEN**: No! That is my boy.

**LADY**: You, Ned, come to me you runaway rascal. (She turns toward Ellen.) I beg your pardon, sir. I was sure it was my boy. I never in my life saw two black pigs more like your boy and my Ned. (Looking at Ellen.) Oh I hope sir that your boy will not turn out to be so worthless as my Ned has. Oh! I was as kind to him as if he had been my own son. Oh, sir, it grieves me very much to think that after all I did for him he should go off without having any cause, whatsoever.

**ELLEN**: When did he leave you?

**LADY**: About 18 months ago an' I have never seen hide nor hair of him since.

**ELLEN**: Did he have a wife?

**LADY**: No sir. Not when he left, though he did have one a little before that. She was very unlike him. She was as good an' faithful as any one would wish to have. But, poor thing, she became so ill that she was unable to do much work, so I thought it best to sell her, to go to New Orleans where the climate is nice and warm.

**ELLEN**: I suppose she was glad to go South for her health.

**LADY**: No, she was not, for niggers never know what is best for them. She took on a great deal about leavin' Ned and the baby; but as she was so weakly I let her go.

**GENTLEMAN MCWELCH**: Was she pretty?

**LADY**: She was quite handsome, and much whiter than I am; and therefor will have no trouble finding a husband. I'm sure I wish her well. I asked the speculator who bought her to sell her to a good master. Poor thing! She has my prayers, and I know she prays for me. Julie was a good Christian, and she always used to pray for my soul. It was through her earliest prayers that I was first led to seek forgiveness of my sins, before I was converted at the great camp meeting.

*She begins to sniffle, blowing her nose in a lacy hanky. Silence.)*

**GENTLEMAN MCWELCH:** As your Julie was such a very good girl. Had served you so faithfully before she lost her health, don't you think it would have been better to have emancipated her?

**LADY:** No indeed! I do not! I have no patience with people who set the Negroes at liberty. It is the worst thing you can do for them. My dear husband, just before he died willed all the Negroes free. But I, and all my friends, knew very well that he was too good a man to have ever thought of doing such an unkind and foolish thing ... had he been in his right mind ... and therefore, we had the will altered ... s it should have been in the first place.

**ELLEN:** Did you mean, Madam, that willing the slaves free was unjust to yourself or unkind to them?

**LADY:** I mean that it was decidedly unkind to the servants themselves. It always seems to me such a cruel thing to turn slaves loose to shift for themselves, when there are so many good masters to take care of them. I have lost more than ten of them since my husband died. Just ruinous. If my son, a good Christian minister, and I could have the value of those runaway slaves, just think what good we could do. We could send missionaries to the heathen who have never heard of our blessed Redeemer.

**GENTLEMAN MCWELCH:** As your son was a good Christian minister, it's strange he didn't advise you to let the poor Negroes have their liberty and go north.

**LADY:** Not strange at all, Sir. My son knows what's best

for the slaves and has always told me that they are much better off as slaves than if they were free men up North. In fact, I don't believe there are any white laboring people who ae well off as the slaves.

**GENTLEMAN MCWELCH:** You are quite mistaken, Madam. My mother, before she died, let her slaves go free. I was up in Ohio last year and visited some of them. They're getting on very well.

**LADY:** Well, freedom may have gone well for your Mama's Negroes, but it will never do for mine, and they shall never have it. That is the word with the bark on it.

**GENTLEMAN MCWELCH:** If freedom will not do for your slaves, Madam, I have no doubt your Ned and the other Negroes will find out their mistake, and return to their old home.

**LADY:** Blast them! If I ever get my hands on them, I will cook their infernal hash and tan their accursed black hides well for them. God forgive me, the Negroes will make me lose all my religion.

**NARRATOR:** It was time for the old lady to get off the train at the next stop.

**GENTLEMAN MCWELCH:** What a damned shame it is for that old whining hypocritical humbug to cheat poor Negroes out of their liberty. If she has religion, may the devil prevent me from ever getting converted.

BLACKOUT

## SCENE 4: BALTIMORE - GOVERNMENT OFFICE

**NARRATOR:** Ellen and William, confronted barrier after barrier. If it wasn't travel officers, it was government offices. When they got to Baltimore, they encountered government officials who were especially concerned about runaway slaves. But it was necessary for them to go to a government office there.

*The officer is seated at desk. Ellen and William enter and cross to desk.*

**ELLEN:** You wish to see me, sir?

**OFFICER**: Yes. It is against our rules, sir, to allow any person to take a slave out of Baltimore into Philadelphia, unless he can satisfy us that he has a right to take him along,

**ELLEN**: Why is that?

**OFFICER**: Because, sir, if we should suffer any gentleman to take a slave past here into Philadelphia; and should the gentleman with whom the slave might be traveling turn out not be his rightful owner, and should the proper master come and prove that his slave escaped on this road, we shall have him to pay for. Therefore, we cannot let any slave pass here without receiving security to show and to satisfy us, that it is all right.

**ELLEN**: No. I bought tickets in Charleston to pass us through to Philadelpihia. Therefore you have no right to detain us here.

**OFFICER**: Are you, sir acquainted with Mr. Ben Bennett, an attorney here in Baltimore who could attest to your legitimacy and that of your slave?

*Conductor enters.*

**CONDUCTOR**: As the gentleman is obviously a slaveholder as well as being an invalid, therefore he should be able to proceed. It would certainly be wrong to detain him any longer.

**OFFICER**: (to Conductor) Was this couple on your train from Charleston?

**CONDUCTOR**: (looking at his watch) Yes they were. I believe their ticket was all the way to Philadelphia.

**OFFICER**: (to Ellen) Well, sir, right or not right, we shan't let you go.

*Silence. Ellen and William look at each other. Conductor exits. The whistle blows to indicate the train was about to start. Ellen stands and is about to start crying, collapses back on her seat. William becomes quite solicitous in a manner not appropriate for a man servant.*

**OFFICER**: (sees her collapse on chair, but doesn't see that she is about to cry, as he looks away and wringing his hands and running them through his hair says.) I really don't know what to do. I calculate it is all right. As he is not well, it is a pity to stop him right here. We will let him go ... with his slave.

**ELLEN**: Thank you!

BLACKOUT

SCENE 5: ON THE TRAIN

*Two men are seated on the train*

**NARRATOR**: Later the train car had two men seated, who appeared rather out of their usual environment.

*Conductor 2 enters (Northern Conductor)*

**CONDUCTOR**: Could I see your tickets please? (They hand him their tickets ... Reading the names on the tickets.) Willis Hughes ... Robert J. Knight ... Where you men from?

**WILLIS**: That information isn't required, is it?

**CONDUCTOR**: Oh no! Of course not. It's just that when I finish collecting the tickets and have some free time, I like to visit with the travelers. You know there are lots of interesting folks traveling by rail these days. (Silence) You know we folks up north get accused of being unfriendly ... particularly to southerners who have a better image of friendliness. (More silence) And I thought you southerners would be more friendly ... like on this trip.

**ROBERT**: How did you know we were southerners?

**CONDUCTOR**: The ticket was issued in NC, was it not? And although it's NORTH Carolina, it's still a southern state, which is a slave-holding state.

**WILLIS**: Yes, but we're not from NC. We're actually from Georgia.

**ROBERT**: You idiot! You didn't have to tell him that.

**CONDUCTOR**: Of course he didn't have to tell me that, but you never know what sympathizers you may have "up north".

**WILLIS**: What kinda sympathizers?

**CONDUCTOR**: About your way of life.

**WILLIS**: You don't hafta beat around the bush. I know you talkin' 'bout the slave trade.

**CONDUCTOR**: Of course. but by time any runaways would get this far above the Mason-Dixon line, they be free men wouldn't they?

**ROBERT**: Not for long.

**CONDUCTOR**: No?

**ROBERT**: Because of the differences between the north and south concerning slavery, congress is working on a law that would give southerners the right to search for their slaves wherever they may be. And if they find them to bring them back.

**WILLIS**: And any one harborin' the black bastards would be arrested and fined or jailed.

**CONDUCTOR**: That's fascinating. But that's not a law yet, is it?

**ROBERT AND WILLIS**: Not yet!

**CONDUCTOR**: Are you looking for any slave in particular?

**ROBERT**: We're looking for a man and a woman from Macon, Georgia.

**WILLIS**: You didn't have to tell him that much.

**CONDUCTOR**: It would be unusual, wouldn't it, for two slaves to be traveling on the railroad?

**WILLIS**: It would, but we've heard that they may be in disguise.

**CONDUCTOR**: What kind of disguise?

**ROBERT**: We don't know for sure, but it's a rumor.

**CONDUCTOR**: Of course this is useful information for someone like myself, who sees many travelers every day ... But if I were to find and identify such fugitives, will I get a reward ... like "Wanted Dead Or Alive $1,000 Reward"?

**WILLIS**: Well, it may not be that much ... but that's the idea.

**CONDUCTOR:** (Moving away) I'll certainly keep my eyes open.

BLACKOUT

## SCENE 6: THE NEXT MORNING

**NARRATOR:** The next morning on the same train, Ellen was in a car, sitting alone. William hadn't been seen in quite a while.

**ELLEN:** (To Conductor) Have you seen anything of my manservant?

**CONDUCTOR:** No I haven't. But you seem to be terribly upset. He's probably just staying away until we reach Philadelphia, for there he'll be able to jump and run ... a free man in the promised land.

**ELLEN:** He would never run away. We have a very special relationship. I'm afraid that he may have fallen or lie hurt somewhere. Someone could have stolen him to enslave him for themselves. He might have been killed somewhere.

**CONDUCTOR:** Sir, I'm much more of an abolitionist than a slave chaser.

**ELLEN:** But I am desperate to find my manservant.

**CONDUCTOR:** That's quite obvious. But how do you suppose I might assist you in your search, when I disapprove of slavery in the first place? (Silence) I talked with a couple of fellows from Georgia. They were rather secretive about their train trip up here.

**ELLEN:** Why was that?

**CONDUCTOR:** They were trying to uncover some tracks, while they were quite diligent in covering their own tracks.

**ELLEN:** Did they say what they were looking for?

**CONDUCTOR:** I assume they were looking for escaped slaves; if my guess was right that they were slave-chasers. They were asking several passengers if they might have seen two potential runaway slaves ... a man and a woman.

ELLEN: I suppose there are lots of runaways ... but probably a slave man and a woman would be far-fetched. If I were to see two such suspects, what should I do?

CONDUCTOR: That depends. If you were to report them to some parties, they would inform the police, who would then probably turn them over to the slave catchers.

ELLEN: Now if they were to get as far as Philadelphia, they'd probably be home free, so to speak?

CONDUCTOR: Why do you say that?

ELLEN: Because Pennsylvania is a free state.

CONDUCTOR: They're about to give the slave owner the opportunity to come to a free state and fetch home their chattel.

ELLEN: After I see the doctor in Philadelphia, I may give my manservant his freedom. I've been giving it a lot of thought lately.

CONDUCTOR: As an abolitionist, I say. "Good for you." But don't tell just everybody that.

ELLEN: Of course not, but I do need to find him now.

CONDUCTOR: I will get some help in finding him.

BLACKOUT

SCENE 7: TRAIN CAR CORNER

NARRATOR: It took some time to find William, but he was asleep in a corner of the car on his carpet bag. Ralph, a colored man, found him.

RALPH BOWEN: Boy, wake up. (Giving him a violent shake.) Your master is scared half to death about you. He thinks you had taken French leave, for parts unknown. I never saw a fellow so badly scared about losing his slave. Now. Let me give you a little friendly advice. When you get to Philadelphia, run away and leave that cripple, and have your liberty.

WILLIAM: No sir, I can't promise to do that.

RALPH BOWEN: Why not. Don't you want your liberty?

**WILLIAM**: Yes sir; but I shall never run away from such a good master, as I have at present.

**RALPH BOWEN**: I have been staying with a man who is an abolitionist. I can recommend a good boarding house, where you will be quite safe. Then if you want to run away, it will be easy to do so. (Writes down a name and address on a slip of paper. Hands paper to William, who takes it and holds it as though not knowing what todo with it.) Just hand this note to any hackney driver, and he'll know how to find it.

**WILLIAM**: (looks at it) You'll have to tell me what it says.

**RALPH**: Is my writing that bad? It's only recently that I learned to read and write.

**WILLIAM**: It's juat that I can't read at all.

**RALPH**: You mean that you're illiterate?

**WILLIAM**: Yassuh. I

**RALPH**: Quit doing that. You don't need to talk like a slave any more. Where are you from before you started this journey?

**WILLIAM**: From Georgia, near Macon

**RALPH**: Did you know the James Smith plantation?

**WILLIAM**: I did.

> *He deliberately says no more.*

**RALPH**: I must visit when you get settled ... But take this note and show it to any hackney driver. Don't tell anyone, even hackney drivers, where you're from. There's lots you're  not telling me right now, and that's ok.

**WILLIAM**: Why so secretive?

**RALPH**: There are a couple of slave hunters looking closely for two escaped slaves, a man and a woman from Georgia.

**WILLIAM**: Thank you for this information and the caution.

**RALH**: I know the folks there, so I'll stop by in a few days to see how things are going.

**WILLIAM**: Yes and meet my partner. Thank you very

much.  That is good information.

*Offstage sound of Conductor shouting, "Next stop, Philadelphia!"*

**NARRATOR**: Ellen and William found each other and began to gather their things to prepare for leaving the train. Everyone else had already left.

**ELLEN**: Thanks be to God, William! We are safe.

**WILLIAM**: Yes but first we must find this boarding house. I'll get a hackney and show him the address.

BLACKOUT.

## SCENE 8: RECEPTION ROOM OF THE BOARDING HOUSE

*The landlord sits at the reception table. Ellen and William enter.*

**HENRY**: Could I help you folks?

**WILLIAM**: I was told ... we were told ...

*He takes out the piece of paper.*

**ELLEN**: (Snatching paper from William.) William ... Rastus I can handle this.

**WILLIAM**: Yassah ... (Bowing as he shuffles backward.) Massah.

**ELLEN**: (Hands paper to Landlord, but she doesn't look at it herself.) Is this your establishment here?

**LANDLORD**: (Taking paper and looking at it.) Yes ... Where did you get this?

**ELLEN**: From a fellow named Ralph, I believe.

**HENRY**: Ralph Bowen ... a colored man?

**ELLEN**: Yes ... I thought he could be trusted.

**HENRY**: Absolutely! ... I see you are a little indisposed ... with your lamed arm there.

**ELLEN**: Yes sir! But we are in dire need of a room. We may be here for quite a while.

**HENRY**: Well you look so everlasting tired. ... From your recent travels, I suppose?

**WILLIAM**: Yassuh My massa not well, so if you could ...

**HENRY**: Yes, of course. We can get the credential s later

... I won't be able to show you your room, as we ae
getting some other guess.

**ELLEN:** Just tell us ...

**HENRY:** Yes. Just take your bags down this hallway, and
the first room on the right with an open door will be
your home as long as you will be staying with us.

**ELLEN:** (Anxious to get out of the public room.) Come,
Rastus, make haste.

**WILLIAM:** Picking up the bags and following her as they
exit.

*Landlord stays and sits, opening a ledger. Robert and*
*Willis enter.*

**HENRY:** Could I help you gentlemen?

**ROBERT:** Have you seen two Negroes today? (Silence) A
man and a woman.

**HENRY:** Oh no. Why are you looking?

**ROBERT:** They're escaped slaves from Georgia.

**WILLIS:** You idiot? You didn't have to say ...

**HENRY:** Are they your slaves?

**ROBERT:** It doesn't matter.

**HENRY:** So you're slave hunters?

**WILLIS:** You're in trouble if you know of their
whereabouts and don't divulge the information to`the
appropriate person.

**ROBERT:** You know the Fugitive Slave Act gives us ...

**WILLIS:** Gives the owner of the escaped slaves, the
opportunity to seize the property and return it to where
it belongs.

**ROBERT:** And it makes no difference where in the
United States the escaped property is found.

**WILLIS:** And whoever harbors such slaves will be severely
punished for interfering with another citizen's property.

**HENRY:** Is there some kind of reward for supplying
pertinent information?

**ROBERT:** Yes, and in the meantime ...

**HENRY:** If that is the Bloodhound Law, I believe that
Congress is still wrangling over that.

**WILLIS:** It will be due for a vote in the near future ... In the meantime, we do need a room.

**HENRY:** (Looking in his ledger) I'm sorry. I've just rented the last room to a couple ...

**WILLIS:** A couple – a man and a woman?

**HENRY:** A couple of men ... A man and his black manservant.

**ROBERT:** We'd like to leave the contact with the U. S. Marshall, who is working with us on this case.

**HENRY:** Yes, of course ... Well good luck in your search ... Your godly mission.

BLACKOUT

## SCENE 9: ELLEN AND WILLIAMS BOARDING HOUSE ROOM

**NARRATOR:** At that point Ellen and William had gone to their room. They felt they had finally arrived to safety.

*Ellen stood as still as a statue. William stretches out his arms for her and takes a step toward her.*

*She turns away, which frightens William. It looks as though she's spurning him. After a short while, she begins taking off her disguise. He still doesn't know why she's acting this way. She takes off her glasses and puts them on a table. She puts the hat on the bed, throws the slling away. She slowly takes off the coat. When she starts taking off her trousers, William could see that her shirt was really the top of a dress. During all of this time, William was quietly watching. She slowly turns around. She picks up the hat, regards it for a few moments, then looks for the first time at William, who is still stoically waiting. She runs to him, grabs him and is about to kiss him, when there becomes a knock on the door, They quickly stand away from each other.*

**ELLEN:** Could I ...

**HENRY:** (Offstage) Could you join us for coffee. There is someone here anxious to meet you.

**ELLEN:** Of course, we 'll be there as soon as we change clothes.

**HENRY**: Wonderful!

*We hear the footsteps walking away.*

**ELLEN**: (To William.) Surely the slave runners aren't the ones wanting to meet us.

**WILLIAM**: He said "someone" not some ones.

**ELLEN**: You're right. How silly of me.

**WILLIAM**: But we must still be careful until we can board the ship for England.

**ELLEN**: (Notices the hat she is still holding, then tries to put it on him, but it doesn't fit. ) Not a very good fit. But at least, I won't have to wear it any more.

**WILLIAM**: There seems to be a lot of things we can now begin to put behind us.

**ELLEN**: Not so quick. There still be a heap of things we gotta go over or around.

**WILLIAM**: Or under or through.

(During this dialogue Ellen continues to finish changing her costume.)

**ELLEN**: William! How do you think this looks? (Not waiting for an answer) I intend to dress as I please now that we're in freedom land.

**WILLIAM**: Don't you s'pose we oughta go meet these nice folk ... in our real person?

**ELLEN**: Of course.

## BLACKOUT

## SCENE 10: THE PARLOR OF THE BOARDING HOUSE

**NARRATOR**: The time had come for them to show their true selves, but it didn't go well at first when they meet the landlord. There was still a suspicion that the slave hunters were close by.

*Ellen and William step into the parlor and are greeted by the landlord and his wife, Helen.*

**HENRY**: (To William) Could I speak to your young Master?

**WILLIAM**: Of course. And here she is. Meet Ellen Craft.

**HENRY**: I'm pleased to meet you. No. I mean the fellow

who came in with you a while ago.

**ELLEN**: I am that fellow who you saw a while ago.

**HELEN**: No. You can't be.

**WILLIAM**: We had to take on these disguises.

**ELLEN**: And pretend that I was a slaveholder.

**WILLIAM**: White of course.

**ELLEN**: Traveling with his manservant.

**WILLIAM**: This was necessary if we were ever to escape.

**HENRY**: Would you sit here for a minute, while I clear up a matter with my wife? She has already poured out some coffee for you.

**ELLEN**: How nice of you to greet us this way.

*Ellen and William sit at a small tabel close to each other, while Henry and Helen retreat to a far corner of the room.*

**WILLIAM**: I really didn"t expect to be treated this well when we got to freedom

**ELLEN**: I've never been so happy in my life.

*They continue to drink their coffee silently, occasionally touching each other affectionately. Henry and Helen have been quietly talking out of hearing distance of the Crafts. Suddenly we hear Helen as she jumps up.*

**HELEN**: Henry Gilley, what in the world are you thinking?

**HENRY**: But, Helen, don't you see ...

**HELEN**: I see that you've become a cold-blooded money-grubber.

**HENRY**: With our debts pilin' up ...

**WILLIAM**: (to Henry) Maybe we should go back to our room.

**HELEN**: No that won't be necessary. Does your room suit you?

**ELLEN**: The room's just fine, and now that we're safer her in Philadelphia ... (looking anxiously at the Henry)

**HENRY**: Only in appearance.

**HELEN**: Are you aware that anyone may be following you?

**ELLEN**: We've heard that two men have come up from

Georgia to take us runaway slaves to the U.S. Marshall to send us back to Georgia.

**WILLIAM:** We knew we were the slaves they were looking for.

**HENRY:** They won't find you here, at least for a little while.

**HELEN:** But you must stay close to the house.

**HENRY:** In fact, it'd be best if you stay in the house ... So they won't get a chance to see you.

**ELLEN:** Are they that close by?

**HELEN:** As a matter of fact, we have just met them ...

**HENRY:** At least we think we've met them.

**HELEN:** Don't be an idiot. You meet two white men from Georgia looking for an escaped slave couple, who we just rented a room ... Of course they ...

**WILLIAM:** Where ...

**ELLEN:** And when did you ...

**HELEN:** Right here.

**HENRY:** Just after you registered and went to your room.

**ELLEN:** We've come this close to freedom and now in a moment we've lost the whole thing. (starts crying) We're married and not married. We're free but not free.

**WILLIAM:** Ellen, I know it looks bad and feels bad, but these good people will protect us until we can find some way out of this predicament.

**ELLEN:** The way out to where? We've no place to go to.

**HELEN:** We, my husband, had a chance to make some money for a reward for your capture.

**HENRY:** Now, I didn't intend to actually ...

**HELEN:** Of course we can't decipher your honest intention.

**HENRY:** Well, to be perfectly honest ...

**HELEN:** That's the key word, PERFECTLY.

**HENRY:** I must admit that ...

**WILLIAM:** How much would the reward ...

**HENRY:** They wouldn't quote an exact amount, but assured me that it would be substantial.

**HELEN**: And my gullible husband ...

**ELLEN**: I'm scared to death. Would we be better off going back and taking our punishment? This runnin' and hidin' tears at my nerves an' clouds my heart.

**WILLIAM**: Ellen, please be comforted. We'll be together no matter what befalls us.

**HENRY**: We, my wife and I, haven't been in this country very long. We have family and friends back in England. Could we help with purchasing passage on a ship to England?

**WILLIAM**: We have enough money. But we'll need some help finding the way.

**HENRY**: I'll be taking the train to Boston next week just before a ship will be sailing to England.

**ELLEN**: Oh! Could we ...

**HENRY**: Absolutely ...

**HELEN**: While we wait for departure, you ... (nodding toward Ellen) ... can help me in the kitchen ... maybe teach me how to cook some of those Georgia dishes.

**HENRY**: But please stay in the house.

**WILLIAM**: I guess the parlor her is not completely safe.

**HELEN**: Yes. True. People come and go all the time here.

**HENRY**: There's a back way between your room and the kitchen.

**HELEN**: My Henry's a good man. He gets a little anxious sometimes. But when the chips are down, he'll do the right thing.

**ELLEN**: Thank you so much. I pray to God that we'll soon find freedom.

*The actors begin humming OH FREEDOM and continue through the Narrator's closing lines.*

**NARRATOR**: They celebrated their plan privately with their new friends even though there were still some obstacles to be overcome. Many years later ... after living in England and learning to read and write, Grandma Ellen and Grandpa William returned to America and even to Georgia ... with their five children and their freedom. There they even wrote their own book, about their path to freedom. Their shared yearning for freedom persisted with other folks into the 20th century. And today continues.

*Projected Visuals with singing. OH FREEDOM is sung with full voice by the full cast.*

**FULL CAST:**

Oh Freedom, Oh Freedom,
Oh Freedom over me, over me.
And before I'd be a slave, I'd be buried in my grave,
And go home to my Lord and be free.
No more weepin', no more weepin',
No more weepin' over me, over me.
And before I'd be a slave, I'd be buried in my grave,
And go home to my Lord and be free.

*The singing and the projections should end together.*

CURTAIN

# E. Reid Gilbert, Ph.D.

Associate Professor Emeritus, Ohio State University

Having been raised in the tobacco hills of North Carolina, Reid left to pursue academic studies at several colleges and universities:

Brevard College, English, AA
Duke University, Sociology, BA
Southern Methodist University, Theology, THM
Union Theological Seminary (NYC), Religious Drama, STM
Wisconsin University (Madison), Asian Theatre, Ph.D.

This journey also included careers in Methodist and Unitarian ministries, two Fulbright Awards (to India and Thailand, respectively), founding and directing the Wisconsin Mime Theatre and School (which the New York Times called the center of mime training in the U.S.), Administrator of International Mimes and Pantomimists, serving on NEA review panels, performing in various solo and full-scripted venues as well as college and university teaching. In 2011 he was awarded the Distinguished Alumni Award at Brevard College.

He has directed more than 40 theatre productions including Shakespeare, Japanese Noh, Commedia del Arte, original and international scripts.

His private study included Storytelling and Folklore with Richard Chase, Modern Dance with Charles Weidman, Mime with Etienne Decroux and Japanese Noh with Sidayo Kita.

Having conducted many classes and workshops on masks, he has taught Architecture as Extended Mask at the Frank Lloyd Wright School of Architecture. He also taught at Union College in KY and Lambuth College in TN. For ten years he directed the Valley Ridge Theatre in Thomas, WV. and taught Movement for Actors at the Ohio State University from which he is now retired.

His most recent creative activities have been in writing: *Trickster Jack*, a collection of tales about the Appalachian trickster, Jack, second edition published by A3D Impressions and *Shall We Gather at the River*, Xlibris Press, a Romeo/Juliet novel set in the Virginia mountains in 1875. It has been written into a screen play.

His book of poetry, *What Matteers*, contains 119 poems, ranging from comic to spiritual. He commemorated his years as the Director of the Wisconsin Mime Theatre and School by publishing *Valley Studio: More than a Place*. which also includes stories from other participants in that nine year adventure in the wilds of Wisconsin.

Reid's memoirs of his early life are shared in his *Twelve Houses of my Childhood*. Next came two books of political limericks: *100 Limericks for 100 Days of Trump* and *Whimsical Limericks from the Age of Trump from All Sides of the Political Aisle*. His later memoirs are contained in *Stories Tell What Can't be Told: My Story*.

All of these books are available at Amazon.com.

E. Reid Gilbert
ergenator@gmail.com

CPSIA information can be obtained
at www.ICGtesting.com
Printed in the USA
FSHW021848101219
64691FS